Windows NT® Cluster Server Guidebook

ISBN 0-13-096019-5

PRENTICE HALL SERIES ON MICROSOFT TECHNOLOGIES

DAVE LIBERTONE

Windows NT® Cluster Server Guidebook

Foreword by MARSHALL BRAIN

Prentice Hall PTR
Upper Saddle River, NJ 07458
www.phptr.com

Editorial/Production Supervision: *Kathleen M. Caren*
Acquisitions Editor: *Michael Meehan*
Marketing Manager: *Kaylie Smith*
Manufacturing Manager: *Pat Brown*
Cover Design: *Scott Weiss*
Cover Design Direction: *Jerry Votta*
Series Design: *Gail Cocker-Bogusz*

© 1999 by Prentice Hall PTR
Prentice-Hall, Inc.
A Simon & Schuster Company
Upper Saddle River, NJ 07458

Prentice Hall books are widely used by corporations and government agencies for training, marketing, and resale.

The publisher offers discounts on this book when ordered in bulk quantities. For more information, contact Corporate Sales Department, Phone: 800-382-3419; fax: 201-236-7141; email: corpsales@prenhall.com
Or write Corporate Sales Department, Prentice Hall PTR, One Lake Street, Upper Saddle River, NJ 07458.

Product and company names mentioned herein are the trademarks or registered trademarks of their respective owners.

All rights reserved. No part of this book may be
reproduced, in any form or by any means,
without permission in writing from the publisher.

Printed in the United States of America

10 9 8 7 6 5 4 3

ISBN 0-13-096019-5

Prentice-Hall International (UK) Limited, *London*
Prentice-Hall of Australia Pty. Limited, *Sydney*
Prentice-Hall Canada Inc., *Toronto*
Prentice-Hall Hispanoamericana, S.A., *Mexico*
Prentice-Hall of India Private Limited, *New Delhi*
Prentice-Hall of Japan, Inc., *Tokyo*
Simon & Schuster Asia Pte. Ltd., *Singapore*
Editora Prentice-Hall do Brasil, Ltda., *Rio de Janeiro*

Acknowledgements

Many people have contributed to make this book possible.
First, I would like to thank Kay and Claudio
at UCI for taking on extra work in my absence.
And in particular, my managers,
Donna and Andrew Scoppa,
who offered me this opportunity.

Next, I would like to thank Larry Jensen,
who, without his efforts, the chapter on implementing
Exchange would not have been possible.
Thanks to Jim Maloney for providing the appendix
on the Cluster API.

Thanks to the many people at Prentice Hall
who have been very helpful and patient in guiding me
through the book writing process.

And last, thanks to my faithful dog Cuda,
who gave up more than a couple of walks
this past winter while I completed this book.

CONTENTS

FORWARD xi

ONE The Data Processing Dilemma *1*
Current Potential Solutions 2

TWO What Is a Cluster? *7*
Clustering Solutions 9
Cluster Models 9
The Quorum Resource 15
An Architectural Overview of Microsoft Cluster Server 16
Virtual Server 23

THREE Building a Cluster *25*
Designing a Cluster 26
Hardware Requirements 26
Software Requirements 31
Installing the Cluster Server Software 32
Removing Cluster Server 53

FOUR Implementing Cluster Available Resources 57

Group Objects   58
Resource Objects   67
The IP Address Resource   72
The Network Name Resource   77
The File-Share Resource   81
The Print Spooler Resource   88
The Generic Service Resource   96
The Generic Application Resource   103
The Physical Disk Resource   107
The IIS Virtual Root Resource   110
The Distributed Transaction Coordinator Resource   115

FIVE Cluster Management   119

The Cluster Administrator Utility   120
Managing Cluster Nodes   127
Managing Cluster Security   129
Cluster.Exe   135
Administrative Tasks   147
Performing a Hardware Upgrade   148
Performing a Software Upgrade   148
Performing Cluster Backups   149

SIX Clustering SQL Server   151

SQL Server – Overview   152
Devices and Databases   152
Microsoft Cluster Server Support for SQL Server   152
Installing SQL Server, Enterprise Edition 6.5   155

Installing Cluster Support for SQL Server   161
Pre-setup Requirements   161
Cluster Support for SQL Server Modifications   169

SEVEN   Clustering Exchange Server   *173*

Exchange Server – Overview   174
Installing Exchange Server, Enterprise Edition   175
Pre-setup Considerations   176
Setup—Primary Cluster Node   185
Setup—Secondary Cluster Node   192
Replacing an existing Exchange Server   194
Supporting Exchange Server, Enterprise Edition   197

EIGHT   Cluster Performance   *205*

Analyzing System Performance   207
Memory   207
Performance Monitor   214
Analyzing Disk Activity   216
Analyzing Processor Activity   219
Analyzing Network Activity   221
Cluster Performance   222

NINE   Cluster Troubleshooting   *225*

Troubleshooting Tools   226
Cluster Troubleshooting   238
Installation Problems   240
SCSI Device Problems   241
Cluster Member Connectivity Problems   242
Client – Cluster Connectivity Problems   244

Group and Resource Failure Problems 245
General Cluster Issues 247
Troubleshooting by Resource Type 248

TEN The Future for Cluster Server 255

The Future for Microsoft Cluster Server 256

APPENDIX A 257

APPENDIX B 259

GLOSSARY 265

INDEX 273

FORWARD

It has been fascinating to watch the evolution of the Windows operating system over the last 10 years or so. I can remember looking at versions of Windows 1.0 and 2.0 running on AT boxes, and clearly the thought was, "This product will never fly." The surge of interest around Windows 3.0 and then 3.1 showed that the product had matured and taken off, but at that point Windows was meant strictly for one-desktop applications, such as word processing and spreadsheet manipulation.

The release of Windows for Workgroups made it possible for small businesses to create peer-to-peer networks easily. This was Windows' first real inroad into the business environment. Then Windows NT version 3.1 was released. As the first secure and robust version of the Windows operating system, you could see that Microsoft had set its sights on the corporate world. However, the 3.1 release of NT was sparse and did not satisfy the needs of real business users. Microsoft kept adding functionality and has over time created a system that is now clearly embraced by large corporate data centers. With the ability to handle multiple processors, gigabytes of memory and terabytes of disk space, high-end NT boxes begin to look something like mainframes. NT proliferates across the business landscape.

With the advent of NT Clustering, Microsoft moves the evolution of its premier operating system to a new level by taking aim at the hardware and software reliability problem. For enterprise-level servers needing 24x7 functionality, clustering is a critical capability because it allows hardware to fail without disabling the server. One part of a cluster may fail, but the cluster as a whole remains active. This is not a new idea—VAX clusters have been around for decades. However, by making the concept available as a standard feature of the NT operating system (as well as adding clustering support to important parts of the Back Office suite), Microsoft moves the concept into the mainstream. Anyone with a couple of NT machines and a SCSI hard disk can create a cluster and significantly improve reliability.

Well, almost. "Anyone with a couple of NT machines" also needs to have some understanding of what clustering is about, how it works and which steps are necessary to set it up. That is where this book comes in. This book is a straightforward and practical guide for anyone who wants to quickly create and utilize clusters of NT servers. The book introduces the clustering concept, talks about some of the prerequisites, and then shows you the steps you must take to create your first cluster (from both a hardware and software perspective). It also takes the important step of showing you how to install and configure the first two cluster-enabled applications: SQL server and Exchange server. The book then wraps up with two of its most important contributions: performance tips and a troubleshooting guide. Both of these topics are especially critical in a clustered setting, both when things are working properly and when they are not.

With this book, a person who wants to set up a cluster—either for experimental or production reasons—can get started quickly. The book walks you step-by-step through the entire process. That makes this book a valuable addition to the library of anyone who is new to the world of NT clustering.

Marshall Brain

ONE

The Data Processing Dilemma

There was a movie once about two computer geniuses; the storyline itself is not important. In the movie, there is a statement by one of them that can be paraphrased as follows, "It's not money that controls the world today, it is the data." Think of how true this is. Have you ever been irritated because an ATM machine is not working, a telephone-based banking system is not available, or your favorite web site is offline? I think the point is clear. We have, as a society, become very dependent upon being online. This is not intended to be a social commentary, just a statement of fact. I have worked in the computer industry for over fifteen years. During that time, I spent five years managing a data center. Systems could be online for six months straight, but the one day a system went offline was always the most important day to the clients.

Business infrastructures need to be online. The banking industry has the potential to lose millions of dollars with even a very small amount of downtime. Even the smallest business loses revenue when its web site is not available to potential customers. Hospitals need access to patient files. It is not an acceptable option to state, "The system will be up tomorrow."

The goal of every system administrator should be to have stable and capable computers online 24 hours a day. Unfortunately, this is not an attainable goal. Systems crash. Hardware needs to be repaired and upgraded. So let's approach this another way. It does not affect the user if a specific computer is online; what impacts him is whether or not its application and data are available.

Current Potential Solutions

There are various potential solutions to the problem of providing high levels of availability of applications or being fault-tolerant. All of the solutions focus on eliminating one or more single points of failure.

UPS

An Uninterruptible Power Supply provides basic protection against system downtime. If the power fails from the primary power source, which is probably the utility company, the UPS provides a few minutes of emergency power until power is restored or can be switched over to a backup power source.

Disk Redundancy

Disk hardware is a major issue when dealing with availability. Speaking from experience, I know a disk crash can have serious implications both in data availability and data protection. There are various levels of protection from disk failures; the first one should always be a regular backup schedule. This is not a book on how to be a good system administrator, but one point needs to be made. Every so often, perform a sanity check on your backups by attempting to restore one or more files, just to make sure that these backups are usable. I have known people who religiously did backups, but when the time came, they were useless.

The next step to increasing the data availability of disks is to possibly implement either disk mirroring or disk striping with parity. Disk mirroring is just what it sounds: two disks that are exact copies, or mirror images, of each other. The operating system sees one drive such as F:, but there are actually two independent disk partitions that represent the data stored on this drive. The operating system issues disk I/O requests to the F: drive. The I/O request is processed by the disk mirroring mechanism and the I/O is issued to one of the physical disks. There are various implementations of disk mirroring, some hardware-based, and some software-based. The hardware version will perform better and put no increased load on the operating system because the work is done at the hardware level, but it may require different hardware. Software implementations will work with most hardware, at the expense of increased operating system activity.

Disk mirroring will protect only against hardware disk failures. If a misbehaving application writes invalid data to a file that corrupts the data, this I/O request will be propagated to both drives and now there are two bad copies of the data. If a hardware malfunction generates an invalid write, this may be isolated to one mirror member, and the data on the other may be intact.

Disk striping with parity logically merges multiple disks into one. When data is read from or written to the stripe set, it is divided into several sections and one section is transferred to each disk in the set, except one. The data that is written to this disk is information that will allow data to be recreated from one of the disks in the set in the event of a failure. This is known as the parity information. Disk striping with parity generally provides protection in the event of a single disk hardware failure, though some new implementations can handle two disk failures.

Transaction Processing

Transaction processing is the concept of treating a group of sub-transactions as one unit. This is common in the database world. For example, if I were to transfer money from my savings account to my checking account, this is really two separate transactions. My bank, however, will want to treat it as one transaction so that all accounts are accurate. Transaction processing guarantees that all sub-transactions or none of the sub-transactions within a transaction block are executed. This protects from downtime by not forcing administrators to do restores of files that are considered corrupt because they are out of sync with each other.

There is another level of transaction processing that can occur at the file system level. Disks maintain pointers to directories, which in turn maintain pointers to files. If the system was interrupted while updating this data, lost files or invalid pointers could exist. This can happen with the FAT file system. Newer file system implementations, such as NTFS on Windows NT, treat updates to the file system as a transaction and therefore provide protection at the disk storage level.

Replication Servers

If 100% availability is required, replicating data to a backup server is an alternative. The replication of data to a backup server introduces additional overhead to the primary server, because it has to push any file update to another system. Also, this method is not without potential risk. In most cases, there will be a small amount of latency involved where a transaction is committed on the primary server and has not yet replicated to the backup server. If a switch to the backup server is made at that time, the possibility of data corruption exists.

Multiprocessors

A multiprocessor is a single computer that has more than one CPU module. The single point of failure of the processor has been removed, and the fact that both processors have direct access to memory means that one processor should have access to any information in memory with which the first processor was working in the case of a failure. Applications may need to be modified to take advantage of moving to another processor in the event of a processor failure. Multiprocessors excel in the area of scalability. When a server becomes fully or over-utilized, it is much more cost-effective to add another processor to a multiprocessor system than to purchase a new and more powerful server. Multiprocessor systems also contain redundant power supplies to eliminate another single point of failure. Applications cannot automatically take advantage of the increased processor resource provided by a multiprocessor configuration. Unless a single application is written to be multi-threaded, there will be no noticeable performance gain in running the application on a multiprocessor platform. Also, in order to restart an application in the event of a failure, either the application itself or another software component must monitor the application and request to restart it when necessary. The one drawback to a multiprocessor configuration is that, to service the system, the whole configuration must be taken offline, which impacts all users of all the resident applications.

The symmetric multiprocessing solution is, by far, the most popular shared hardware architecture today. Whether this is a reflection on the capabilities of multiprocessors or a lack of viable alternatives is the question. The law of diminishing returns begins to apply to most SMP configurations as they move beyond an eight-processor configuration. As the number of processors in a multiprocessor configuration increases, it is not a one-to-one relative increase in the total number of transactions that the system as a whole can process. This diminishing return factor can be accounted for by the overhead introduced as the number of processors in the SMP configuration increases.

The Requirements

Any fault-tolerant and high availability solution must support four major features in order to be effective:

- Removal of single points of failure. The solution needs the ability to avoid interruption of services to clients if a hardware or software component fails.
- Performance scalability. The solution needs to be easily expandable without requiring a total replacement of existing hardware to increase processing levels.
- System and resource failover protection. It must be possible for any component resource to be taken over by another cluster member.
- Resource sharing. There must exist the option for offering resources to clients such as files, printers, and applications.

Microsoft Cluster Server

The solution offered by Microsoft is Microsoft Cluster Server, or MSCS. Microsoft Cluster Server is unique as a clustering solution in a couple of ways. First, it avoids any issues of proprietary hardware. This makes the software an option in almost every possible situation where fault tolerance or high availability is necessary. Second, it digresses from the one prevalent cluster concept where multiple computers in the cluster can access a device at the same time. By following this approach, the Cluster Server software has less complexity, and less complexity implies less overhead.

TWO

What Is a Cluster?

The industry's standard definition of a cluster is, "two or more independent computer systems that are addressed and managed as a single system." The cluster concept was originated by Digital Equipment Corporation in the mid- to late 1980's with the introduction of the VAXCluster. The VAX can be classified as a mini-computer. The main idea behind the design of the VAXCluster was "no single point of failure." This meant totally parallel hardware with multiple CPUs, disks, and disk controllers. The network controllers were redundant because each computer had a separate Ethernet connection. Redundant hardware was not a requirement to run a VAXCluster, but it was necessary to be able to allow any component hardware failure without affecting the services offered by the cluster as a whole. See Figure 2-1 for a sample VAXCluster design.

The main bus of the cluster was a device known as a star coupler. The star coupler accepts connections from processors and special controller units. Notice in the diagram that there is no redundant star coupler. The star coupler is a passive device without a power supply. It can be considered a patch panel or passive hub.

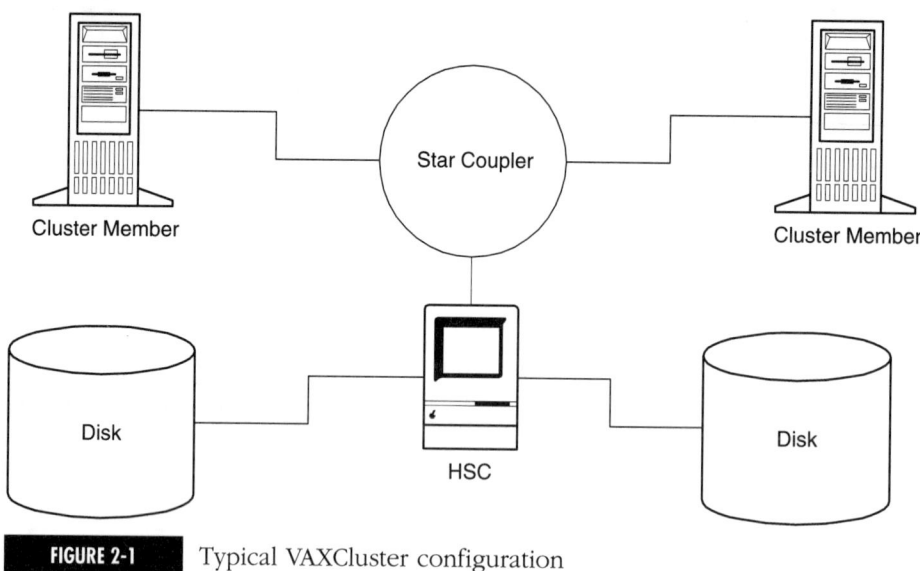

FIGURE 2-1 Typical VAXCluster configuration

The specialized controller units are known as hierarchical storage controllers, or HSCs. The HSC handles disk and tape drive I/O. In order to provide disk redundancy, the VAXCluster supports what is known as volume shadowing. This is a mirroring product that keeps the data on two disk drives the same. Any writing of data is performed to both drives, but data reads need to be done to one drive only, since they contain the same information. By connecting one member of the shadow set to a different HSC, there is now redundancy at the disk and controller levels. Since all processors in the VAXCluster have access to the HSCs via the star coupler, there is not a single point of failure in the hardware. Still to be solved, however, is software failover. For example, let's assume that a process is running on VAX A and is serving as some sort of daemon. If VAX A were to crash, the software needs to be smart enough to realize this and start the process daemon running on another member of the cluster.

There are four basic components to the functionality of a cluster. First is the removal of any single point of failure. A user connection should never run the risk of being dropped due to a failure of any cluster hardware or software component. Second, the cluster should provide scalability. It should not be necessary to replace computers with more expensive, faster computers; the cluster should allow for the introduction of more processing power without sacrificing the processors that are already in place. Third, the cluster must provide for resource failover between processors. If a directory is currently being accessed through one cluster member and that cluster member goes offline, the directory resource should be made available on another cluster member. Finally, the cluster must provide sharing of resources such as disks, printers, etc.

Clustering Solutions

Active/Passive

In an active/passive clustering solution, a standby server monitors a continuous signal from the active server. The standby server remains in a backup, passive mode until it recognizes that the active server has failed. It then comes online and takes control of the cluster. When the primary server comes back online, manual intervention by the administrator may be necessary to revert the systems to their original state. Depending on the implementation, the cluster may have to go offline to return to its primary configuration.

Active/Active

In an active/active configuration, all servers in the cluster can run applications and act as backup servers to the other cluster members. There is no concept of a primary or standby server. All servers can dynamically assume either role.

Cluster Models

Cluster implementations can be placed into one of two categories. The cluster can be a shared resource cluster. This means that a resource, such as a file, can be physically accessed by more than one cluster member simultaneously. The term, "physical," here implies a computer issuing an I/O request on a disk controller. The other cluster implementation is referred to as a shared nothing cluster. In this implementation, only one computer can access a disk. Both implementations have advantages and disadvantages.

Chapter Two • Windows NT Cluster Server Guidebook

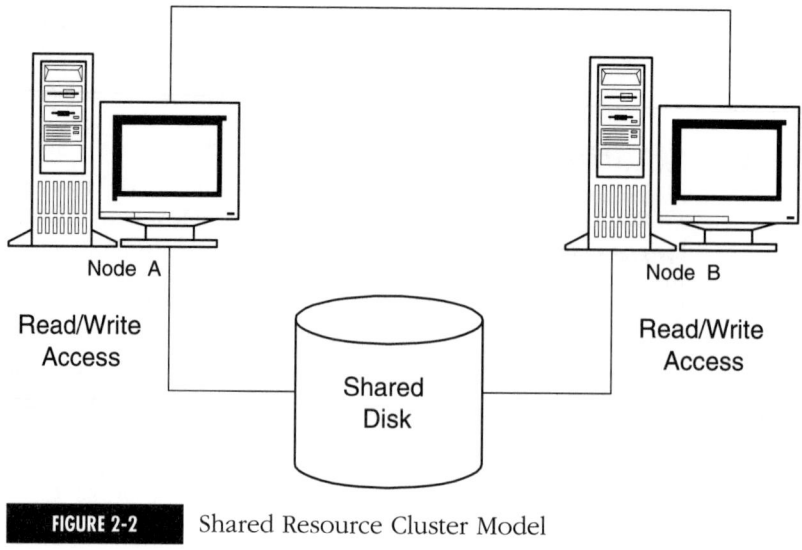

FIGURE 2-2 Shared Resource Cluster Model

As was stated earlier, in a shared resource cluster, multiple cluster members are allowed independent access to the same resource. The most common example is a file. See Figure 2-2. Let's assume the cluster consists of two computers, NODEA and NODEB. Let's also assume that processes on both members want to open the same file named LOTTO.NUM. First, it is necessary to understand what happens when an application program opens a file. When the application requests to open the file, it specifies the level of access it needs, such as read or read/write. It also states what level of sharing it will allow on a file. This is also something like read, or read/write. This information is kept in memory in a structure known as a lock block. Let's look at a couple of examples.

For our first example, we will use only one computer. Suppose USERA runs an application that opens a file for read access and allows no shared access. A lock block is created in memory with this information. Now, USERB runs another application that needs to open the same file. When the application USERB is running attempts to open the file, the lock block is checked and it is determined that access to the file is denied because USERA specified no shared access. The message that commonly would be displayed by the application is "Access denied" or "Error 5."

For our second example, we will still work with only one computer. Now, USERA runs an application that opens the file for read access and allows shared read access. Now, USERB runs an application that wants to open the file for read access and allows no shared access. Even though USERA has allowed the access that USERB desires, the application that USERB is running will fail because it specifies no shared access and USERA already has the file open. If the operating system allowed USERB to open the file, the application would be running under the assumption that no other process has the file open, when in fact USERA has it open.

All the previous examples have simply dealt with how locking works on a single computer. For the next example, let's assume there is a two-member cluster consisting of NODEA and NODEB. Now, USERA from NODEA opens a file for read access and allows no shared access. A lock block is created in memory. Now, USERB from NODEB attempts to open the same file. The problem is, there is no lock block resident in memory on NODEB. A method is needed to supply information to NODEB that the file is already open and the lock block that needs to be checked is on NODEA. There needs to be an operating system component to manage file access among the various computers.

Distributed Lock Manager

The distributed lock manager is the software that coordinates resource access between cluster members. Generally, a distributed lock manager consists of two structures. See Figure 2-3. First is a table that points to all the lock blocks that currently reside on the system. This structure is referred to as a lock ID table. The second structure is a table of resources and what cluster member the lock for the resource can be located on. This structure is known as a resource table. The two tables are used to implement distributed locking as follows. A process on NODEA requests a lock on a resource. The local computer examines the resource table to locate the computer that should manage the lock. A request for access is then sent to the computer that is managing the lock, based on the information from the resource table, in this case NODEB. The computer maintaining the lock generates a positive or negative acknowledgement to the lock request, which is then delivered to the requesting process.

Chapter Two • Windows NT Cluster Server Guidebook

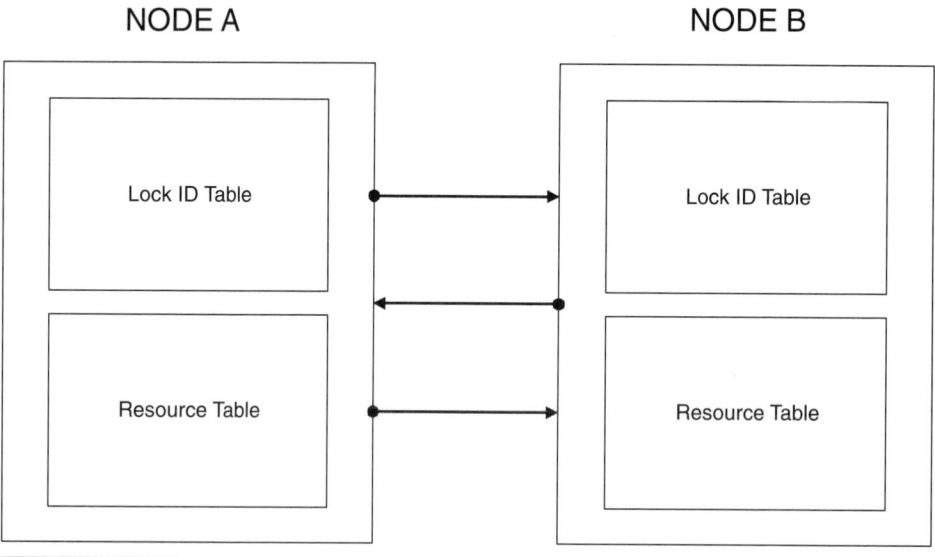

FIGURE 2-3 Distributed lock manager communications

There are two major disadvantages to running a distributed lock manager. The first is the complexity of distributing the lock database and making sure it is accurate among all processors using the distributed lock manager. Locks are constantly being validated by the operating system. The traffic generated by this lock request and acknowledgement could overload an already busy network. This assumes that the lock messages are transported over the standard network media. This is not always the case. Some cluster implementations allow the administrator to designate a path for this type of traffic. Also, what happens when a computer participating in the distributed locking mechanism goes offline? Any lock blocks that were owned by this computer could now have invalid references on other members. The distributed lock manager has to be able to handle this by recognizing that the owning computer is not reachable and creating a new lock block on one of the remaining members. All this needs to occur before user processing can continue. Whenever a member exits a cluster, the cluster suspends all non-critical processing temporarily. During this time, the cluster is performing a variety of tasks to return the cluster to a usable state. If a distributed lock manager is being used, all the lock blocks that were owned by the exiting computer must be moved to another member. But how can lock blocks be relocated when the computer that owned the lock block has crashed? What really happens is that the remaining members must process their entire resource table, and any references to the member that has gone offline will be reestablished on one of the remaining members, not necessarily on the member with the entry in the resource table. The distributed lock manager allows participating members to be given priority values that determine what percentage of the distributed locks they should manage. This allows the administrator to use more powerful processors effectively. This process of the cluster's suspending activity while it relocates various resources and structures is known as cluster transition. Cluster transitions can take anywhere from 5 seconds to minutes, depending on the number and type of resources that were owned by the departing computer. This brings us to an important point. Since cluster transitions are a known and accepted characteristic of a cluster, a cluster may not be the best platform to implement a realtime, critical application. For example, if a computer was controlling metal pieces that were getting stamped on an assembly line, what happens to the assembly line during cluster transition? Does the arm stamping the metal stop? Does the whole assembly line stop? Here is an even more critical environment: Should a cluster control a nuclear power plant? Obviously, cluster transitions would be unacceptable in that type of environment! Clusters offer many benefits, but they are not the solution to every problem.

The second disadvantage to running a distributed lock manager is in the area of operating system caching. Accessing the disk is one of the most expensive operations in regards to overall performance. To reduce the amount of time spent on disk activity, operating systems will maintain one or more caches. Caches are chunks of memory used to store various information from the disk such as directory entries and the actual file data. In the case of a distributed lock manager, multiple systems can be accessing files. Each system will have its own caches. The lock manager is responsible for making sure that all systems are caching valid data. For example, two computers, NODEA and NODEB, could be accessing a file and have the same data records in memory. If NODEA updates one of these records, the distributed lock manager must update the information in the data cache on NODEB. Again, if this is happening constantly, extra messaging traffic is being introduced onto the network.

The distributed lock manager hides the fact that an application is running in a cluster environment at the expense of a larger, busier operating system. A distributed lock manager allows access to files to be coordinated through the native file system. No additional code needs to be generated for an application to perform I/O. An application would need only to be cluster-aware if it is necessary to create a shared resource of a type other than file. Also, a distributed lock manager allows for easy scalability and load balancing.

The main arguments for a distributed lock manager are the scalability it provides and the capability to load balance a single application. As the demands on the cluster grow, additional CPUs and disk can be easily added. Since the same file can be accessed by multiple computers, users can be spread among the processors so as not to overload one processor while another sits idle.

14 Chapter Two • Windows NT Cluster Server Guidebook

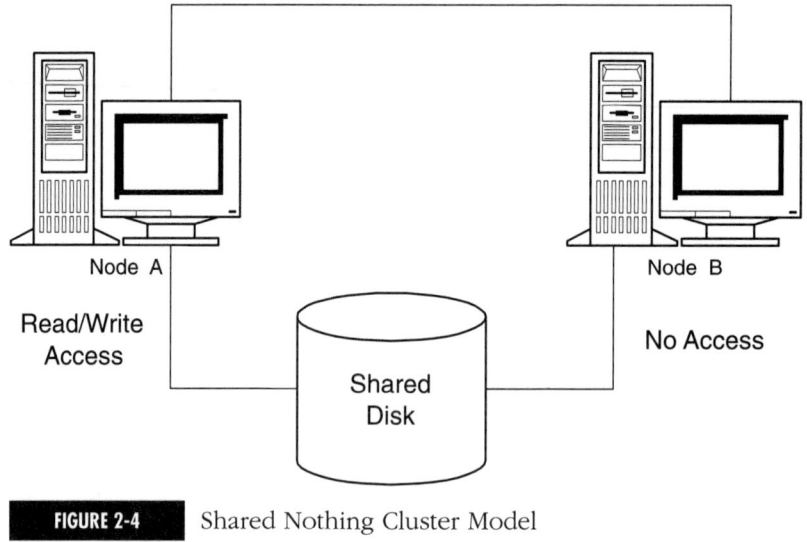

FIGURE 2-4 Shared Nothing Cluster Model

The alternative to a shared resource cluster model is a shared nothing cluster model. As its name implies, in this implementation resources are not simultaneously shared between the cluster members. In this model, each node of the cluster will own a subset of the hardware resources of which the cluster consists. See Figure 2-4. As a result, only one node can own and access a given resource at one time.

There are advantages and disadvantages to the shared nothing cluster model. The advantage to this model is that it avoids the overhead associated with a distributed lock manager. This makes the cluster software smaller and less complex.

Disadvantages of the shared nothing model include load balancing and resource failover. Since a resource can be accessed by only one cluster member, it is not possible to spread the processing load for a given resource across the cluster members. There is no capability to perform dynamic load balancing. The only load balancing possible is known as static load balancing. Here, it is the responsibility of the administrator to spread the different applications across the cluster members in order to balance the user-processing load of each system. This leads to another issue. A disk is a resource and can therefore be accessed by only one cluster member. To support cluster-based applications running on each cluster member, it is necessary to have multiple physical disks, or multiple RAID sets, so that each cluster member can "own" the disk that contains the application resources the cluster node is running.

The second disadvantage is in the area of resource failover. In a shared resource model, a resource can be accessed by a cluster member without the issue of which cluster member "owns" the resource. Therefore, if one cluster member becomes unavailable, the resource is still available, usually immediately, through another cluster member. In the shared nothing model, the cluster node must own the resource in order to offer the resource to clients. It is therefore necessary to move resource ownership among cluster members. This is called resource failover. When a resource moves among cluster members, there will be a temporary stoppage in user processing while the resource is being relocated to another cluster member. Also, the client may be required to reestablish its connection to the resource. The exact requirements of the client will be specific to the type of resource being used.

The Quorum Resource

When a cluster member is booted, it must determine whether the cluster to which it belongs is already running. If it is, then the booting cluster member simply joins the existing cluster. If the cluster is not running, then the booting cluster member must establish the cluster as an entity on the network. The danger occurs when two or more cluster members are restarting at the same time. Administrators will not generally do this. It is usually caused by a power outage. When the computers restart, a situation could occur where all the booting members do not detect a cluster and decide to form their own. This is referred to as a partitioned cluster. All proper synchronization to resource access is lost, whether this is a shared resource or shared nothing cluster. Data would probably be corrupted in a short period of time as computers are independently modifying files and allocating disk space.

Various methods have been devised to avoid this situation, and they generally involve some use of a quorum resource. The definition of quorum is majority. One implementation of a cluster and quorum involves allocating votes to various cluster members. Really democratic! A quorum value is calculated from all the outstanding votes. If the current members of the cluster own more than "quorum" number of votes, the cluster is allowed to function. Otherwise, the cluster goes into a paused state until more cluster members rejoin. The problem with this implementation is that the entire cluster could be paused when there were numerous servers up and running.

Microsoft Cluster Server solves the partitioned cluster problem by using one of the features of a shared nothing cluster model. One disk is selected as a quorum resource. Since only one computer can access a disk in a shared nothing cluster, the rule is as follows. When a cluster member is booting, if it owns the quorum disk, it creates a new cluster. If the cluster member is booting and does not own the quorum disk, it must join an existing cluster. If the computer that owns the quorum resource were to fail, the resource will be relocated to another cluster member, and when the failed cluster member restarts, it will join the existing cluster.

To avoid any potential problems, it has been recommended that the boot delay times on the Microsoft Cluster Server members be modified so

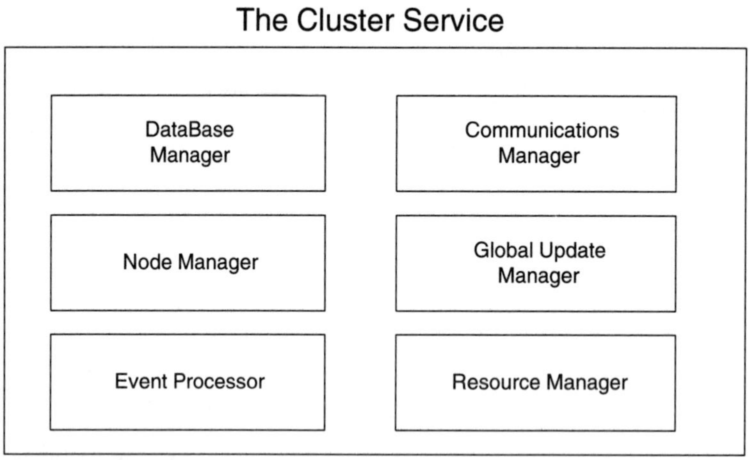

The Cluster Service

```
┌─────────────────────────────────────────────────┐
│                                                 │
│   ┌───────────────┐        ┌───────────────┐   │
│   │   DataBase    │        │ Communications│   │
│   │   Manager     │        │   Manager     │   │
│   └───────────────┘        └───────────────┘   │
│                                                 │
│   ┌───────────────┐        ┌───────────────┐   │
│   │ Node Manager  │        │ Global Update │   │
│   │               │        │   Manager     │   │
│   └───────────────┘        └───────────────┘   │
│                                                 │
│   ┌───────────────┐        ┌───────────────┐   │
│   │Event Processor│        │Resource Manager│  │
│   └───────────────┘        └───────────────┘   │
│                                                 │
└─────────────────────────────────────────────────┘
```

FIGURE 2-5   Cluster Service Components

that they are not the same. This will give one member enough time to allocate the quorum resource in the event of a power failure.

Microsoft Cluster Server uses the quorum disk to store what is referred to as the quorum log. The quorum log stores changes that have been made to the cluster configuration, such as a group or resource being added. A log is necessary to store the changes if one of the cluster members is offline at the time configuration changes are made. When a cluster member boots, it checks the quorum log for any changes and updates its registry information.

An Architectural Overview of Microsoft Cluster Server

The Microsoft Cluster Server software has two primary components. One is the Cluster Service. As its name implies, this program runs as a Windows NT service. The Cluster Service carries out six very distinct and separate tasks. Each component of the cluster service is known as a manager. See Figure 2-5. Every manager runs as one or more threads within the context of the Cluster Server process.

The Cluster Service on a node can be in one of three possible states. These states are different from the Windows NT service states. They are the status of the service from the cluster server software's perspective.

- **Offline** If the state is offline, the node is not a functioning member of the cluster. The node may not be started, the Cluster Service may have failed during startup, or the Cluster Service may not have been configured to start.

- **Online** If the state is online, the node is a functioning cluster member. It is participating in group and resource ownership, and it is generating, or responding to, heartbeats.
- **Paused** In a paused state, the node is also a functioning cluster member. The difference between this state and the online state is that a paused node cannot own any groups or resources. The purpose for the paused state is to provide the ability to upgrade applications without interfering with cluster activity. A paused cluster member can be rebooted without severely impacting the cluster because there are no groups and resources to failover. Cluster transition times would be minimal in this case.

The Database Manager

The Database Manager is responsible for maintaining the cluster database. The cluster database contains information such as the cluster name, resource types, groups, and resources. The cluster database is stored in the registry of each cluster member. The registry key for cluster-related data is HKEY_LOCAL_MACHINE\Cluster.

The Database Managers on each cluster member coordinate with each other to maintain consistent cluster configuration information. It is also the responsibility of the Database Manager to supervise changes to the cluster database. For example, the characteristics of a resource should not be modified at the same time for multiple cluster members.

The Event Processor

The Event Processor is responsible for the Cluster service initialization process and any cleanup that needs to occur when a cluster member exits. To implement this control, the Event Processor implements two substates that the Cluster Service can have. These states are internal to the Cluster Service and are not viewable from the operating system level via the graphical interface.

- **Initializing** The Cluster Service is in the process of starting. After the Event Processor puts the Cluster Service into this state, it calls the Node Manager to continue the initialization process.
- **Exiting** The Cluster Service is in the process of cleaning up before exiting.

The Event Processor acts as a dispatcher. It is an interface between an application and the cluster service. For example, a cluster aware application may request all available cluster resources to be enumerated, or listed. This could occur when an application needs to create a new cluster resource and is verifying that any dependent resources already exist. The application makes the request to the cluster via an API call. These API calls are discussed in detail in a later chapter. The request is accepted by the Event Processor and is handed off to the appropriate module of the cluster software.

The Node Manager

The Node Manager is responsible for tracking the status of other cluster members. If a cluster member goes offline, it will be necessary to relocate any resources that were owned by the failed member. The Node Manager tracks the status of cluster members by listening for "heartbeats." A heartbeat is defined as a message that is sent regularly by the Cluster Service between nodes in order to detect node failures. The heartbeat functions more like a PING. The first computer to boot into the cluster assumes the responsibility for generating the heartbeats. As other members join the cluster, the first node starts sending them heartbeats. If the secondary computers fail to respond to a heartbeat, the cluster considers the member offline and starts moving any resources that it owned. The heartbeat messages are generated at one-half second intervals. This is not necessarily a large amount of traffic, but the capability exists to send all cluster communications traffic on an isolated segment. This is discussed in the chapter on building a cluster.

The Node Manager is also involved when a computer is forming or joining a cluster. As a cluster member is initializing the cluster service, it goes through several "state" transitions in the context of being a cluster member. These states are totally separate from the Cluster Service states and are not visible outside the Cluster Service. The possible states include:

- **Member Search** The node is attempting to locate an online cluster member. This is used to determine if a cluster already exists; it can then be used to join the cluster.
- **Quorum Disk Search** The node is attempting to locate a quorum disk with which it can synchronize its cluster configuration from the registry in order to form a cluster.
- **Dormant** The node has been unable to find an online cluster member or a quorum disk. If neither of these components can be located, the member cannot form or join a cluster and goes into a "sleeping" state.
- **Forming** The node could not locate an online cluster, but it was able to locate the quorum disk and is in the process of creating a cluster.
- **Joining** The node has discovered an online cluster member and is doing the negotiation to join the cluster. If the negotiation is not successful, the Node Manager returns a failure message to the Event Processor.

One interesting situation is this. If the network connection between the cluster members fails, each cluster member will act as if it were the only cluster member and will want to take control of all resources. The problem is solved using the quorum resource. If communications between cluster members fail, the node with control of the quorum resource brings all resources online. Nodes that do not own the quorum resource will take all their resources offline.

The Communications Manager

The Communications Manager functions as a low-level transport mechanism for all other cluster server components to communicate between nodes. Most, if not all, of the other managers use the communications manager as their underlying message delivery mechanism. For example, the communications manager is responsible for:

- Heartbeats
- Resource group push and pull
- Resource state transitions
- Cluster connection requests, such as with the Cluster Administrator utility
- Nodes joining or exiting the cluster.

This component is also known as the Cluster Network Driver.

The Global Update Manager

The Global Update Manager also functions as a dispatcher. It provides a mechanism for other cluster service components to initiate and manage updates. For example, an administrator has the capability through the cluster administrator to change the state of a resource or group between online and offline. All cluster members need to be notified of the change in resource or group status. The notification process is performed by the Global Update Manager.

The Resource Manager

The Resource Manager is responsible for all control interaction with resources. This includes bringing a resource online, taking a resource offline, and performing failovers of resources to other cluster members. The Resource Manager depends on information from other managers such as the Node Manager and one or more resource monitors for cluster, node, group, and resource status.

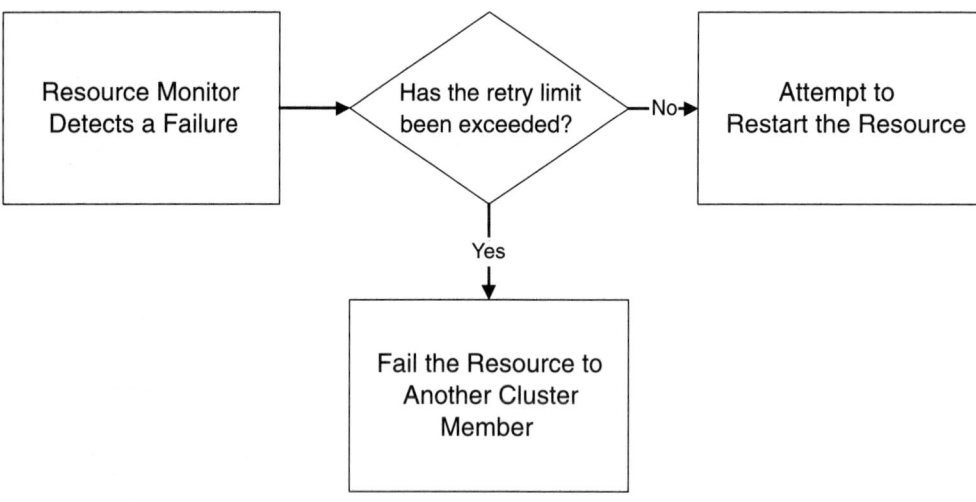

FIGURE 2-6 How the cluster handles a resource failure

FAILOVER

The Resource Manager is responsible for moving resources among cluster members in order to keep the resource online as much as possible. One event the Resource Manager handles is when a cluster member goes offline. In this case, the Resource Manager will relocate all cluster resources onto any remaining cluster members, as long as the remaining cluster member has been identified as a possible owner of the resource. For example, there may be a very CPU intensive cluster resource. The decision needs to be made as to whether this resource should be moved and started on another cluster member in the event of a system failure. Do any remaining cluster members have enough available processor time to support the new application without severely impacting the clients they are already servicing? This is a hardware capacity planning decision.

The next situation is when an application fails and the cluster member is still active. The cluster provides two options here. See Figure 2-6. First, the application can be restarted on the same processor. Obviously this provides the fastest recovery if the application can restart successfully. Eventually, after a definable number of restarts, the resource is moved to another cluster member. There may be situations where it makes more sense to fail over the resource immediately, as in cases where it may be acceptable to be offline for five seconds but not ten. By immediately failing the resource over, downtime could possibly be minimized. This is very application and installation specific and would require on-site testing to determine the best possible approach.

FAILBACK

Failback is the process of moving resources back to their original cluster member that owned the resource. Failback can occur only after a failover of a resource. Failback can be disabled to avoid resources being moved at non-convenient times. The cluster administrator can then manually move the resource back to the original cluster member at some point. Also, failback can be configured to occur only during certain hours of the day, such as midnight until six a.m. This allows resources to be automatically returned to their original cluster member at a time when the impact on clients should be less.

Resource Monitors

The Resource Monitor is the second major component of the Cluster Server software. Resource Monitors and dynamic link libraries, or DLLs, reside between the cluster service and a resource. They handle any communication between the cluster service and the resource. A DLL is basically a set of routines, or functions. A term used throughout this book and in the Microsoft Cluster Server documentation is "cluster-aware." A "cluster-aware" application has been written to handle the possibility of running in a clustered environment. Cluster-aware applications make use of the cluster API. The cluster API is a collection of functions implemented by the cluster software that can be used by a cluster-aware application to manage the cluster. This includes adding new resources, checking to see what resources exist, and bringing a resource online. For example, assume an application runs on the cluster that serves multiple databases to clients. With the standard resource types supplied by the Cluster Server software, the database server application would need to be the resource. Remember, this is a shared nothing model. Since a resource can be running on only one cluster member at a time, only one cluster member could function as the database server. If the database were defined as a new resource type, however, now the component that is allocated to a given cluster member is a specific database. The database server software could now run on multiple cluster members, each offering different databases to the clients. As a general rule, when an application is no longer the resource, an instance of the application can be running simultaneously on different nodes, each with its own set of resources. The cluster API is discussed in much more detail in Appendix B.

    The Resource Monitor runs as a process of the operating system. One Resource Monitor can support one or more resources. Resource Monitors are created by the cluster service as resources are brought online. The default for the cluster service is to control as many resources as possible in one Resource Monitor. This consumes as few system resources as possible. Situations could arise where a poorly written application causes the Resource Monitor to hang. Any other resources under the control of the same Resource Monitor could possibly become inaccessible to the cluster service. To work around this problem, a resource can be configured to run in a separate Resource Monitor. This should be used only when there is a misbehaving application, or when there is no shortage of system resources such as memory.

Resource Monitors track the online/offline state of resources. If a resource state changes, the Resource Monitor does not take any action of its own. Instead, it notifies the Resource Manager that will take the appropriate action of restarting the resource or initiating a failover of the resource to another cluster member.

Every Resource Monitor contains a "poller" thread. These threads are used to detect resource failures. There are two polling intervals used by the thread. They are:

- **LooksAlive interval** This is a quick check by the Resource Monitor to determine if a resource is still running.
- **IsAlive interval** A more detailed check is made to verify the state of the resource. Polling occurs at this interval whether the resource is online or offline. This allows for automatic recovery if a resource is able to correct the problems that were preventing it from responding to the LooksAlive poll.

If the Resource Monitor fails to receive a response from the LooksAlive message, the IsAlive check is performed. If the Resource Monitor does not receive a response to the LooksAlive check, the monitor notifies the Resource Manager that the resource has failed. The Resource Manager then decides whether to restart the resource or perform a failover to another cluster member.

The Time Service

The Time Service is a cluster resource running as a Windows NT service that synchronizes the date and time among the cluster members. There is only one Time Service in the cluster, and extra time service resources should not be created.

The Time Service resource synchronizes the date and time when two nodes join to form a cluster. The date and time are synchronized again within an hour of cluster establishment, then eight hours later, then every twelve hours. The computer that owns the time service resource is treated by the cluster as having the correct time and pushes the date and time information to any other cluster members.

Virtual Server

A virtual server is the logical equivalent of a file or application server. There is no physical component in the Microsoft Cluster Server software that is a virtual server; it is made up of two separate resources: a unique network name and a unique TCP/IP address. A resource is associated with a virtual server by linking it with the network name and TCP/IP address. At any point in time, different virtual servers can be "owned" by different cluster members. The virtual server entity can also be moved from one cluster member to another in the event of a systems failure. Since the virtual server appears exactly like a physical server to clients, it is not necessary for the users to learn anything new in order to use clustered resources. In fact, they do not even need to know that the system they are using is a cluster. The clients will use the network name assigned to the virtual server just as they would normally use a computer name. For example, if a user ran applications from a server named ADMINSERVER, before a cluster is implemented, the administrator can create a network name of ADMINSERVER on the cluster, limiting the impact to the client.

The administrator could take this one step further, however. Whereas in a standard configuration there is a limit of one computer name per server, in a clustered environment that limitation no longer exists. The administrator can create user-friendly network names for virtual servers that are easy for clients to remember and use.

THREE

Building a Cluster

Installing the necessary hardware and software to run Microsoft Cluster Server requires a thorough knowledge of both Windows NT and SCSI device configuration. With regard to SCSI device configuration, it is necessary that devices and cabling be configured in such a way that it will probably be very new, even though you may have been working with SCSI devices for years. Your knowledge of Windows NT can be as rudimentary as how to create a user account, but if problems occur during the installation process, the more experience you have with Windows NT, the better.

The installation process is initiated by first identifying the hardware and software configurations that will support Microsoft Cluster Server. The hardware configuration is a more complicated task than the software configuration to implement a successful installation. There are many web sites available to provide useful information regarding hardware requirements for Windows NT and SCSI specifications, which play a very important role in the operation of a cluster.

Designing a Cluster

Before cluster hardware is acquired and software loaded, it is useful to do some planning to guarantee that Cluster Server is implemented to achieve the desired results. Is the main goal to provide redundancy in the event of a system failure, to offload some of the activity of a file server, or offload a server-based application such as SQL Server? While all of these goals can be attained with a single installation of Cluster Server, hardware configurations will vary slightly with each goal.

If the main purpose of implementing a cluster is to offload activity from a file or application server, there is an important concept to understand at this point. The physical disk on which a shared resource resides can be accessed by only one computer at a time. Therefore, if the goal is to load balance the file and application server load among the cluster server members, it will be necessary to have more than one physical disk on the shared SCSI bus. It will then be possible to allocate various resources among the cluster members. See Figure 3-1 on page 29. When determining the processor size and memory necessary for a cluster server member, the worst possible scenario should be used. Assume all resources are running on one server. What will be the expected system load and user response time in this situation? Realize that the situation is temporary. If one server cannot handle the total expected load, how much degradation in performance will your client base and management accept?

Hardware Requirements

The hardware requirements can be broken down into two categories. First, since the Cluster Server software runs on top of Windows NT Server Enterprise Edition, it is necessary to comply with the hardware requirements for the operating system. Second, Cluster Server has some unique requirements in the area of peripheral device configuration.

Disk fault tolerance is not a hardware requirement but rather a design issue and needs to be discussed. Most of the resources that the cluster offers to clients involve some level of disk access. The cluster is designed to eliminate certain single points of failure such as memory and the processor. It does not address the disk as a failure point mainly because there are already numerous fault-tolerant disk implementations from which to choose. One of the more popular solutions is the use of RAID, or redundant array of inexpensive disks. Although Windows NT has the capability to implement RAID at a software level, this feature is not supported by the Cluster Server software. The software RAID supported by Windows NT is very flexible. A fault-tolerant disk driver can be loaded by the operating system. Devices on any disk controller can be combined into a stripe or mirror set, including IDE disks. Since the Cluster Server software supports only SCSI, not all configurations of Windows NT–based mirroring and striping can be supported. It will be necessary to implement the hardware RAID solution. Remember that the overall configuration is only as reliable as its weakest component. Any cluster designed with the goal of maximum uptime and online availability in mind will need to include some level of hardware RAID.

Windows NT Server Enterprise Edition— Hardware Requirements

The general requirements published to support Windows NT Server 4.0, Enterprise Edition and Microsoft Cluster Server are:

- Two PCI-based systems, minimum Intel processor of P90, or an Alpha system. It is not possible to mix an Intel and Alpha system in the same cluster.
- Each server should have at least 64MB of RAM, at least 500MB of available disk space.
- Other hardware requirements are discussed in the next section.

If possible, perform some capacity planning from whatever data is available about the applications that will run on the cluster. For example, the plan may balance the applications across the cluster members, and this may run with 10-15MG of RAM free at any time. But planning should be made for the worst possible case. What will happen to the processor load if one of the cluster members is down and the other has to take over its application load while supporting its own? Will the remaining cluster member provide adequate response times to the client base? Different applications have widely varying requirements for the basic system resources of memory and processor. Sadly, information to help capacity planning in this manner is generally not available, so we must depend on our previous experience with software products or just load up the system and see how it runs!

Microsoft Cluster Server Hardware Requirements

Microsoft Cluster Server is currently supported in a two-computer hardware configuration. Both computers must comply with the Windows NT Server Enterprise Edition hardware compatibility list. As usual, this list can be interpreted as the hardware that Microsoft has certified will work and which they will support. Just because your hardware does not appear on the compatibility list does not mean that it definitely will not work. My advice would be to perform a software installation on the hardware in question. Chances are good that you will be successful.

Following are the hardware requirements for each computer that will run the cluster server software:

- More than one disk controller such as IDE and SCSI
- One or more SCSI adapters
- An external SCSI disk
- SCSI cables and terminators
- One or more network adapters.

In addition to the above requirements, it is strongly suggested that similar hardware be used on all cluster server members, at least with regard to the disk controllers and network adapters. There is a hardware compatibility list published specifically for cluster server software.

DISK CONTROLLERS

A hardware requirement for a valid cluster server configuration is that the computer must contain more than one disk controller. Of these controllers, at least one must be a SCSI adapter which will service peripheral devices that will be accessible by all cluster members. One reason for the two adapters is to hide the disk that contains the Windows NT installation. Windows NT cannot be installed on a disk that is connected to the shared SCSI controller. This is not really true. Windows NT will install, but when it comes time to install the Cluster Server software, the device and controller that Windows NT is resident on will not be available drives for the Cluster Server software installation. So, basically, one disk controller is required for the Windows NT installation and a second disk controller, which must be SCSI, will be required for cluster server operations.

SCSI BUS AND DEVICE CONFIGURATION

To properly configure the SCSI devices and controllers for operation in a cluster, it is necessary to understand some of the basics of SCSI operation. Every SCSI bus can be viewed as a single cable that is terminated at both ends. See Figure 3-1. Some SCSI controllers provide an option for internal termination so that the SCSI cable can be plugged directly into the back of the computer. This is a nice and clean configuration for a standalone server, but it can cause problems in a cluster environment. First, if the SCSI bus ever loses termination, it is likely that all devices on the bus will be unreachable. In a clustered environment, one of the features is the ability to take a computer down for maintenance without affecting clients and the resources they use. If a cluster member is providing internal termination to a SCSI bus and the SCSI bus is unplugged from the computer because the computer is going to be upgraded, the bus has now lost termination and all devices would be unavailable. Second, not all SCSI devices have the ability to provide termination without power to the card. In this case, a single point of failure now

Three • Building a Cluster 29

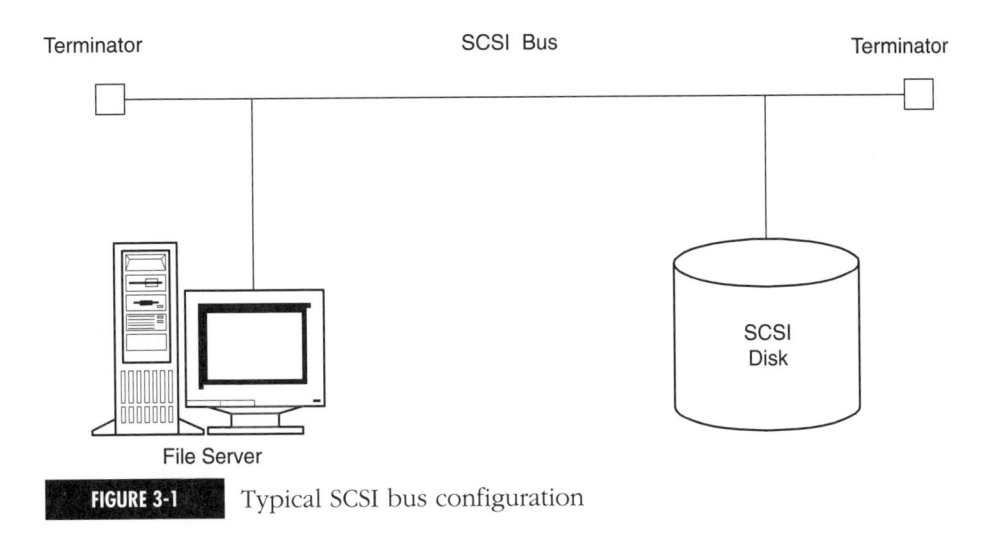

FIGURE 3-1 Typical SCSI bus configuration

exists: the power supply. A better configuration is to use either a SCSI Y cable or a trilink connector. Either of these options allows the SCSI bus to be terminated outside the cluster server members. Now the SCSI bus can be disconnected from one or more cluster members without affecting the physical termination of the bus. These cables are not available from all cable vendors and will take some explanation when attempting to order them. One supplier is Digital Equipment.

All devices on a SCSI bus require a unique SCSI ID. This includes the SCSI controller and all peripherals on the bus. By default, most SCSI controllers are configured to use SCSI ID 7. Since the SCSI bus connects to more than one SCSI controller, one of the controller SCSI ID values must be changed. See Figure 3-2. This is done via the setup utility supplied with the SCSI controller card and can vary slightly between vendors. Furthermore, it is documented in the Cluster Server release notes that the controllers in the two cluster members must use SCSI IDs 6 and 7 to insure proper bus arbitration. If other SCSI IDs are used, timeouts on the SCSI bus could occur, leading to errors in the cluster server software.

Some SCSI controllers generate a bus reset at boot time. Normally it would be a good idea to clear the bus before booting, but with a cluster, resetting the bus could again cause errors in the Cluster Server software. Use devices that do not generate a bus reset or at least provide the ability to turn off the feature in the BIOS of the controller.

Devices on a SCSI bus use one of two available transmission methods: single-ended or differential. Single-ended transmission establishes a signal connection using two leads, one data and the other ground. This method is more susceptible to noise problems and all cable distance rules must be strictly followed. Differential transmissions establish a signal connection

FIGURE 3-2 Cluster SCSI bus configuration

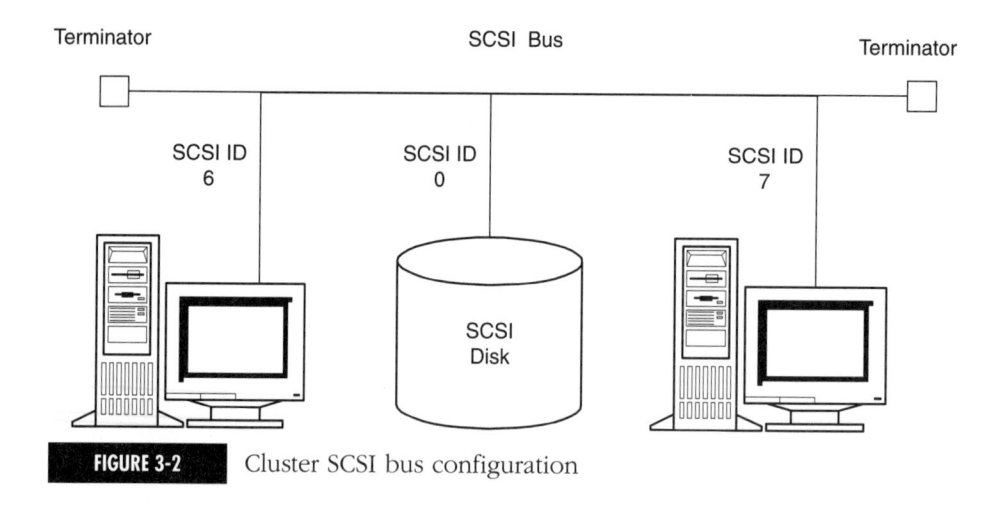

where neither lead is at ground. This is a more stable configuration. It allows for longer cables and faster bus speeds. All devices on the same SCSI bus must use the same transmission method. If it is necessary to mix the transmission methods on the same bus, it will be necessary to use a signal converter. Signal converters convert single-ended SCSI signals to differential SCSI signals. Mixing transmission methods on the same bus without a signal converter can severely damage hardware.

The requirement that the SCSI disk be an external disk is more of a recommendation than a strict requirement. Internal SCSI disks can use two cables just like an external disk, but the cable is slightly different. It is a flat ribbon-like cable. An internal SCSI disk can be used as a cluster disk, but it is not recommended. First, it is possible to run the ribbon cable between two computers, but this is rather messy. There is no connection point on the back of the computer to use. The second and more critical reason for not using internal drives is that they draw their power from the computer power supply. Even if the controller were cabled properly to another cluster member, turning off power to the computer will spin the disk down. This violates the goal of having the capability to allow access to resources independent of whether a specific cluster member is available. It would not be possible to remove the computer from the shared SCSI bus without impacting users and access to resources.

The requirement for one or more network adapters exists because cluster communications occurs over the network. Although the amount of extra traffic generated due to cluster communications is not excessive, cluster server does provide the ability to isolate the traffic on a separate segment. A short piece of thinwire Ethernet is very useful here because no hub is necessary.

This next statement is very important. DO NOT connect the shared SCSI bus to both computers at the same time until at least one has the Cluster Server software installed. It is the Cluster Server software that restricts both computers from accessing the disk simultaneously. Failure to follow this rule can easily corrupt the integrity of the disk, because both computers will be independently accessing the drive and maintaining their own file caches.

Software Requirements

Windows NT Server Enterprise Edition

Windows NT Server Enterprise Edition is an upgraded version of Windows NT Server 4.0 bundled with products like Microsoft Cluster Server. The goal is to be an all-inclusive product suite for enterprise environments. The major new features of the Enterprise edition include:

- Support for eight-way symmetric multi-processing
- More virtual memory for application—3gb
- Enterprise products including Cluster Server Message Queue Server, and Transaction Server.

INSTALLING WINDOWS NT SERVER ENTERPRISE EDITION

Most likely, the computers that are going to be used to run Microsoft Cluster Server are not already running the Enterprise edition software, so it must be installed. If the target systems to be used are already running Windows NT Server 4.0, it is possible to upgrade the operating system to the Enterprise edition. There are two methods of upgrading the operating system. The one to use depends on what Service Pack the system is currently using. The current Service Pack can be determined be running the Windows NT Diagnostics program in the Administrative Tools group. If the current Service Pack is 2 or later, then the program WINNTUP should be used to upgrade to the Enterprise edition of the software. The reason for this is that the WINNT32 program installs the operating system at Service Pack 1, but a large number of files have already been modified by later Service Packs that have already been applied. If the program WINNT32 is used to upgrade a machine that is running Service Pack 2 or later, when Service Pack 3 is installed, the system may not function properly. One disadvantage of the WINNTUP program is that it does not modify the number of supported processors for the operating system. If it is necessary to support more than four processors and the computer is already running Service Pack 2 or later, it will be necessary to perform a new installation of Windows NT Server, Enterprise Edition. All previous configuration information will be lost.

If systems are being upgraded from Windows NT 4.0, their role as a domain controller or member server has already been decided, because whether or not they function as a domain controller cannot be modified during an upgrade. If the cluster members are being newly loaded, then some decisions must be made about the role the cluster member will assume on the network. It is obvious that the cluster members will perform the tasks of a file, application and print server. The basic rule has usually been not to have the same computer perform the tasks of a domain controller and a file and application server. Applications such as SQL Server recommend not installing on a domain controller for best performance. There are three supported configurations for Windows NT Server Enterprise Edition within a cluster. The possible configurations are:

- Both computers can be member servers. This means they will not assume the burden of client logon validation and account database synchronization. Both nodes must be members of the same domain.
- Both computers can be backup domain controllers in an existing domain.
- One computer functions as the primary domain controller, the other as a backup domain controller.

The most efficient configuration is to use the primary/backup domain controller configuration in a domain that consists only of cluster members. This alleviates the domain controller load of logon validation support and also avoids any file permission issues that could arise from member servers maintaining their own account database. In order to allow users access to the cluster resources, a trust relationship must be established with the domain that contains the enterprise account database.

Service Pack 3 must be installed to complete the installation of Windows NT Server, Enterprise Edition; it is provided with the software distribution.

Installing the Cluster Server Software

Preliminary Steps

Before the Microsoft Cluster Server software can be installed, there are a few tasks that must be performed. First, verify that the drive letters for the shared SCSI disk partitions are the same on both servers. Remember that both systems cannot be running at this time with the shared SCSI bus connected. Boot one system first and verify the drive letter for each partition. It may be useful to use the Disk Administrator utility to assign drive letters that are higher in the alphabet. This leaves room for future local drive additions and the ability to keep local drive letters contiguous. If the shared SCSI drives are not viewable while one machine is powered off, this may be due to internal termination being used from the SCSI adapter, preventing the adapter from providing the termination with the power off. To work around this, boot the second computer, then at the boot menu press the up or down arrows. The boot process will stop at this point. Now check the drive letters on the first computer and make any desired changes. Next, reverse roles and configure the drive letters on the second computer to be exactly the same, at least for the shared SCSI devices. It is not required, but it may be useful to have all partitions with the same drive letter assignments whether they are shared or not. Microsoft Cluster Server supports the NTFS format only on shared disks, so perform a format from one of the computers either in Disk Administrator or from a command prompt. If there is pre-existing data that needs to be preserved on the drives, the drive can be converted to NTFS format. Open a command prompt window and issue the command "CONVERT drive:/FS:NTFS," where drive is the drive letter to be converted. The switch "/FS::NTFS" is necessary even though there are currently no other options. If there are files open on the drive, the conversion process cannot take place and will be run during the next reboot of the system.

The Cluster Server software runs as a Windows NT service, and services run under the context of an account that can be specified. The installation process requires that an account and password be already created for this purpose. The account can be created using the User Manager for Domains program in the Administrative Tools group. The documentation states that this account does not require any special privileges, but this is not entirely true. The account does need the advanced user right to log on as a service, but the installation program grants the privilege automatically. However, if the privilege were to be revoked manually at a later time, the cluster service would fail to start. Make sure that there are no restrictions enabled on the account that require password changes and the option to force the password to be changed at next logon. Since this account will not be used interactively, this would again cause the cluster service to fail at startup.

Installing the Software—First Cluster Member

Now that the preliminary steps have been completed, the installation of the Microsoft Cluster Server software can be performed. There are two methods to start the installation. A new installer program is shipped with Windows NT called NHLOADER. This tool is an interface to install the products that ship with Windows NT Server Enterprise Edition that reside on Disk 2 of the distribution. The other option is to invoke the Setup program in the directory MSCS/CLUSTER/I386 or ALPHA, depending on your hardware platform. The installation process will begin. See Figure 3-3.

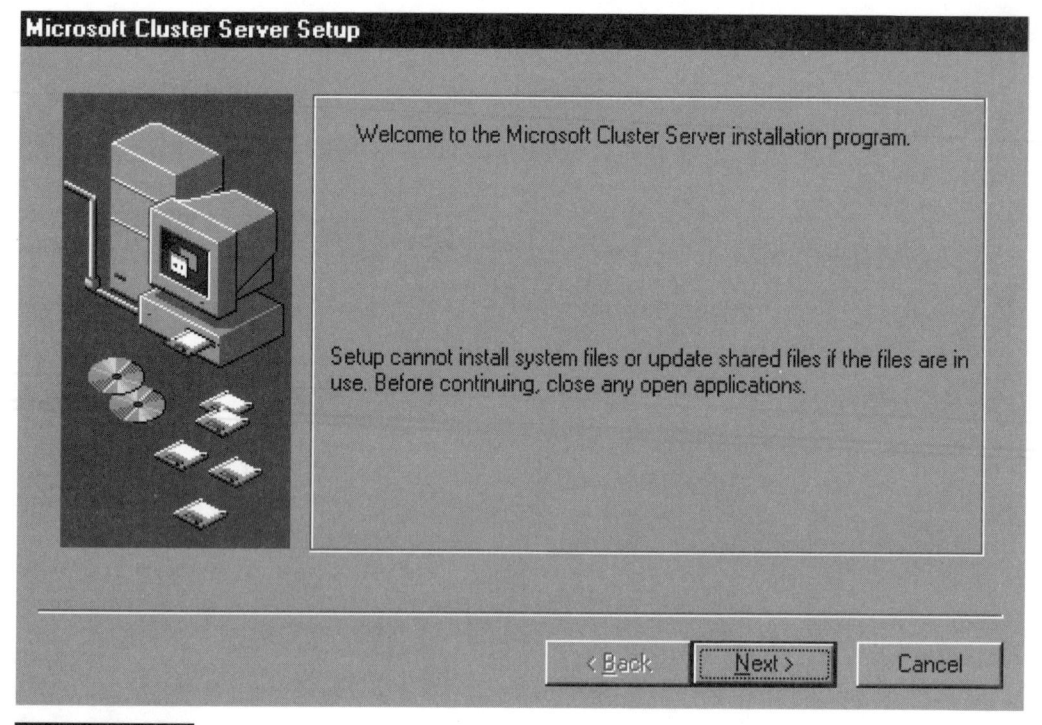

[Screenshot: Microsoft Cluster Server Setup — Welcome to the Microsoft Cluster Server installation program. Setup cannot install system files or update shared files if the files are in use. Before continuing, close any open applications. Buttons: < Back, Next >, Cancel]

FIGURE 3-3 Cluster Server Installation—Screen 1

Windows NT cannot update files that are currently open. With files such as DLLs, it may not be obvious which application is currently using it. The safest thing to do is to shut down all unnecessary applications during the Cluster Server installation.

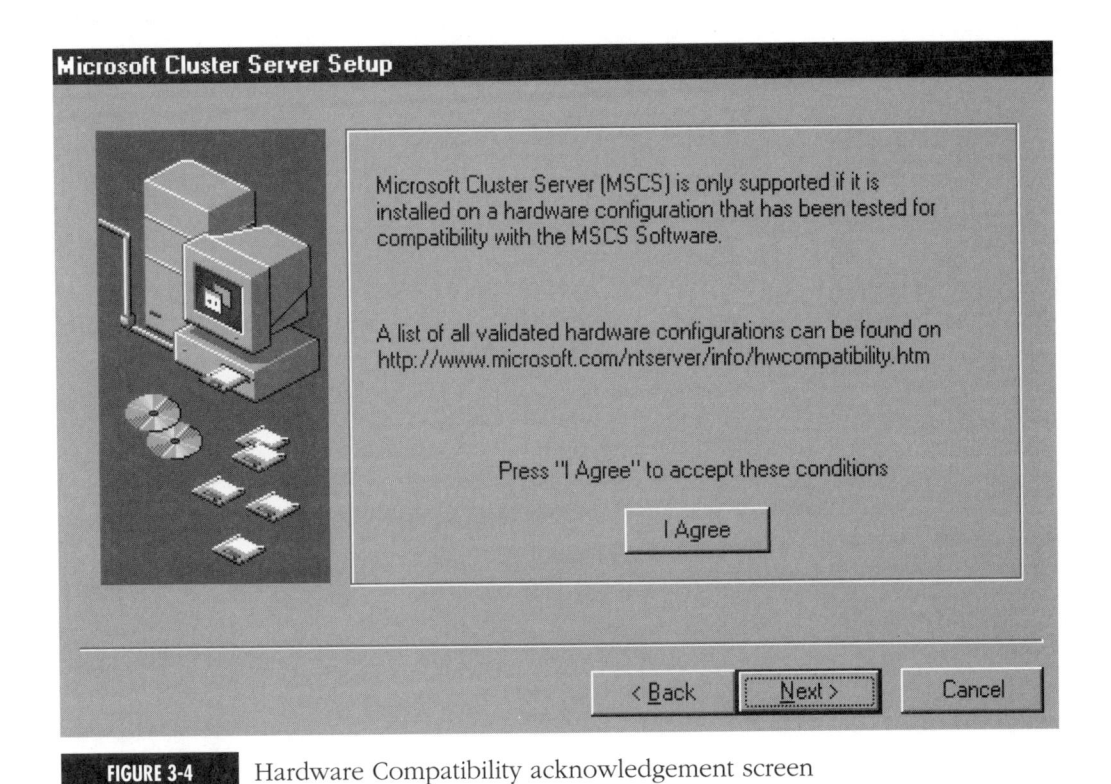

FIGURE 3-4 Hardware Compatibility acknowledgement screen

There are published hardware compatibility lists for both Windows NT Server Enterprise Edition and for the Cluster Server products. Confirm that the Cluster Server software is being installed on approved hardware by selecting the "I Agree" button. See Figure 3-4. The safest method is to use only hardware that is listed. My experience with hardware compatibility lists has been that most hardware that is not listed will work, but there is no guarantee. Be aware that if Cluster Server software is loaded on non-approved hardware, Microsoft technical support may not be able to aid in troubleshooting problems that may arise. Most of the hardware issues associated with Cluster Server deal with the SCSI controllers and adapters. If possible, use the same same model SCSI controller in all cluster members. If this is not possible, at least make sure that the controllers use the same transmission method as discussed earlier in the chapter. Also, only use controllers with the same data path size. Do not mix 8-bit, 16-bit and 32-bit controllers.

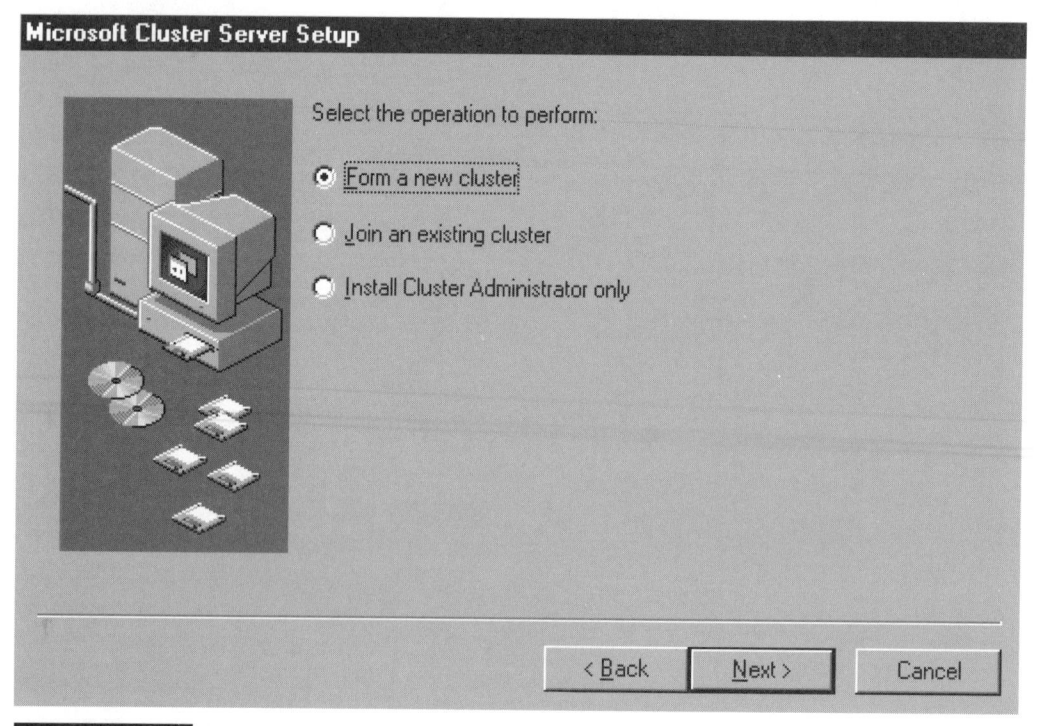

FIGURE 3-5 Specifying the type of installation

It is necessary to declare whether this Cluster Server installation should create a new cluster or participate in an already formed cluster. See Figure 3-5. Which option should be chosen here depends on whether this is the installation of the first cluster member or secondary cluster members. Since this is the installation of the first cluster member, the option, "Form a new cluster," should be selected. If this is an installation of a secondary cluster member, the option, "Join an existing cluster," would be used. Both of the options to "Join an Existing Cluster" and "Install Cluster Administrator only" are discussed in more detail later.

If the computer receiving the first node installation is not the primary domain controller for its domain, the PDC must be running and available in order for the Cluster Server installation to complete successfully.

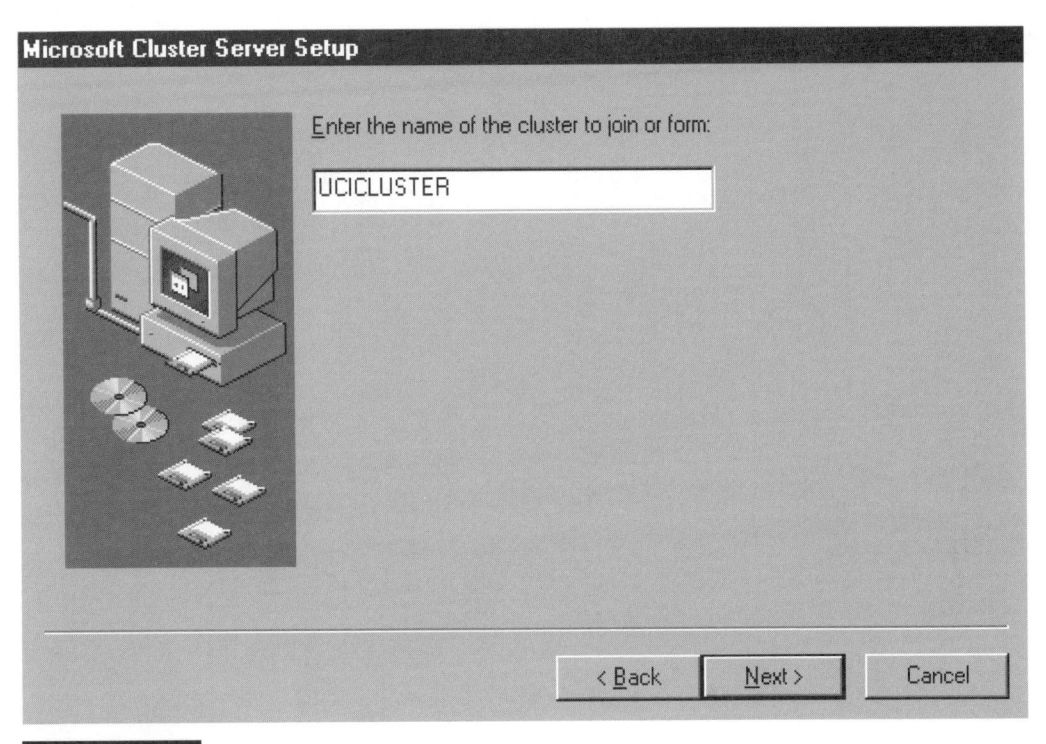

FIGURE 3-6 Specifying the cluster name

When either the option to join a cluster or form a cluster is selected, it is necessary to supply the name of the target cluster. See Figure 3-6. Enter the name of the cluster to be created if this is the installation of the first cluster member. If this is a secondary cluster member, enter the name of the cluster to join. Also, in the case of a secondary member installation, the initial cluster member must be up and the cluster server must be running.

The only restriction on naming the cluster is that it must follow typical NetBIOS naming conventions. It cannot be longer than fifteen characters, and the name must not already exist on the network. From personal experience, I find that the installation process attempts to determine whether the name supplied already exists as a NetBIOS name on the network. The normal NetBIOS name resolution methods are used, including WINS and broadcast.

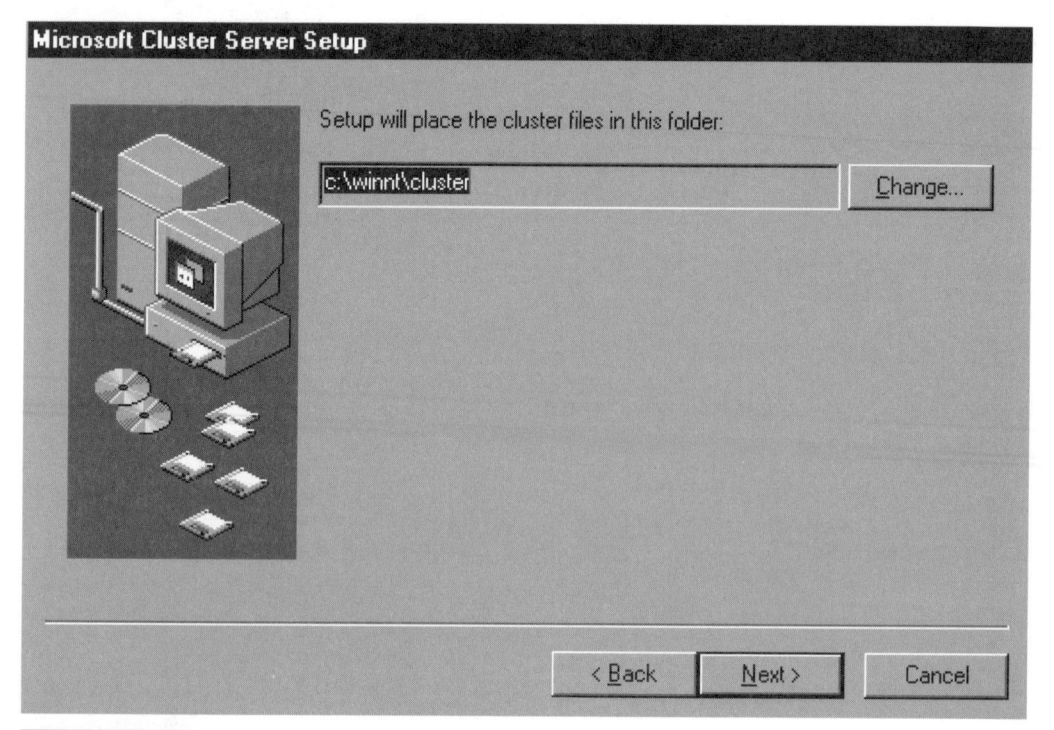

Chapter Three • Windows NT Cluster Server Guidebook

FIGURE 3-7 Cluster Server files location

The Cluster Server installation process requires two different file locations. The first directory will contain the Cluster Server software. See Figure 3-7. Enter the path to the folder that will contain the Cluster Server files. This is the location of the executables, not the location of the quorum files. The path must contain a local disk and not a shared SCSI device.

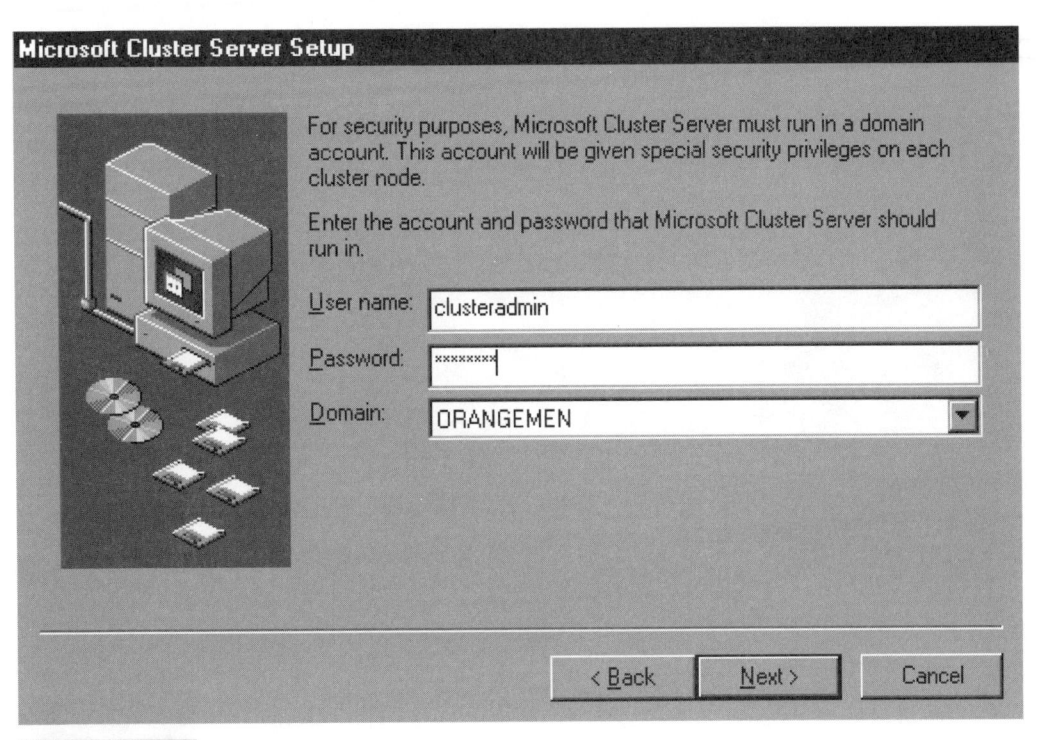

FIGURE 3-8 Cluster Server service account

The primary Cluster Server component runs as a Windows NT service. Valid logon information must be supplied during the installation. See Figure 3-8. Enter the username and password that have been designated as the Cluster Service account. As was stated earlier, the account does not need any special privileges when it is created. The installation process modifies the account to have the necessary rights and permissions. Because the installation process must modify the account permissions, the primary domain controller for the domain to which the cluster member belongs must be online during the installation process. This is because all account database changes are applied to the primary domain controller for a domain, and then these changes are propagated to any backup domain controllers. Also, if the service account does not reside in the local domain account database and resides in a trusted domain database, a domain controller for the trusted domain must be accessible during the installation process. This is not a recommended procedure, because the account information must be verified every time a cluster member is booted. The recommended configuration is to have the cluster members be domain controllers in a separate domain, and set up any necessary trusts to allow access to the cluster resources.

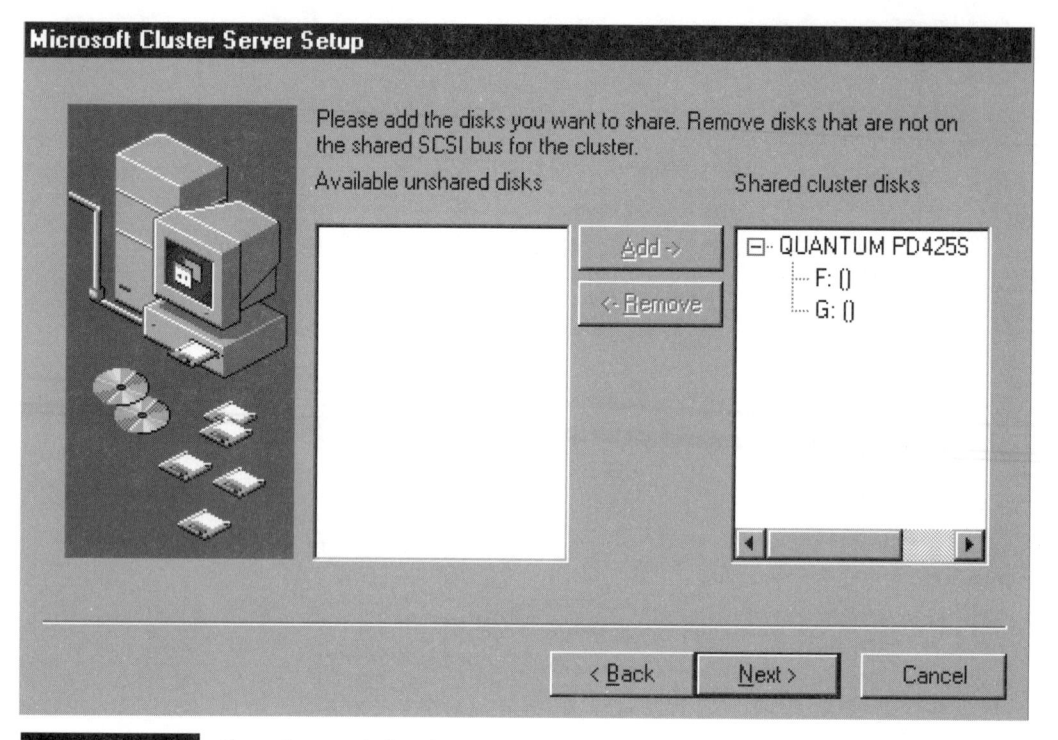

FIGURE 3-9 Shared SCSI disk selection

It is necessary to have at least one shared SCSI disk. If there is none, the installation cannot continue. The Cluster Server installation program displays the available SCSI devices. See Figure 3-9. By default, all SCSI disks on SCSI buses other than the bus that contains the Windows NT installation will appear on this screen. The Cluster Server software has no method to determine which SCSI disks are on shared controllers and which disks are not. The only assumption the Cluster Server software makes is that no disk on the bus with the Windows NT installation disk can be a cluster-shared disk. Make sure that any SCSI disks that are not going to be on a shared SCSI bus do not appear in the Shared Cluster Disks window.

Notice in the example that the SCSI Quantum disk consists of two partitions of F and G. It is not possible to have one partition treated as a shared cluster disk and the other partition not be shared. Cluster Server supports only NTFS formatted drives. If devices are on the shared SCSI bus but are not allowed to be a cluster shared disk, check the disk format and, if necessary, format or convert the disk to the NTFS format. In the two partition configuration in the example, the Quantum disk was not selectable as a shared cluster disk until both partitions had an NFTS format.

FIGURE 3-10 Quorum resource location

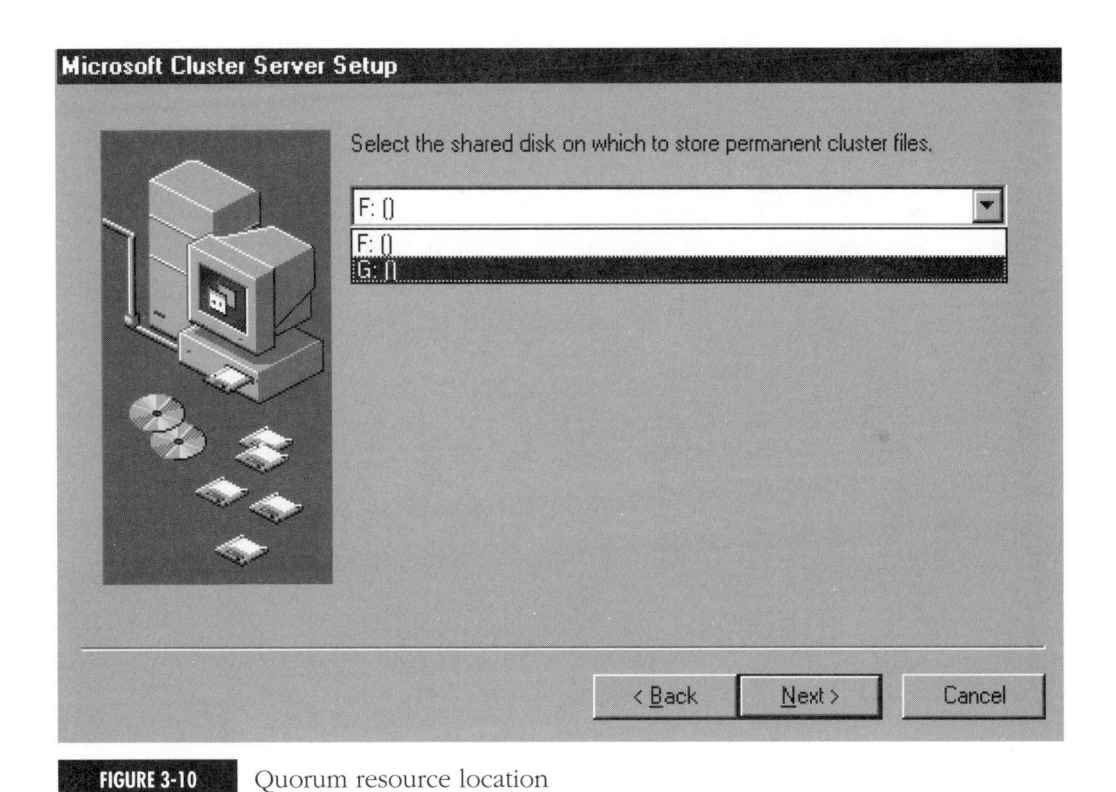

The second disk specification required by the Cluster Server installation is the location of the quorum resource. Any disk configured to be a cluster-shared disk can store the quorum resource. See Figure 3-10. Select the disk that will store the quorum resource. The quorum resource is designed to keep the cluster members from booting up and forming separate, independent clusters. If it becomes necessary, the disk designated as the quorum disk can be changed later through the Cluster Administrator utility. The use of the quorum resource is discussed in detail in Chapter 2.

Microsoft Cluster Server Setup

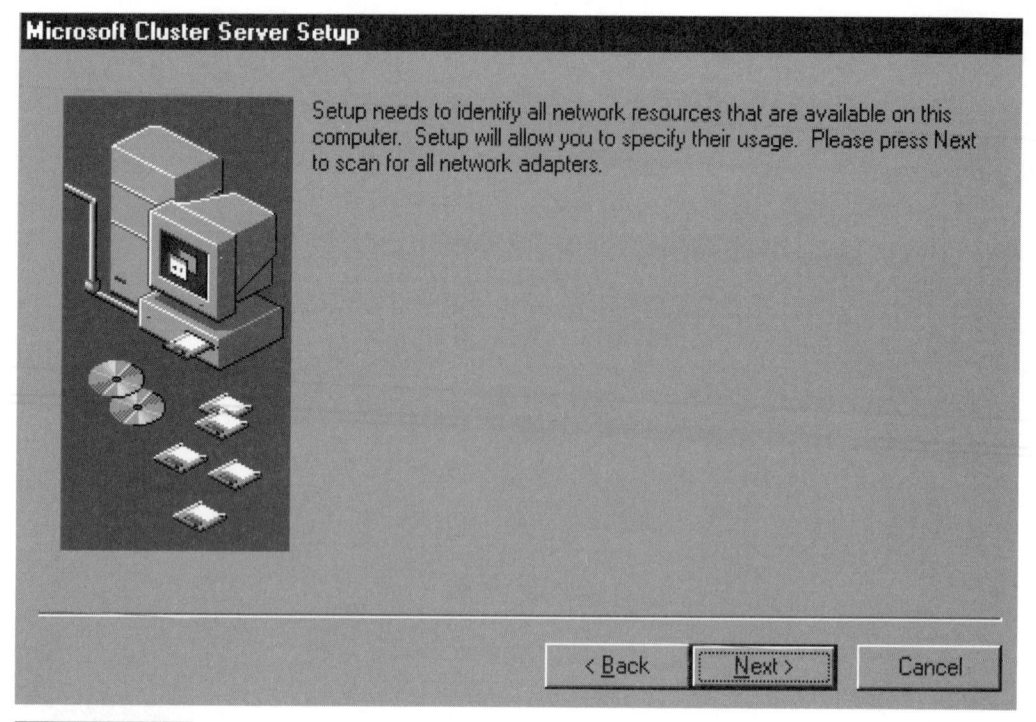

Setup needs to identify all network resources that are available on this computer. Setup will allow you to specify their usage. Please press Next to scan for all network adapters.

FIGURE 3-11 Network adapter search

At this point, the installation program will detect all network adapters on the computer. See Figure 3-11. It is useful in a cluster configuration to have more than one network adapter. One adapter could be used solely for the cluster communications traffic. This could be a totally isolated network segment. This avoids extra traffic over your company network.

Three • Building a Cluster   **43**

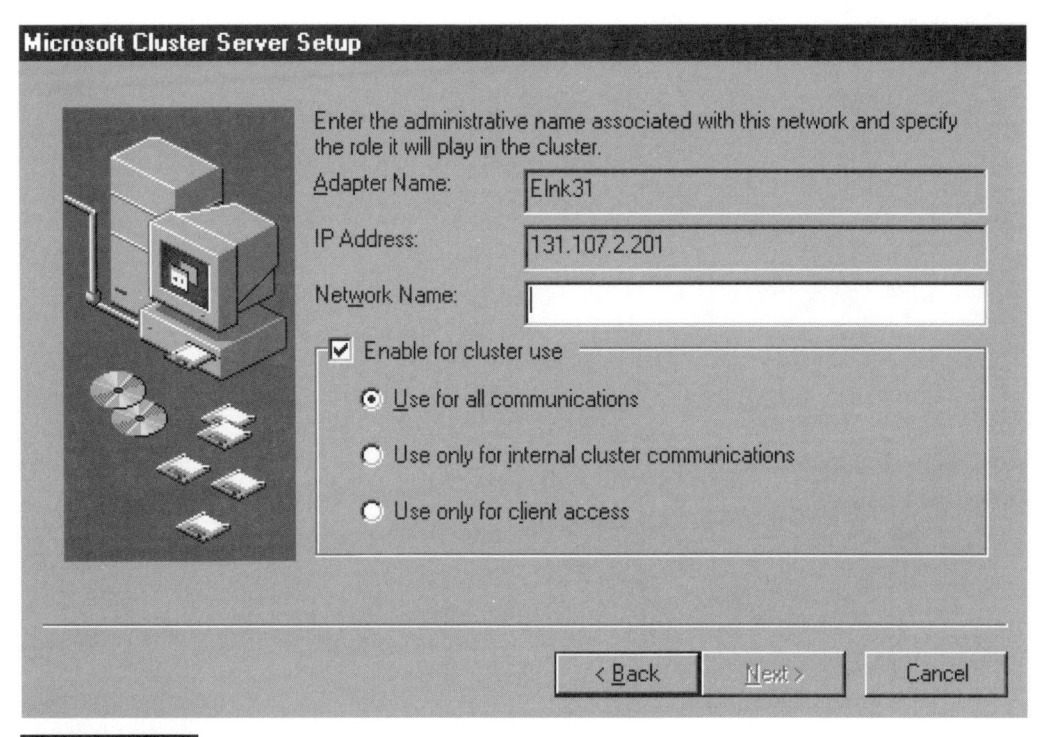

FIGURE 3-12   Network adapter configuration

After the network adapter detection process has completed, the installation process allows each adapter to be configured independently. See Figure 3-12. For each network adapter detected, assign a descriptive name. Also, the software allows each adapter to be designated as to what type of traffic it can carry. First, make sure the box, "Enable for Cluster Use," is checked. Select the option, "Use only for internal cluster communications," if the adapter is connected to a separate network with the intention of isolating the underlying cluster traffic. Select the option, "Use only for client access," to not allow the cluster to send internal heartbeats and messages via this network. And select the option, "Use for all communications," to allow all traffic. This would be the case if there is only a single network adapter in the cluster member.

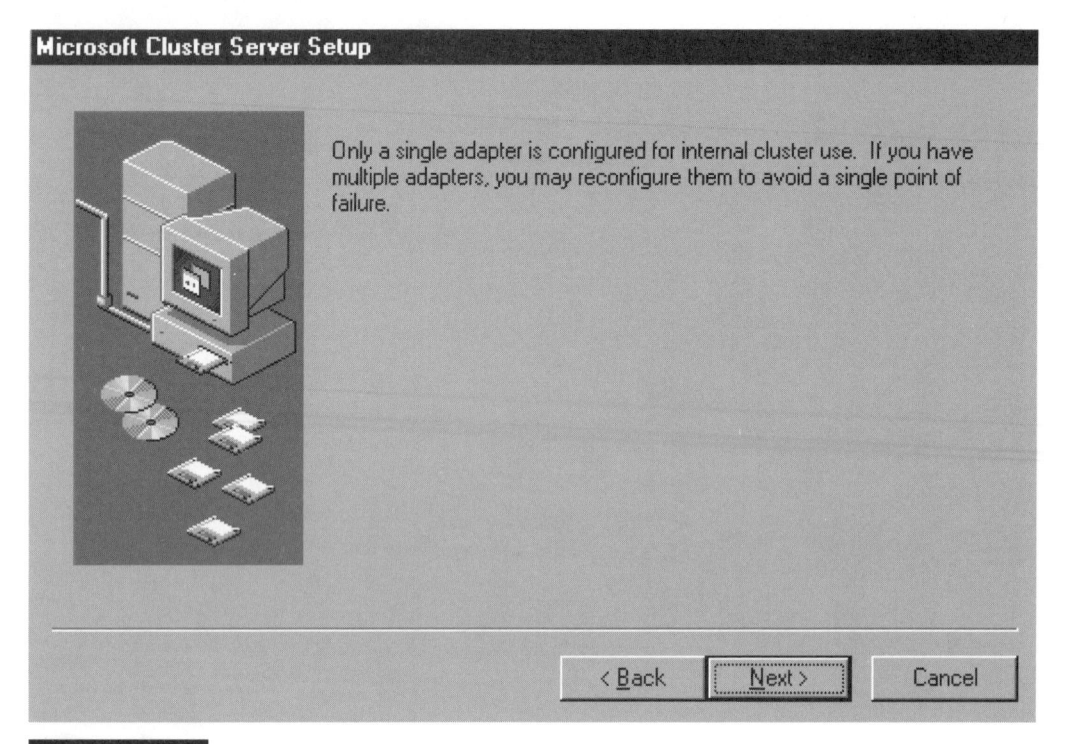

[Screenshot: Microsoft Cluster Server Setup dialog with message "Only a single adapter is configured for internal cluster use. If you have multiple adapters, you may reconfigure them to avoid a single point of failure." with Back, Next, and Cancel buttons.]

FIGURE 3-13 Network adapter prioritization

If there are multiple network adapters with cluster communications allowed, at this point the installation will allow those adapters to be prioritized. See Figure 3-13. For example, there may be two network adapters, both with cluster communications allowed but only one with client access allowed. To do this, select, "Use for all communications" on one adapter and "Use only for internal cluster communications" on the other. If both networks are available, it makes sense to split the load by having the cluster traffic use the adapter designated for internal cluster communications only if the network is available. This can be accomplished by ordering the networks, top being given the highest priority, in the order the networks should be used for internal cluster communications.

Three • Building a Cluster

Microsoft Cluster Server Setup

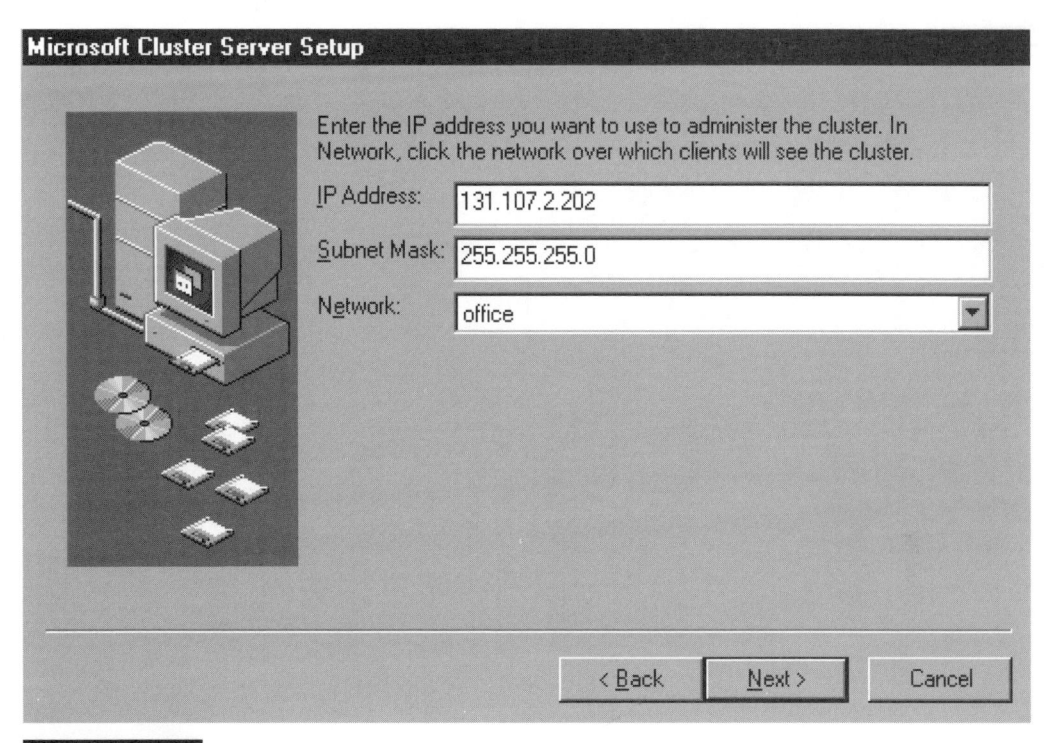

Enter the IP address you want to use to administer the cluster. In Network, click the network over which clients will see the cluster.

IP Address: 131.107.2.202
Subnet Mask: 255.255.255.0
Network: office

FIGURE 3-14 TCP/IP configuration

It is necessary to assign a static TCP/IP address and subnet mask to the cluster. See Figure 3-14. This becomes the Cluster IP address resource and is one method of referencing the cluster. The cluster IP address resource should not be used by clients connecting to cluster resources because there is no guarantee that the same cluster member will own the cluster IP address resource and the resource the client is attempting to access. The address is used by administrators to connect to and manage a cluster with the Cluster Administrator utility.

FIGURE 3-15 Completing the installation

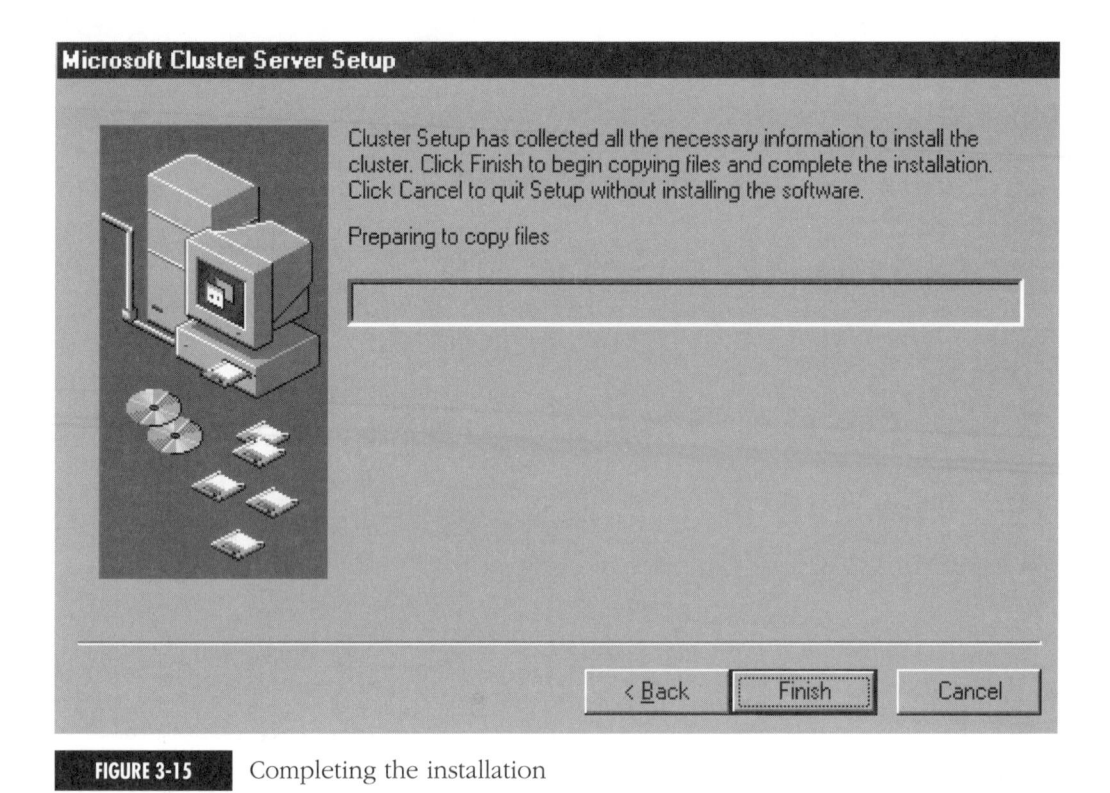

At this point, all necessary information has been supplied to the installation program. Select "Finish" to complete the installation. See Figure 3-15.

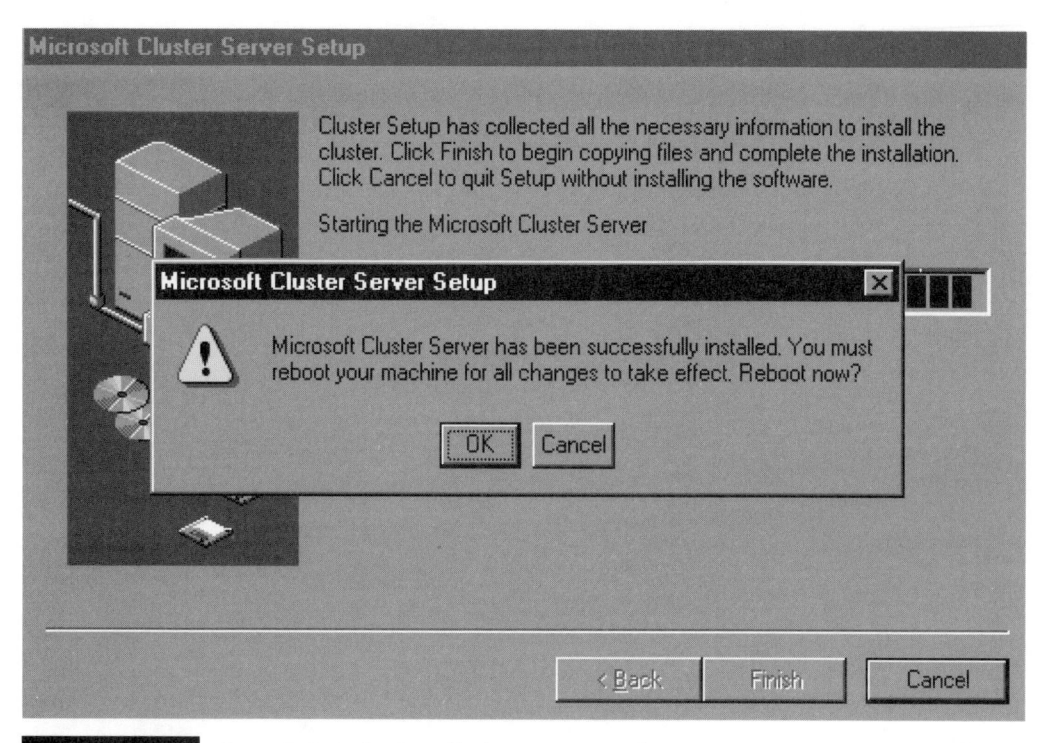

FIGURE 3-16 Completing the installation, continued

If the installation is successful, it is necessary to reboot the system to start the cluster server software. See Figure 3-16. To verify the installation after the computer reboots, start the Cluster Administrator utility in the Administrative tools group. If a timeout occurs, wait a few seconds and try again. The Cluster Server software starts in the background and sometimes is not completely running when the desktop is displayed.

Another check for a successful installation is to verify the "Cluster" key has been created in the HKEY_LOCAL_MACHINE section of the registry.

Installing the Software – the Second Node

Installation of secondary nodes in the cluster is a very simple process with limited input required from the administrator. As with the first node, the hurdle is getting the SCSI controller and devices configured properly. Remember the basic rule that both computers should not be booted until at least one has the Cluster Server software installed. Once one system is a functioning cluster member, it will lock the disk from access by the other planned cluster member until the Cluster Server software is loaded successfully.

![Microsoft Cluster Server Setup screen with options: Form a new cluster, Join an existing cluster (selected), Install Cluster Administrator only]

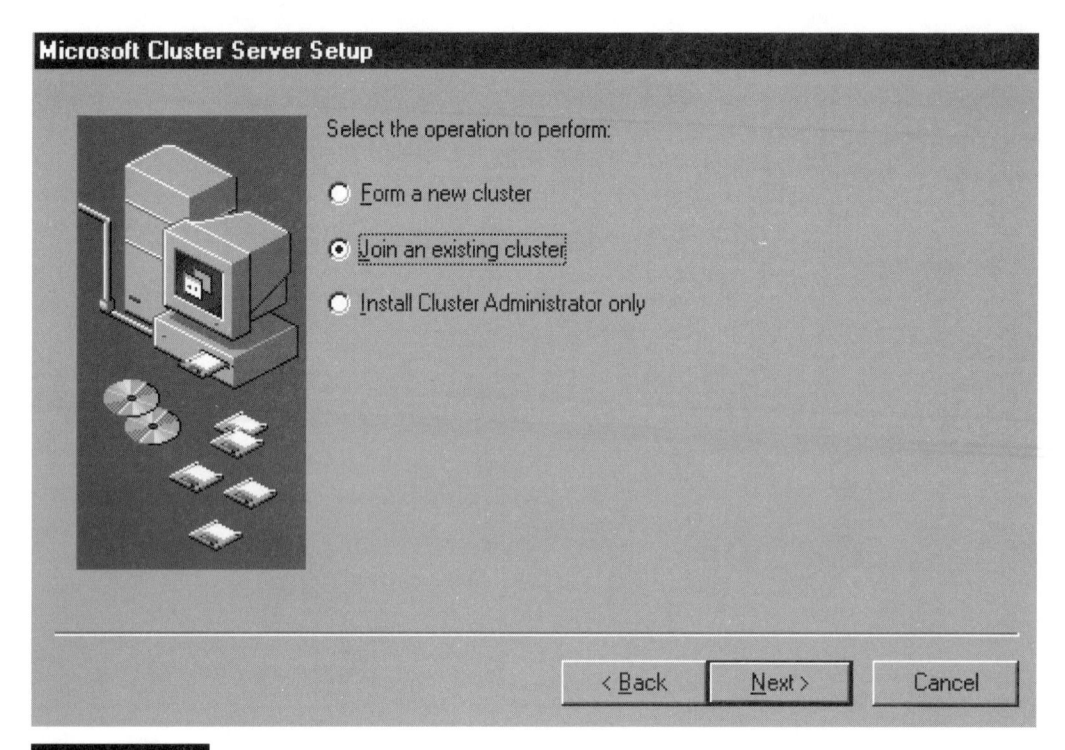

FIGURE 3-17   Specifying the type of installation, second node

    As mentioned previously in the section on preliminary steps, the disk drive letter assignments to the devices on the shared SCSI bus should be verified. It is necessary that the drive letters be the same on both cluster members. If not, shut down the computer running Cluster Server to make the devices available to the new potential cluster member. Run Disk Administrator and configure the drive letters to be the same as on the first node.

    At this point, the installation of the second node can be started. Be sure to reboot the existing cluster member. This may require the second node be shut down to release the SCSI devices. If the boot process stalls at the SCSI device detection then displays the message, "Device timeout," the second node must be shut down to release the devices to the existing cluster member. Once both cluster members are running the program SETUP.EXE in the directory MSCS/CLUSTER/I386 or ALPHA from disk 2 of the Windows NT Server, Enterprise Edition distribution can be executed. See Figure 3-17. Installation screens that are the same as the installation of the first node have been left out, in order not to be too repetitive.

Three • Building a Cluster   49

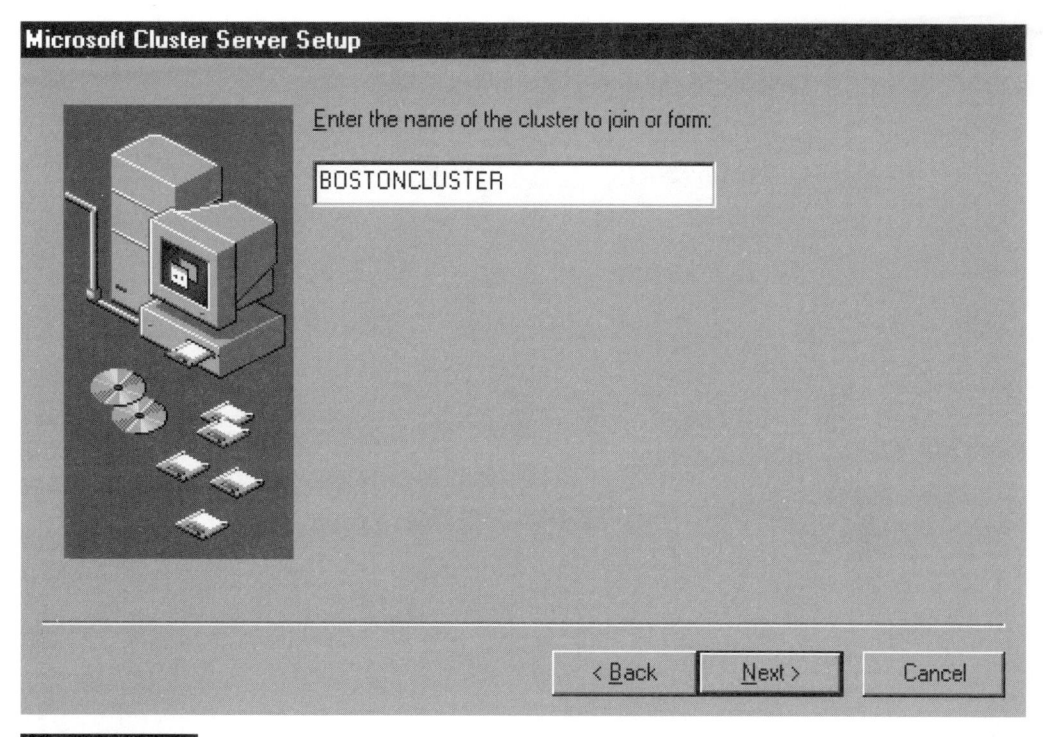

FIGURE 3-18   Specifying the cluster name, second node

For the installation of the second node, the option 'Join an Existing cluster' should be selected.

Enter the name of the cluster to join. See Figure 3-18. At this point, the first node in the cluster needs to be online. If the first node is not the primary domain controller of the domain the computers are members of, it also must be online. If either server is not available, the cluster server installation will fail.

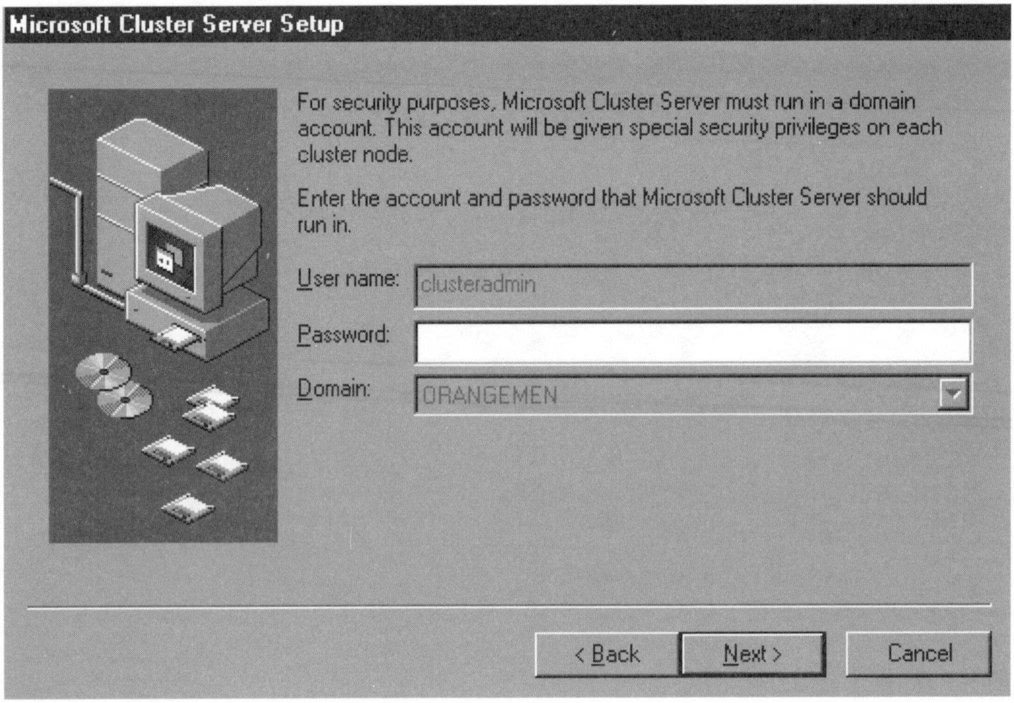

FIGURE 3-19 Cluster Server service account, second node

After completing the screen requesting the location for the cluster software, the password to the cluster service account is requested. See Figure 3-19. Notice that both the username and password fields are grayed. The username and password used for the Cluster Service must be exactly the same on both nodes. As a security check, the installation requires the password to be entered. In the situation where both cluster members are domain controllers, the account used for the cluster service has already been granted the right to log on as a service. If the cluster nodes are member servers, it is a good idea for the administrator to make sure the account has been granted the proper privileges.

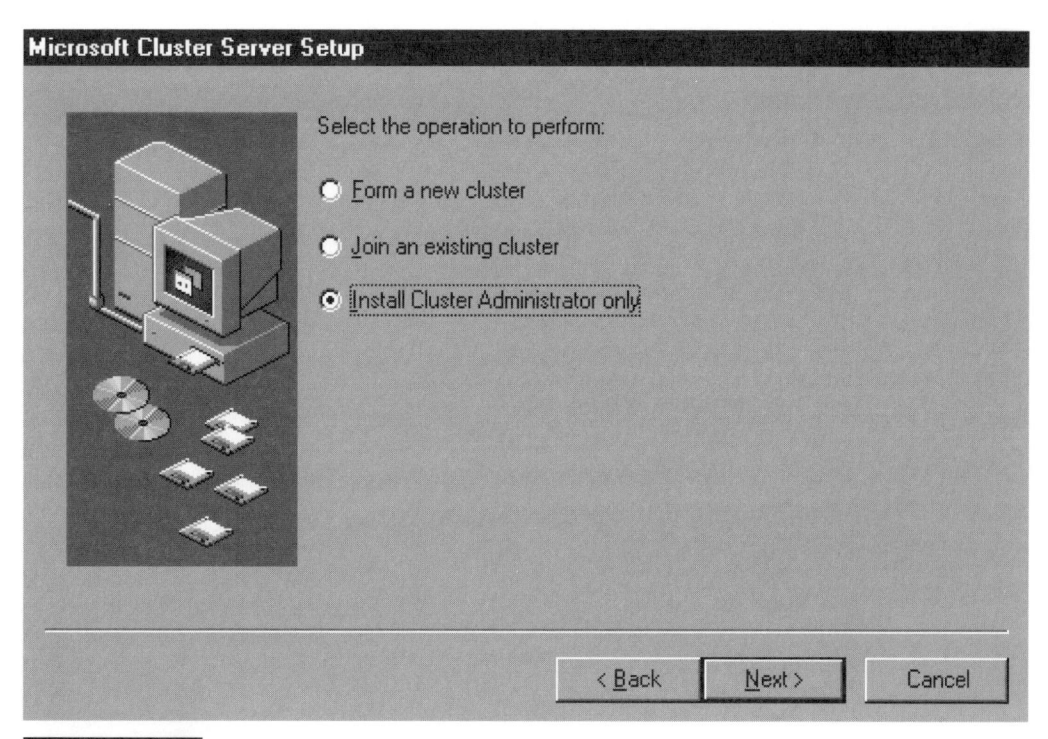

FIGURE 3-20   Installing the Cluster Administrator tool

Installing the Cluster Administrator tool

In most data processing organizations, an individual does not usually use the application and file servers as a regular system on a daily basis. Generally, servers are placed in strategic locations, sometimes to get the system onto a specific network segment, sometimes to get the servers out of the flow of user traffic to avoid the accidental bumps and coffee spills. In any case, it is not practical for the administrator to be sitting physically at the cluster in order to carry out configuration tasks after the initial installation. The Cluster Server software allows the installation of the Cluster Administrator tool, which is the same program installed on the cluster nodes, to be installed separate from the rest of the software. This allows the administrator to perform configuration and monitoring tasks from their desk.

To install the Cluster Administrator tool, start the Cluster Server installation program and select the option "Install Cluster Administrator only" option. See Figure 3-20.

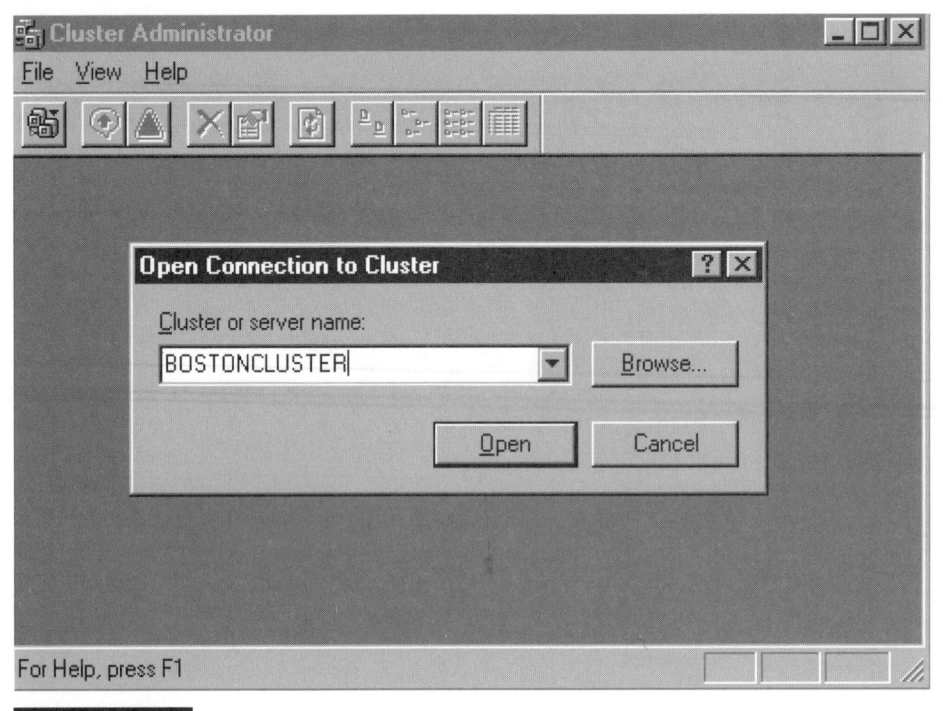

FIGURE 3-21 Using the Cluster Administrator program

The Cluster Administrator tool can be installed on any computer running Service Pack 3 with version 4.0 of either Windows NT Workstation or Windows NT Server. Cluster Administrator can also be installed on any computer running Windows NT Server, Enterprise Edition.

The Cluster Administrator utility is installed into the Administrative Tools group. When the program is run for the first time, Cluster Administrator prompts for a cluster name. See Figure 3-21. If the cluster name does not work, attempt to connect with either a node name or TCP/IP address, or the TCP/IP address assigned to the cluster. The Cluster Administrator utility will automatically restore any connections to clusters that are left open at the end of the most recent session. Connections can be established to multiple clusters by requesting to open another cluster without closing the current connection. It is not possible to establish to connections to the same cluster in this manner, but the same result can be achieved by using the Window, New option from within the Cluster Administrator program. This can be useful; it allows the administrator to set up a separate window for each cluster member.

Removing Cluster Server

If it ever becomes necessary to permanently remove a node from the cluster, it is accomplished as follows:

- Move all resources to the remaining cluster member. If a cluster member is being replaced, it is not possible to install the new node until the old one is removed. By moving all resources to the remaining cluster member, the interruption, or cluster transition time, of the users will be minimized.
- Use Cluster Administrator to evict the node being removed.
- De-install the software on the node.

Evicting the Removed Node

The first step in removing the cluster server software should be to move any groups and resources that are owned by the node that is being removed to the node that will remain a cluster member. This can be done via the Cluster Administrator program. When the software is de-installed on the cluster member, it does not remove itself from the cluster configuration database. This is accomplished by evicting the node from the cluster. This is performed in the Cluster Administrator. See Figure 3-22.

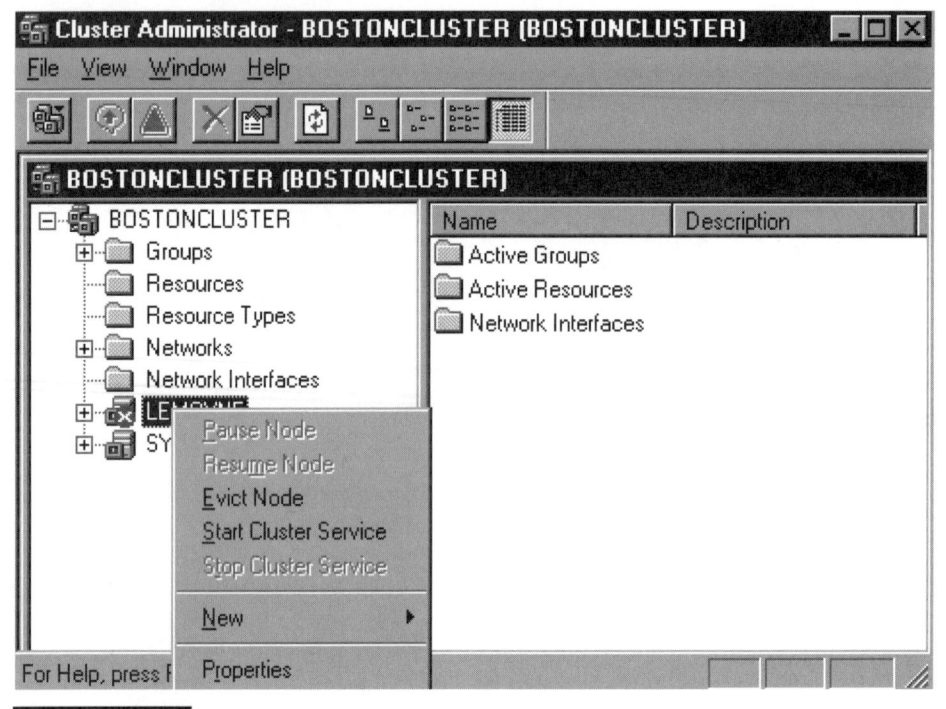

FIGURE 3-22 Configuring a cluster member

De-installing the Software

The Cluster Server software does not have its own un-install option, but it does install with InstallShield which allows software to be removed via a standard application. To remove the Cluster Server software, use the option, "Add/Remove Programs," from Control Panel. A screen will appear with the list of installed software that can be removed with this method. See Figure 3-23.

Three • Building a Cluster 55

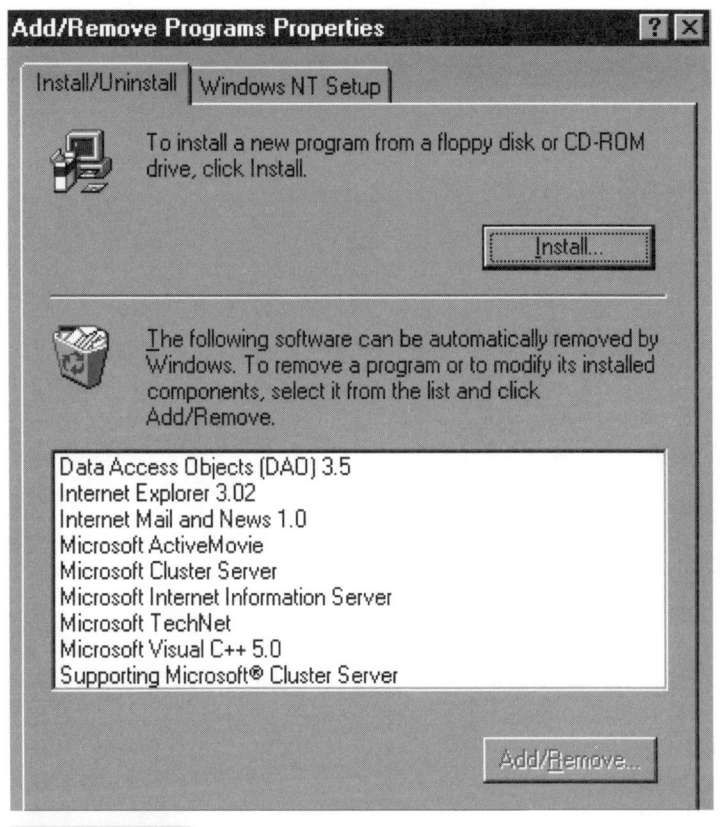

FIGURE 3-23 Removing Cluster Server

Select the entry for "Microsoft Cluster Server" and then the "Add/Remove" button. The software should be removed. If the software is being removed with plans to immediately re-install, perhaps as a troubleshooting option, be sure to reboot at this point before attempting to re-install the software.

FOUR

Implementing Cluster Available Resources

Once the cluster is built, the administrator can begin the process of configuration. This includes placing resources such as applications, shared directories, and printers in the cluster to take advantage of the fault tolerance the cluster can provide. Many cluster components must be created, such as TCP/IP addresses and network names. It will take some planning to implement the cluster resources in a method that includes both the cluster features of load balancing and fault tolerance. For example, in a non-cluster implementation, the availability of a file-share depends upon the current status of the file server. In a cluster, the availability of a file-share is based upon the overall status of the cluster. A resource should still be available to clients as long as one member of the cluster is operational. This is a loose definition of fault tolerant. Client access to their data or application should not depend upon a cluster member computer's encountering a hardware or software "fault." In a properly configured cluster, it will be transparent to the client what cluster member is serving their request. The administrator implements this by configuring the resource and all the necessary parameters on the cluster. This chapter discusses the various resources that can be offered to clients as cluster resources and the necessary steps to properly configure the resource.

The steps necessary to implement cluster available resources include planning and creating groups to contain resources, configuring the actual resources, and defining fail-over and fail-back policies for both the groups and resources.

Group Objects

Groups Defined

A group is a collection of dependent or related resources that are managed as a single entity. A group typically contains all of the resources necessary to run a specific application. For example, a file-share resource allows a directory to be accessed over the network by using the standard NetBIOS method. At a lower level, the disk that holds the file resource is also a resource. Microsoft Cluster Server resources can be accessed by one member only since this is a "shared-nothing" cluster model. If one cluster member controls the disk resource while another cluster member owns the file-share resource, neither cluster member will have access to the file-share. The only member that could possibly have access is the one that owns the file-share. But since it does not own the disk the file-share resides on, it has no ability to perform any disk I/O.

Standard Cluster Groups

There are two groups created during the installation process: the Cluster Group and Disk Group 1. The Cluster Group contains the Cluster Name, Cluster IP address and Time Service resources. The specifics regarding these resources will be discussed later in this chapter. The Disk Group 1 group contains the disk devices selected for cluster access. See Figure 4-1.

The group Disk Group 1 is selected in the left pane, and the member resources of Disk Group 1 are displayed in the right pane. Notice there are two disks, F: and G:, that are displayed. The software shows the two disks as one resource. That is because they are two partitions of the same physical disk. Remember that only one cluster member can own a disk. This is true at the physical disk level, not logical disk. If the system allowed these resources to be separately managed, one resource could fail over to another cluster member and become inaccessible. Another important note is that disks should not be repartitioned once they are cluster resources. In reality, the disks can be repartitioned, but be careful of drive letter changes affecting certain types of resources such as a file-share or printer server.

Planning Groups

Obviously, the applications that are contained in the groups will probably supply the majority of the workload to the cluster members. It is, therefore, very important to perform some planning at this stage, if not earlier.

1. Since a group will usually provide underlying resource support for one or more applications, list all the applications that are to be installed on

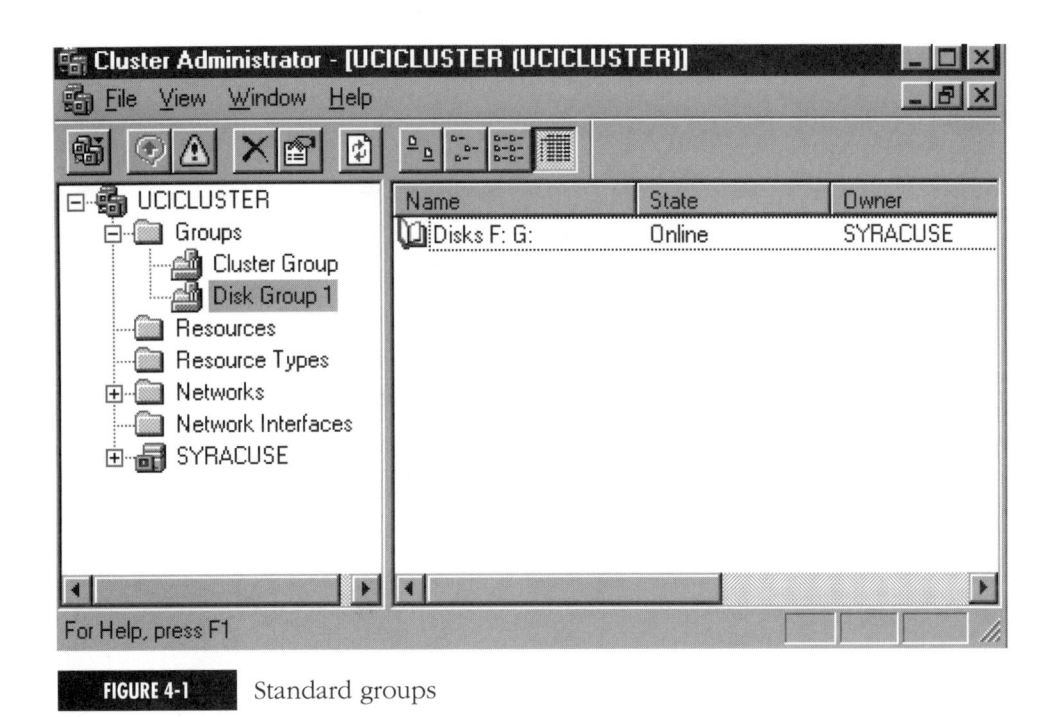

Four • Implementing Cluster Available Resources

FIGURE 4-1 Standard groups

the cluster members. The total resources, such as memory and processor for the total cluster, must be greater than the total required by the application list created and the resources consumed by the Windows NT operating system.

2. Determine which applications can be configured to use the Cluster Server failover feature. The requirements for an application capable of using the failover feature of the cluster are:

   - The application must support TCP/IP as a transport protocol, and
   - The application must be capable of specifying a location for data storage outside the Windows NT installation directory tree. In order for the application to failover properly, the application must be able to use one of the shared SCSI devices and not depend entirely on the Windows NT system directory, since the Windows NT directory cannot be on the shared SCSI bus.

3. List all the resources that can be implemented that are not generally associated with an application, For example, this will include print spoolers and file-share resources. The print spooler and file server applications are not failing over between cluster nodes. One of the resources supported by these operating system components is. It is important to realize that these resources, while not specific applica-

tions, still impact the system resources consumed by a cluster member. For example, a print spooler resource will consume memory to format and buffer the print job, and generate disk I/O as it fetches the print job from the disk. A file-share resource also introduces disk I/O and will consume memory.

4. List all known dependencies for a given resource. This information will be covered for each resource later in this chapter. For example, a file-share resource uses a NetBIOS name and a directory. The NetBIOS name is a network name resource, and the disk that holds the directory is a physical disk resource. For a quick summary of resources and their dependencies, see Appendix A. Two guidelines here are:

- A resource and all its dependencies must be in the same group.
- A resource cannot span groups. For example, if several applications require the same disk resource, they must be in the same group.

Creating Groups

To implement new resources in the cluster, the best approach is to create new groups to contain the resources to be offered. The default groups could be used, but this is not recommended. In addition, it is not recommended to use the cluster name and IP address as resource dependencies. We will discuss this in the section on resources.

Do not take the task of creating groups lightly. Even though it is a fairly simple process, groups impact the cluster's ability to load-balance and provide a level of fault-tolerance. As with Windows NT and user groups, planning the cluster groups ahead of time provides a foundation for the rest of the cluster configuration.

One question to be answered in the group planning phase is:

- Is the main goal of the cluster to load-balance or provide fault tolerance?

While this question really needs to be answered during the cluster hardware planning phase, it also impacts the group planning. If load balancing is a primary objective, then multiple physical disks must be part of the cluster hardware configuration, and all disks cannot be members of the same fault tolerant disk set. By definition, load balancing implies that all cluster members will be doing some level of work. Remember, in the shared-nothing cluster implementation, only one cluster member has access to a cluster disk. In order for cluster members to offer resources to clients simultaneously, each cluster member must be able to own at least one disk. This means that there must be at least as many independent disk devices as cluster members. Next, each of these disk resources must be placed in separate groups. The cluster software offers the ability to influence which group should be owned by which cluster member when all members and

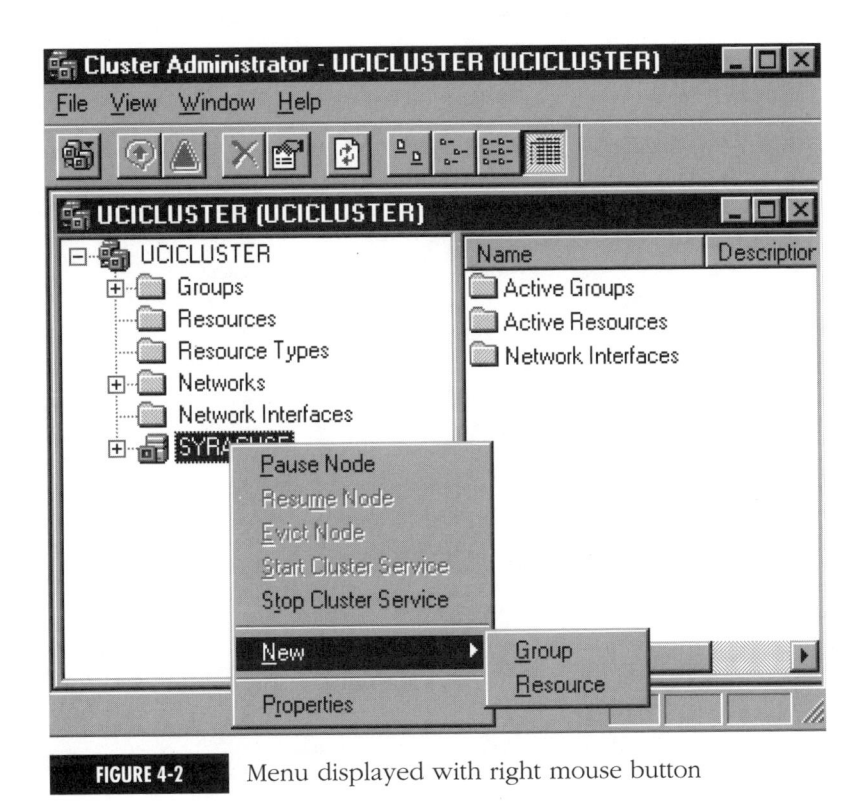

Four • Implementing Cluster Available Resources 61

FIGURE 4-2 Menu displayed with right mouse button

resources are available. This is known as "preferred ownership" and will be discussed shortly.

To create a new group, simply right click with the mouse, somewhere in the cluster administrator utility and select New, Group. See Figure 4-2. The New Group screen appears. Enter a name and description for the new group. Be as descriptive as possible to help when managing the cluster at a later date. See Figure 4-3.

Optionally, preferred owners can be defined for the group. A preferred owner is a cluster member that should become the owner of the group when multiple cluster members are available. This is how it is possible to do some balancing of the total workload of a cluster. Let's assume there are two cluster members, NodeA and NodeB. Let's also assume that there are two applications called App1 and App2. To balance the load between the cluster members, create two groups, App Group 1 and App Group 2. Now place the App1 resource in the App Group 1 group and make the preferred owner NodeA. Place the App2 resource in the App Group 2 group and make the preferred owner NodeB. If both members of the cluster are online, App1 and App2 are split among the cluster members. If Node1 or Node2 goes offline, the other node can take ownership of the group as long as it is listed

FIGURE 4-3 Configuring group names

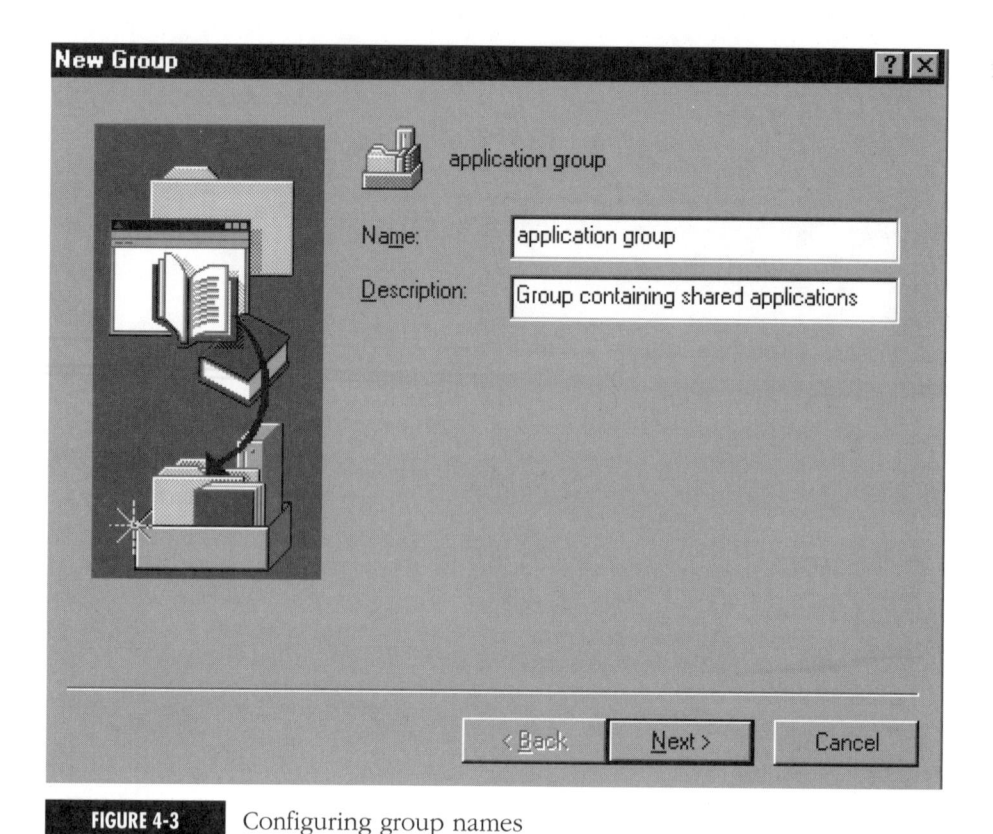

as a possible owner for the resource. This is slightly confusing. Possible owners are defined at the resource level. Preferred owners are defined for the group. When the offline node returns to the cluster, it will take ownership back of any groups where the node is the highest ranked preferred owner. It is possible to have multiple preferred owners. Use the Move Up and Move Down buttons to specify their relative priority status. See Figure 4-4. Click Finish to complete the creation of the group. In the main Cluster Administrator window, the group will appear with a yellow symbol next to it. This is tagging the group as offline.

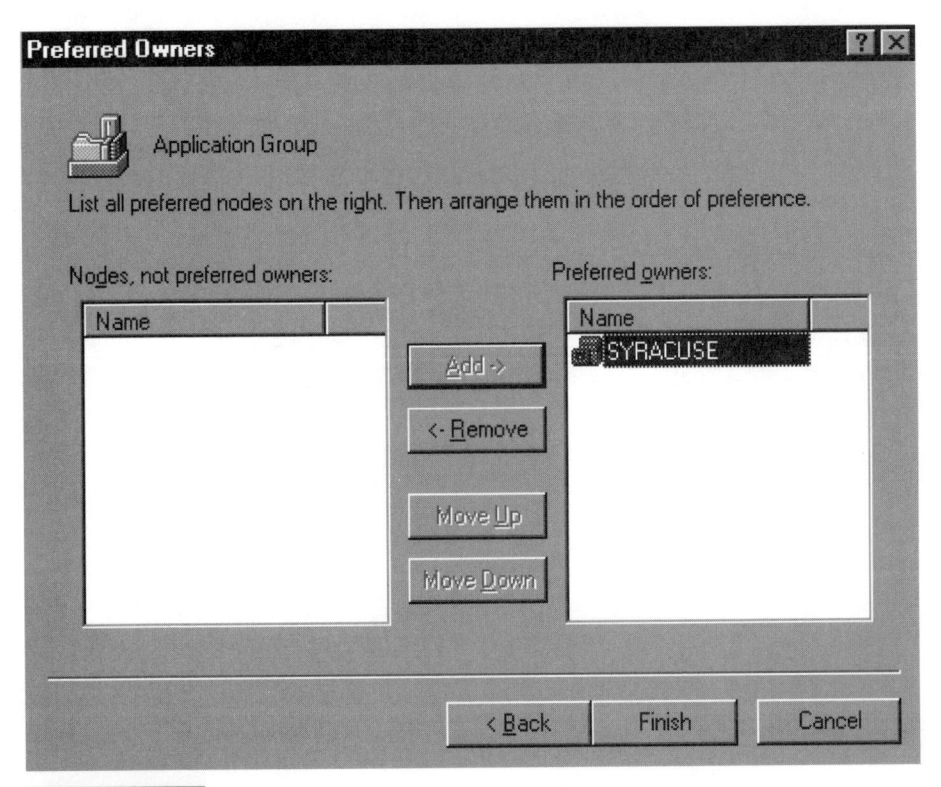

Four • Implementing Cluster Available Resources **63**

FIGURE 4-4 Preferred owners list

Working with Groups

In the normal operation of the cluster, very little maintenance is needed on the groups that have been defined. There are situations, however, when hardware or software maintenance needs to be performed. One of the benefits of a cluster is that it should be transparent to users what actual computer in the cluster is functioning as their server. But what happens if maintenance needs to be performed, or the administrator wishes to do a hardware upgrade? One method is to unplug the cluster member for maintenance and let all the resources fail-over to the other cluster members. The only problem is that there will be a slight delay while the cluster attempts, first, to restart the resource, then decides it cannot restart the resource, then moves the resource to another cluster member. This is a form of cluster transition.

Rather than letting the cluster detect the failure, it is a smoother operation to move the group manually from the member that is going offline for maintenance to a remaining cluster member. To do this, right mouse click on the group or groups in question and select the "Move Group" option. See Figure 4-5.

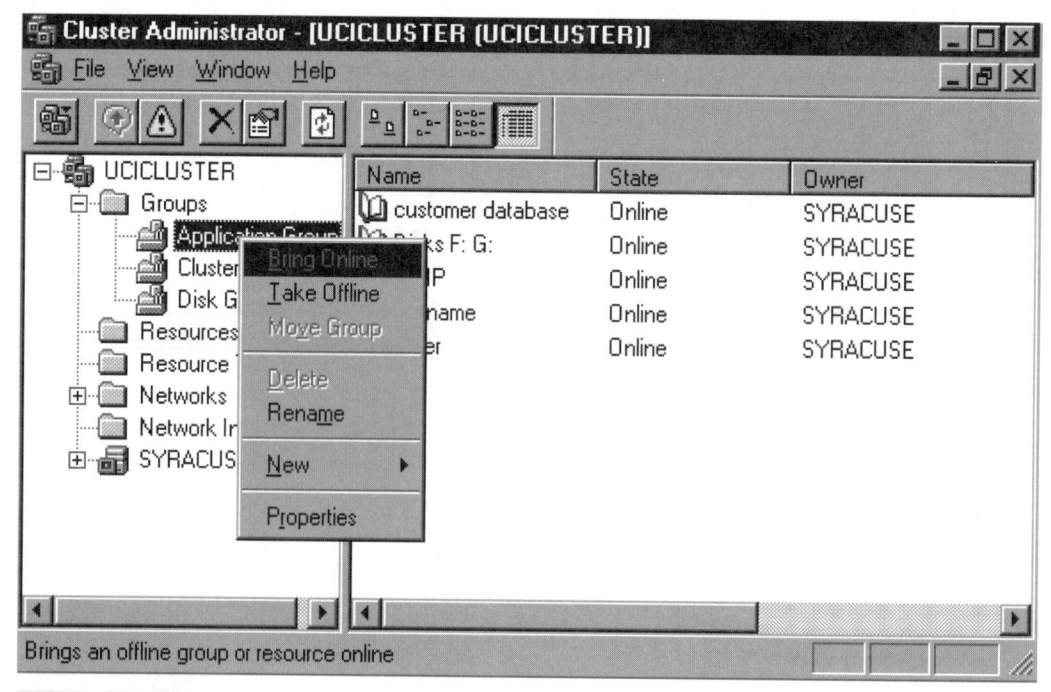

FIGURE 4-5 Group options menu

Entire groups can be brought online or taken offline. An example of when an administrator may want to take a group offline is when a software upgrade to a resource in the group is going to be applied. The administrator can take the group offline. The resources in the group will be unavailable to clients. The software can be upgraded, and the resource can be brought back online. When a request is made to bring a group online, all the resources in the group are brought online. If one or more resources cannot be brought online for some reason, the group still goes online with the resources that are available. Likewise, groups can be taken offline. When a group is requested to go offline, all resources will also be taken offline. I once accidentally requested that the group with the quorum disk be taken offline and the software took all the resources except the quorum disk offline.

In the situation where it is necessary to pull a member out of the cluster for maintenance, all groups should be moved to another cluster member. Select the "Move Group" option. Unfortunately, it is not possible to use the Ctl or Shift keyboard keys to select multiple groups at one time to be moved. There is a "Pause Node" option by right mouse clicking on the cluster member itself, but all this does is stop any new activity from being moved to that member. All groups must still be manually moved to another member of the cluster.

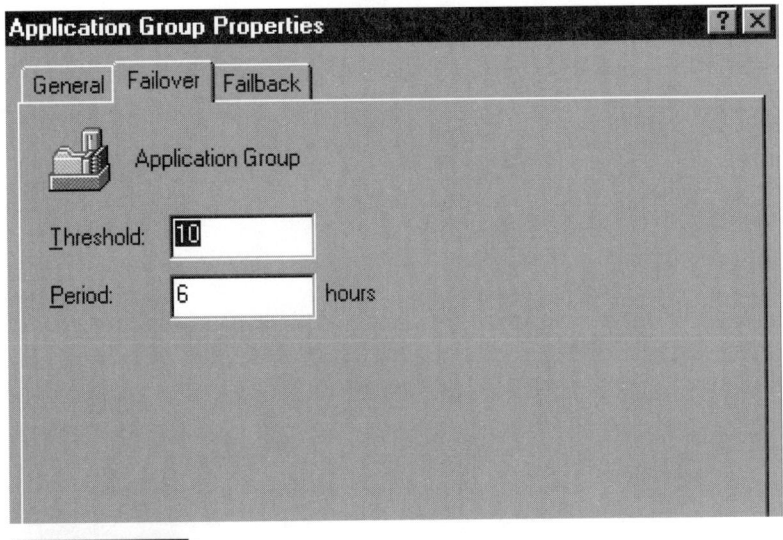

FIGURE 4-6 Group fail-over configuration

Setting Group Properties

Two important features of groups are their fail-over and fail-back functions. Fail-over happens when a resource becomes unavailable on the cluster member that is the current owner. The group that contains the resource is moved to another cluster member that has been configured as a potential owner of the resource in question. In that respect, fail-over is associated more with resource settings, which we will discuss later. As far as a group is concerned, there are two parameters that deal with fail-over. Examine Figure 4-6.

The threshold parameter is the number of times the group is allowed to fail-over to another cluster member. The period is the number of hours to monitor for the threshold number of times a fail-over of a group has occurred. For example, the default threshold is 10 and the default period is 6 hours. If a group is constantly bouncing between cluster members, the group will be taken offline on the eleventh failure as long as all the failures occurred in a period of less than six hours. The assumption is that one or more of the group resources is not behaving properly and it is better to take the group offline rather than affect the properly behaving resources of the cluster.

Fail-back is the function of moving a group back to the original cluster member. So fail-back occurs only when a fail-over has already taken place. See Figure 4-7. Fail-back can be prevented. This option is useful if the cluster constantly services requests for the resources of the group in question. Any time a group is moved from one cluster member to another, a delay is experienced. This delay is a form of cluster transition. For a period of 5-20 seconds, the

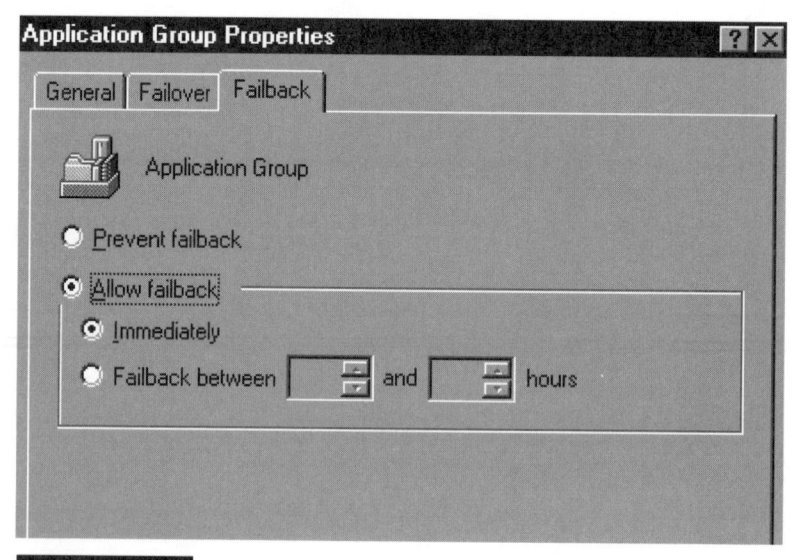

FIGURE 4-7 Group failback and configuration

cluster will be unresponsive. This time period can be greater or less, depending upon the configuration, the number of connected users, etc. In order to avoid users' experiencing this delay, fail-back can be delayed or disabled. In this case, the administrator must manually move the group back to the target cluster member at a convenient time, perhaps when no processing is occurring. Otherwise, fail-back can be enabled. In order to avoid the cluster transitions during normal working hours, fail-back can be configured to occur only between certain hours of the day. For example, setting the fail-back hours between zero and 6 would postpone all fail-back operations until between the hours of midnight and 6 a.m., when there is probably less activity on the cluster.

Resource Objects

Resources Defined

A resource is defined as a physical or logical entity managed by a cluster node such as a file or printer. A resource provides a service to clients in a client/server environment. The Cluster Server software organizes resources by type. Several common resource types are supported. In addition to files and printers, Windows NT services and Internet Information Server virtual servers are two very useful resource types. Resources are implemented by providing a resource DLL that has the capability of communicating with Resource Monitors and the Cluster Service.

Resources can have dependencies. A dependency can be described as follows. If resource A is dependent on resource B, if resource B is unavailable, resource A will not attempt to start. Resources are members of groups, and when a group fails over to another cluster member, all resources move with it. Resources can define only dependencies on other resources in their same group. Since dependent resources must be members of the same group, the cluster server software is guaranteed that the resources will be available to the same cluster member. When planning resources and groups, the dependency is a very important concept. In order to allow for fault-tolerance, a resource such as a file-share must be a member of a group with the shared cluster disk that contains the directory it shares. In order to allow for load balancing, there must be separate groups to allow one or more groups to be on each cluster member. One of the most critical resources is the shared SCSI disk. Since the disk resource can be in one group only, in order to have applications simultaneously running on the different cluster members, there must be more than one physical disk. There is one slight variation to this. If the application is installed on a local disk of each cluster member, a disk does not have to be included as a dependency, and the entire dilemma of needing a SCSI disk per group is avoided. Now the application must be manually configured on each cluster member.

Standard Cluster Resources

A number of resources are defined at the time the cluster server software is installed. They are members of the Cluster group and should not be modified. Since we have not discussed the types of resources and their characteristics, a detailed description of these resources will not be given at this time. However, the individual resources will be discussed in the appropriate section of this chapter. The Cluster IP address, Cluster Name, Time Service, and disk resource are the resources defined at installation time.

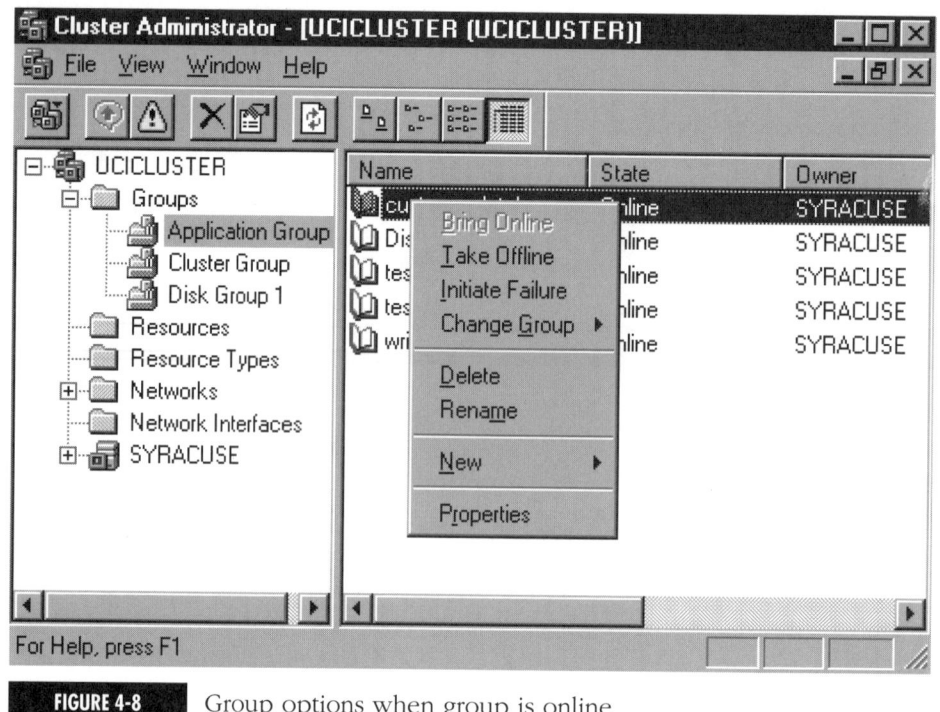

FIGURE 4-8 Group options when group is online

Working with Resources

Resources of different types have specific parameters that must be supplied during the configuration process. For example, a file-share resource needs the disk and directory it is sharing, but an IP address resource needs the TCP/IP address and subnet mask that it represents. Because of this, a discussion of resource properties will cover each type of resource. There is one group of settings that is consistent among all resources. The common setting will be found in the "Advanced" page of the "Properties" screen; we will discuss those shortly.

Working with resources after they are created is a standard procedure that will be discussed now. To manage a resource that is already defined on the cluster, locate the resource in the Cluster Administrator utility and right-mouse click on it. A menu appears. See Figure 4-8.

Some options may be grayed out or unavailable because the action would be redundant. For example, if a resource is already online, it makes no sense to select the "Bring Online" option. The option to bring a resource online first checks for resource dependencies. Any dependent resources that are not online are brought online. Only when all dependent resource are online will the cluster server bring the target resource online. For example, assume there is a network name resource called APPSERVER that has a dependency on an IP address resource called APP IPADDRESS and both are offline. If the "Bring Online" option is selected for the APPSERVER resource, the cluster server must first bring the APP IPADDRESS resource online. If the IP address resource cannot be brought online for any reason, such as encountering a duplicate TCP/IP address on the network, the network name resource of APPSERVER will also not be brought online.

The second option, "Take Offline," basically works opposite of the "Bring Online" option. Again using the example with the network name resource of APPSERVER and the IP address resource of APP IPADDRESS, let's now assume both resources are online. If the APPSERVER resource is selected and the "Take Offline" option is selected, that is exactly what happens. If the IP address resource is taken offline while both resources are online, the cluster server will also take the network name resource of APPSERVER offline because one of its dependent resources has gone offline. There is no warning by the cluster server software; the resources are simply taken offline. In the Cluster Administrator utility, a yellow warning symbol next to the resource is the only notification of what resources are now offline. The basic rules are:

- When a resource is taken offline, any resources that are dependent on the resource's being taken offline must also go offline.
- When a resource is brought online, any resources that it is dependent upon must be brought online first.

The next option is "Initiate Failure." It may seem strange to include an option that forces a resource that has been added to the cluster to fail! However, this provides the perfect method of testing what happens to a resource if it does fail instead of waiting for a failure to occur while in production. In order to determine what happens when the "Initiate Failure" option is selected, it is necessary to examine the configuration settings for the resource. By selecting "Properties" from the menu displayed when the right mouse button is pressed, it is possible to view the policies regarding what actions the Cluster Server software should take if the resource is considered to have failed. These settings can be examined by selecting the "Advanced" property page from the resource "Properties" screen. See Figure 4-9. The first option defines whether the resource should be automatically restarted after a failure has occurred. It is convenient that a resource can be restarted without any administrator intervention except in the case of a resource that is severely impacting the operating system performance or integrity. In this case, it may be better not to have the resource restarted. The resource could be taken offline manually, but the resource's automatically starting and stopping can make troubleshooting even more difficult than it already is.

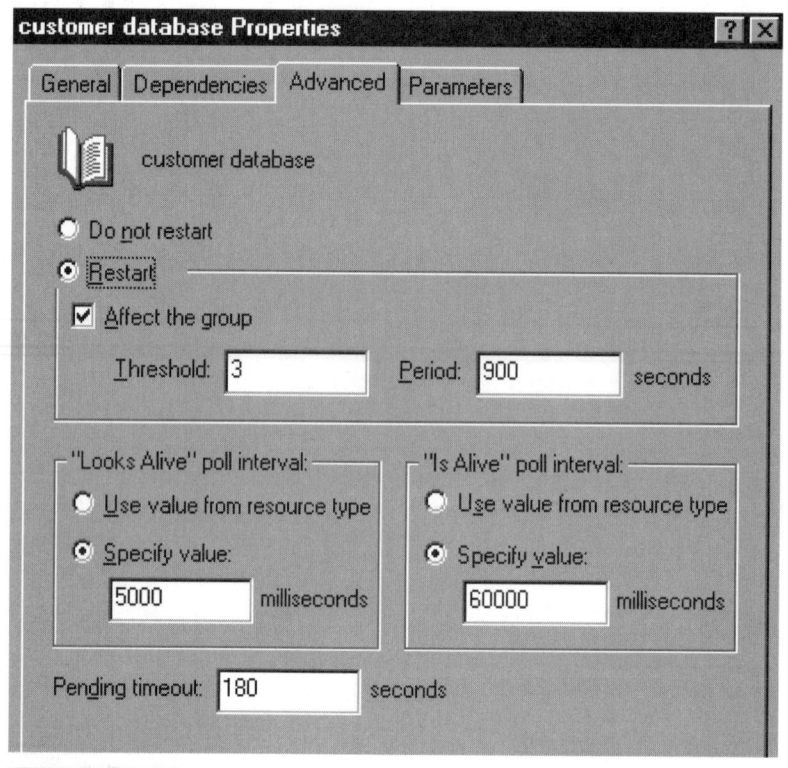

Chapter Four • Windows NT Cluster Server Guidebook

FIGURE 4-9 Advanced resource properties

If the resource is configured to automatically restart, the checkbox "Affect the group" determines whether the resource and its group should be moved to another cluster member after a certain number if failures. The threshold defines the number of failures and the period is the amount of time to monitor for "threshold" number of failures.

The default for the threshold is 3, and for the period it is 900 seconds or 15 minutes. When the resource fails for the fourth time within 15 minutes, the resource will be moved to another cluster member. If there is not another cluster member that can take over the resource, the resource goes into a "failed" state and can be brought back online only manually. When a resource is brought back online, the failure count is not cleared. For example, if a resource has failed 4 times and has gone into a "failed" state, then the administrator manually brings the resource online. If one more failure occurs with the 15-minute window, the resource again goes into a "failed" state.

The next two settings are the "Looks Alive" and "Is Alive" timers. The "Looks Alive" timer indicates how often the cluster service checks to see whether the resource has had activity. This is a very cursory check to see if a resource appears to be online. The "Is Alive" timer is a more thorough check to see if a resource is online. When a resource is offline, the "Is Alive" polling still happens so that if the resource goes back online without intervention, the cluster service will be notified and the resource status updated.

The pending timeout defines how long a resource can be in an "Online Pending" state. If a request is made to bring a resource online, this timer allows the request to fail rather than continue attempting to bring the resource up indefinitely.

The next option from the main Cluster Administrator window is "Change Group." Even with the best planning, a resource may need to be moved from one group to another. When a resource is moved to another group, the Cluster Server software will move any dependent resources. It must also move any resources that have dependencies on any resources that are going to be relocated to the new group. For example, assume there are a file-share resource and a print spooler, both with dependencies on the same physical disk resource. If the file-share is moved to another group, it is obvious that the disk resource must also be moved. If these two resources were moved, the print spooler resource would not work. The Cluster Server software will also move the print spooler resource to ensure that it will have access to all its dependent resources. Moving one resource to another group could start a chain reaction and move every resource in the initial group. If this is the case, it would be simpler to add the new resource to the existing group. An easy method to move a resource between groups is drag-and-drop. Highlight the resource in the right Cluster Administrator window and, while holding the mouse button down, drag it to the target group in the left window.

The "Delete" option is simple, but it can also do more than expected. When this option is selected, the software will also delete any resources that have dependencies with the resource that is being deleted. It asks the administrator to confirm this action. The proper sequence to delete a resource is to first remove any dependencies on the resource and then delete it. This option can be useful in finding what resources have dependencies on the resource that is to be deleted.

The final "Properties" option allows for modification of the information that was supplied when the resource was created, such as dependencies, possible owners, and resource specific parameters. The properties screen has already been discussed.

The IP Address Resource

What Is an IP Address Resource?

An IP address resource is defined as a 32-bit number in dotted decimal notation that represents an Internet Protocol (IP) address and is supported as a cluster resource by a resource DLL provided in the Cluster Server software.

If a network device supports TCP/IP as a protocol, a unique TCP/IP address must be allocated to it. (The scheme of TCP/IP addressing and subnetting is complicated and will not be discussed in this book; there are many other books on the subject.) All network devices contain an on-board address referred to as a MAC, hardware, or Ethernet address.

When one computer requests a TCP/IP connection to another host, that request may be made by computer name, or by TCP/IP address. Network communications at a low-level works only with hardware addresses. When a computer name or TCP/IP address is used, some translation must occur. For our example, assume that the connection request from one computer to another is generated using a computer name. In this case, two levels of translation must occur. First, the computer name must be translated to a TCP/IP address. There are various methods to perform this translation, including DNS (Domain Name Server, WINS (Windows Internet Name Server), and files such as HOSTS and LMHOSTS. Once the computer name is translated to a TCP/IP address, the next translation can occur. The TCP/IP address must be converted to a hardware address. This is done via a mechanism known as ARP, or address resolution protocol. ARP broadcasts on the local segment requesting the computer that owns the TCP/IP address in question to respond with its hardware address. To speed up the process, ARP maintains an ARP cache. This cache holds recently resolved TCP/IP addresses and their corresponding hardware addresses. Once the computer that initiated the request has a hardware address of the target system, network communications can commence.

The whole process works quite well, as can be seen by the size of the Internet. When an IP address resource is created on a cluster, a moving target has been introduced into the IP address resolution mechanism. This is the potential situation. A client makes a request to connect to the cluster via some IP address. Of our two nodes in the cluster, assume NODEA responds to the request. At this point, the hardware address for NODEA is written to the ARP cache in the client for future lookups. Now, NODEA goes down and the IP address resource fails over to NODEB. Here is where the problem is. NODEB has a different hardware address. If our client made a request, a connection failure would occur.

This problem is solved by following the recommendations outlined in RFC (request for comment) 826. RFCs are the documentation for how TCP/IP works. RFC 826 states that all systems receiving an ARP request must update their IP address to hardware address mapping for the source of the request. Because ARP requests contain both the IP address and the hardware address of the source of the request, it is possible to update the address mappings.

As part of the TCP/IP registration process, the Windows NT TCP/IP driver broadcasts an ARP request on its subnet. This request is made to determine TCP/IP address conflicts on the local segment. When this ARP request is generated, Windows NT specifies the IP address being registered as the source of the request. Therefore, all systems on the subnet will update their ARP cache with the new information. The result is that the registering computer becomes the new owner of the address. When an IP address resource is being brought online, the cluster member that now owns the resource will broadcast an ARP request. This request forces all computers on the subnet to update their ARP cache. This results in computers now being able to access the new cluster member via the same TCP/IP address in the case of a failover. This solves one of the resolution steps. Host name to IP address resolution is discussed in the section on Network Name resources.

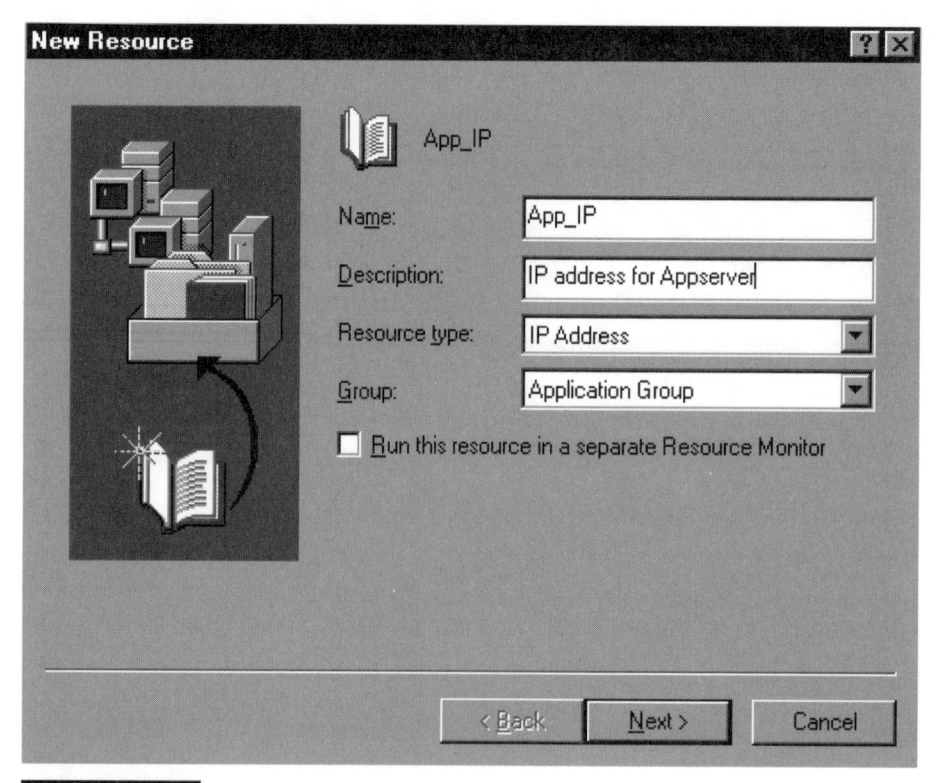

FIGURE 4-10 Creating an IP Address resource

Creating an IP Address Resource

To create an IP Address resource, right mouse click in the Cluster Administrator utility and select "New, Resource." Supply a descriptive name and description, and be sure to select a resource type of IP Address. See Figure 4-10.

Include all possible owners of the resource, and define any dependencies. There are no required dependencies for an IP address resource. It is difficult to remember what resources require which dependencies. A chart of resources and their dependencies has been included in Appendix A.

[TCP/IP Address Parameters dialog box showing:
- App_IP
- Address: 131.107.2.205
- Subnet mask: 255.255.255.0
- Network to use: network 1
- Buttons: < Back, Finish, Cancel]

FIGURE 4-11 IP address resource parameters

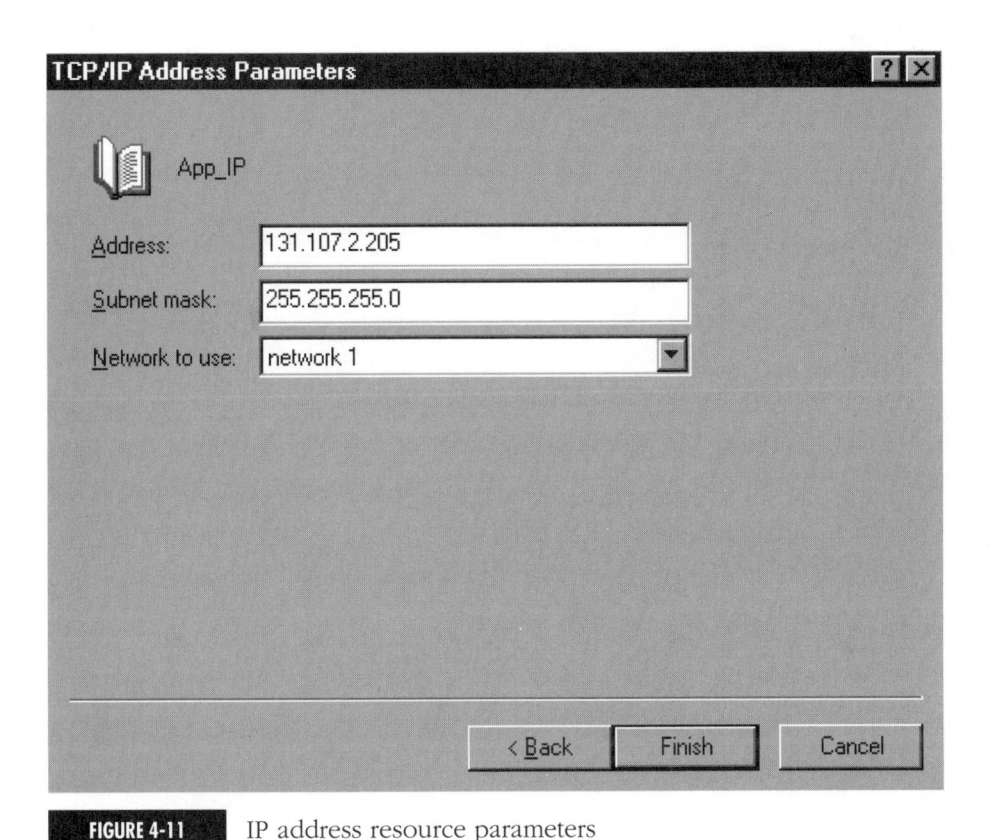

The final screen is the TCP/IP parameters screen. See Figure 4-11. Supply the TCP/IP address and subnet mask that the resource should represent. Do not arbitrarily enter an address. If you are not the administrator of TCP/IP addresses on your network, request a valid address and subnet mask from the network administrator. Entering an invalid address could make the cluster member or the entire network unreachable. In the "Network to Use" option, select which network to associate with the IP address. Selecting the wrong network could cause just as much trouble on your network as supplying an invalid address and subnet mask.

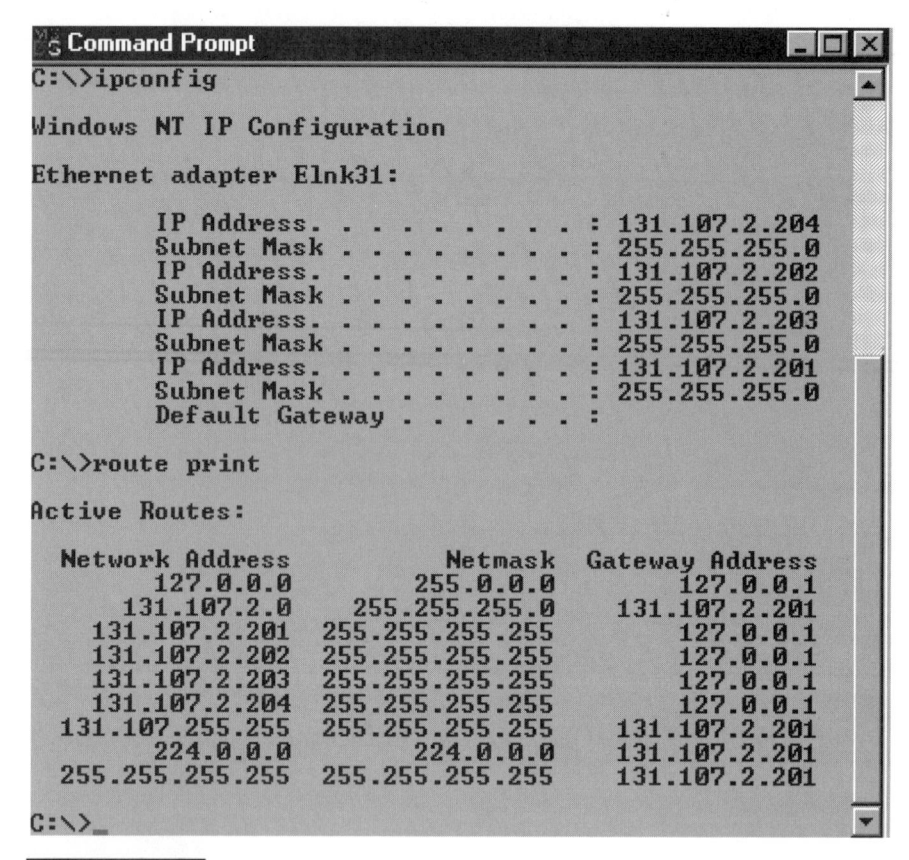

```
Command Prompt
C:\>ipconfig

Windows NT IP Configuration

Ethernet adapter Elnk31:

        IP Address. . . . . . . . . : 131.107.2.204
        Subnet Mask . . . . . . . . : 255.255.255.0
        IP Address. . . . . . . . . : 131.107.2.202
        Subnet Mask . . . . . . . . : 255.255.255.0
        IP Address. . . . . . . . . : 131.107.2.203
        Subnet Mask . . . . . . . . : 255.255.255.0
        IP Address. . . . . . . . . : 131.107.2.201
        Subnet Mask . . . . . . . . : 255.255.255.0
        Default Gateway . . . . . . :

C:\>route print

Active Routes:

  Network Address          Netmask    Gateway Address
        127.0.0.0        255.0.0.0         127.0.0.1
      131.107.2.0    255.255.255.0     131.107.2.201
    131.107.2.201  255.255.255.255         127.0.0.1
    131.107.2.202  255.255.255.255         127.0.0.1
    131.107.2.203  255.255.255.255         127.0.0.1
    131.107.2.204  255.255.255.255         127.0.0.1
    131.107.255.255 255.255.255.255    131.107.2.201
        224.0.0.0        224.0.0.0     131.107.2.201
  255.255.255.255  255.255.255.255    131.107.2.201

C:\>
```

FIGURE 4-12 Verifying an IP address resource with the IP config and route print commands

To verify the functionality of an IP address resource, different tests can be performed. One is to use the "Ping" utility from a non-cluster member computer. Another check that can be performed by the administrator is to issue the command "ipconfig" from the cluster member that currently owns the resource. This command is issued from a command prompt window and will return data similar to Figure 4-12. Notice that associated with the single network adapter there are four different TCP/IP addresses. These addresses represent the standard address assigned in the operating system network properties, the cluster IP address assigned at the time the cluster server software was installed, and two IP address resources. One last piece of information is the output from the "route print" command in Figure 4-12. This command displays the routing table information for TCP/IP. Notice that all four addresses have a gateway of 127.0.0.1, which is a local loopback address. The routing table is updated automatically when an IP address resource is started.

The Cluster IP Address Resource

The Cluster IP Address resource is defined at the time the cluster server software is installed. It is an IP address resource. It does not have any special functionality. It is used to connect to the Cluster for administrative purposes through the Cluster Administrator utility.

The Network Name Resource

Network Names Defined

Network names are defined as friendly names for devices that exist on a network. It is an alphanumeric string associated with a specific network address. For example, it is probably much easier for a user to remember that his database is accessible via the name WIDGETDATA as opposed to remembering the address 194.73.18.162. Since network names are not necessary in order to establish a network connection, they can be classified as an optional resource; in reality, everyone uses them because of their convenience. Some may argue that UNC names, names in the format of \\server\share, require a name. This was true in earlier versions of Windows NT, but now using a TCP/IP address in the server field works.

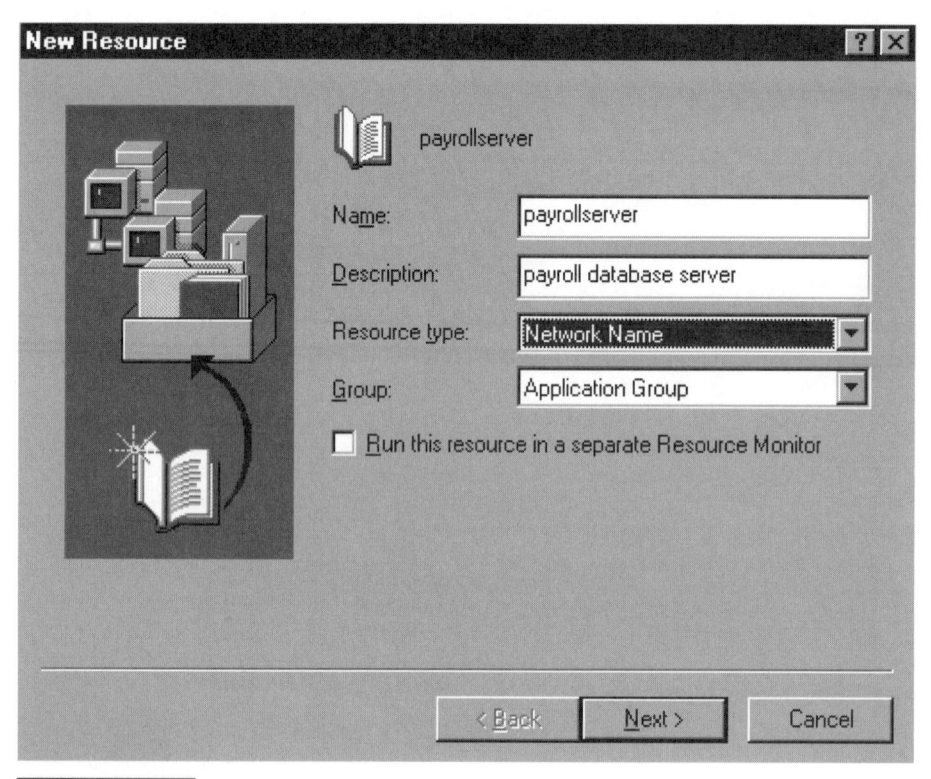

FIGURE 4-13 Creating a network name resource

Creating a Network Name Resource

Use the standard procedure to start the processing of creating a new resource, and select a resource type of "Network Name." See Figure 4-13.

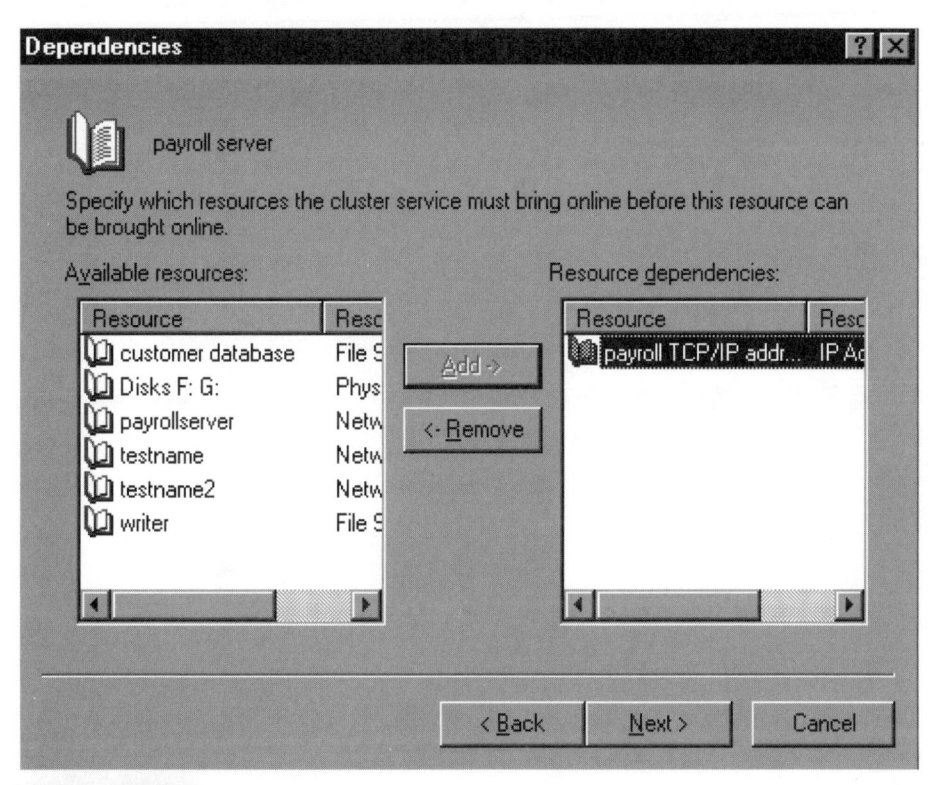

FIGURE 4-14 Defining dependencies for a network name resource

Since a network name resource is a character representation of a TCP/IP address, an IP address resource is a necessary dependency. This is the only dependency required. Remember that the IP address resource must be in the same group. See Figure 4-14.

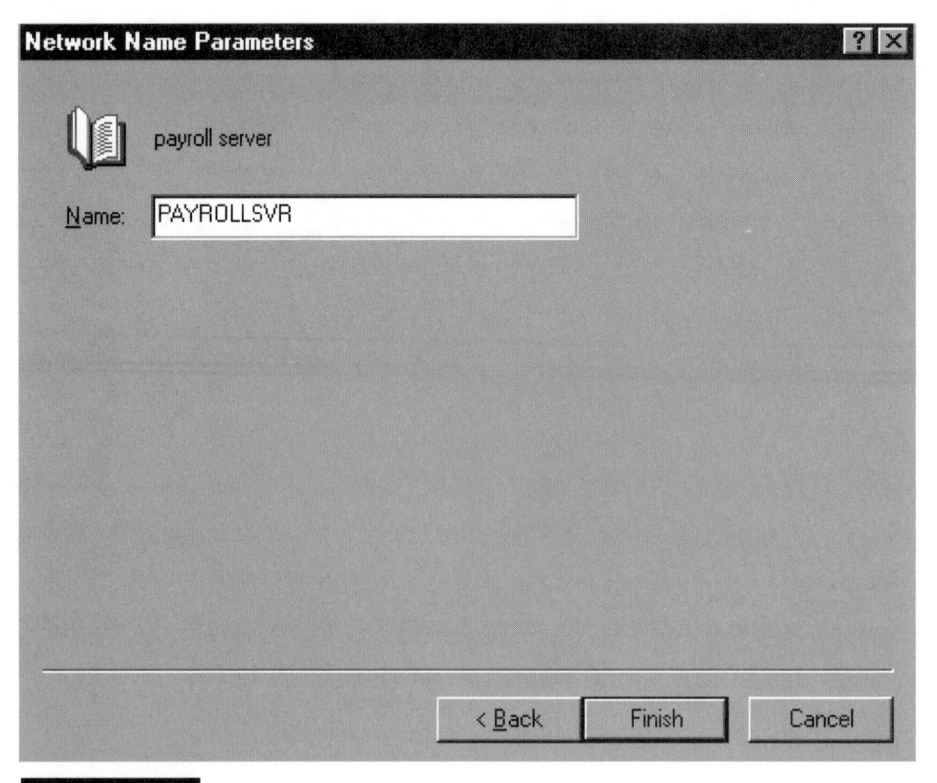

FIGURE 4-15 Network name resource parameters

    There is only one parameter to supply for a network name resource: the character string to associate with the IP address resource. The parameter must follow the standard conventions for NetBIOS names, such as limiting the string to 15 characters. See Figure 4-15.

    Now that there is a network name that represents a TCP/IP address, there is one problem that must be resolved. The mechanism of TCP/IP address resolution that is provided by ARP resolves only TCP/IP addresses to physical addresses. Given a network name, there must be a resolution of that name to an address. Various mechanisms exist to perform this task, such as WINS, DNS, LMHOSTS, HOSTS and a broadcast message requesting name resolution. This last method will work only if the client is on the same physical network segment as the cluster. The LMHOSTS and HOSTS files are text files that contain network name and TCP/IP address entries. Is there a problem using these files for resolution because the name resource has the potential to move between cluster members? The answer is "No" because the IP address resource will move with the network name. For example, assume an IP address resource has been created of 190.35.172.15, and a network name resource of WIDGETSVR is dependent on this resource. Making an entry in a HOSTS file connecting these two components will be valid because the cluster member that owns the IP address resource will also own the network name. The only disadvantage of using a file such as HOSTS or LMHOSTS is that they are resident on the client. If there are 500 clients, that is a lot of files to maintain. Some administrators have implemented code in a login script that gets executed when the user logs in that copies a HOSTS file from a central server to the local client. This works and is an excellent way to make sure all clients have the same information.

The best solution that is currently available is to have the cluster members be configured with WINS server addresses. To summarize, WINS is software that runs on Windows NT Server that maintains a database of TCP/IP addresses and computer or NetBIOS names. It is very similar to DNS except for one very important feature. The WINS database is dynamic. With DNS, entries need to be manually entered and updated. WINS servers depend on their clients to register and de-register the name and TCP/IP address they are using. This was originally designed to support DHCP, dynamic TCP/IP address assignment, but it also allows network name resources to be translated to their IP address equivalent. When a cluster member brings a network name resource online, the network name and TCP/IP address are registered with the WINS Server defined in its TCP/IP properties.

The Cluster Name Resource

The Cluster Name Resource is a standard network name resource. It is similar to the Cluster IP Address resource in that the intended use for the Cluster Name is for remote management. The Cluster Name resource is dependent on the Cluster IP Address.

The File-Share Resource

What Is a File-Share?

A file-share resource is a shared directory that is available to one or more cluster members. File-share resources can be accessed by only one member of the cluster simultaneously. This means that the file-share resource is available only through one cluster member at a time. Load balancing, which is servicing multiple requests for a given resource through multiple cluster members simultaneously, is not an option at this time.

An example of using a file-share is a situation where the goal is to provide the maximum online availability for an application or database. Think of a file-share as a directory, except that instead of residing on the client computer, it resides on the cluster. The client may need to establish a network connection to the cluster to use the files in the file-share, but it will be transparent to the client which cluster member is actually providing access to the resource.

When a file-share resource is defined, a device and directory path needs to be provided. In regards to files, there are only two major levels of access: read, and read/write. In a situation where read/write access must be allowed to the file-share, the device and directory associated with the resource must be one of the shared SCSI devices. This is because, if the data is going to be updated, we must guarantee that there is only one version of the files. We do not want a situation where there are multiple data files being updated. There is no easy way to keep the files accurate. If the file-share resource needs to be located on a shared SCSI disk, only the cluster member that currently owns the disk would be able to successfully offer the file-share. In this situation, a dependency of the disk resource on the file-share would be a proper configuration. The problem with this is that there is no way to load balance client requests simultaneously among the cluster members, because the disk resource is available only through one member at a time.

In a situation where the access to the data is read-only, synchronizing changes to the data is not an issue because no changes are occurring. If the device and directory supplied for the file-share resource is a local path available on all cluster members, such C:\APPS, then multiple file-shares could be created. Now there is the capability of doing some static load balancing. Static load balancing means that the administrator must configure the client connections to balance the users across the different file-share resources. If one of the cluster members goes offline, the file-share resource that was resident will fail-over to another cluster member. Since the path is local to all cluster members, clients will see no disruption in service. At this point, we have loaded the one cluster member with more work, but only temporarily until the other cluster member goes back online.

Four • Implementing Cluster Available Resources **83**

FIGURE 4-16 Creating a new resource

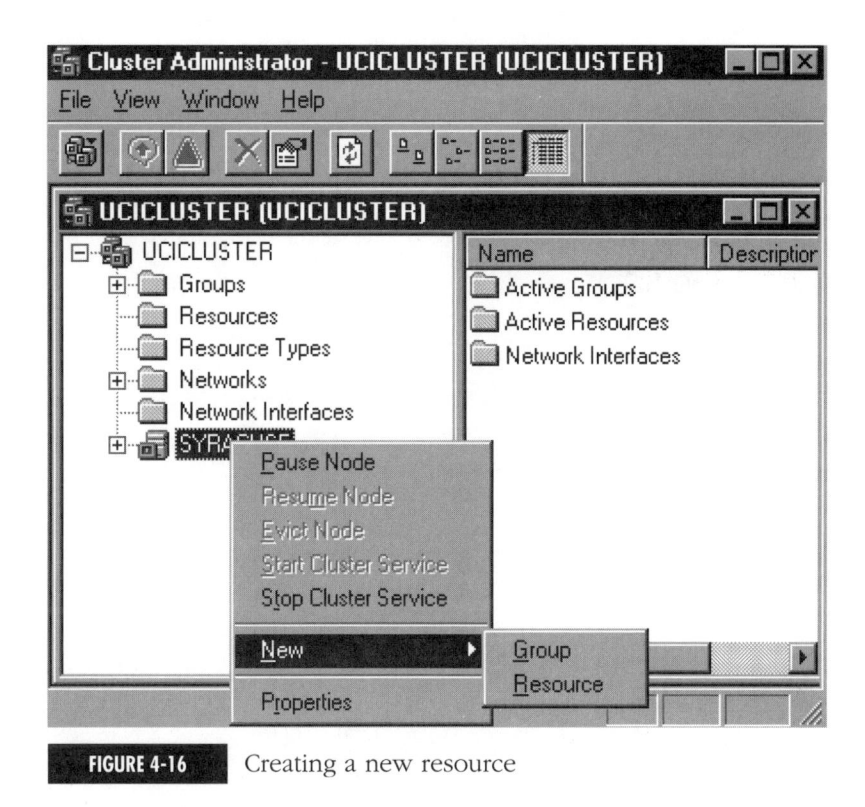

Creating a File-Share Resource

To create a file-share resource, right mouse click somewhere within the Cluster Administrator window. Select New, Resource and complete the screens that follow. If the group is selected before right mouse clicking, the resource is automatically associated with that group. This is not a necessity, because during the resource definition, the owning group can be specified. See Figure 4-16.

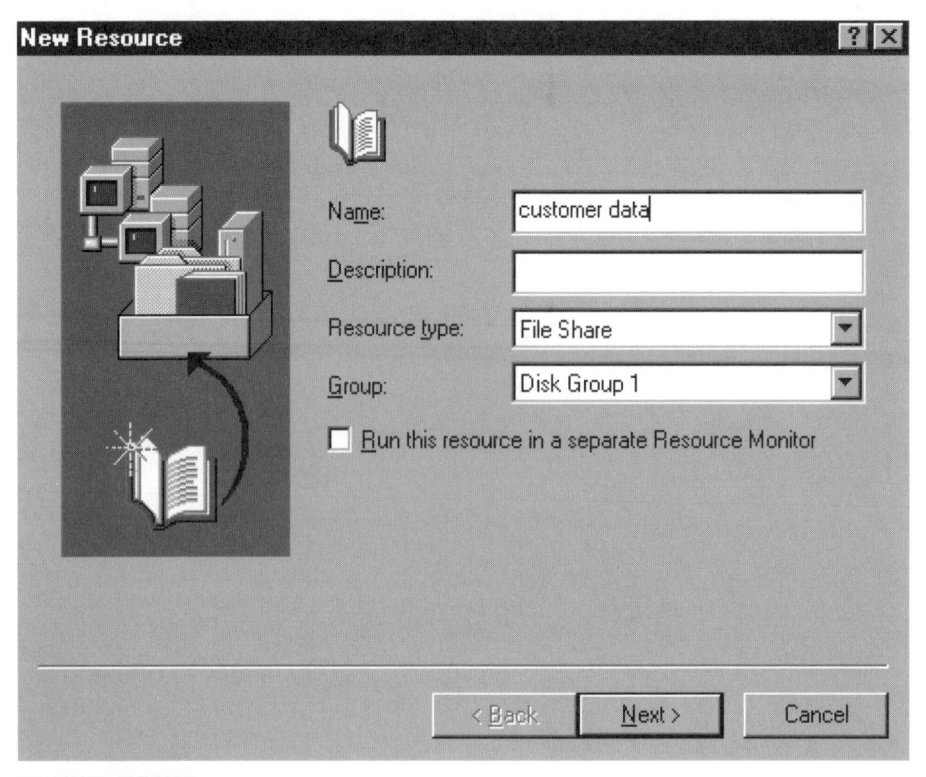

FIGURE 4-17 Available resource types

Enter a resource name and description, and select a resource type of file share. Be as descriptive as possible with the name and description. The option, "Run this resource in a separate resource monitor," should be selected only if a resource is crashing and restarting. Each resource monitor is a process. When the resource monitor process is launched, the specific dynamic link library, or DLL, is loaded to support that type of resource. There are standard dynamic link libraries that ship with the cluster server product to support all the available resource types. Also, vendors have the capability to develop their own resource DLLs. This is discussed in the chapter on the Cluster API. Therefore, each resource monitor will consume system resources such as memory and CPU cycles. See Figure 4-17.

Next, specify what nodes in the cluster are allowed to own the file-share resource. If the file-share is to be supported by various members of the cluster, some planning must be done. The file-share resource associates with a specific disk and directory. The disk is treated as a separate resource by the cluster software. It is the responsibility of the cluster administrator to guarantee that the disk and file-share resources will always be owned by the

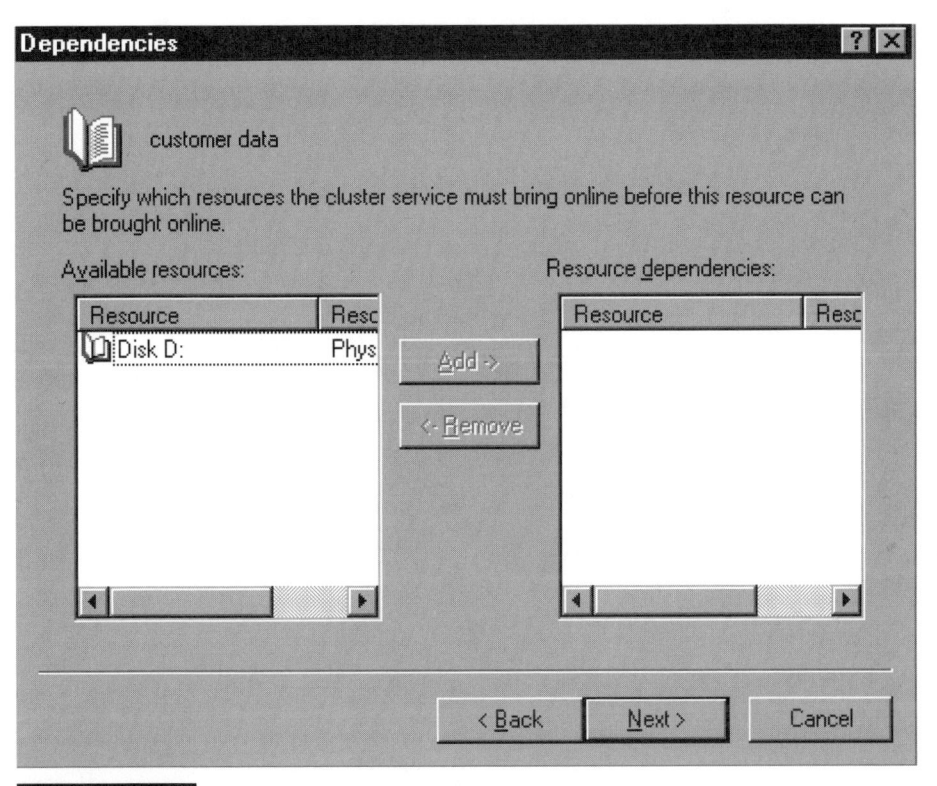

FIGURE 4-18 Defining file share resource dependencies

same cluster member. To guarantee that the resources reside on the same cluster member, they must placed in the same group. Remember, groups are moved during a fail-over, not individual resources. See Figure 4-18.

Also, it does not make sense to attempt to bring a file-share resource online if the shared disk the file-share resides on is offline. To prevent this, the administrator can define a dependency between the file-share resource and the disk resource. See Figure 4-18.

With one or more dependencies defined, the resource in question is not brought to an online state unless all the dependent resources are online. In the case of a file-share, a disk dependency should be defined in all situations except when the file-share resource is referencing non-shared disk. Optional resource dependencies include network name and IP address resources. It is not necessary to define both network name and IP address resource dependencies. The network name must have a dependency of an IP address resource. When a resource is requested to be brought online, the Cluster Server software also attempts to bring online any dependent resources. This has a cascading effect. If the file-share resource is dependent

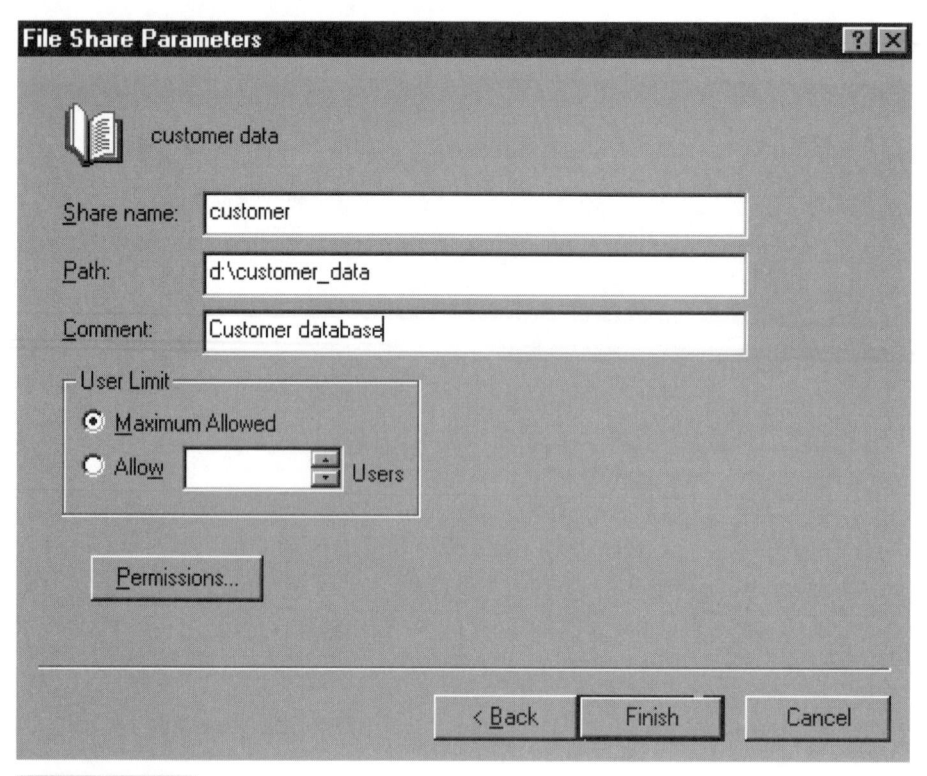

FIGURE 4-19 Defining file share resource parameters

on a network name, which we know is dependent on an IP address, simply requesting to bring the file-share online will automatically request that the network name and IP address also be brought online. This will work unless any of the resources in the dependency tree are unavailable, in which case the file-share will not be brought online.

The Parameters page defines the characteristics of the network share point. See Figure 4-19. In the share name box, enter the name that is to be offered on the network. This is the name that users will reference with a UNC name to map a network drive. The path field contains the physical device and directory which the file-share represents. This can be either a local device or a shared SCSI device. One point should be made about the path: the software does not verify whether the device and directory are valid. That test is not made until the resource is brought online. Then only a failure, no message, appears on the screen. I also attempted to use a network drive in the path. The resource failed when I tried to bring it online. I do not know exactly how this could have been used. Since it did not work, I did not pursue it further.

The User Limit defines the number of simultaneous users that can be connected to the resource. This controls the number of NetBIOS sessions that are allowed against the resource. The permissions button allows the administrator to build an access control list defining allowed and disallowed users and groups.

Using a File-Share Resource

Users will request a connection to a file-share resource just like any other shared directory on the network. If the Network Neighborhood program is used, the Network Name resources that have been created and brought online will appear as standard computer names. From a command prompt, the "NET VIEW \\network_name" and "NET USE \\network_name\share_name" work as usual. Substitute the network name and share name that have been created for the resource. Be aware that a file-share resource may appear under multiple network names. For example, let's go back to our NODE1 and NODE2 example. Let's assume the cluster name is WIDGETWORLD, that we have created a file-share dependent on the network name WIDGETAPPS, and that the cluster name, network name, and file-share are all owned by NODE2. Our file-share, WIDGETAPPS will show as an available shared resource under all three names in the Network Neighborhood program. Why? All three network names are internally associated with the MAC address of the network card in the NODE2 computer. The argument is whether to create network names for all file-share resources or to let the users map via the cluster name. There is no guarantee that the cluster name and network name to be used for the file-share resource will always be owned by the same cluster member unless both names are located in the same group. It is also suggested not to use the cluster group for any add-on resources other than what was placed in the group during the Cluster Server software installation. To limit the number of network names users need to remember, one option may be to create a file-share that is associated with an application root directory. The actual applications can then reside in subdirectories. Users need only to remember one network name. One disadvantage to this method is that all applications will be owned by one cluster member. The load will not be balanced. If the goal is to spread the processor activity, multiple groups, file-shares and network names must be defined. Any load balancing must be done at the group level.

What Happens During a Failover

Up to this point, we have discussed how to implement a file-share resource. But what really happens when a user is in the middle of an update through a file-share resource and a failover occurs?

While setting up for the first test that I made, I discovered something by accident. I had originally created a file-share with Read permission and wanted to change it. A properties screen can be accessed by right mouse clicking on the resource. I attempted to change the permissions on the resource and the system did not complain, but the change never actually was applied. If the properties were checked again, the old permissions were still intact.

The first test made was a simple one of mapping a drive and opening a file with the Edit program. After the file was opened, a resource failure was initiated by again right mouse clicking on the resource and this time selecting "Initiate Failure." After the failure completed and the file-share resource was back online, an attempt to save the file by using the File-Save option failed. Upon examination through the Server Manager utility, the NetBIOS session that was created to support the network drive no longer appeared. Attempting to save the file with the File – SaveAs option was successful as long as the network drive letter that was mapped was selected. The fact that the second attempt to save the file worked is due to the fact that network drive connections will be reestablished automatically when they are used. This is sometimes referred to as a persistent connection.

The Print Spooler Resource

Print Spooler Resource Defined

The print spooler resource is defined as one or more printer queues that provide access to network based printers. This resource gives a method for centrally managing print queues, rather than creating and maintaining print queues on every client computer. Functionally, the print spooler resource is similar to the file-share resource. One difference, however, is that there is no limit on the number of file share resources that can be created, whereas only one print spooler resource can be defined. This is not the same as allowing only one print queue. One spool process is created, and that spool process can support multiple printers.

Creating a Print Spooler Resource

Resources up to this point have been generally self-contained; create the resource and it is available to the client via the cluster. This is not true with a print spooler resource. Once a print spooler resource is created, the administrator has to carry out the task of creating print queues that use the cluster spooler. The creation of the print spooler resource will be discussed first. As usual, the first step is to invoke the "New Resource" wizard by right mouse clicking in the Cluster Administrator utility and selecting New, Resource. Select a resource type of Print Spooler. The print spool resource will need a disk and directory to which to spool jobs. Therefore, it will require a disk dependency. Make sure the owning group for the print spool resource con-

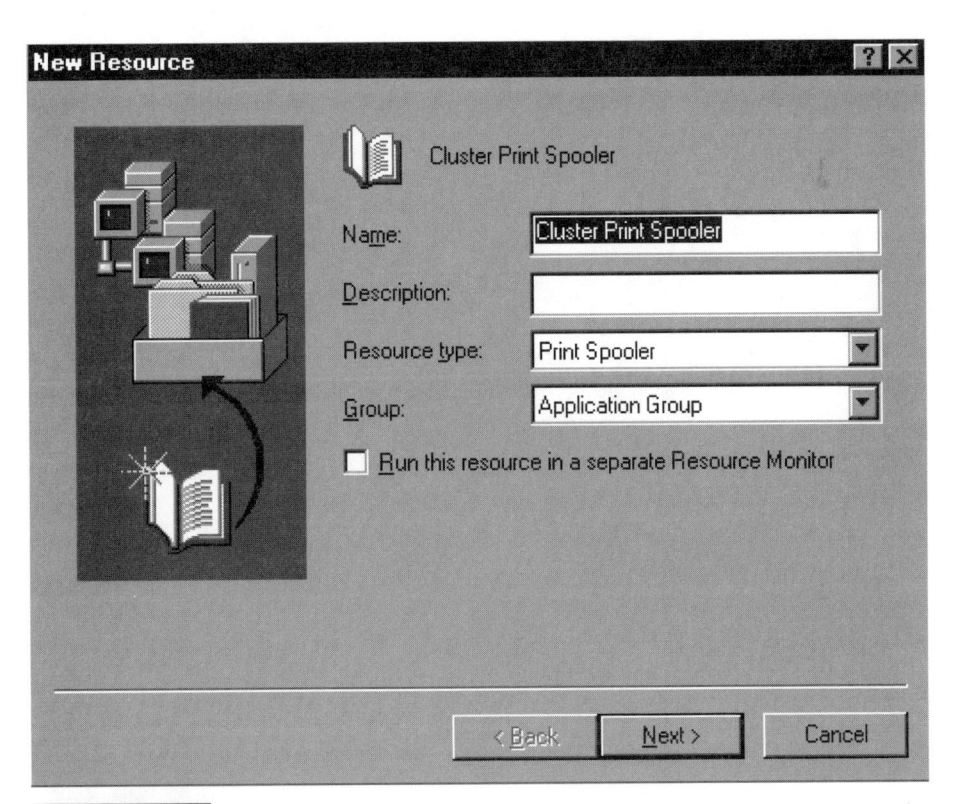

Four • Implementing Cluster Available Resources **89**

FIGURE 4-20   Creating a Print Spooler resource

tains at least one disk resource. See Figure 4-20. Along with a disk dependency, the print spooler resource requires a network name. This will be the target for client print jobs. Since there is a network name dependency, an implied IP address dependency exists. Because the network name already has a dependency on the IP address, it is not necessary to define it again. See Figure 4-21.

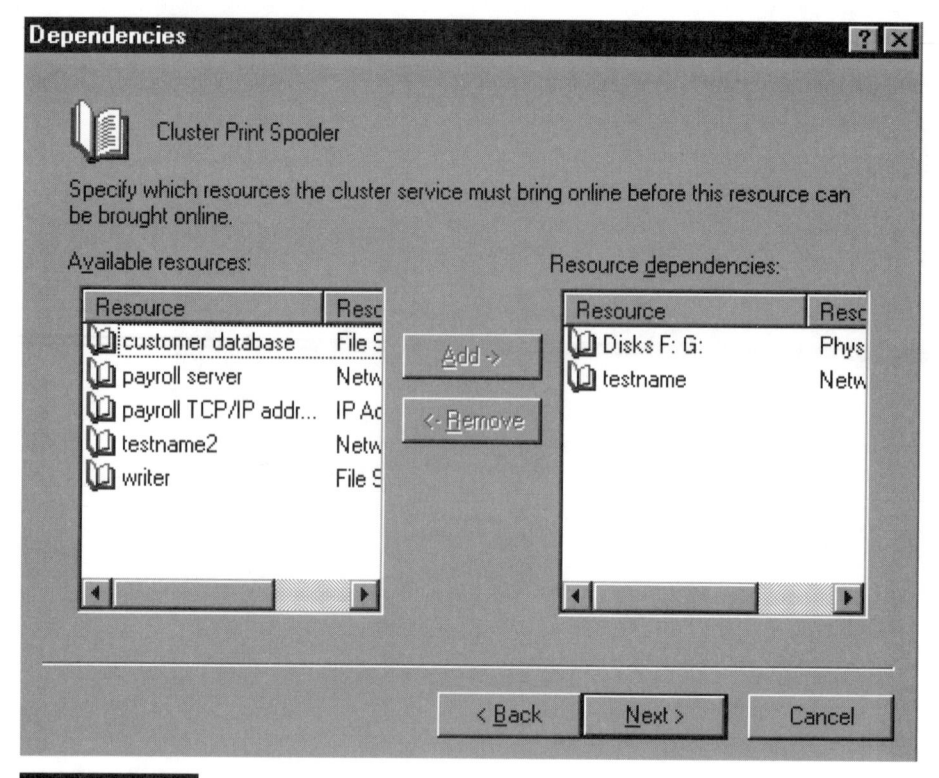

FIGURE 4-21 Defining Print Spooler resource dependencies

There are only a couple of parameters required for a print spooler resource. See Figure 4-22. First is the spool folder. This is the disk and directory to use as jobs are spooled. Spooling is basically an intermediate holding area for a print job between the user application and the physical printer. It allows the user to continue to work as his application does not need to wait until the entire print job is done printing. It is not necessary to create the spool folder in advance. If the directory does not exist, the cluster server software will create it. One point of interest here is that the cluster server software does not give any notification that the device and directory supplied are invalid. If the spooler resource is started and the supplied spool folder location is invalid, the resource is started using a directory in the Windows NT system directory structure. The second parameter is the job completion timeout. Job completion timeout controls how long a document takes to get from the cluster member with the print spool resource to the physical printer. If this timer expires, the printer stops printing the document.

At this point, there is a cluster-wide print spooler. If the network name is viewed with "Network Neighborhood," it would not yet display any avail-

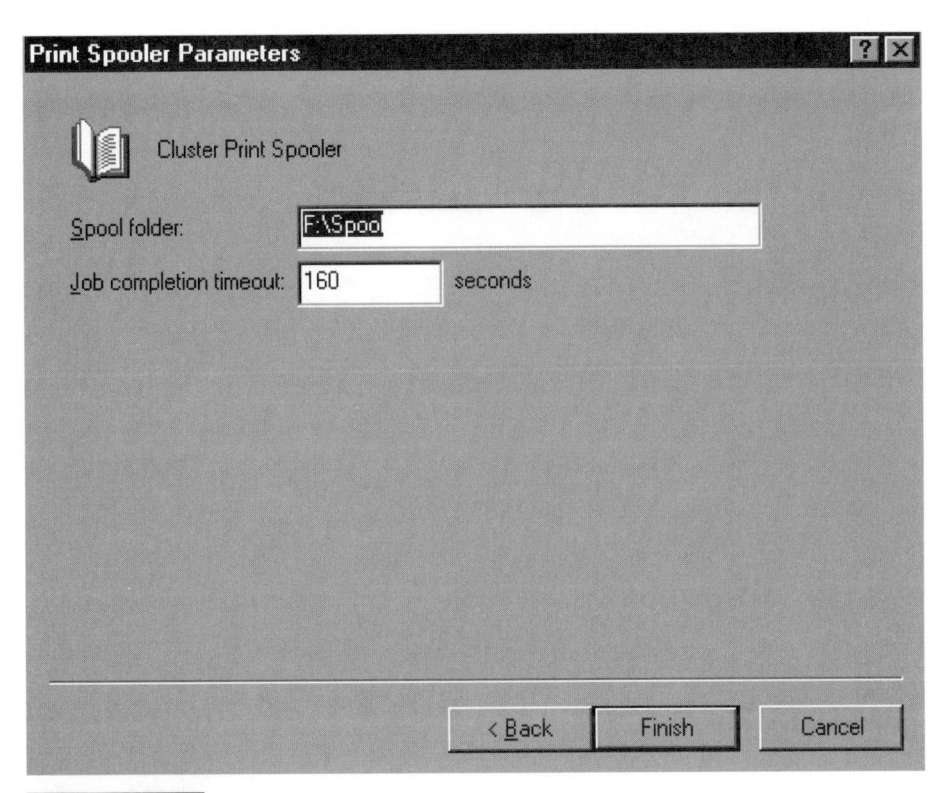

FIGURE 4-22 Specifying Print Spooler resource parameters

able printers. This can be slightly confusing. If there are locally defined printers, they will display here when a network name resource is browsed on the network. This is because the network name resolves to a TCP/IP address and the "Network Neighborhood" program displays all shared resources available via that address. To have printer resources that can failover between cluster members, it is necessary to define new printers via a special method that will be discussed next.

Configuring Cluster Print Devices

CREATING PORTS

Even though a cluster-wide print spooler is supported, there is no method of configuring and mapping ports such as LPT1 and various LPR ports cluster-wide so that all members are aware of the port mappings. Currently, all print device configurations and all device drivers must be manually configured on all nodes in the cluster. This is not a complex task, but there are very specific steps that must be followed.

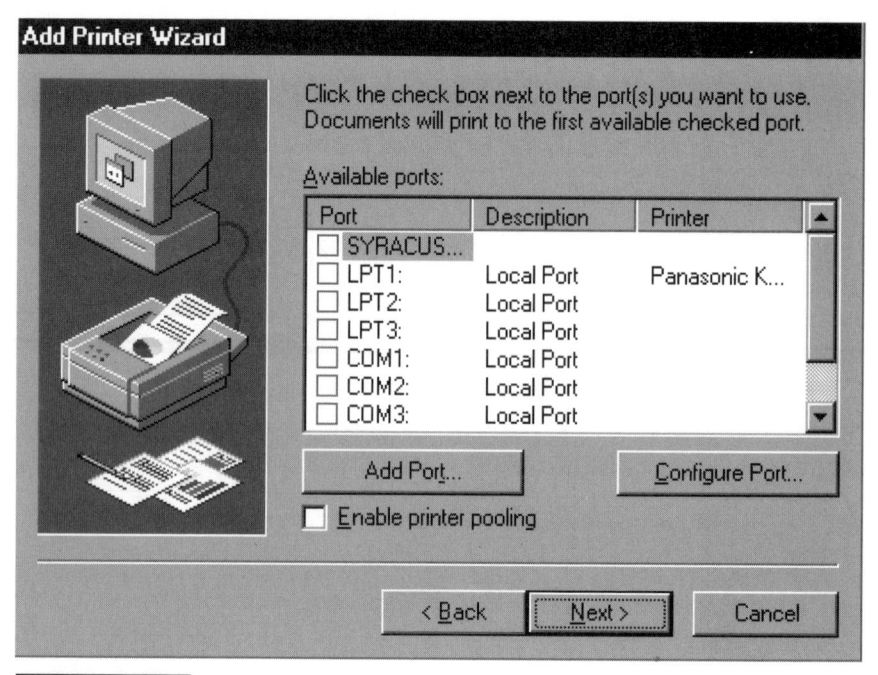

FIGURE 4-23 Creating printer ports for the cluster print spooler resource

First, all printer ports must be defined on each member of the cluster that will support the print spooler resource. To initiate this process, click Start, Settings, and Printers. Next invoke the "Add Printer" wizard. Make sure the "My Computer" radial button is selected. The object is to define any ports that are going to be used for cluster-wide printing. See Figure 4-23. At this point, does it make sense to select a physical port such as LPT1, which is a hardware component of one cluster member? The printer would be directly cabled to that specific computer. If the print spooler failed over to another cluster member, the printing device would be inaccessible by the current owner of the printspooling resource, and any print processing to that device would fail. There is one possibility, however. If a splitter cable were used to cable the printer to both cluster member LPT1 ports, printing should work well no matter which member currently owned the spool resource. This is a standard configuration mechanism that can be used in cluster server configuration. If the resource is not going to be a physically shared resource, then all cluster members must have the exact same configuration information regarding the resource. Another example is the file-share resource, which can be defined to map to a local disk and directory as long as all cluster members have the same disk and directory resident on their local disks.

Generally, however, network printer ports or LPR ports will probably

FIGURE 4-24 Creating printer ports, continued

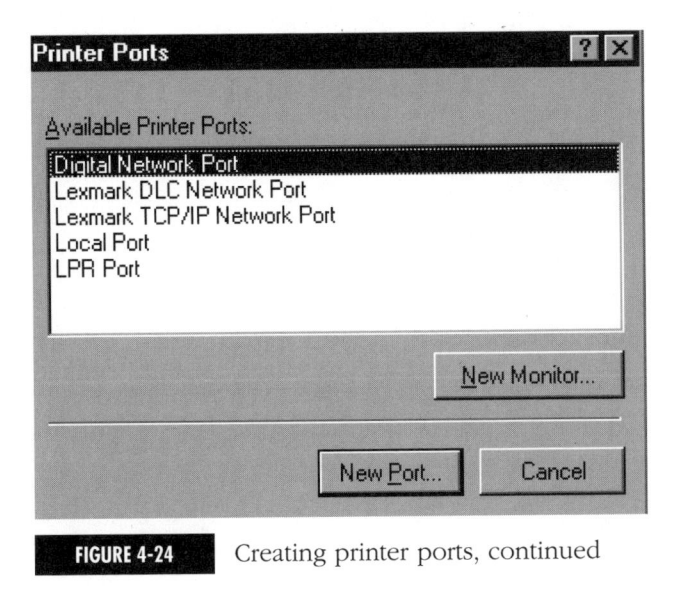

be the target ports for cluster print devices. The best I could determine is that LPR stands for Line Printing Utility. It has been a standard component of UNIX systems for many years and is a nice feature of Windows NT. The LPR software actually consists of two components: a client and a server. The client utilities are LPR, which allows a client to submit a print job, and LPQ, which allows the client to view a print queue. The server side is known as the TCP/IP Printing Service and can be viewed in the Control Panel, Services program. This software component is not loaded by default. If "LPR Port" does not show as available option when adding a printer port, this is a sign that the TCP/IP printing service has not been loaded. See Figure 4-24. To load the service, activate the Network properties screen, select the Services tab and add Microsoft TCP/IP Printing. Select LPR Port, and New Port. The "Add LPR compatible printer" screen appears as displayed in Figure 4-25.

Enter the TCP/IP address or the hostname of the computer that is providing the print queue. This can either be a TCP/IP address of a computer running an LPR service, or it can be the TCP/IP address of a network connected printer, such as a printer with an HP Jetdirect card. The "Name of Printer" field is optional and would be used only if the host of the printer has the capability to assign names to the printer it manages. One example would be a UNIX served printer. Clients would use a printer resource offered by the cluster, and totally transparent, the print request would be routed to the UNIX server. This is beneficial because it allows the administrator to control all client access through the cluster and not have to configure clients to have direct access to other systems on the network such as a UNIX server, which may require additional software to be installed on the client.

Figure 4-25. Associating the printer port with a physical device

Once the port information has been defined, do not continue with the printer creation. Cancelling the print creation process does not affect the ports that have been configured. They are permanently defined unless the administrator manually removes them.

LOADING PRINTER DRIVERS

The next step in the printer configuration process is to load printer drivers on each cluster member that will support the print spooler resource. There is no clean way to do this, so the method used is to step through the screens in the "Add Printer" wizard and create a printer. This has the effect of loading the necessary printer drivers. Select any available port; the printer is just temporary. It is not necessary to share the printer or print a test page because as soon as the printer is created, it can be deleted. The printer drivers are not deleted along with the printer. Make sure to load all necessary printer drivers on each cluster member. Now that the printer ports are created and the printer drivers loaded, the actual process of creating cluster-based printers can take place.

FIGURE 4-26 Creating a shared printer

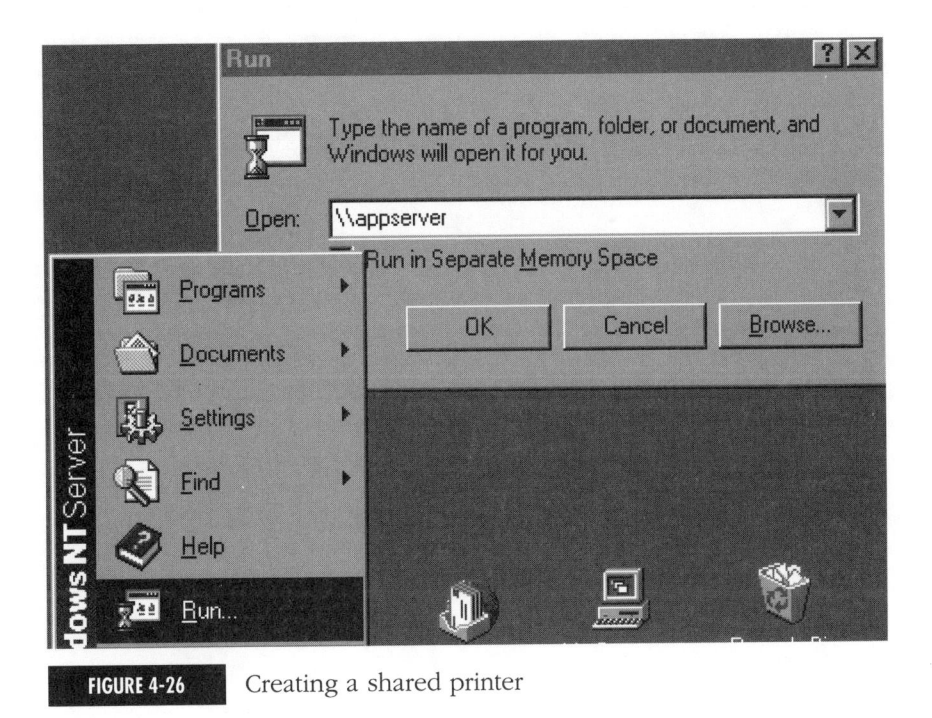

Installing Cluster Printers

The final step is to create the printer as a shared resource of the network name that was associated with the print spooler resource. This network name is sometimes referred to as a virtual server. It is a server because it offers resources to clients. It can be considered virtual because it is not a physical server of its own. It is a logical entity managed by the cluster.

If the printer were to be created by invoking the "Add Printer" wizard on one of the cluster members, the resource would be associated with that cluster member and not the network name or virtual server. In order to have the printer resource be "owned" by the virtual server, it is necessary to run the "Add printer" wizard under the context of that virtual server. Since it is not a physical computer that can be logged on to, it is necessary to perform this task over the network. From the Start menu, select "Run" and enter the text "\\virtual_server," where virtual_server is the network name resource created for the print spooler. See Figure 4-26. A window will display the shared resources for this network name. One of the resources is the "Printers" folder. From this folder, the "Add Printer" wizard can be executed and the printer created in the appropriate context. Since we are now working at the cluster level, this step needs to be performed only once, not once

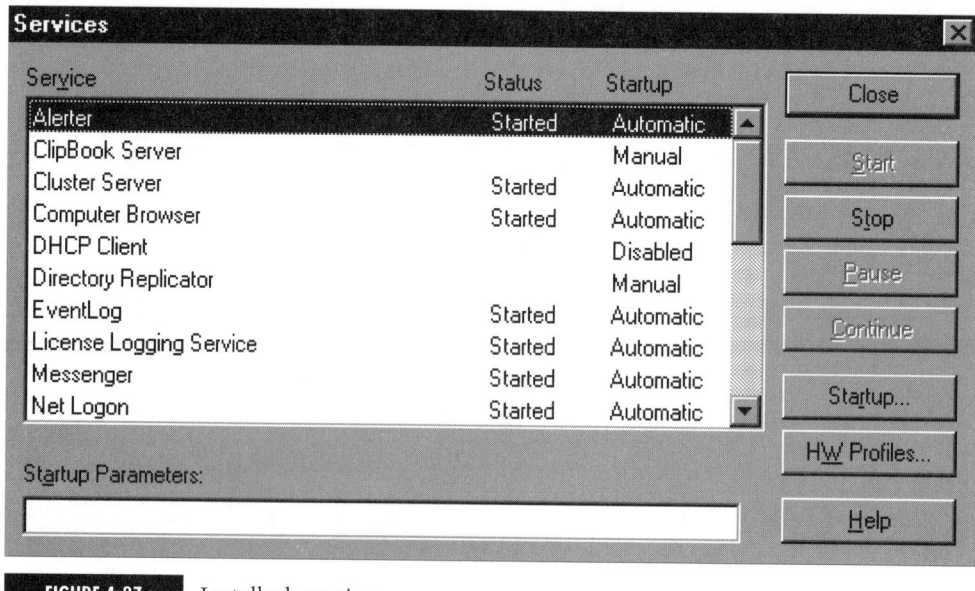

FIGURE 4-27 Installed services

per cluster member as the previous steps did. When creating the printers, make sure to use the ports and printer types configured for use by the cluster.

The Generic Service Resource

What Is a Service?

A service is a powerful feature of the Windows NT operating system. It is basically an application running in the background or not associated with the desktop window and user. In the UNIX world, a service is very similar to a daemon. The operating system makes extensive use of services to support the low-level functions that it provides. One example of a service is the Server service. This application is responsible for accepting NetBIOS based connection requests from clients. The list of configured services can be viewed through the Services icon in Control Panel. See Figure 4-27.

Before discussing how to configure a service to run in a cluster, it is important to understand how a service is implemented by the operating system. A service is an application program that is written following some very specific rules. Approximately 80-90 percent of a service program is standard; therefore, it is fairly simple to have a program sometimes referred to as a *wrapper*. In this case, the wrapper program takes an existing application and allows it to run as a service. This will not work for all applications, but it is a nice feature for those applications it will support. We will discuss the specifics of implementing our own service later.

A service can run as a separate process or as a thread in the context of the primary Services process. The primary difference is that every process has unique security information, or access token, whereas a thread inherits the access token of the process to which it belongs. It is important to realize that the standard Windows NT security mechanism applies to services when an operating system resource is accessed. Windows NT security can be summarized as follows: the access token of the process, or thread, must match a granted access in the access control list of the resource. The Services interface in Control Panel provides the option to define the user context to use when creating the service process. Double-click on the service to be configured, and the following screen appears (see Figure 4-28):

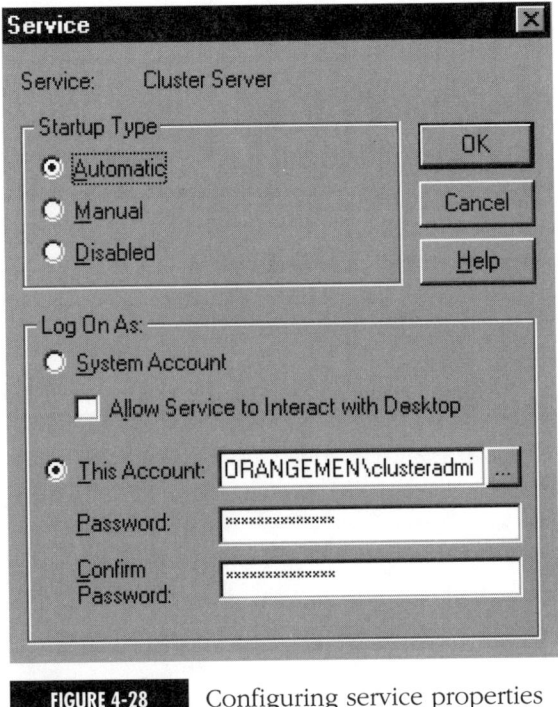

FIGURE 4-28 Configuring service properties

Provide the username and password in the fields provided. The password supplied is actually stored in the registry in association with the service parameters, so if the password on the account is ever changed in the user account database, the properties of the service must be updated.

Applications sometimes store information in the registry. As was stated in an earlier section on generic applications, registry information can be replicated between cluster members. This takes the burden away from the application developer or system administrator. The replication process assures that every cluster member computer has up-to-date registry information. In addition to the application specific information in the registry, the operating system also stores all the necessary information to start the service. To view this information, use the REGEDT32 utility provided with Windows NT. Some administrators prefer the utility REGEDIT. Both ship with Windows NT. The REGEDIT utility has a couple of nice features. First, it represents the registry as one large structure as opposed to five or six separate structures such as REGEDT32. It also allows searches on components other than key names, which is a big drawback to REGEDT32. The one feature the REGEDIT utility lacks is any security menu. Access control lists are supported on registry objects just as any other object. This is because the REGEDIT utility originated in Windows 95 where less emphasis is placed on security. The registry path to view service settings is HKEY_LOCAL_MACHINE\SYSTEM\CurrentControlSet\Services. Under this registry location is a separate key entry for every service installed in the operating system.

Service Resource in Microsoft Cluster Server

A service resource object in a cluster is a service that has been installed on all members in the cluster. The service may or may not be in a running state on all members. There are situations where an application runs in the context of a service. Microsoft SQL Server is a good example. SQL Server functionality is mainly supported by two services, SQLSERVER and SQLEXECUTIVE. Specifics on how to manage SQL Server are discussed in a later chapter. Associating a cluster service resource with a Windows NT service allows for fail-over of the service to occur. When a cluster member goes offline and that cluster member owns a service resource, the cluster software will move the service resource to another member in the cluster. Realize that this function involves a process' or thread's being terminated on one system and a similar process' or thread's being recreated on the new owning cluster member. Any object handles will become invalid and must be corrected by the application.

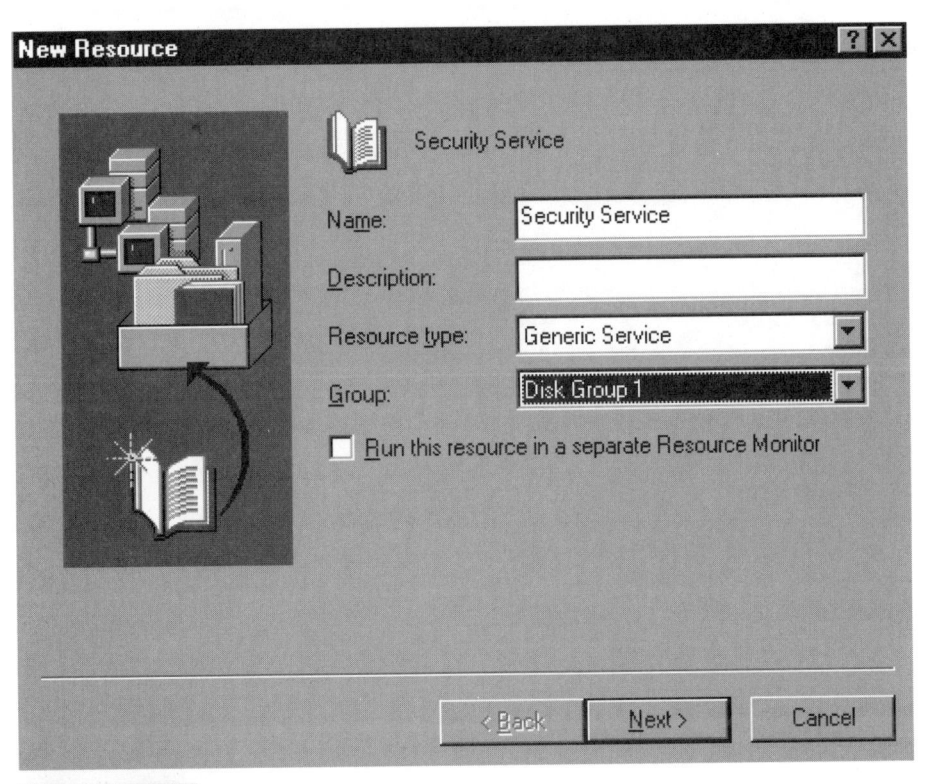

Four • Implementing Cluster Available Resources **99**

FIGURE 4-29 Creating a generic service resource

Configuring a Generic Service Resource

To configure a service to run as a cluster resource, the following tasks must be carried out:

- Create or designate the group of whom the service resource will be a member.
- Provide the text name of the service. This is the text displayed from the Services program in Control Panel.
- Define any necessary registry replication.

To create a generic service resource, invoke the New Resource wizard (see Figure 4-29).

Enter a text name and description for the resource. Take advantage of the name and description fields. Many situations can be avoided with this feature that is often ignored by administrators, not just in Cluster Server, but in many products. For example, six months from now, if an administrator examines Cluster Administrator, is he more likely to remove a resource

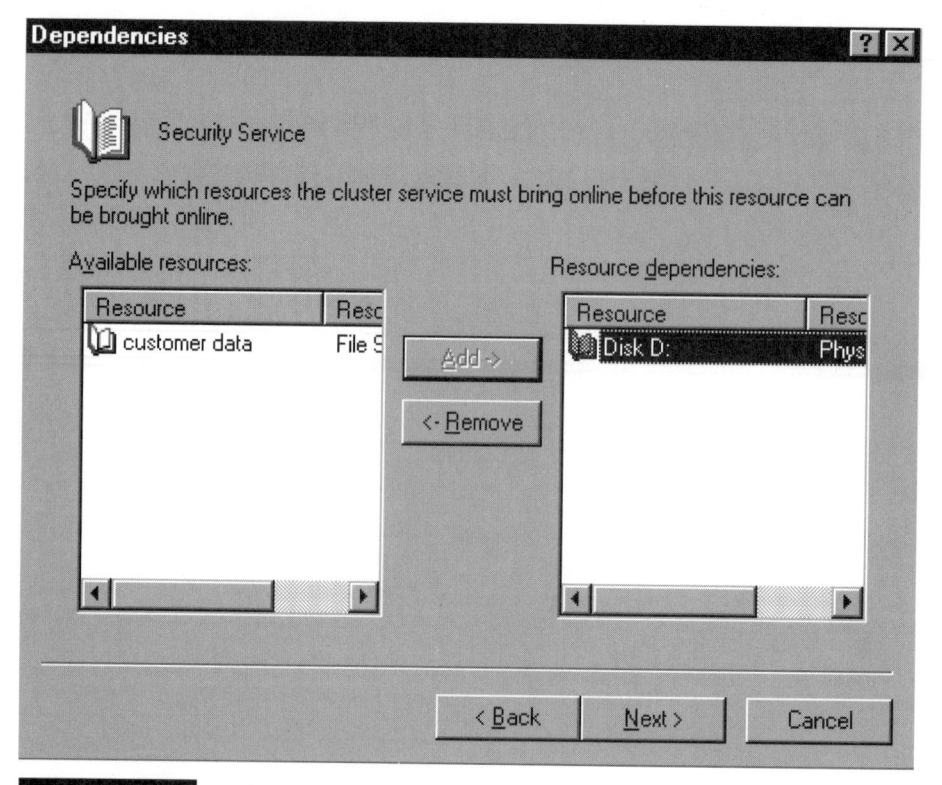

Chapter Four • Windows NT Cluster Server Guidebook

FIGURE 4-30 Defining generic service resource dependencies

called APP1 or a resource called Customer Database? Take the time to generate useful names at this point and avoid potential problems later.

The checkbox, "Run this resource in a separate resource monitor," was probably originally designed specifically for two types of resources: generic services and generic applications. Since both of these resource types allow many different programs to run as a resource, the risk of introducing a poorly behaving resource to the cluster increases. To protect the other cluster resources from interference, consider running these resources in separate resource monitors. This will consume more system resources, however. The decision whether to run the resource on a separate resource monitor requires that the application in question be tested in a cluster environment. Make sure to test failover for the resource.

Select all members of the cluster that will be capable of running the service. This means defining what cluster members can possibly own and run the service resource. This is not defining the preferred owner. Preferred owners are associated with groups, not resources. If all members of the cluster are intended to be possible owners of a service resource, the service application

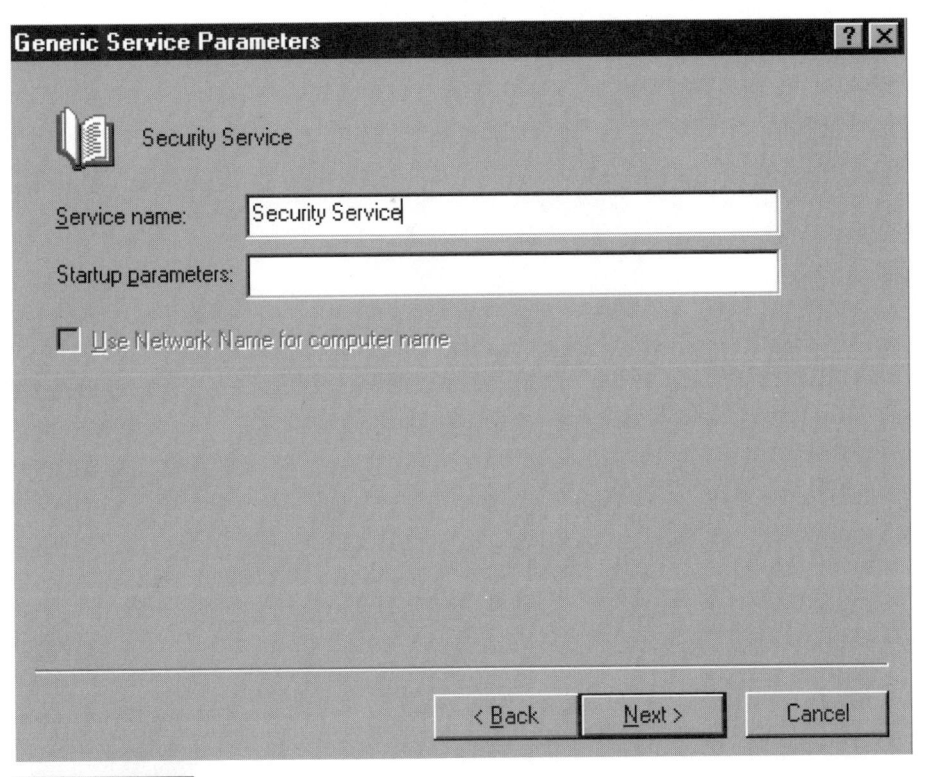

[Screenshot: Generic Service Parameters dialog — Service name: "Security Service"; Startup parameters: (blank); checkbox "Use Network Name for computer name"; buttons < Back, Next >, Cancel.]

FIGURE 4-31 Configuring a generic service resource parameters

must either reside on one of the shared SCSI devices or it must be installed locally on each member that is listed as a potential owner of the resource.

Select any resources that must be running in order for the service to function properly. See Figure 4-30 on page 100. In the case of a generic service resource, no dependencies are required, but can be included. For example, if the service runs a program that is on one of the cluster shared SCSI disks, then the disk resource should be a dependency of the service.

Only two parameters must be supplied for a generic service resource. See Figure 4-31. Enter the Service name. This is the text string that is displayed by the Services program in Control Panel. The text is specified when the service is installed and is simply an entry in the registry.

Enter any startup parameters. These will be application specific and must be documented by the programmer. A startup parameter is data that is passed to the program when it starts. The application then uses that data to decide what tasks it needs to perform. For example, an application that performs as a security monitor may need to be supplied for the disk and/or directory to be monitored.

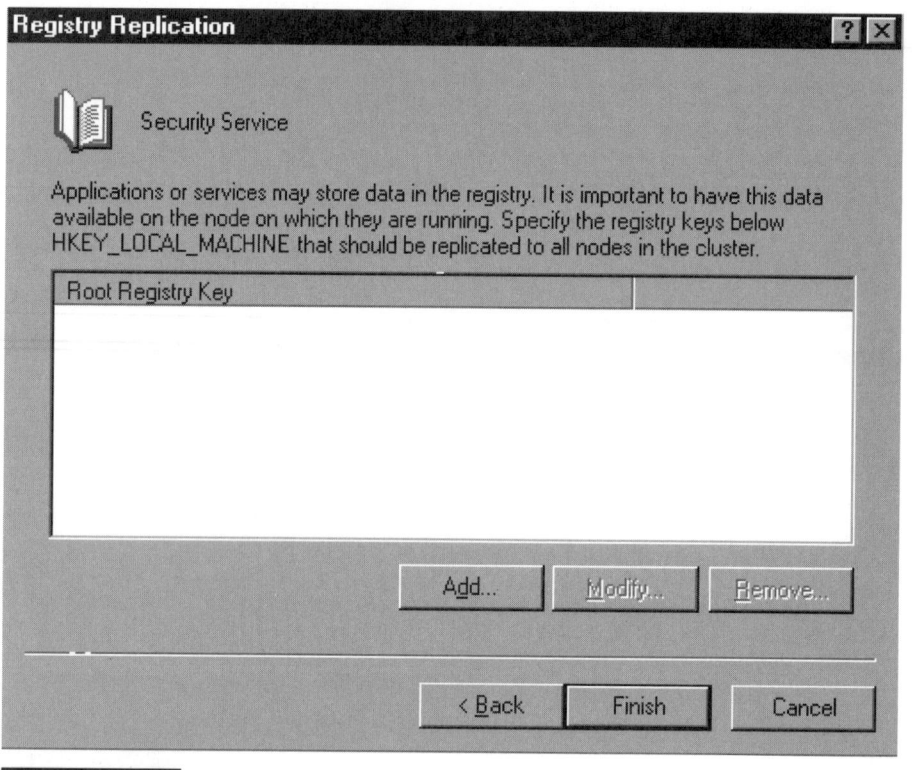

FIGURE 4-32 Configuring registry replication

Another method of providing data to a service application is to store data in the registry. Since each cluster member has a unique registry, it will be necessary to replicate the registry data between cluster members. See Figure 4-32. In this screen, supply the root, or starting point, for the registry information that needs to be replicated. For example, if a service named FileMon has been installed, and a registry key named FileMon has been created in HKEY_LOCAL_MACHINE\SOFTWARE section of the registry, the root registry key to be entered would be HKEY_LOCAL_MACHINE\SOFTWARE\FileMon. This would replicate any data in the FileMon key and any subkeys.

When the service resource is created, it is not brought online automatically. In order to bring the resource online, right click on the service resource and select the "Bring Online" option.

The Generic Application Resource

Generic Application Resource Defined

The generic application resource allows a program to run as a resource. Conceptually, it is very similar to a generic service resource except that it does not require all the extra code in the program to interact with the service control manager. The generic application resource can be useful when the administrator wants to guarantee that a program will always be running. For example, assume that a disk defragmentation utility offers the ability to perform work while the computer is in normal operation. A generic application resource can be created with the appropriate command to start the disk software. This guarantees that if the software for some reason is stopped or terminates, it will be restarted automatically by the cluster server software. Notice that this is not taking advantage of any load balancing or fault tolerance, but is simply using the auto-restart capability of a resource. To continue with the example, a generic application resource should be created for each cluster member, in order to execute the disk maintenance software on all systems. Obviously, in this example, there is no need to configure any failover. Another example of an application that works well here is a program that performs security monitoring. A security program does not provide any benefit if it is not running. With the monitor defined as a generic application, the cluster server software will always attempt to restart the program if it fails.

The program associated with the generic application resource is required to be a program that runs indefinitely. It should not complete. If the program completes, the cluster server software assumes the resource has failed and needs to be restarted. After the failure threshold for the resource has been reached the resource will be moved to other cluster members, if the resource configuration allows, and will eventually be taken offline due to the large number of failures detected.

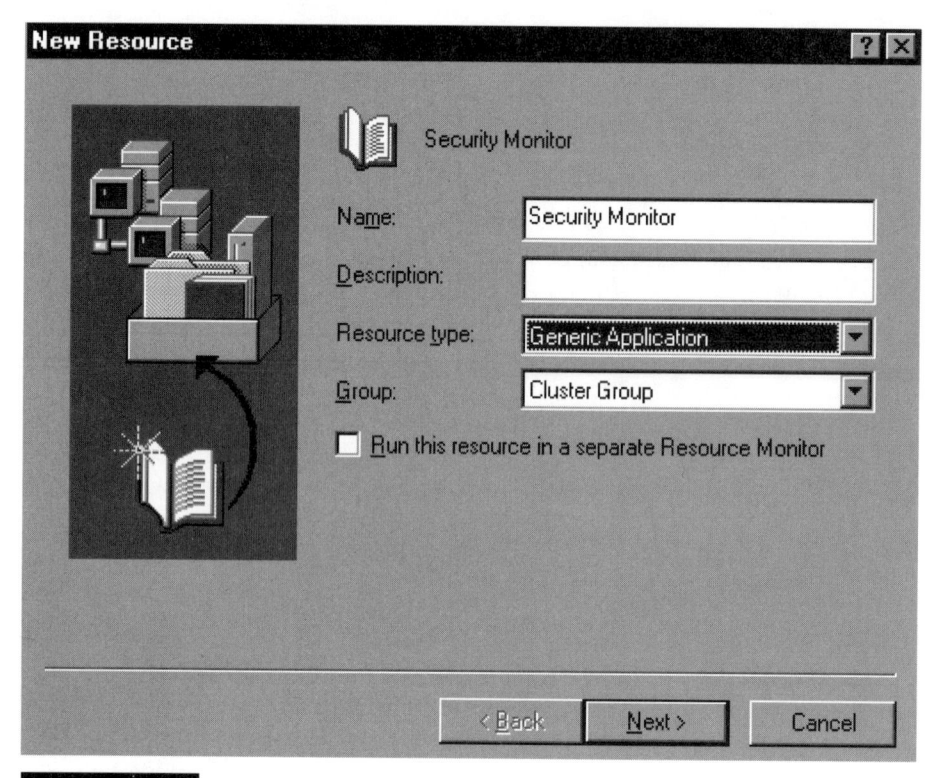

FIGURE 4-33 Creating a generic application resource

Creating a Generic Application Resource

To create a generic application resource, invoke the New Resource wizard and select a resource type of generic application. See Figure 4-33.

Take full advantage of the name and description fields. Assigning meaningful names and descriptions at this point will avoid potential confusion later.

Place the resource in the group that holds any dependent resources it will require. For example, if the generic application resource runs an executable on one of the shared SCSI disks, then the physical disk resource associated with the SCSI device should be a dependency. See Figure 4-34. Do not rely on the Cluster Server software to determine which resources need to be dependent or which resources need to be in the same group. The Cluster Administrator tool will allow a generic application resource, or any resource, to be associated with a directory or executable without requiring that the physical disk resource that contains the directory or executable to be a dependent resource. The Cluster Server software only enforces a

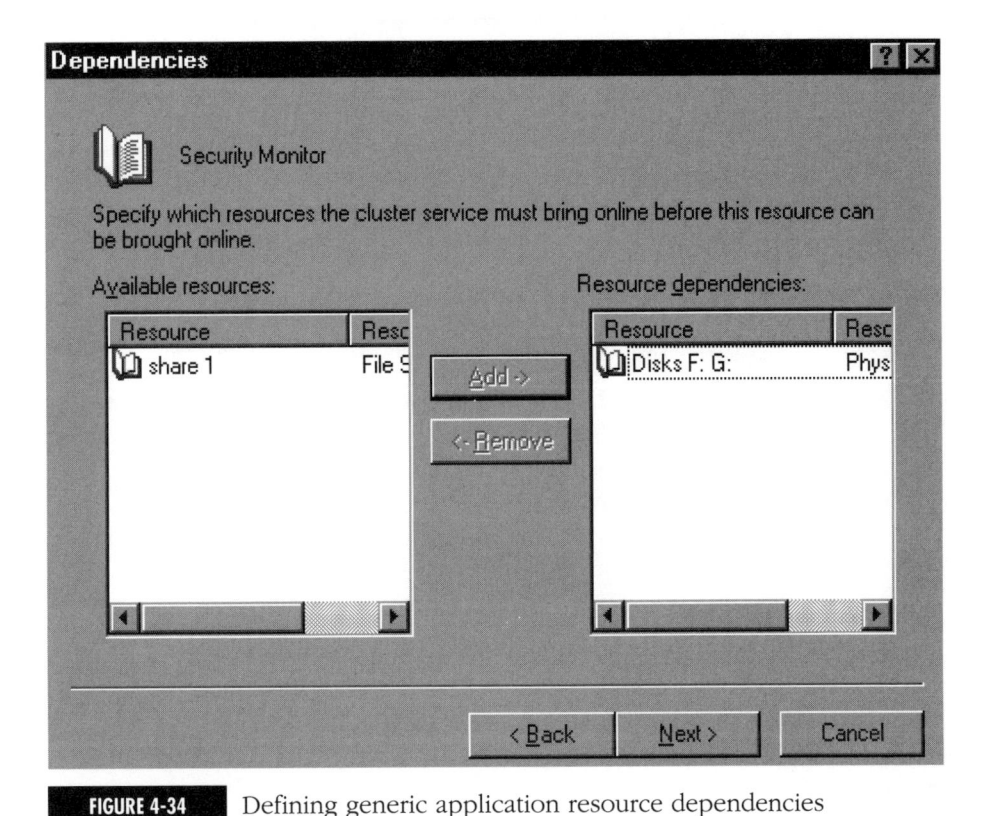

FIGURE 4-34 Defining generic application resource dependencies

type of dependency, such as a network name resource which is dependent on an IP address resource.

Since the generic application is a file level resource, it may seem reasonable that a disk resource be required, but this is not the case. Similar to the file-share resource, the generic application resource can reside on a local disk of the cluster member. This is useful when an application has been installed on all the cluster members and is bound to a specific directory, such as under the Windows NT root directory.

Because the generic application resource does not require a disk resource, load balancing, by application, can be achieved without having to dedicate important disk resources to a specific application. For example, in a cluster configuration consisting of one SCSI disk RAID array, all disk resources will be owned by one cluster member or the other since the RAID array needs to be treated as a single resource. This forces one of the cluster members into a passive mode since it does not have any disk resources. By using generic application resources that are configured to use Executables on the local disks, the passive cluster member can now be put to work.

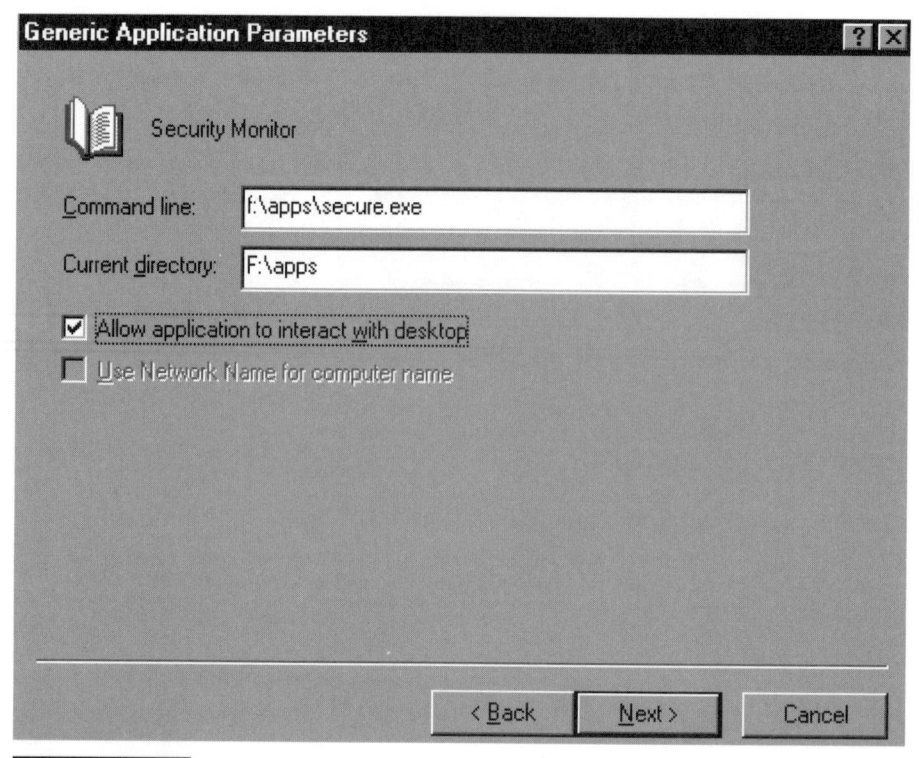

Figure 4-35: Generic Application Parameters dialog

- Command line: `f:\apps\secure.exe`
- Current directory: `F:\apps`
- ☑ Allow application to interact with desktop
- ☐ Use Network Name for computer name

FIGURE 4-35 Configuring generic application resource dependencies

If the generic application is located on a local member disk, remember to install the application in the same directory for each cluster member that is a potential owner of the resource.

The configuration of a generic application resource is very simple. See Figure 4-35. Enter the command line that invokes the program to be executed. The current directory is the default directory the application will run under. This means that if the application requests access to any files, the current directory will be searched first.

The checkbox, "Allow application to interact with desktop" allows or disallows the application to open a window to display its output. If an application normally opens a window and this box is not checked, the resource does not fail. It will be running as a background process. To verify whether this mistake has been made, the "Processes" tab of the Task Manager utility can be used. The Task Manager utility can be invoked by right mouse clicking on an open area in the Taskbar.

Many applications are using the registry as a storage location for small amounts of data such as configuration information, for example, on how many simultaneous clients the application should support. Since the registry

[FIGURE 4-36] Configuring registry replication

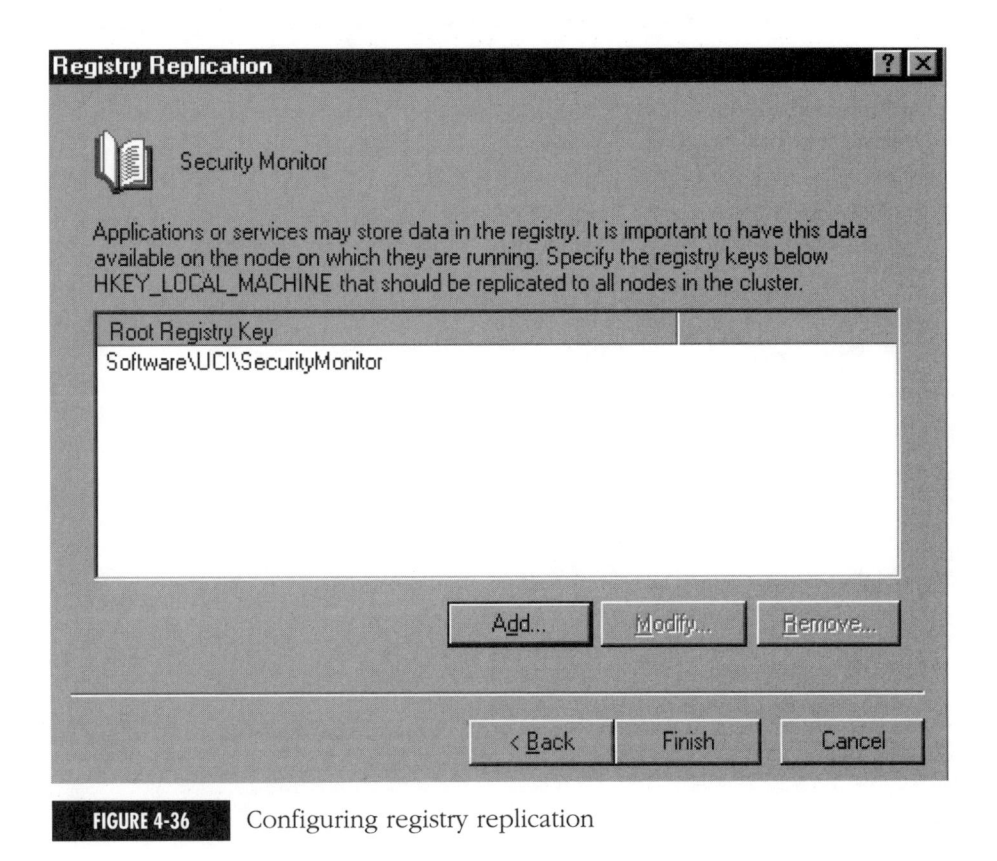

is computer-specific data, the portion of the registry that the application uses must be copied to other cluster members in case the application were to failover to another cluster member at some time.

To configure replication of various registry keys, select the "Add" button. See Figure 4-36. Next, supply the registry path that is to be replicated among the cluster members.

The Physical Disk Resource

The Physical Disk Resource Defined

The physical disk resource is defined as a SCSI-attached disk used for shared folders or storage. At least one physical disk resource is defined at installation time. This is a requirement because the quorum resource must be stored on a physical disk resource. The quorum resource is discussed in Chapter 2. The physical disk resource is linked to physical disk hardware, not logical disk partitions.

FIGURE 4-37 Creating a physical disk resource

Creating a Physical Disk Resource

Creating a new physical disk process is a straightforward task. The only work that must be performed before adding the physical disk resource is to connect the hardware, create one or more disk partitions with the Disk Administrator utility, and format the partitions as NTFS. The Cluster Server software supports only NTFS formatted drives. When the new SCSI disk is connected to the shared bus, remember to assign a unique SCSI ID to the device. How this is done is disk specific; usually it is accomplished by configuring one or more jumpers, toggle switches, or a thumbwheel. Once completed, invoke the New Resource wizard and select a resource type of Physical Disk. See Figure 4-37. The only parameter is the disk device itself, which is selected from a pull-down menu. At this point, the disk is available as a shared cluster device.

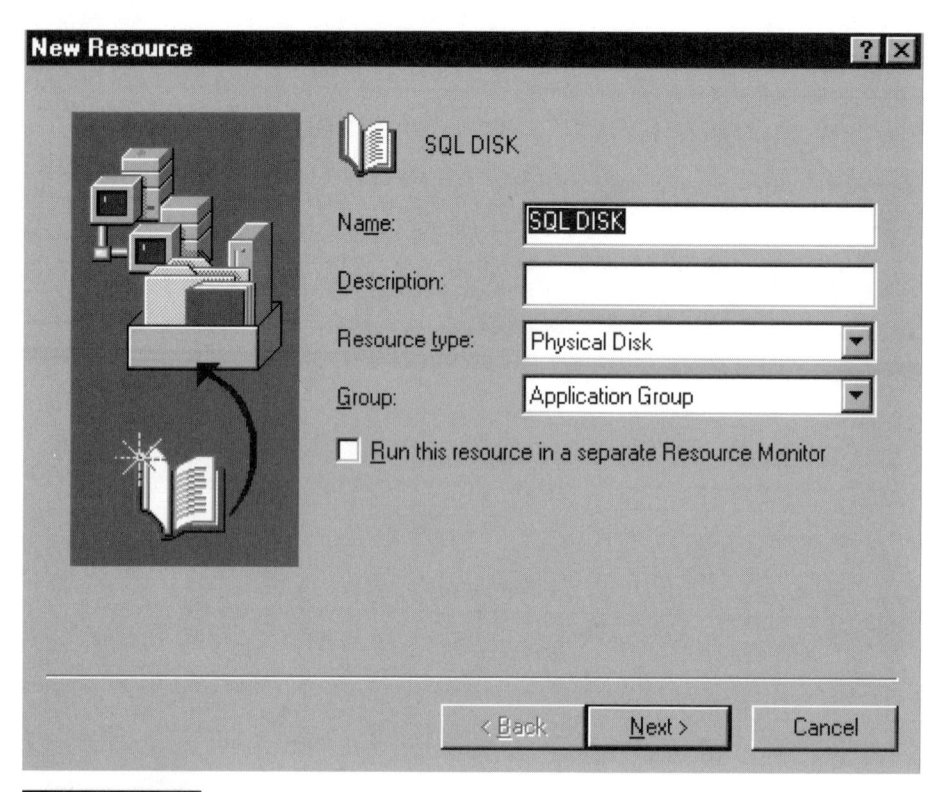

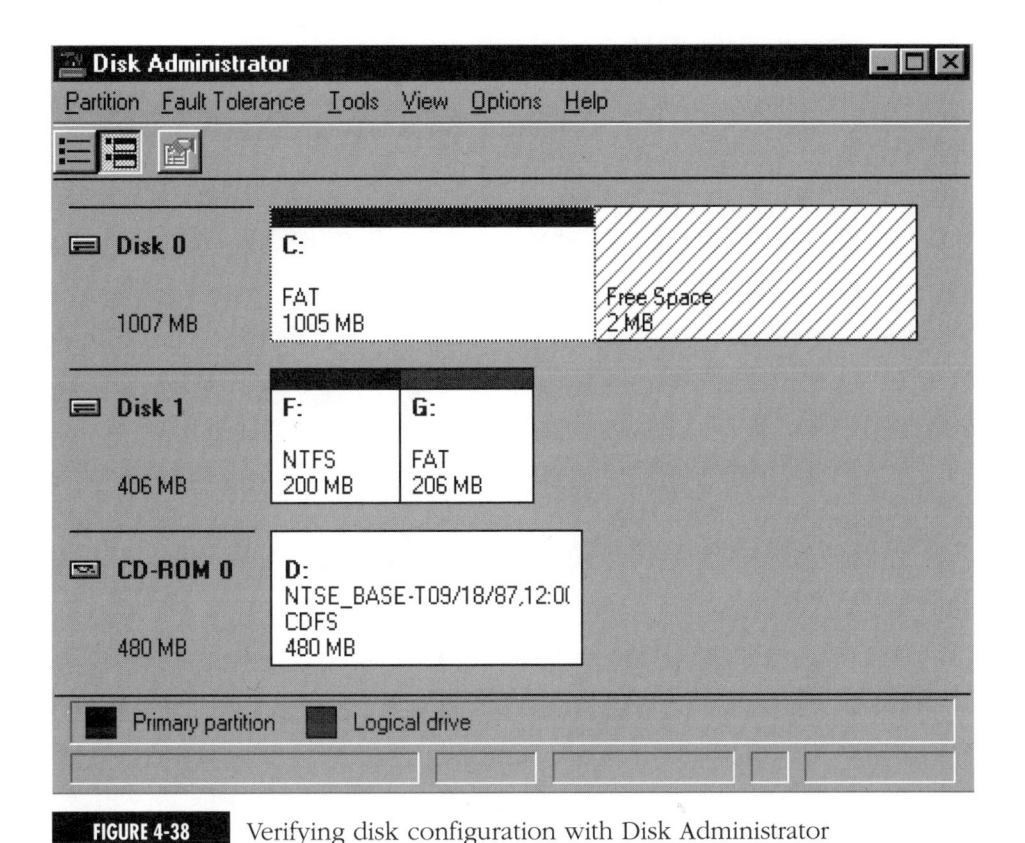

FIGURE 4-38 Verifying disk configuration with Disk Administrator

In order to verify which cluster member currently owns a disk resource, the Cluster Administrator utility can be used. When troubleshooting, it may be beneficial to determine whether the Windows NT operating system on a given cluster member has control of a disk resource. The best utility to do this is Disk Administrator. See Figure 4-38. Any disk resources not owned by the cluster member will display the message "Configuration information is not available."

The IIS Virtual Root Resource

The IIS Virtual Root Resource Defined

By default, each domain name, such as www.ucicorp.com, represents a unique computer on the Internet. It is possible to take a single computer and make it appear as multiple servers, such as schedule.ucicorp.com, registration.ucicorp.com, etc. These secondary domain names are virtual servers defined within Microsoft Internet Information Server. The advantage of this is that multiple, independent Web sites can be offered from a single computer. It is efficient from an administrative perspective to manage only one physical Web server. Also, with security on the Web being a major concern, the fewer servers a site has on the Internet, the less likely they are to be the target of a hacker. A virtual server is nothing more than a TCP/IP address bound to the network adapter and an entry in a DNS that associates the TCP/IP address with a domain name. There are various methods for host name resolution, but only two of those methods work with fully qualified domain names. An FQDN is a name in the format www.ucicorp.com. The two methods for resolving this type of name are DNS, or a HOSTS file. Both of these methods require manual updates and maintenance by the network administrator, although rumors of a dynamic DNS with a future version of Windows NT are common. Install these virtual servers as cluster resources and the result is fault tolerant Web servers that can be served by any cluster member. This is especially important to companies that depend on the Internet for their revenues by taking orders via one or more Web pages, for example.

In addition to virtual servers, the Internet Information Server software also supports virtual directories. A virtual directory is a directory that one of the three services, WWW, FTP, or GOPHER can use to publish data. These directories can be scattered across various disks and even be network drives, but the client will be presented with one "virtual" directory tree, with the home directory as the root and each virtual directory addressed as if it were a subdirectory of the home directory. Physical subdirectories of these virtual directories are also available to the client.

Creating an IIS Virtual Directory Resource

Before an IIS virtual directory resource is defined, verify that the Internet Information Server software is loaded. From the desktop "Start" menu, select Programs, and there should be an option of Microsoft Internet Server. If there is not, install the Internet Server software either by selecting the icon on the desktop labeled "Install Internet information Server" or by running the program Inetstp that is found in the Inetsrv directory under the appropriate hardware directory, such as I386, on the Windows NT Server distribution media. Once the Internet Server software is loaded, it is useful to examine

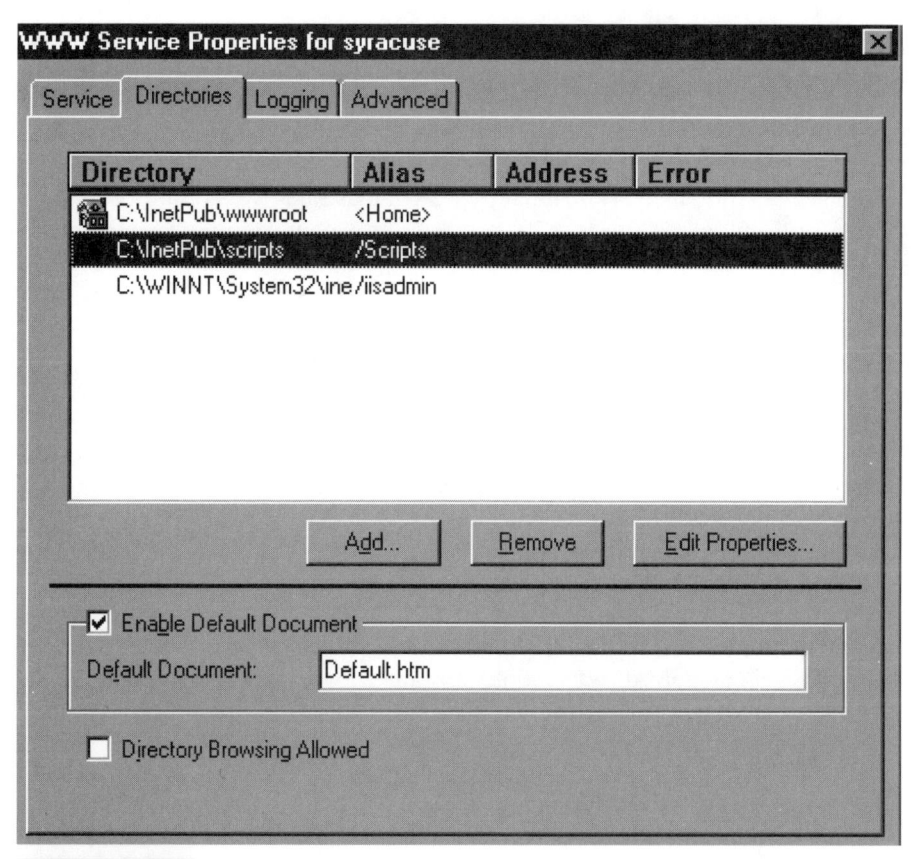

Four • Implementing Cluster Available Resources **111**

FIGURE 4-39 WWW service properties

some of the settings before defining virtual directory resources. Invoke the Internet Service Manager program from the Microsoft Internet Server group. Display the properties for the WWW service and select the Directories tab. See Figure 4-39. There should be a total of three entries after the software is loaded. First is the "home" directory. This directory is the "root" directory for the service. By default, the home directory and all folders in it are available to users. This is the location of the file default.htm. There are also two virtual directories. The scripts directory is used to store batch files or executables associated with the web pages offered by the server. The iisadmin directory stores product documentation.

The process to create a virtual server differs between a cluster member and a standalone server. On a standalone server, it is necessary to define a new TCP/IP address by modifying the network property settings for the computer. Also, there would be no capacity to provide any failover for the address. On a cluster member, this is replaced by an IP address resource.

In order to provide a friendly URL name to the TCP/IP address such as www.ucicorp.com, it is necessary to configure one of the host name resolution methods that Windows NT provides. Of the methods available, the most useful ones are DNS, WINS or a HOSTS file. DNS or domain name server has been an industry standard for many years in the TCP/IP environment. It involves making an entry manually in a database that will reside on one or more domain name servers. A lookup request is generated by client software known as a resolver. The Internet, with regard to domain names, can be viewed as a large tree structure, each branch consisting of subdomains from a parent domain such as COM or GOV. When a client resolver request occurs, many internal requests may need to be made to traverse the domain tree being referenced. This may seem cumbersome, but the response time is remarkably short when it is understood what is actually happening.

Another method of host name resolution is WINS or the Windows Internet Naming Service. As its name implies, WINS is available only on Microsoft operating systems. One advantage of WINS is that it is dynamic. Clients register their names and addresses at boot time. This is useful if a method such as DHCP is being used to allocate addresses. One disadvantage of WINS is the inability to understand fully qualified domain names such as www.hamptonbeach.com. In a situation where a fully qualified domain name is being resolved, WINS looks up only the string up to the first period, in this case www. This could obviously give erroneous results as there are www hosts in many domains.

The last option is to maintain a HOSTS file. The issue with a HOSTS file is that it resides on the client computer. In a network of 5000 clients it would be impractical to manage such a large number of files. One interesting workaround is accomplished using a login script. A login script is a file that is executed every time a client logs onto the network. A line can be placed in the login script to download a HOSTS file from some central location on the network. Now only one file is maintained, but all clients will have the information resident on their computers.

No matter which method is used, the only task of the administrator is to make the entry in the database associating the TCP/IP address with the appropriate domain name. Since host name resolution deals with translating a name to a TCP/IP address, it is transparent at this level which member in a cluster owns the resource. It does become an important issue at the level of TCP/IP address resolution, where TCP/IP addresses are mapped to Ethernet, or MAC addresses. How this is accomplished in the cluster is discussed in detail in the section on IP address resources.

To create a virtual directory resource, first create a directory on one of the cluster shared disks. It is necessary to place this directory on the shared disk for failover to work properly. Next, create an IP address resource that will function as the address of the virtual server. The virtual root resource has a dependency of an IP address resource. Now the virtual root resource

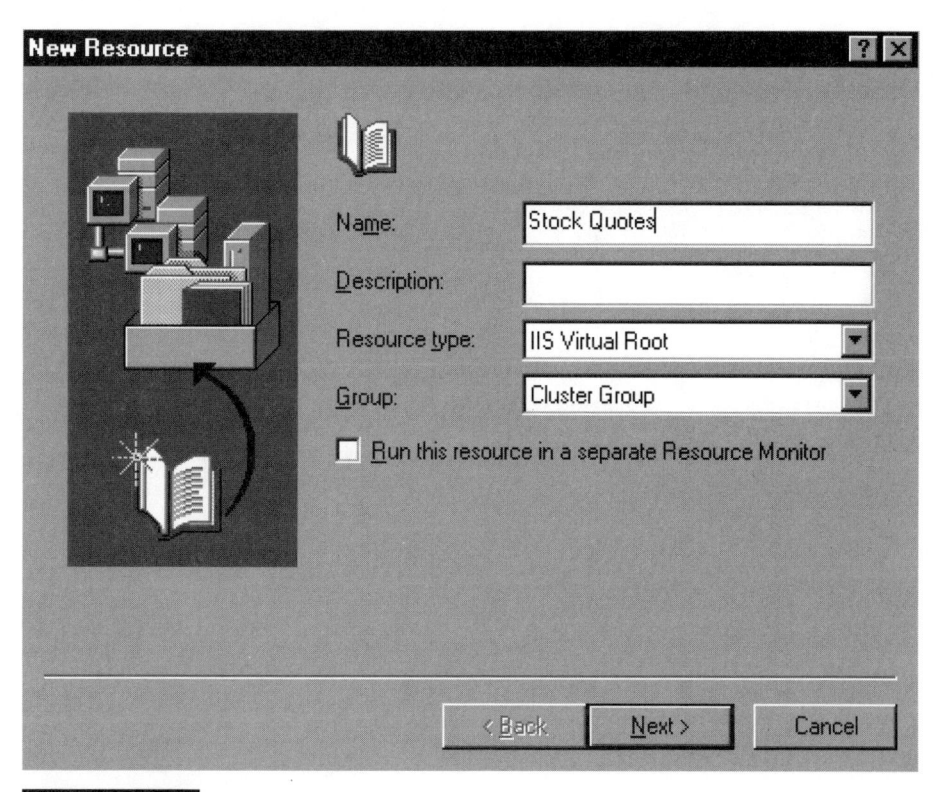

Four • Implementing Cluster Available Resources   113

FIGURE 4-40 Creating an IIS Virtual Root resource

can be created. Invoke the New Resource wizard and select a resource type of IIS Virtual Root. See Figure 4-40. As mentioned earlier, a dependency on an IP address resource is required. Also, if the resource uses a directory on one of the shared SCSI disks, there should also be a disk dependency defined, although one is not required. This is likely for the same reason that a file-share resource does not have a disk dependency. If the data is to be read-only, separate copies could be placed on local disks of the cluster members as long as the path names were consistent, for example, D:\web-data. It would then be necessary to implement some process to guarantee that all copies of the data in question were the same. Not having the disk dependency can be useful when trying to force some level of load balancing on the cluster.

[FIGURE 4-41] Configuring IIS Virtual Root resource parameters

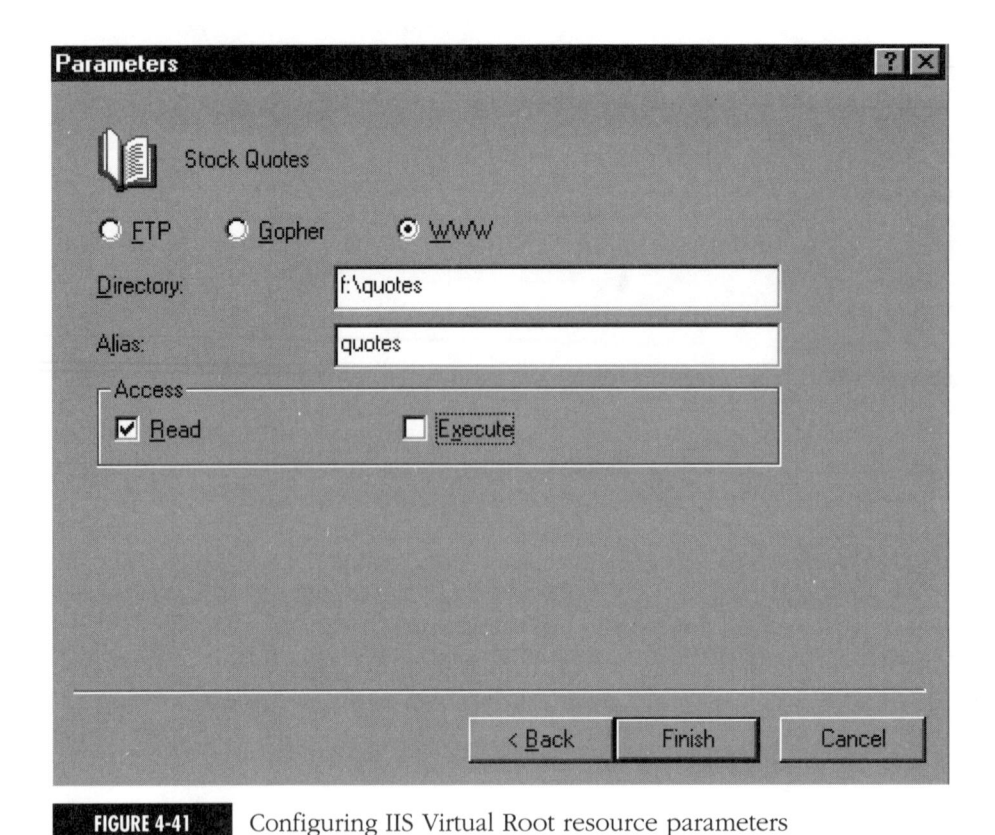

The Parameters screen accepts the details for the virtual root. See Figure 4-41. First, specify whether the directory should be an FTP, GOPHER, or WWW directory. Next, provide the physical path for the directory, such as F:\WEBDATA. An alias is also required. Remember that this directory, no matter where the physical location, is going to appear as a directory under the Web, FTP, or gopher site. The alias name will be used by clients to access this directory and all its subdirectories. Last, specify the level of access, either read or execute.

The Distributed Transaction Coordinator Resource

The Distributed Transaction Coordinator Defined

Distributed transactions are transactions that update data on two or more systems. The primary problem with distributed transactions is how to protect the integrity of the data on the various computers from corruption due to network or system failures while in the middle of processing the transaction. The possibility exists that a transaction will be completed on one participating system but not on another. There must be a guarantee that either the entire transaction is processed or no part is processed. The transaction needs to be "atomic." This problem is resolved by using the Microsoft Distributed Transaction Coordinator. There are various components that work together to provide the functionality of distributed transactions.

Resource Managers

A resource manager is the software that actually manages the data to which transactions are being applied. For example, SQL Server is a resource manager. When a resource manager starts, it contacts its local transaction manager to declare the resource manager's existence. The resource manager then waits for execution requests from applications. When a request arrives, the resource manager contacts the transaction manager and enlists in the transaction. By enlisting in the transaction, the resource manager will be notified by the transaction manager when the transaction commits or aborts.

Transaction Managers

A transaction manager is responsible for controlling transactions by performing the following tasks:

- Creates transaction objects at the request of applications
- Accepts requests by resource managers to join a transaction
- Tracks the status of the transaction among the resource manager and either commits or aborts the transaction.

Every system has a local transaction manager. When a transaction involves multiple computers, the transaction manager communicates with the other transaction managers involved to coordinate the activity.

The transaction manager uses a method known as a two-phase commit when requested to commit a transaction. In phase one, the transaction manager requests that all resource managers involved in a transaction prepare the transaction. Depending on the results of phase one, the transaction manager requests that all the resource managers either commit or abort the transaction.

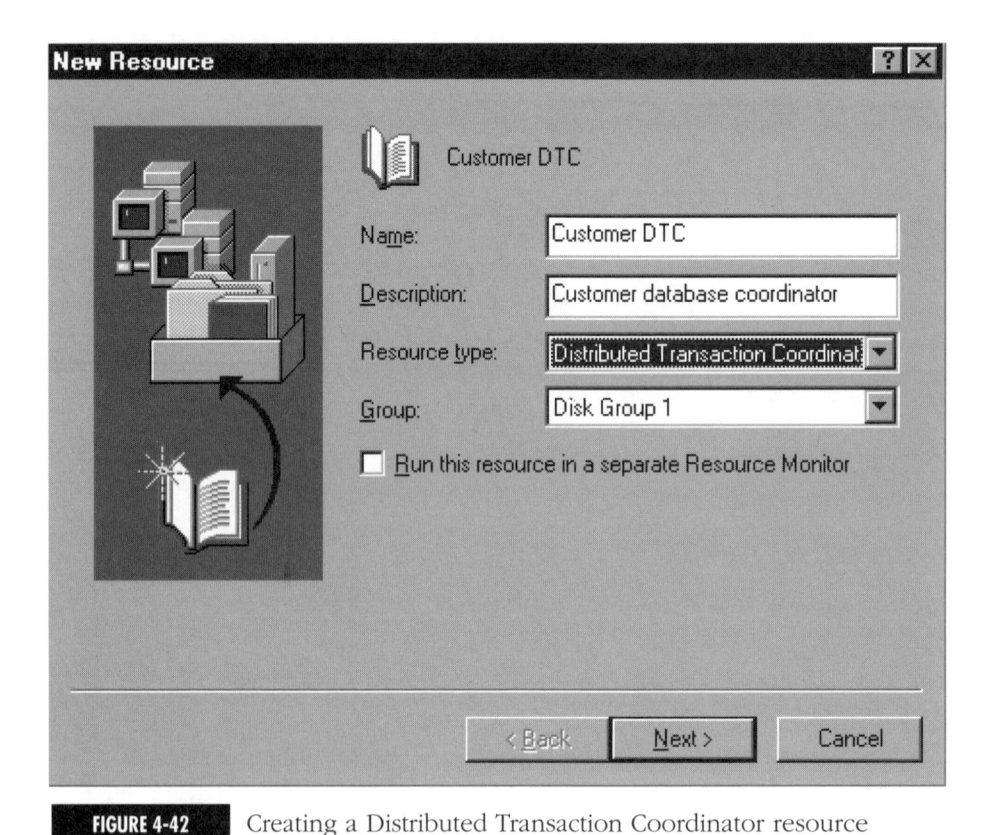

FIGURE 4-42 Creating a Distributed Transaction Coordinator resource

Creating a Distributed Transaction Coordinator Resource

The Cluster Server software supports the distributed transaction coordinator as a cluster resource. The failure of a distributed transaction coordinator resource can have a wide-ranging impact. If one transaction coordinator were to fail, the entire transaction will need to be aborted, which could impact numerous other servers and clients. For this reason, running this resource in a separate resource monitor will provide another layer of protection by isolating the resource from potential problems due to another resource's using the same monitor. See Figure 4-42.

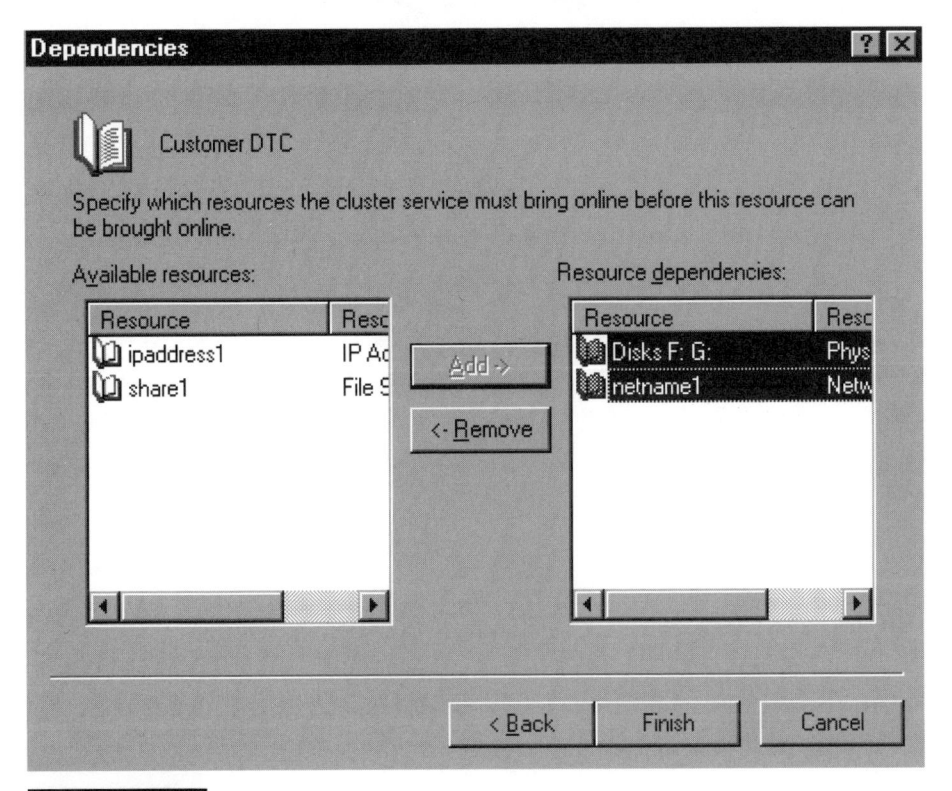

FIGURE 4-43 Defining DTC resource dependencies

The distributed transaction coordinator keeps a log on disk. This log is a sequential file that records transaction events. For this reason, a transaction coordinator resource requires a disk dependency. See Figure 4-43.

A network name dependency is required since transaction coordinators communicate with each other on the network as transactions are being processed. The network name resource supplied as a dependent resource should also be the name registered in the SQL Enterprise Manager to perform configuration of the coordinator.

Cluster Management

By this time, a fully functional cluster should be running smoothly. The challenge and excitement of something new has probably worn off. But building the cluster is only one step in supplying clients with a high degree of application availability and fault tolerance. The cluster is now in production and the goal is to keep it there.

Cluster management tasks can be divided into three categories. The first is the normal administrative tasks such as performing hardware upgrades, software updates, and backups. The second is performance monitoring and the third is troubleshooting. These may overlap somewhat, for example; one of the troubleshooting steps may include performance monitoring.

Some standard procedures that your organization follows may need to be modified slightly to take advantage of the features that the cluster provides. For example, a documented software installation policy may require that it be performed during off-peak hours due to the possibility of system corruption or failure. Since the cluster concept eliminates the server as a single point of failure, software installs and updates can be performed during normal business hours. Another policy that will probably need some revision is the backup procedures, which will be discussed in detail later.

The Cluster Administrator Utility

The Cluster Administrator utility is the primary tool for the system administrator to manage a cluster. The tool is installed on any system that uses the Cluster Server software. It is also possible to install only the Cluster Administrator tool on a desktop to perform remote cluster management. Any system that is running Windows NT Workstation V4.0 or Windows NT Server V4.0 with Service Pak 3 or later, or any system running Windows NT Server, Enterprise Edition, can run the Cluster Administrator tool. To install Cluster Administrator, run the standard Cluster Server setup program and select the Cluster Administrator utility option.

The options in the Cluster Administrator utility that deal with groups and resources have been discussed in a previous chapter; there are many additional features that are useful. Before these options are covered, it is important to understand the different icons that may appear in Cluster Administrator. The icons are context sensitive; i.e., an icon will be interpreted slightly differently depending on the object it is marking.

The most common icon is a yellow triangle that looks like a yield traffic sign. This icon is a signal that a resource or a group has been manually taken offline. When a resource encounters a failure, the cluster server software will attempt to restart it. After the configured number of failures, the resource is either moved to another cluster member or marked as "failed," which is denoted with a different icon. Keep in mind that if a resource or group is marked as offline and you did not do it, this means someone else did. Do not bring the resource or group back online without first checking with the person who was privileged to perform the operation. (This symbol is also used to mark a cluster member that has been paused.)

The next icon is a red circle with an "X" in it. This represents a variety of situations, depending on what cluster object it is associated with. First, if a resource is marked with this icon, it means the resource is in a "failed" state. This occurs when a resource encounters failures and has been restarted by the cluster for the configured number of times. Next, the resource will be moved to another cluster member, if possible. If there is no other cluster member available to take the resource, the resource is classified as "failed."

This symbol, when associated with a group object, denotes that one or more of the member resources is not online. The resource could either be in an offline or failed state. The remaining members of the group will still function normally.

When this symbol is associated with a node object, the cluster server has determined the cluster member as down. A cluster member could be classified down if the computer is shut down or if the network between the cluster members is not functioning.

Cluster Administrator Options

There are many other options in the Cluster Administrator used to perform configuration tasks. There are three methods to modify the properties of a cluster object. First, the object can be highlighted and the right mouse button depressed. The second option is to highlight the object and select the "File" option in the menu bar. Either method leads to the same options available to configure an object.

The third method is the toolbar, which is limited in its options. It is object sensitive in the options that it provides. For example, the "Bring OnLine" toolbar button will be available only when a resource or group that is currently offline is selected. Since it is limited in the options it provides, I never use the toolbar.

One option in Cluster Administrator that is not object sensitive is the "Open Connection" option from the File menu. This option establishes connections to remote clusters for administration purposes. This may concern administrators that their cluster can be managed remotely; however, the Cluster Administrator utility provides the option to define what users and Windows NT groups have permission to connect remotely.

Cluster Object

The first entry in the left pane of the Cluster Administrator is the cluster object. There are only two options. See Figure 5-1. The first is "Rename." As its name implies, the name of the cluster can be changed with this option. When changing the name of the cluster, make sure to follow the NetBIOS naming rules, such as no more than fifteen characters. Also, if the cluster name has been defined in a DNS database, it must be changed. This should not be a problem with a WINS database because the registration process is dynamic. The new name of the cluster will be automatically registered. Finally, the new name assigned to the cluster will not take affect until the Cluster Name resource is taken offline and put back online. Notice the options "Open Connection" and "Close," which are the options an administrator uses to connect to a remote cluster.

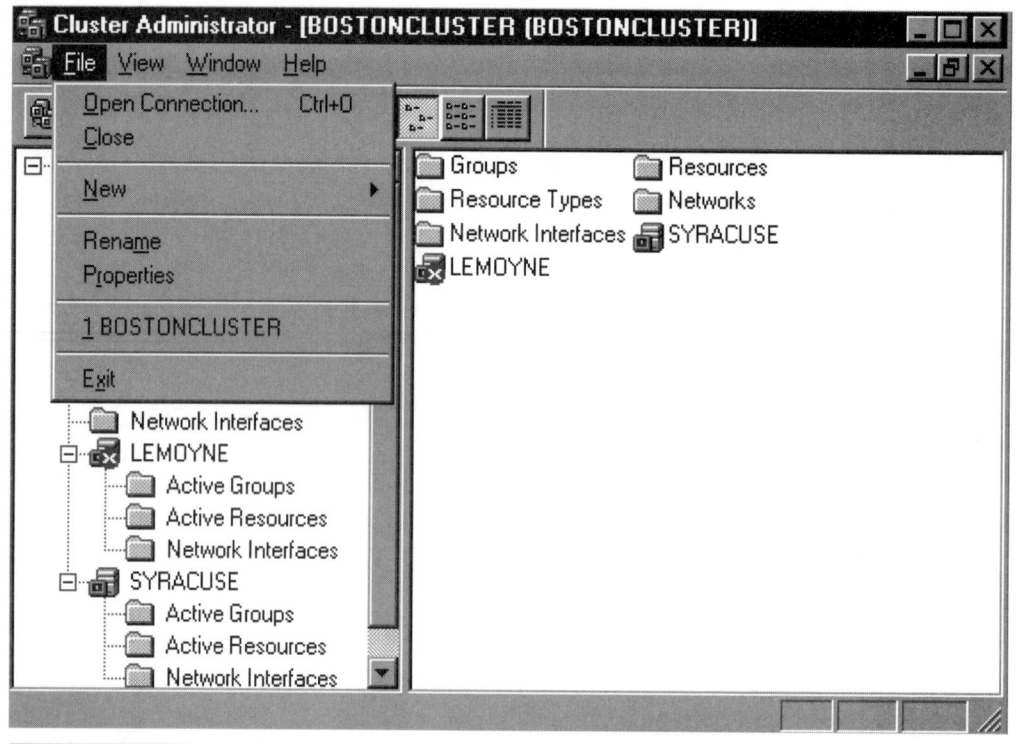

FIGURE 5-1   Configuring the cluster's properties

Cluster Properties

The configuration of the cluster can be modified by selecting the "Properties" option from the File menu (see Figure 5-2).

Through the general tab in the cluster properties, the cluster name and cluster description can be modified. The most important feature on this page is the "permissions" option, which allows the cluster administrator to define what users or groups can manage the cluster, not which users can connect to resources. Resource permissions are managed through the "permissions" option provided by the type of resource. For example, the only resource at this time that provides a permissions option is the file share resource. Since the file share resource parallels the NetBIOS file-sharing mechanism of Windows NT, the permissions are applied in the same method the operating system uses. Not all resource types provide this feature, and when they do, there is no guarantee that the security interface will be the same.

Other management tasks pertaining to security are discussed in detail in this chapter.

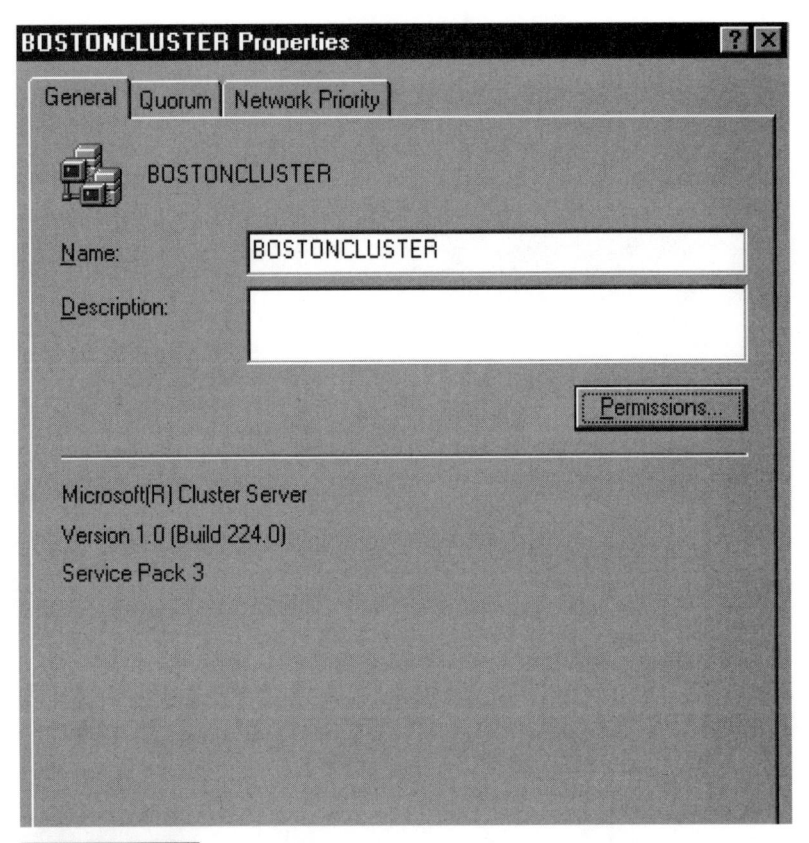

FIGURE 5-2 Configuring cluster properties, continued

To assign specific users or groups the ability to manage the cluster, select the "Permissions" button to bring up the standard Windows NT permissions screen. See Figure 5-3. The only entry after an installation allows the Administrators group management access to the cluster. To modify this list, use the "Add" and "Remove" buttons. Selecting the "Remove" button removes the currently highlighted entry from the access list. When the "Add" button is selected, a list of the groups and users from the Windows NT user accounts database is displayed. Select the users or groups to be given access and select OK. Full control is the only type of access that can be granted.

FIGURE 5-3 Configuring cluster administration access

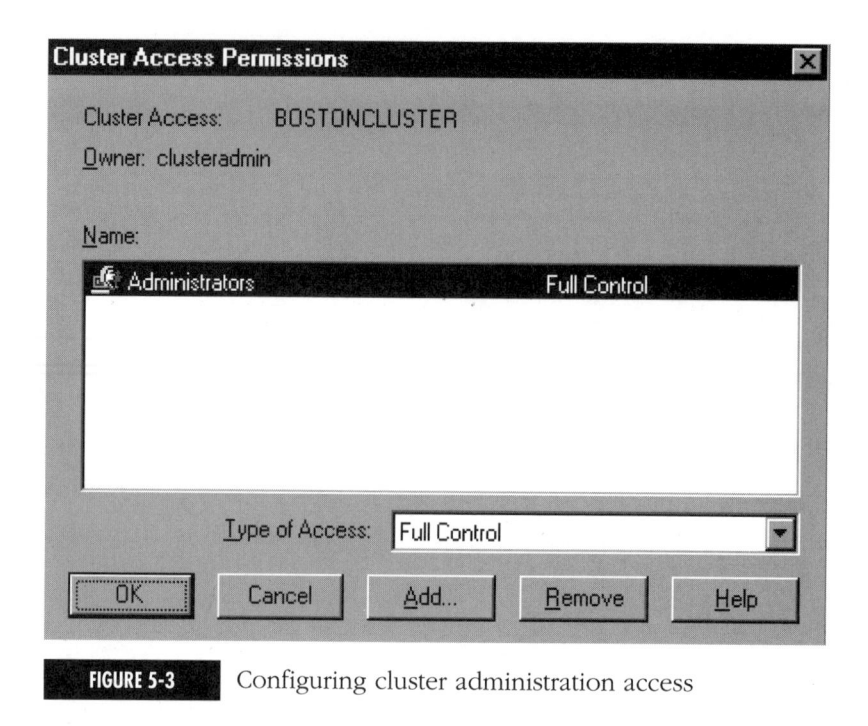

The quorum resource location is defined during the cluster installation process. It is possible to change the location of the quorum resource if the disk configuration in the cluster is changed. See Figure 5-4. Select a partition on the shared SCSI bus from the pull-down menu and if needed, change the root path. If the cluster is started and the quorum files do not exist or are corrupt, the necessary files are created by the cluster service at startup time. Do not modify the access permissions on the disk that contains the quorum resource. The Cluster Server software must have full access to this device.

The quorum log saves configuration changes made to the cluster. This is necessary since changes could occur while one of the cluster members is offline. In the event a cluster member is planned to be offline for an extended period of time, or if cluster configuration changes appear to be getting lost, the size of the quorum log should be increased from its default size of 64KB.

The Cluster Server software provides the ability to use multiple network adapters. A typical configuration has two adapters in each cluster member. If there is more than one physical network connecting the cluster members, one or more of these network interfaces can be designated to handle the internal cluster traffic. Only one adapter is used for cluster communication at any time, but this allows another level of fault tolerance to be designed into the cluster configuration. This traffic consists of the heartbeats that occur at the rate of two per second between the cluster members and any resource

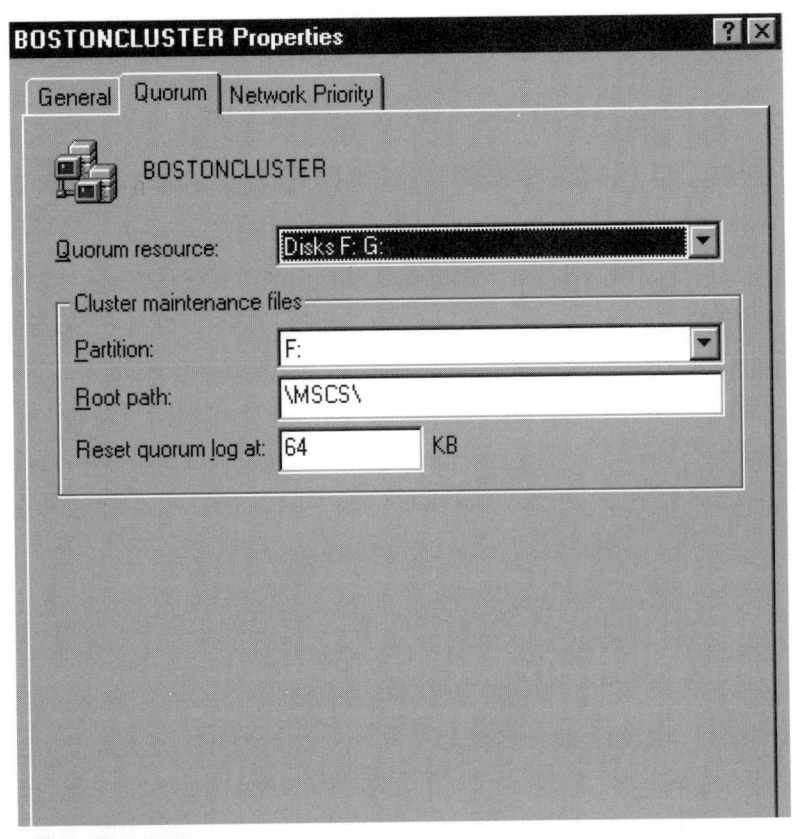

FIGURE 5-4 Modifying the quorum resource properties

failover or failback traffic. When more than one network adapter is configured to handle the internal cluster traffic, the adapters can be prioritized to define which should be used. A small thinwire segment is a perfect configuration for the internal cluster communication network. Use the "Move Up" and "Move Down" buttons to define the order of precedence of adapters used for internal cluster traffic.

A network interface can be used for internal cluster traffic only, client traffic, or only for both. Client traffic consists of access to all the cluster resources and therefore can be very heavily used, so isolate the user traffic from the internal cluster traffic, if possible. If there are two network adapters on the cluster members, configure only one for client access, and configure both for all communications. Then prioritize the adapters so that the adapter not used for client access will be used first for cluster communication traffic. See Figure 5.5. The net effect is that there are fault tolerant

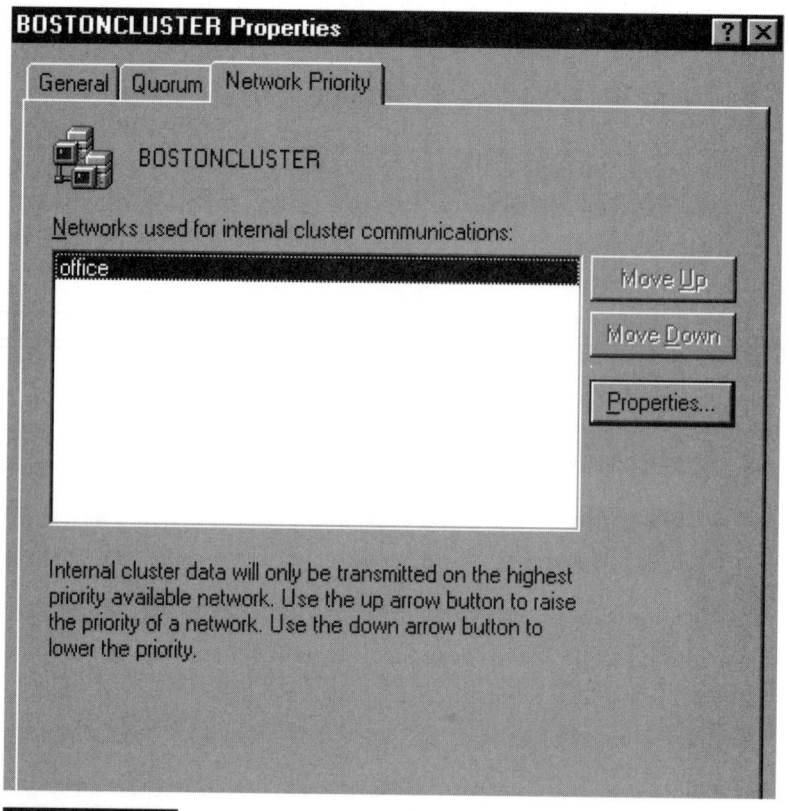

FIGURE 5-5 Changing the network to be used for cluster communications

paths for the cluster communication, but only one path for client access. If the network adapter on the client network fails, the cluster resources can be manually failed over to the other node and users can regain access to their resources.

To configure what type of traffic is allowed on the network interface, highlight the interface and select the "Properties" button to view the network properties screen. See Figure 5-6.

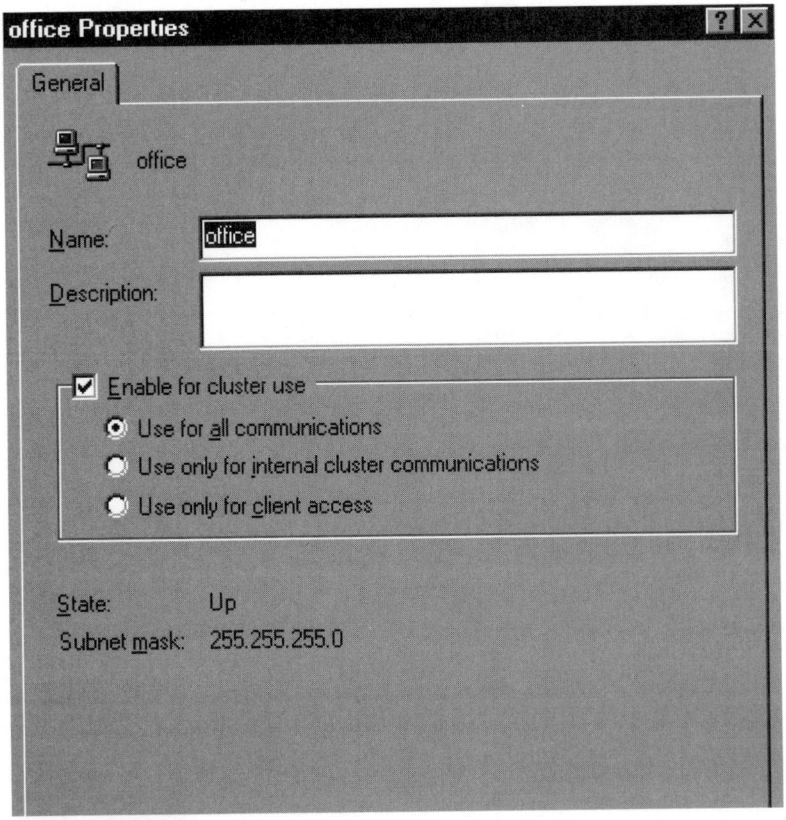

FIGURE 5-6 Configuring network properties

Managing Cluster Nodes

Pause Node

The pause node option allows existing groups and resources to stay online, but does not allow any additional resources or groups to be brought online. See Figure 5-7. This option can be used to gradually move resources and groups to other cluster members. If a node has reached its processing capacity, pausing the node prevents it from taking over additional cluster resources. One recommended sequence for performing maintenance on a cluster member is as follows:

- Pause the node requiring maintenance.
- Move remaining groups and resources to other cluster members.
- Perform the maintenance on the paused node.
- When the maintenance is complete, select the "Resume Node" option.

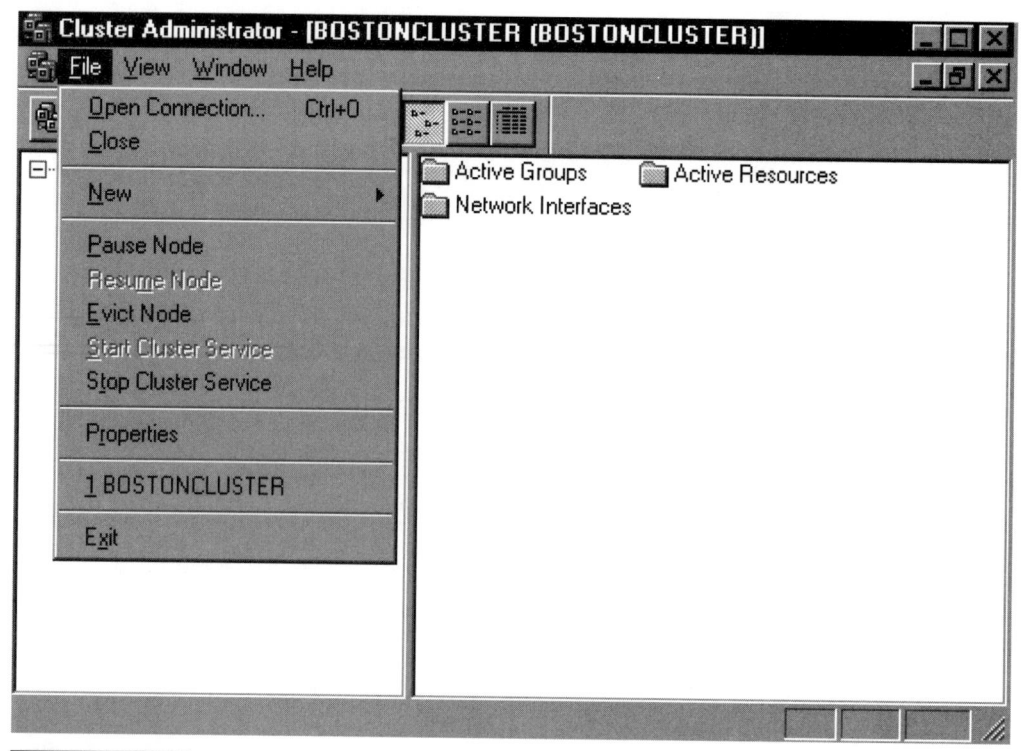

FIGURE 5-7 Managing a cluster member

Make sure that the SCSI bus termination is not interrupted during the maintenance process. It is recommended that Y cables be used so that the cluster member can be disconnected from the SCSI bus and proper termination is preserved.

Evict Node

The Evict Node option is used to permanently remove a node from the cluster. See Figure 5-7. It does not de-install the cluster software; it removes the node information from the cluster database. The Cluster Server software must be removed manually by using the "Add/Remove Programs" option in Control Panel.

Start/Stop Cluster Service

When the Cluster Service is stopped on a node, all groups will be moved to the other node, as long as the group policies allow. See Figure 5-7. All client access to resources on the cluster member is immediately terminated. This is an easy way to fail all resources at once to the other cluster member and can be used when a cluster member is going to be shut down, for maintenance. Even if the computer is not going to be shut down, e.g., there are other reasons to disconnect all users. Perhaps a software upgrade will be applied that will affect only the local disks, but the upgrade will not succeed with connected users. In this case, when the upgrade is complete and the node is ready to become a cluster member again, simply select the "Start Cluster Service" option.

Managing Cluster Security

The Microsoft Cluster Server product depends on Windows NT security at all levels of communication, from communication between nodes to client access to cluster resources.

Windows NT Server offers two types of accounts and groups: local and global. A local group in Windows NT, not to be confused with a cluster group, is a group of users that is known only to that specific Windows NT Server, hence the term "local." A local user is a user account that is known only to the owning Windows NT Server. Windows NT assigns a unique identifier to every user account or group. This identifier is called a security ID, or "SID." All Windows NT permissions are granted to "SIDs," not to usernames. Usernames exist for our benefit. Local account and groups are an issue on Windows NT Servers that are running as member servers because every member server has its own account database. Windows NT Servers functioning as domain controllers share their account database. Therefore, all accounts and groups have a valid security context between domain controllers. Whenever assigning permissions in a cluster, it is imperative not to use local accounts and groups. This would be an issue only if the cluster nodes are running as member servers and not domain controllers.

Earlier in this chapter, it was discussed how to specify which Windows NT users and groups can manage the cluster. Other tasks relating to security that may need to be carried out by the administrator include:

- Changing the account under which the Cluster Service runs
- Changing the password to the account under which the Cluster Service runs
- Limiting access to shared data (file share resources)
- Auditing access to shared data
- Taking ownership of files or folders.

Changing the Cluster Service Account

The Cluster Service must run under a domain user account, as opposed to the system account, which is the default account with which Windows NT services are configured to run. There are certain restrictions and a number of privileges that must be applied to the account to be used:

- The account must be a domain account, not a local account. This means that a member server must use an account from a domain account database.
- The Cluster Service must run with the same account on both nodes. This guarantees that the Cluster Service on both nodes will have the same security context and will be capable of accessing files created by the other node's Cluster Service. If the two nodes do not have the same account, they will not join to form a cluster.
- The account must be in the Administrators group on both nodes. Violation of this restriction is more likely to happen when the nodes are member servers and have their own account database and, therefore, their own Administrators group. However, it is possible to encounter this situation between domain controllers if the account being used is newly created or modified and the two domain controllers have not yet performed an account database synchronization with the new account information.
- The account must have a variety of privileges. Some, but not all, of these privileges will be inherited when the account is placed in the Administrators group. The Cluster Server installation process performed the initial privilege allocation.

If the account is changed, the privileges must be granted manually. The privileges required by the Cluster Service account are:

- Back up files and directories
- Increase quotas
- Increase scheduling priority
- Load and unload device drivers
- Lock pages in memory
- Logon as a service
- Restore files and directories.

Rather than create a brand new account and assign all the privileges, it may be an acceptable option to rename the account in the User Manager utility. This would modify the username but preserve the security context and privileges that are required. Once the account has been granted these privileges, the following procedure can be used to change the account:

1. Verify with the User Manager utility that only the following restrictions are set:
   - User cannot change password
   - Password never expires.
2. Stop the Cluster Service on both nodes by using the Services option in Control Panel.
3. With the Cluster Server service highlighted, select "Startup." Mouse-click in the grey box at the end of the line titled "This Account." This will allow the domain and account database to be browsed and the username selected. Enter the password and reconfirm the password.
4. Perform step 3 on the other cluster member.
5. Restart the Cluster Server service on both nodes.
6. Verify that the cluster is functional by using Cluster Administrator to check that both cluster members are online.

Changing the Password to the Cluster Service Account

The security policy of some companies requires that passwords be changed every so often. This task is less complex than changing the username and password. To change the password for the Cluster Service account, perform the following tasks:

1. Use the Services option from Control Panel to stop the Cluster Service on both cluster members.
2. With the User Manager utility, change the password to the Cluster Service account. Make sure that the "User must change password at next logon" option is not selected.
3. In the Services program, double-click on the Cluster Server service to bring up a startup properties window. Enter the new password and confirm it.
4. Perform step 3 on the other cluster member.
5. Restart the Cluster Server service on both nodes.
6. Verify that the cluster is functional by using Cluster Administrator to make sure both cluster members are online.

Setting Security on File Share Resources

Security is set on file share resources through the same interface used from Windows NT to assign permissions to shared directories. Make sure that permissions are assigned through the Cluster Administrator interface and not through the standard Windows NT permissions interface. Permissions assigned to file share resources from Windows NT will be lost when the resource is taken offline and put back online because the assigned permissions were not stored in the cluster database.

The Cluster Server software requires that the shared SCSI disks be formatted as NTFS. The NT file system supports its own level of security, also known as access control lists. When the permissions assigned at the NTFS level conflict with the permissions assigned to the share directory, a network connection to the resource will provide the most restrictive permissions from the two access control lists. For example, if the NTFS security is set to allow the group Domain Users read access to a directory, but the file share resource allows Change access, users will be given the most restrictive permission, which in this case is Read. Security would be compromised if the granted access were not handled in this manner.

One interesting discovery is that if the NTFS permissions allow "No Access," the Cluster Server software fails when attempting to bring the resource online. However, it does not fail when the NTFS permissions allow "Read" and the file share resource allows a higher level permission such as "Change."

Auditing Access to Data

Windows NT offers an audit function that records various successful or failed events generated by the operating system. With regard to data protection, auditing can record access to files. Windows NT supports only file-level auditing in NTFS partitions, which means that any disk on the shared SCSI bus is a candidate for auditing. Auditing of file access can be enabled at the drive, directory, or file level. Also, it is not necessary to audit every user's access to a file; the users to be monitored can be specified by the administrator. Audit information can be viewed with the Event Viewer utility.

To enable auditing on a file, directory, or drive, right mouse click on the object and select properties. A security tab should be one of the options to choose, but if it is not, the object is probably not stored on an NTFS partition. Select the security tab, then select the Auditing box. An audit configuration screen will appear. See Figure 5-8.

Use the "Add" button to select the users and groups to be audited. Select the events to be audited by selecting the appropriate success or failure boxes. Be aware that auditing consumes system resources. The saying, "There ain't no such thing as a free lunch," applies here. The more security features that are enabled on a system, the greater impact the security logging has on the overall performance of the system. The new load is mainly in the

Five • Cluster Management   **133**

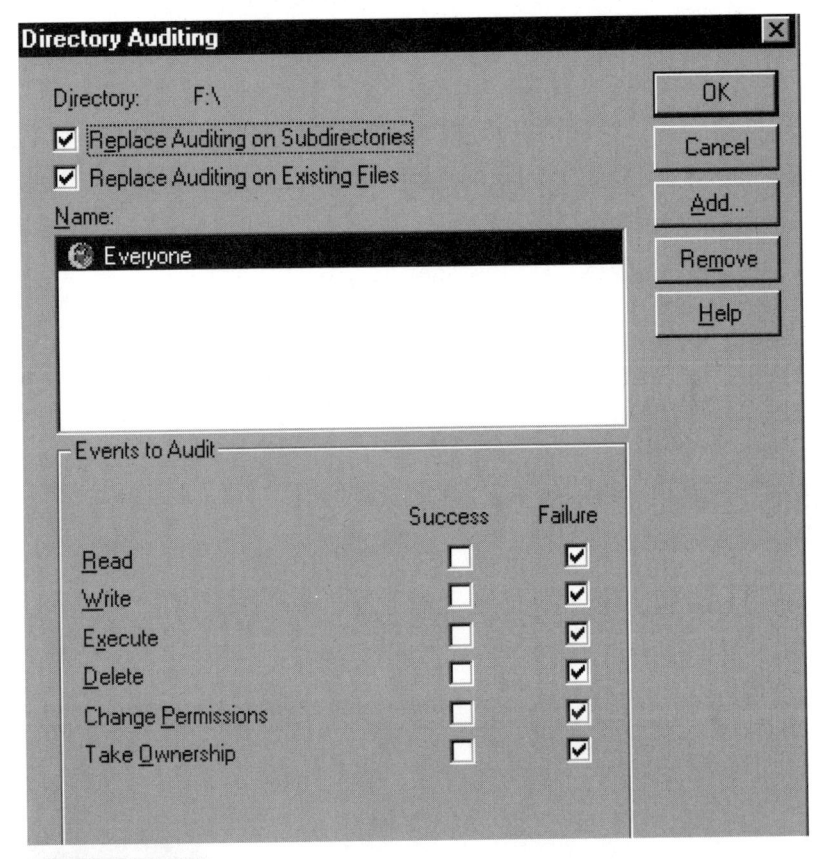

FIGURE 5-8   Audit configuration screen

areas of processor and disk I/O. The load introduced by enabling auditing can be minimized, however, by choosing wisely the events to audit. For example, do not choose to audit successful file accesses by everyone. This can slow down your system to the point where it could hang. By limiting the users and event to audit, you can make the audit utility a useful tool for security monitoring.

The auditing utility needs to be enabled. It is not enabled when Windows NT is installed. If the audit utility is not already enabled, when the audit configuration screen shown in Figure 5-8 is closed, a warning message will appear. See Figure 5-9.

To enable the audit utility, use the User Manager utility. Select the options, Policy, then Audit. The screen in Figure 5-10 will appear.

Notice that there is no reference to usernames or groups in this screen. All this screen does is enable or disable the component of the operating system that collects the selected audit information. Here again, the events to be

FIGURE 5-9 Message when auditing is disabled

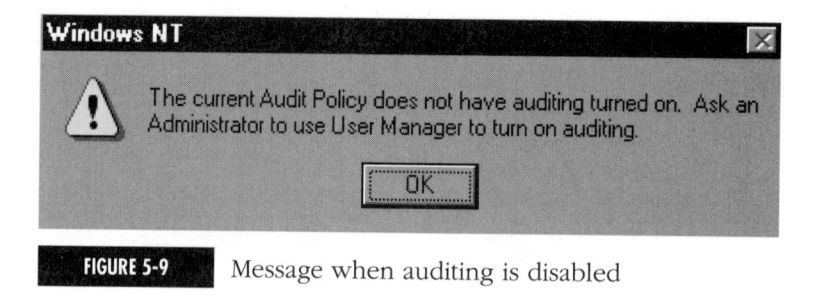

audited can be limited. In this example, only failed file access has been selected. It is probably better to limit what is collected at this point rather than to limit what is actually reported. Why configure the operating system to collect information that it will not use?

After auditing is enabled, it should be reviewed periodically by the administrator. The audited events are written to a log file that can be viewed with the Event Viewer utility. The Event Viewer works with three different log files. To examine the collected data, in Event Viewer, select the Log option, then Security. This will display any audited events. See Figure 5-11. To view

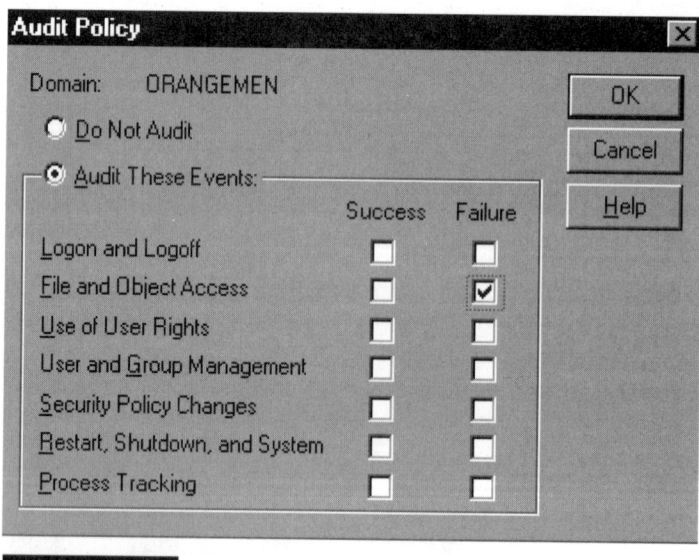

FIGURE 5-10 Audit policy configuration

more detail for any event, double-click on it. The file accessed and the username that requested the access are some of the detail information available.

Five • Cluster Management

FIGURE 5-11 Results of auditing

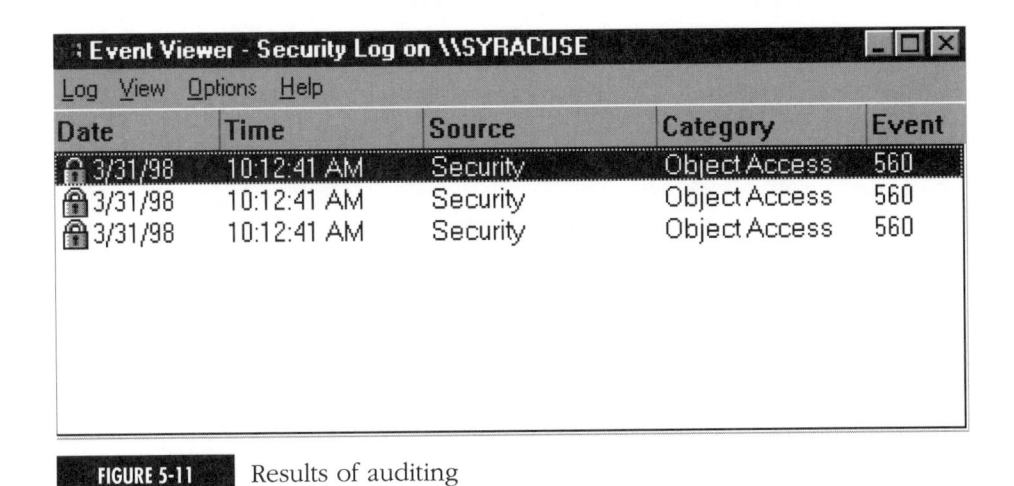

Cluster.Exe

The Cluster Server software contains a utility that allows for many of the same tasks that can be done through the Cluster Administrator utility to be performed via the command line. The command is "cluster" and it has a variety of options. One advantage to the command line version is that batch files can be written and scheduled to execute on a repeating basis in order to automate many of the cluster administration tasks.

Some objects have common settings. For example, all resources can define dependencies. Other settings are object specific. An IP Address resource requires a TCP/IP address, whereas a Network Name resource requires a NetBIOS name.

Cluster

The "Cluster" command can be used to modify the cluster object. The syntax is:

```
CLUSTER [cluster name] /option
```

The cluster name is optional. Supply a cluster name to execute a configuration command on a remote cluster. Any arguments in square brackets are optional parameters.

TABLE 5.1 Options for the "Cluster" command

Option	Description
/RENAME:cluster name	Renames the cluster.
/VERSION	Displays the cluster server software version number.
/QUORUM_RESOURCE:resource name /PATH:path][/MAXLOGSIZE:size]	Change the name or location of the quorum resource, or the size of the quorum log.
/LIST:[domain name]	

EXAMPLE: To view which device is the quorum resource:

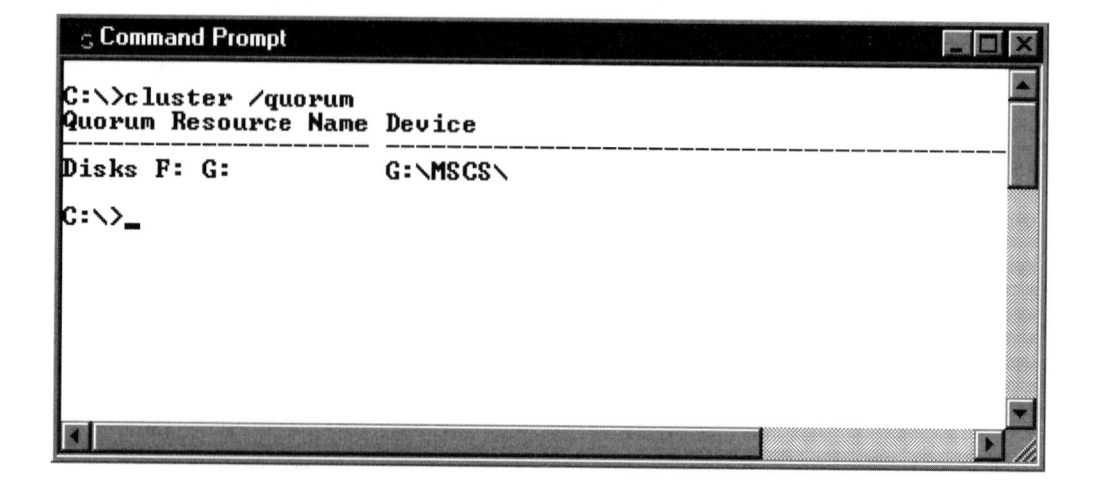

```
C:\>cluster /quorum
Quorum Resource Name   Device
--------------------   ------
Disks F: G:            G:\MSCS\

C:\>
```

Cluster Node

The "Cluster Node" command is used to configure cluster member nodes. The syntax is:

```
CLUSTER [cluster name] NODE [node name] /option
```

The node name is optional only for the /Status command.

TABLE 5.2 Options for the "Cluster Node" command

Option	Description
/STATUS	Displays the cluster node status, such as up, down, or paused.
/PAUSE	Pauses a node.
/RESUME	Resumes a node.
/EVICT	Evicts a node from the cluster.
/PROPERTIES	

EXAMPLE: To display a status of each node in the cluster:

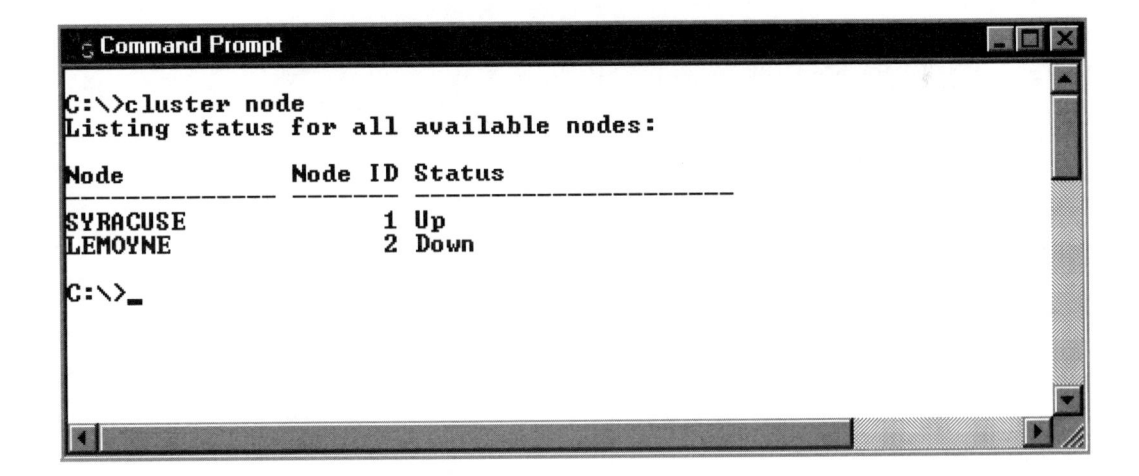

```
C:\>cluster node
Listing status for all available nodes:

Node            Node ID  Status
-------------   -------  --------------------
SYRACUSE              1  Up
LEMOYNE               2  Down

C:\>_
```

Cluster Group

The "Cluster Group" command is used to display and configure group settings. The syntax is:

```
CLUSTER [cluster name] GROUP [group name] /option
```

TABLE 5.3 Options for the "Cluster Group" command

Option	Description
/STATUS	Displays the status of a group such as Online, Offline, or Partially Online.
/NODE: nodename	Displays all the groups on a specific cluster member.
/CREATE	Creates a new group.
/DELETE	Deletes a group.
/RENAME: new group name	Renames a group.
/MOVETO: nodename	Moves a group to another node and displays the
/WAIT: timeout	amount of time to wait for the move to complete.
/ONLINE: nodename	Brings a group online.
/WAIT	
/PROPERTIES	Displays a group's properties.
[propname = propvalue]	Uses the property names returned to set new values.
/PRIVPROPERTIES	Displays the private properties for a group.
[propname = propvalue]	Sets private group properties.
/LISTOWNERS	Displays the list of preferred owners.
/SETOWNERS: node list	Specifies a preferred owner list.

There are no groups that contain private properties, but software developers can take advantage of this feature to store data pertinent to a group's functionality.

Five • Cluster Management **139**

EXAMPLE 1: To display all groups on specific node:

```
C:\>cluster group /node:syracuse
Listing status for all available resource groups:

Group                Node                Status
------------------   -----------------   -------
Cluster Group        SYRACUSE            Online
Disk Group 1         SYRACUSE            Partially Online

C:\>_
```

EXAMPLE 2: To display the configured properties for a group:

```
C:\>cluster group "Disk Group 1" /prop
Listing properties for 'Disk Group 1':

R  Name                              Value
-  -------------------------------   --------------------------
R  Name                              Disk Group 1
   Description
   PersistentState                   1 (0x1)
   FailoverThreshold                 10 (0xa)
   FailoverPeriod                    6 (0x6)
   AutoFailbackType                  0 (0x0)
   FailbackWindowStart               -1 (0xffffffff)
   FailbackWindowEnd                 -1 (0xffffffff)
   LoadBalState                      1 (0x1)

C:\>_
```

Cluster Resource

The "Cluster Resource" command is used to display and configure cluster resource settings. The basic syntax of the command is:

```
CLUSTER [cluster name] RESOURCE  [resource name]
/option
```

TABLE 5.4 Options for the "Cluster Resource" command

Option	Description
/STATUS	Displays the status of a resource such as Online, Offline, or Failed.
/CREATE	Creates a new resource.
/GROUP	Indicates group of which the new resource should be a member.
/TYPE:resource-type	Indicates the resource type for the resource such as "File Share."
[/SEPARATE]	Specifies that the resource should run in a separate resource monitor.
/DELETE	Deletes a resource.
/RENAME : new resource name	Renames a resource.
/ADDOWNER : node name	Adds a node name to the list of possible owners.
REMOVEOWNER : node name	Removes a node name from the list of possible owners.
/LISTOWNERS	Displays the possible owners of the resource.
/MOVETO : group	Moves the resource to the specified group.
/PROPERTIES [propname = value]	Displays the common properties of a resource. Uses propname = value to modify a common property, such as the RestartPeriod for a resource.
/PRIVPROPERTIES [propname = value]	Displays the private or resource specific properties for a resource, such as the Address for an IP Address resource. Uses propname = value to modify a private property.

Some properties are common to all types of resources. For example, all resources have a restart threshold, which indicates how many times to restart the resource on the same cluster member before moving the resource to another node. These properties are displayed and modified with the "/PROPERTIES" option.

TABLE 5.5 Properties that can be modified with the "/PROPERTIES" option

Common Property Name	Description
Description	Changes the text that describes the resource.
DebugPrefix	Defines which debugger should be used for the resource.
SeparateMonitor	Indicates whether or not the resource should run in a separate resource monitor. Valid entries are true or false.
PersistentState	Is the last known state of a resource. For example, if a resource is taken offline and the system is rebooted, the resource will still be offline because of its persistent state.
LooksAlivePollInterval	Indicates the interval in milliseconds that the Cluster Service should perform a quick check to see if the resource "looks" operational. If there is no value for this property, a default value is taken from the same property for the resource type.
IsAlivePollInterval	Indicates the interval in milliseconds that the Cluster Service should perform a more thorough check to determine whether a resource is online. If there is no setting for this property, a default is taken from the property for the resource type.
RestartAction	Defines what action should be performed if the resource fails. ■ 0 – Do not restart the resource. ■ 1 – Allow resource restarts, but not failover. ■ 2 – Perform restarts and failovers.
RestartThreshold	Defines how many times Cluster Server will attempt to restart the resource before failing the group to another node.
RestartPeriod	Specifies the monitoring interval for resource restart attempts to reach the RestartThreshold before Cluster Server fails over the group to another cluster member.
Pending Timeout	Indicates the period of time that a resource can stay in a Pending Online or Pending Offline state without correcting itself. When this timer expires, the resource is placed in an Offline or Failed state.

Properties displayed with the /PRIVPROPERTIES switch are known as private properties and are unique to the resource type. These properties correspond to the "Parameters" tab displayed in Cluster Administrator when the properties for a resource are requested.

TABLE 5.6 Properties that can be modified with the "/PRIVPROPERTIES" Option

/FAIL	Initiates a resource failure.
/ONLINE	Brings a resource online.
/OFFLINE	Takes a resource offline.
/LISTDEPENDENCIES	Lists all the dependencies for a resource.
/ADDDEPENDENCY : resource	Adds a new dependency for a resource.
/REMOVEDEPENDENCY : resource	Removes a dependency for a resource.

EXAMPLE 1: To display a list of all resources, their owner node, and current status:

```
C:\>cluster resource
Listing status for all available resources:

Resource                Group                 Node            Status
--------                -----                 ----            ------
Disks F: G:             Disk Group 1          SYRACUSE        Online
Cluster IP Address      Cluster Group         SYRACUSE        Online
Cluster Name            Cluster Group         SYRACUSE        Online
Time Service            Cluster Group         SYRACUSE        Online
share1                  Disk Group 1          SYRACUSE        Online
ipaddress1              Disk Group 1          SYRACUSE        Online
netname1                Disk Group 1          SYRACUSE        Online
Customer DTC            Disk Group 1          SYRACUSE        Offline
NTFS share              Disk Group 1          SYRACUSE        Failed

C:\>
```

Five • Cluster Management **143**

EXAMPLE 2: To initiate a resource failure:

```
C:\>cluster resource ipaddress1 /fail
Failing resource 'ipaddress1'...

Resource                  Group                  Node                  Status
--------------------      --------------------   --------------------   ------
ipaddress1                Disk Group 1           SYRACUSE               Online

C:\>
```

EXAMPLE 3: To change a parameter setting for a resource:

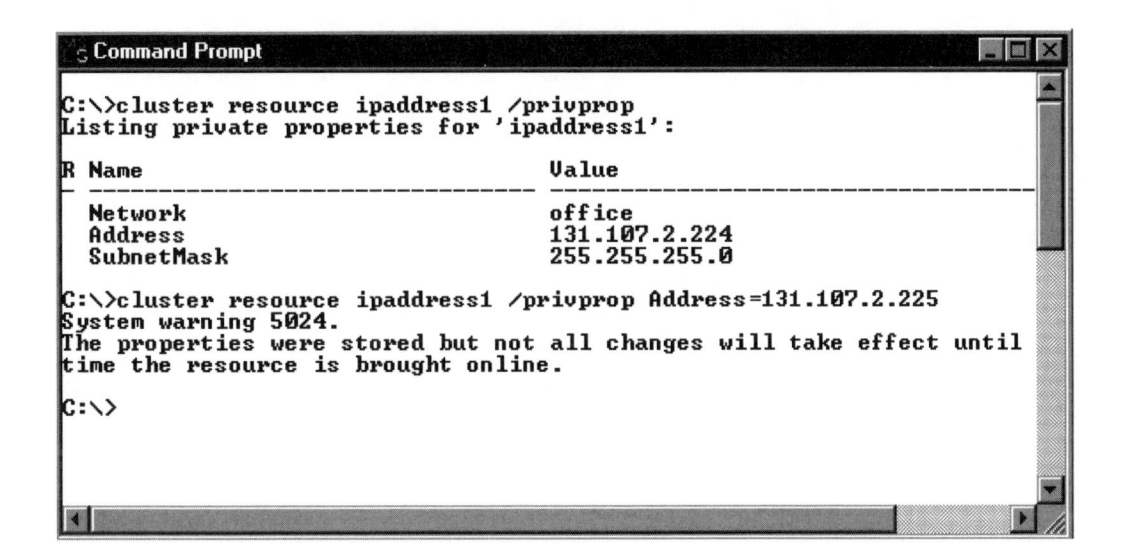

```
C:\>cluster resource ipaddress1 /privprop
Listing private properties for 'ipaddress1':

R Name                                          Value
- --------------------------------------        --------------------------------
  Network                                       office
  Address                                       131.107.2.224
  SubnetMask                                    255.255.255.0

C:\>cluster resource ipaddress1 /privprop Address=131.107.2.225
System warning 5024.
The properties were stored but not all changes will take effect until
time the resource is brought online.

C:\>
```

Cluster Resourcetype

The "Cluster Resourcetype" command allows the administrator to display or modify properties for a resource category such as an IP address. The properties for a resource type are sometimes used as default settings for an instance of the resource. For example, if a resource is created without specifying a LooksAlivePollInterval, the value from the resource type is used. The basic syntax of the command is:

```
CLUSTER [cluster name] RESOURCETYPE [resource type name] /option
```

TABLE 5.7 Available options for the "Cluster Resourcetype" command

Option	Description
/LIST	Lists the installed resource types.
/CREATE	Creates a resource type.
/DLLNAME : dllname	Specifies the filename of the resource DLL.
/TYPE : type name	Assigns a type name.
/ISALIVE : interval	Defines a default IsAlive timer.
/LOOKSALIVE : interval	Defines a default LooksAlive timer.
/DELETE	Deletes a resource type.
/PROPERTIES [propname=value]	Displays or modifies the common properties for a resource type.
/PRIVPROPERTIES [propname=value]	Displays or modifies the private properties for a resource type.

TABLE 5.8 Common properties available for use in the CLUSTER RESOURCETYPE command

Property	Description
Name	Changes the resource type display name.
Description	Changes the text that describes a resource type.
DllName	Specifies the name of the DLL (Dynamic Link Library) for the resource type.
DebugPrefix	Specifies the debugger to use for the resource type.
AdminExtensions	Indicates one or more class identifiers for Cluster Administrator extensions.
LooksAlivePollInterval	Specifies the interval that the Cluster Service uses to check the resource of this resource type to determine if the resources "look" operational. This is a very superficial check.
IsAlivePollInterval	Specifies the interval that the Cluster Service should use to perform a thorough check to determine if the resource of this resource type is functional.

There are currently no private properties for the standard resource types, but programmers may use this feature to store appropriate information when implementing new resource types.

EXAMPLE: To change the default IsAlivePollInterval for a file share resource:

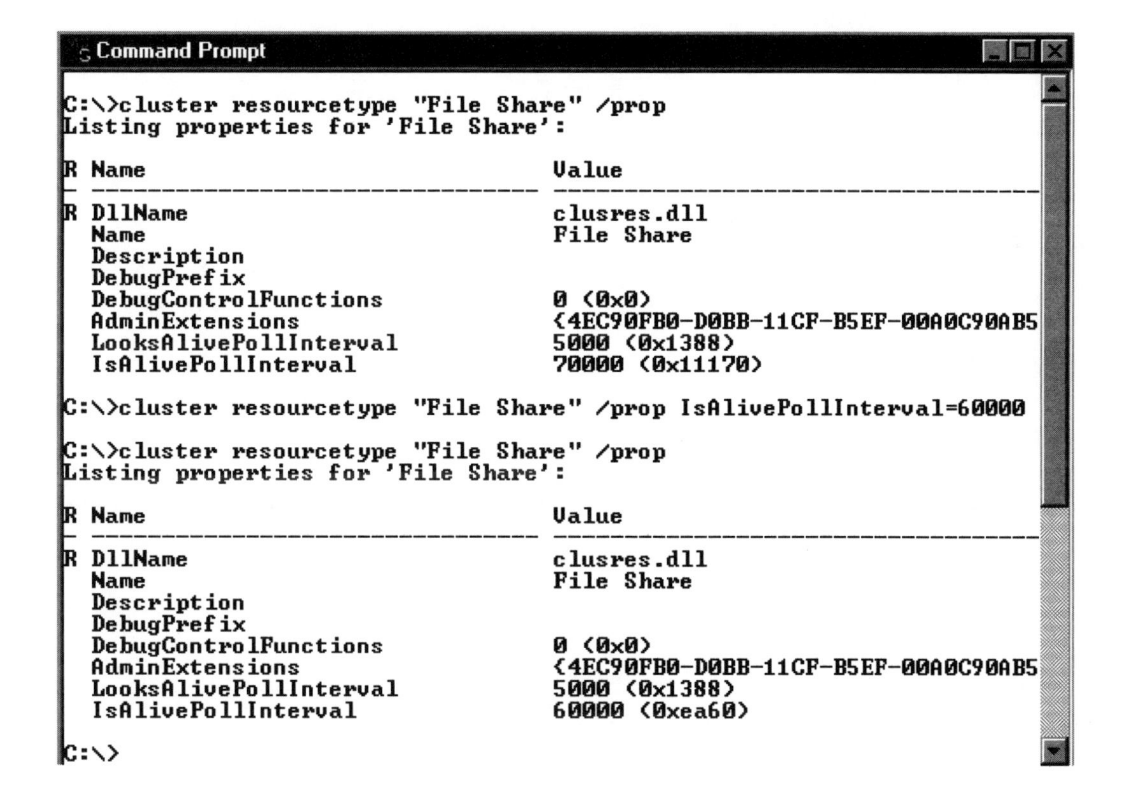

```
C:\>cluster resourcetype "File Share" /prop
Listing properties for 'File Share':

R Name                              Value

R DllName                           clusres.dll
  Name                              File Share
  Description
  DebugPrefix
  DebugControlFunctions             0 (0x0)
  AdminExtensions                   {4EC90FB0-D0BB-11CF-B5EF-00A0C90AB5
  LooksAlivePollInterval            5000 (0x1388)
  IsAlivePollInterval               70000 (0x11170)

C:\>cluster resourcetype "File Share" /prop IsAlivePollInterval=60000
C:\>cluster resourcetype "File Share" /prop
Listing properties for 'File Share':

R Name                              Value

R DllName                           clusres.dll
  Name                              File Share
  Description
  DebugPrefix
  DebugControlFunctions             0 (0x0)
  AdminExtensions                   {4EC90FB0-D0BB-11CF-B5EF-00A0C90AB5
  LooksAlivePollInterval            5000 (0x1388)
  IsAlivePollInterval               60000 (0xea60)

C:\>
```

Cluster Network

The "Cluster Network" command allows the administrator to display or configure any networks used by the Cluster Server software. The basic syntax of the command is:

```
CLUSTER [cluster name] NETWORK [network name]
/option
```

TABLE 5.9 Options available for the "Cluster Network" command

/STATUS	Displays the status of the network(s), such as up or down.
/RENAME	Allows the text name of a network to be modified.
/LISTINTERFACES	Displays the cluster nodes for a given network and the status of each node. The network name is not optional for this command.
/PROPERTIES [propname = value]	Displays or modifies the common properties of a network resource.
/PRIVPROPERTIES [propname = value]	Use to modify the private properties of a network. There are no private properties for a network in the standard release of Cluster Server. The capability exists to store private properties and may be used in future releases or by software vendors.

TABLE 5.10 Common properties that can be modified

Name	The text name assigned to the network.
Address	The network portion of the IP address assigned to the network.
AddressMask	The subnet mask assigned to the network.
Description	The text description of the network.
Role	The communication role the network provides to the cluster represented by a numeric code: ■ 1 – Use only for internal cluster communications ■ 2 – Use only for client access ■ 3 – Use for both cluster and client communications.

EXAMPLE: The first command displays the networks defined in the cluster. The second command displays the network status for each cluster member.

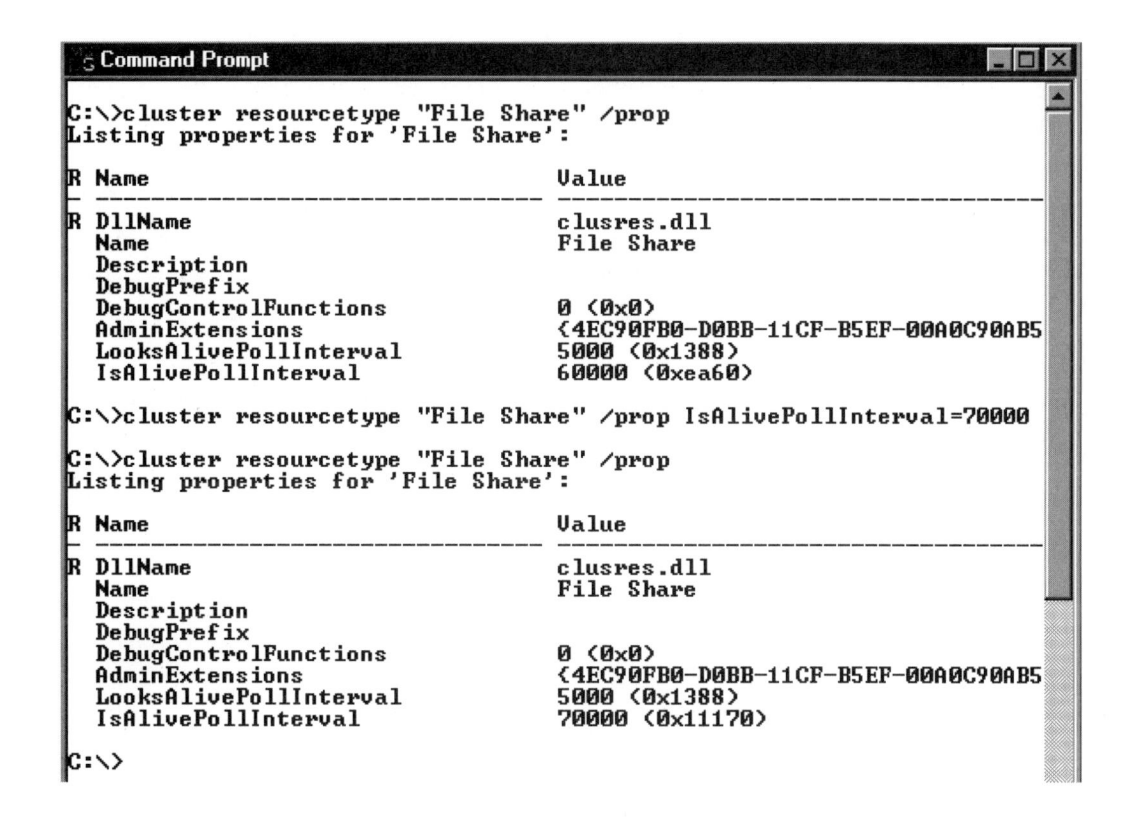

```
C:\>cluster resourcetype "File Share" /prop
Listing properties for 'File Share':

R  Name                                    Value
  --------------------------------------------------------------------
R  DllName                                 clusres.dll
   Name                                    File Share
   Description
   DebugPrefix
   DebugControlFunctions                   0 (0x0)
   AdminExtensions                         {4EC90FB0-D0BB-11CF-B5EF-00A0C90AB5
   LooksAlivePollInterval                  5000 (0x1388)
   IsAlivePollInterval                     60000 (0xea60)

C:\>cluster resourcetype "File Share" /prop IsAlivePollInterval=70000

C:\>cluster resourcetype "File Share" /prop
Listing properties for 'File Share':

R  Name                                    Value
  --------------------------------------------------------------------
R  DllName                                 clusres.dll
   Name                                    File Share
   Description
   DebugPrefix
   DebugControlFunctions                   0 (0x0)
   AdminExtensions                         {4EC90FB0-D0BB-11CF-B5EF-00A0C90AB5
   LooksAlivePollInterval                  5000 (0x1388)
   IsAlivePollInterval                     70000 (0x11170)

C:\>
```

Administrative Tasks

System administrators are responsible for providing a processing platform for clients that meets their always changing needs. Hardware and software become outdated at an increasingly more rapid rate. The impact on the administrator is in the area of hardware and software upgrades. One benefit of a clustered environment is the ability of the administrator to perform tasks during normal business hours that in the past had to be postponed until all business was completed for the day. Attempting to perform upgrades during non-workday hours sometimes becomes an adventure because often the technical support for the upgrade is unavailable after hours, or, at best, the wait times for technical support may double or triple. In a clustered environment where all applications are implemented as cluster resources, a cluster node can be shut down and removed from the cluster for maintenance without adversely affecting the client base. This statement holds true as long as every cluster member has sufficient resources, specifically memory and CPU speed, to support all resources with acceptable response time.

Performing a Hardware Upgrade

For the first example, let's assume a hardware upgrade needs to be performed, such as a CPU upgrade. The node can simply be shut down. At this point, all resources will fail over to the remaining cluster node and still be available to clients. The computer that has been shut down can be taken apart and any new hardware can be installed.

A couple of precautions need to be followed. First, the shared SCSI bus must maintain termination when disconnected from the computer that is being shut down for maintenance. The second precaution is when configuring a system to use more than one SCSI adapter.

Supporting More Than One SCSI Adapter

Multiple SCSI adapters are supported, including multiple shared SCSI adapters. There is a lightly documented problem that can occur. Most SCSI controllers have BIOS that can be enabled, which is usually the default. If the controller contains the boot disk, the BIOS should be enabled. On all SCSI controllers, the BIOS should be disabled. If it is enabled, seemingly unrelated error messages can occur.

Performing a Software Upgrade

Clusters offer the concept of what is sometimes called a rolling upgrade. What this means is that it is not necessary to upgrade all operating systems or applications on a cluster at the same time; they can be upgraded independently. The benefit of a rolling upgrade is that many software upgrades require system reboots, and it is advantageous not to reboot all cluster members at the same time. The idea is to perform the installation on one cluster member and perform the required reboot. When the upgraded cluster member has rejoined the cluster, the upgrade process is now performed on the next cluster member, always making sure there is, at least, one running cluster member. If upgrades can be performed successfully on one cluster member at a time, the impact to clients is minimized. Clients will experience cluster transitions and possibly some degraded performance as one cluster member is forced to own all cluster resources while the other cluster member is rebooted to complete a software installation or upgrade, but all cluster resources will still be available.

Since MSCS is a new product, there has been no release of Windows NT to attempt a rolling upgrade.

Performing Cluster Backups

The procedure to backup the operating system files for a cluster node is no different from any other installation of Windows NT Server. Perform a backup of the boot and system drives and the registry. Use the RDISK utility to keep a current repair disk for all cluster nodes.

The backup procedure for the shared SCSI devices must be handled slightly differently. It is not possible to schedule the backup to run on one of the cluster nodes because there is no guarantee which cluster node will own the disk resource at a given time. If the backup procedures are performed via batch processing, one possible solution is to include a "CLUSTER GROUP/MOVE" command that moves the disk resource to the system that the backup procedure will be performed on.

Another solution is to perform a network backup of the shared SCSI devices. A network name can be created and placed in the same group as the disk resource. To hide the resource name from the network browse lists, end the name with a "$," such as DiskF$. This naming convention allows network connections to the sharepoint, but it does not expose the name in the list of available shares returned to a network browse request. Now backups can be performed over the network via the network name and will succeed no matter which cluster member owns the disk resource.

Restoring a Backup

The hardware settings and disk signatures for the devices on the shared SCSI bus are stored in the Windows NT registry. For this reason, a backup of Windows NT cannot be successfully restored to another computer. If a cluster member fails and the computer is replaced, Windows NT Server, Enterprise Edition, must be reinstalled. Then use Cluster Administrator on the functioning cluster member to evict the node that is being replaced. Now reinstall Cluster Server on the new node and join the cluster. Any applications and data can now be recovered from backups. Be aware of applications that have modified the registry during their installation, because that registry information no longer exists. There are methods of saving registry key information with the REGEDT32 utility.

Clustering SQL Server

There is a statement from the movie, "Sneakers," that can be paraphrased as follows: "It's not money that leads to ultimate power these days, it is control of the data." It is almost scary to think how accurate that statement is. Unavailability of data can be directly translated to loss of revenues.

At the time this book was being sent to press, Cluster Server is a new product, probably released only three or four months ago. Previous chapters have detailed the somewhat generic resources that can be implemented through a cluster.

The next step in the growth of clusters occurs as applications are specifically written to take advantage of features, such as fault tolerance, that a cluster can provide. Some applications can be implemented simply as generic applications or generic services and will not require rewrites, but as new versions of software become available, they will include some level of cluster support. There are a few applications that have built-in support to the Cluster Server software. For example, one resource type that will be discussed in a later chapter is the Distributed Transaction Coordinator. This product is bundled with Windows NT Server, Enterprise Edition along with Cluster Server. Other products have a separate release that includes cluster support. The Microsoft products that include cluster support are the "enterprise" editions of products. Two such products with an enterprise edition release are SQL Server and Exchange Server. The SQL Server enterprise edition will be discussed here and Exchange Server in the next chapter.

SQL Server – Overview

Before discussing the implementation of SQL Server in a clustered environment, a brief overview of SQL Server in a standard environment is necessary for comparison purposes. In a typical standalone SQL Server installation, three services are installed: a SQL Executive, SQL Server, and MSDTC (Microsoft Distributed Transaction Coordinator) service. Each service performs specific tasks within the SQL Server umbrella. For example, the SQL Executive is responsible for executing scheduled SQL tasks, such as backups. Standard client access to data is provided by the SQL Server service.

Devices and Databases

A device is a pre-allocated area of a disk that SQL Server will use as a storage device. From Windows NT's perspective, an SQL device is a file. From SQL Server's perspective, the device is like a logical drive. SQL Server can create and store multiple databases on a device. A 100 megabyte device might only be five to ten percent utilized, but Windows NT sees only the 100 megabyte file and must back up the entire device. This is why it is not practical to perform a Windows NT backup of an SQL Server device.

A database consists of tables, which are the basic unit of data storage for SQL Server. Databases are created on an SQL device. Outside of SQL Server, databases are hidden, residing in the file that represents the SQL Server device.

There are a number of devices and databases created during the installation process. The most common device is the master device, which holds the master, model, pubs, and tempdb databases.

Microsoft Cluster Server Support for SQL Server

The Microsoft Cluster Server software supports two types of SQL Server configurations. The configuration used depends upon the desired result of the cluster/database administrator. The type of SQL Server implementation desired also influences the hardware required by the cluster, specifically the shared SCSI disks. The two configurations possible are known as active/active and active/passive configurations. Both configurations use symmetric virtual servers.

A Symmetric Virtual Server is an instance of a SQL Server. Each symmetric virtual server can be linked to a standard SQL Server installation. To the client, the virtual server is referenced by a server name as is any other SQL Server. The difference is that the SQL virtual server is a group of

FIGURE 6-1   Symmetric virtual server configuration

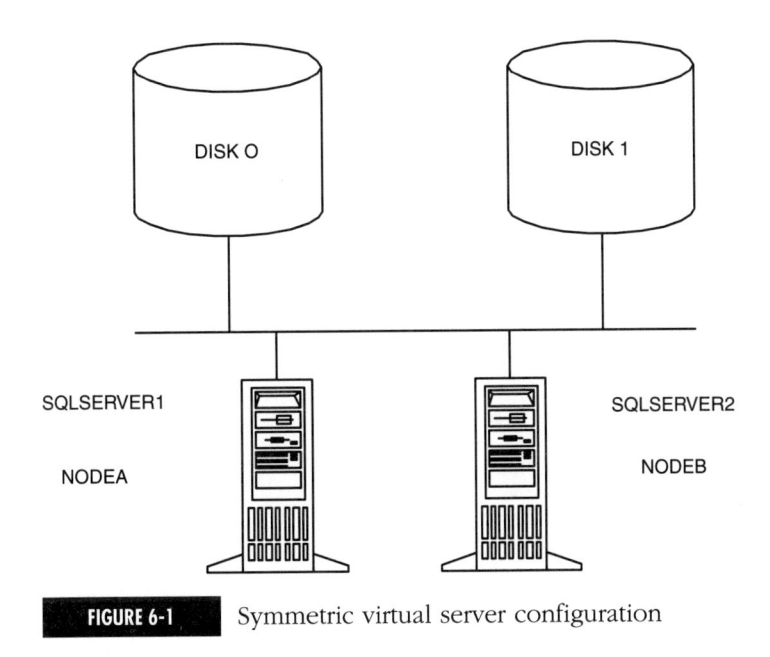

resources on the cluster that can be owned by any cluster member. This equates to a fault tolerant SQL Server, at least from a hardware perspective, because the resources that implement the virtual server can fail over between cluster members. Since SQL virtual servers have their own installation, they also have their own master, model, tempdb, and user databases. One cluster node has the ability to simultaneously run one or more virtual servers.

Examine Figure 6-1. Assume two SQL Server installations have been performed along with Cluster support for SQL Server and the virtual server names are SQLSERVER1 and SQLSERVER2. The two SQL virtual servers are serving access to totally independent databases. If NODEA fails, the virtual server SQLSERVER1 will be moved by the cluster software to NODEB along with all the supporting resources, such as the physical disk. To a client application, it is equivalent to turning NODEA off and then immediately back on. The client will lose all connections to the SQL Server and all uncommitted transactions are rolled back. The client application must reconnect to the server SQLSERVER1. The fact that the virtual server is now running on NODEB will be transparent to the client. The server environment is preserved as the virtual server is moved from NODEA to NODEB. Information in all open databases and logs will be consistent after the failover. In reality, the new server is working with the same data, because the physical disk that stores the devices is now owned by NODEB. Any SQL registry information is kept consistent between nodes with registry replication.

Client applications may require slight modification to take full advantage of SQL Server cluster functionality. They should be written to reestablish lost connections when the server fails. Connections to an SQL Server can be state-oriented or stateless. Any state or data associated with a connection is lost when the connection is broken. This includes any uncommitted transactions and temporary tables. If the connection to the SQL Server is stateless, such as with Microsoft Access or Internet Information Server, the client can reconnect and continue processing with no loss of data. Stateless clients provide a more seamless failover and recovery of the SQL virtual server.

Active/Passive Configuration

In an active/passive configuration, only one cluster member is running SQL Server (the active server), and the other cluster member is available as a backup if the active SQL Server fails. The second server is the passive server. Refer to Figure 6-1. To implement an active/passive configuration, install SQL Server on NODEA only. On NODEB, install the SQL Server utilities. Now one virtual server can be created, associated with the SQL Server installation on NODEA. This implementation offers fault tolerance and requires no additional hardware. The SQL Server installation, along with the master device, must be located on one of the shared SCSI devices. This allows the SQL virtual server to fail over successfully between cluster members.

Active/Active Configuration

In an active/active configuration, there are multiple instances of SQL Server running as symmetric virtual servers. The cluster support for SQL Server allows more than one instance of SQL Server to be running on a node in the cluster. In a typical two-node cluster, there can be two SQL virtual servers. Normally they can be load-balanced by defining appropriate preferred owners. If one of the cluster nodes goes offline, the SQL virtual server resource will fail over to the remaining cluster member and will still be reachable by clients.

An active/active configuration requires additional hardware. There must be multiple installations of SQL Server, one per virtual server. The SQL Server installations must be on separate SCSI devices on the shared bus. In order to distribute the SQL processing load among the cluster nodes, the SQL Server installations must be on separate disk resources that can be owned independently of each other.

Installing SQL Server, Enterprise Edition 6.5

Upgrading from SQL Server 6.5 to SQL Server, Enterprise Edition 6.5

It is possible to upgrade an SQL Server 6.5 installation to SQLServer, Enterprise Edition 6.5. The one major consideration is replication. If replication is in use, all replicated transactions in the distribution database must be distributed before upgrading to SQL Server, Enterprise Edition 6.5. If it is unclear whether all replicated transactions have been processed, users should be unsubscribed before installation and resubscribed after the upgrade has been completed.

It is recommended that all servers which function as replication Publishers and Distributors be upgraded to either SQL Server 6.5, service pack 3, or to the Enterprise Edition version. A Distribution server running service pack 3 or Enterprise Edition can communicate properly with Publishers run versions of SQL Server earlier than service pack 3. The reverse is not true, however. A Publisher running service pack 3 should not run against a Distributor running an earlier service pack.

Replication depends extensively on server names for each node in the replication configuration. Renaming of a server involved in replication is not supported. When clustering support for SQL Server is installed, a new server name is created. In order for replication to function properly, it must be de-installed prior to configuring the SQL Server cluster support, and re-installed after the the configuration is complete.

Installing SQL Server, Enterprise Edition 6.5

Installing SQL Server is a straightforward process. There are some special installation requirements when installing SQL Server to be run in a clustered environment.

FIGURE 6-2 Installing SQL Server

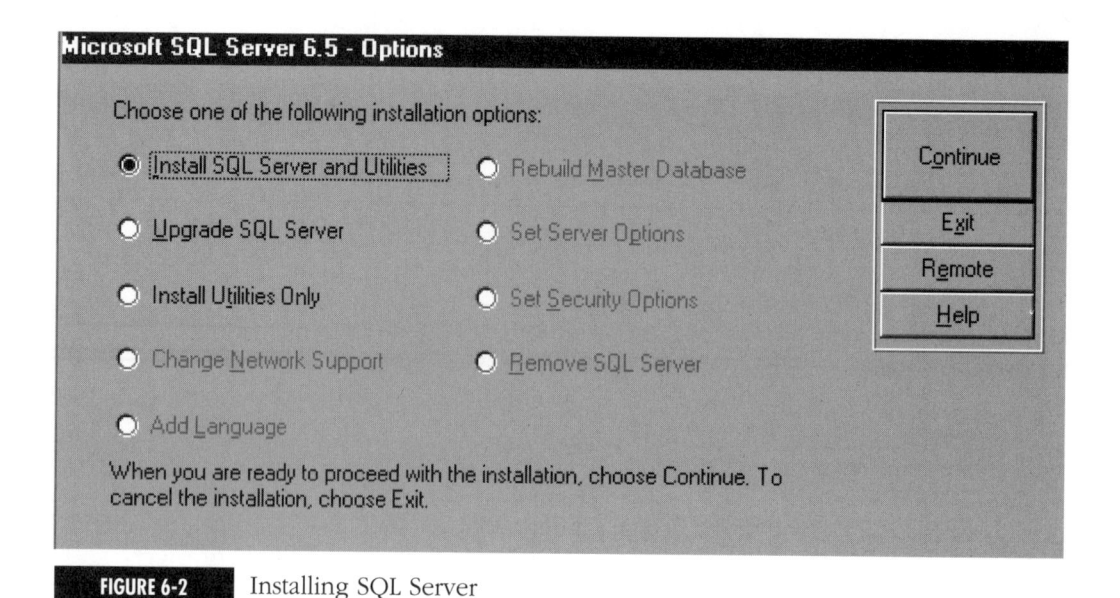

For every virtual server desired, there must be a corresponding SQL Server installation. An active/passive configuration requires one installation; an active/active configuration requires two installations, one on each cluster node. In an active/passive configuration, install the utilities such as Enterprise Manager on the passive node by selecting the option, "Install Utilities Only." To install SQL Server on the active node, run the setup program from the SQL Server distribution. Select the option "Install SQL Server and Utilities." See Figure 6-2.

FIGURE 6-3 SQL Server installation location

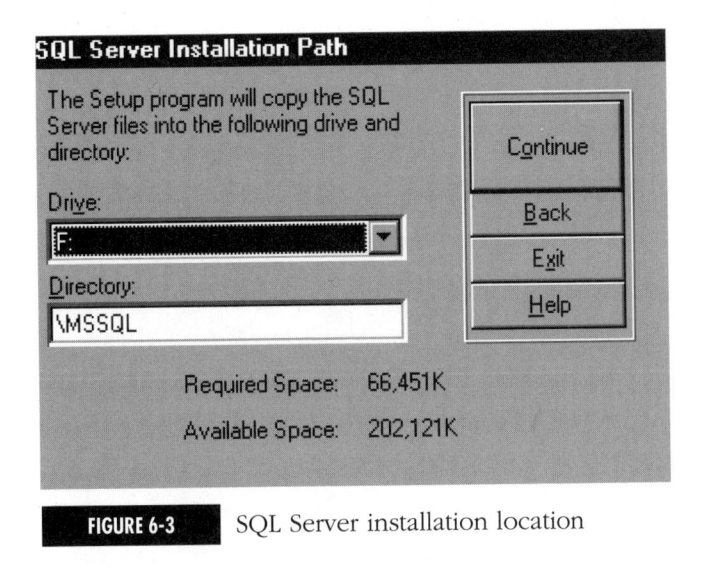

For a symmetric virtual server to be successfully implemented, SQL Server must be installed on one of the shared SCSI disks. See Figure 6-3. If an active/active configuration is being implemented, the two SQL Server installations must be on separate shared SCSI devices in order to allow independent failover of the virtual servers. The virtual server resource will be automatically placed in a group with the disk resource that contains the SQL Server installation. Since only one cluster node can own a disk resource, having two installations of SQL Server on the same disk does not allow SQL Server to be running simultaneously on both cluster nodes.

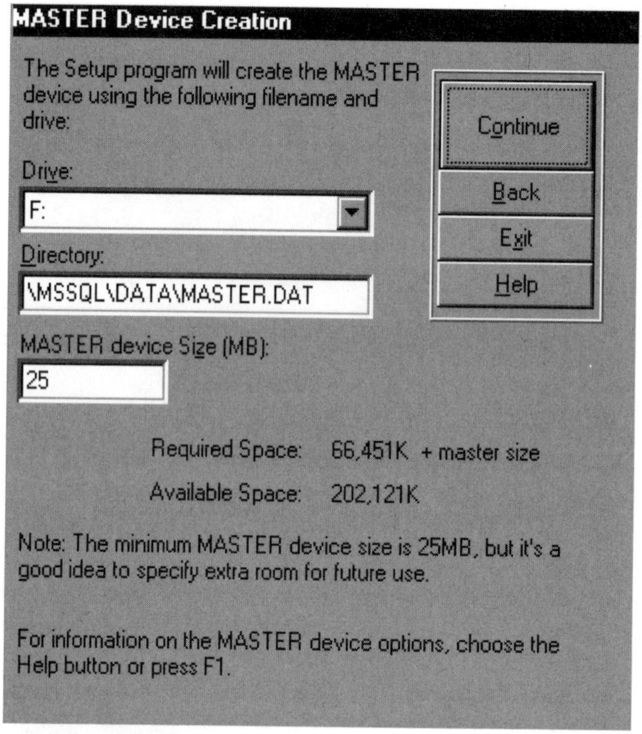

FIGURE 6-4   MASTER device location

The master device must be located on a shared SCSI disk for the virtual server to fail over properly. The default location for the master device is a subdirectory under the device and directory specified as the main SQL Server installation directory entered in Figure 6-3. Specify the disk and directory that will be used to store the MASTER device. See Figure 6-4.

From a performance perspective, separating the SQL Server Executables and databases can be useful. This is because disk I/O traffic can be spread amongst multiple physical disks. However, when configuring SQL Server to run in a clustered environment, all files and devices should be located on one physical disk in order to minimize the number of shared SCSI disks that must be moved between cluster members in the event of a failover.

FIGURE 6-5 SQL server installation options

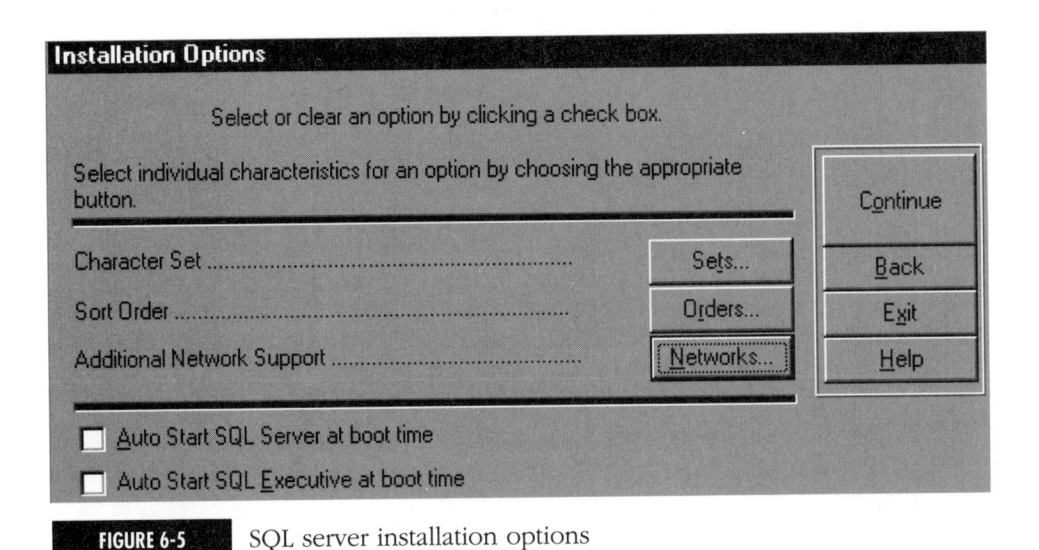

Do not configure the SQL Server and SQL Executive services to start automatically, because they must be stopped anyway when SQL cluster support is installed. See Figure 6-5. Standard SQL Server offers many options for network support. SQL Server running in a cluster supports only TCP/IP, Multiprotocol, and Named Pipes. In addition, the SQL Cluster installation program uses only named pipes for connectivity. Therefore, the named pipes protocol must be installed, at least until the SQL Cluster Support software is installed, then it could be removed. Selecting the "Networks" button in Figure 6-5 presents the network protocols screen in Figure 6-6.

FIGURE 6-6 SQL server network support

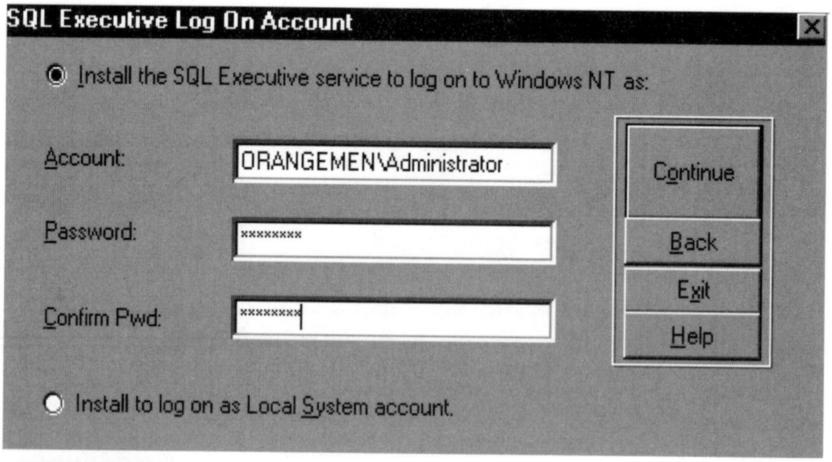

FIGURE 6-7 SQL Executive service account

The main component of SQL server runs as a Windows NT service; therefore, a username and password must be supplied for the service to start. See Figure 6-7. If an active/active configuration is being implemented, the username and password must be the same for the SQL Executive service for both SQL Server installations. The username specified for the SQL Executive service can be verified with the Services option in Control Panel. The password for the account can also be re-entered. If the password for the account is changed in the User Manager utility, it must be manually updated in the Services program in order to work.

Service Packs and Hot Fixes

SQL Server, Enterprise Edition, supercedes service pack 4 and earlier. As a result, applying any service pack other than service pack 5 or later, or any hot fixes to these service packs, can corrupt the SQL Server installation.

Installing Cluster Support for SQL Server

Pre-setup Requirements

Before the SQL Server Cluster software can be loaded, there are pre-requisite tasks that must be performed. Some tasks are only recommendations, whereas others will block a successful installation if not carried out. These crucial tasks are as follows:

- There must be a two node functioning cluster. The cluster support for SQL Server will not install if it does not detect a two node cluster, and both must be up and running.
- SQL Server, Enterprise Edition, must be installed on at least one node in the cluster. If SQL Server is not installed on both nodes, the SQL Server utilities must be installed on the second node.
- Stop the SQL Server and Internet Information Server services on both nodes. Use the SQL Service Manager utility in the SQL Server program group to stop the SQL Server services. Stop the MSDTC, MSSQLServer, and SQLExecutive services. Use the Internet Service Manager to stop the WWW, FTP, and Gopher services.
- Proper licensing currently requires SQL Server licenses on both cluster nodes, even if only one SQL Server process will be running on the cluster. There are rumors of cluster licenses for software, but at the time of this writing, they are not yet available.
- If there are multiple virtual servers, designate which shared disks belong to each virtual server. In order to have multiple instances of SQL Server running, each needs its own disk on the shared SCSI bus.

Cluster Support for SQL Server – Setup

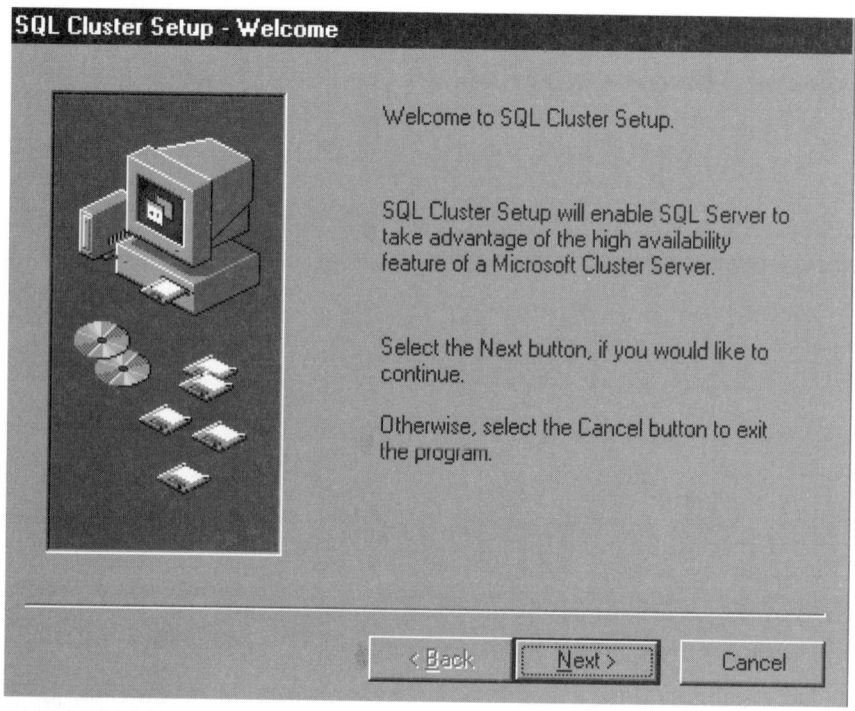

FIGURE 6-8 Installing Cluster support for SQL server

On the SQL Server, Enterprise Edition CD, switch to the appropriate platform directory, either Alpha or I386. In the Cluster subdirectory, start the installation program named "SQL CLUSTER SETUP." The screen in Figure 6-8 appears.

If a message appears at this time stating that the computer is not a member of a cluster, make sure the other cluster member is up and shows online in the Cluster Administrator utility.

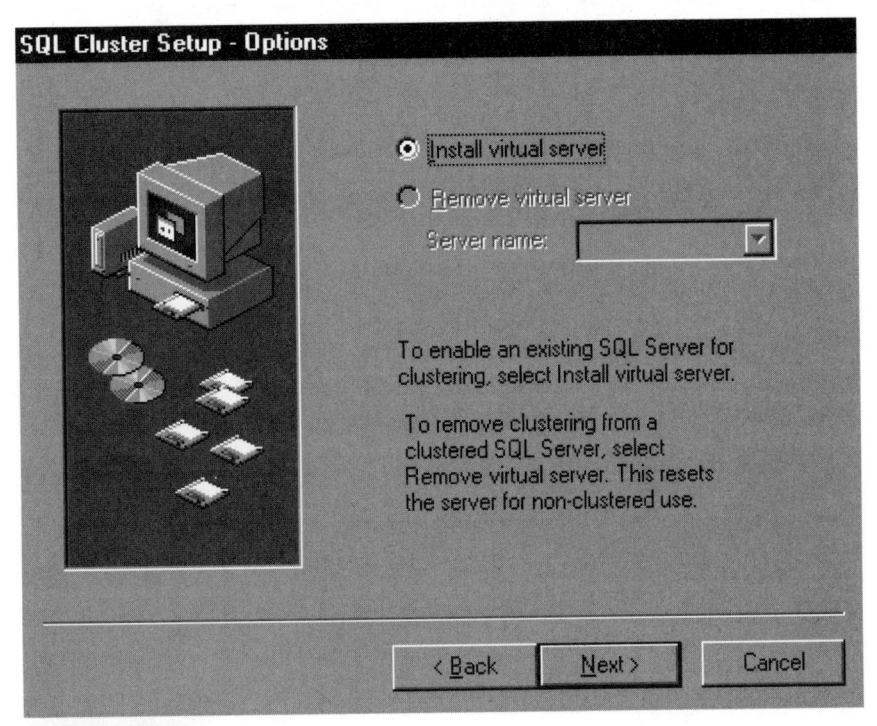

FIGURE 6-9 Installing Cluster Server support for SQL server, continued

There are only two possible installation options: install or remove a virtual server. To install cluster support for SQL Server, select the option "Install virtual server." See Figure 6-9. If this is an initial installation, it is the only option available. If cluster support for SQL Server has already been installed, the "Remove Virtual Server" option can be used to de-install the software. Resources are also removed with this option, so do not remove the SQL Server resources manually through Cluster Administrator.

Multiple virtual servers cannot be installed unless there are separate disks available on the shared SCSI bus. The software allows a maximum of one virtual server per shared SCSI disk. You cannot use separate logical drives on the same SCSI disk and install multiple virtual servers. The physical disk is a single resource and can be accessed by only one member of the cluster. There must be an SQL Server installation associated with each virtual server specified in this screen.

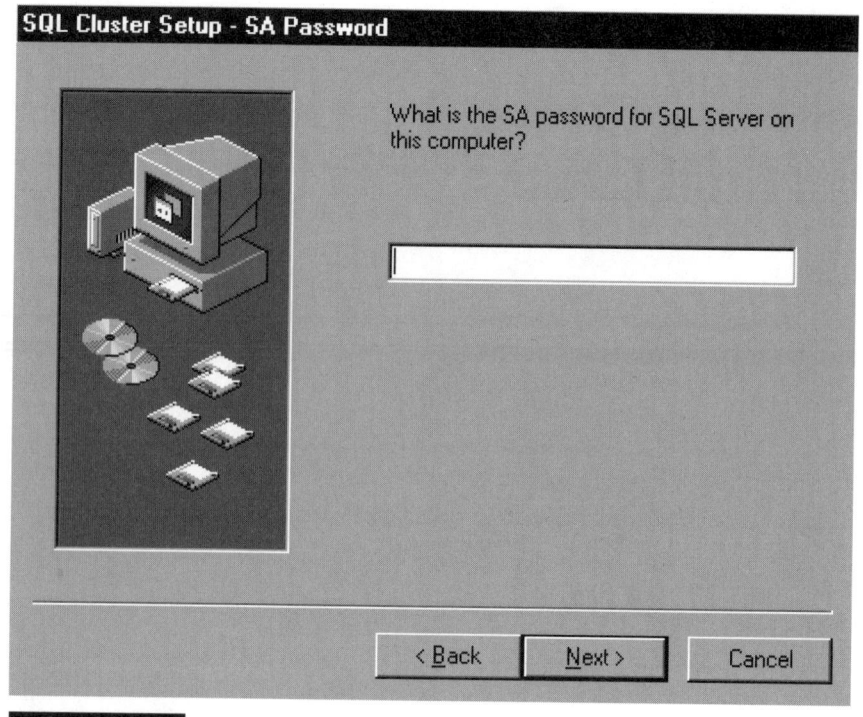

Chapter Six • Windows NT Cluster Server Guidebook

FIGURE 6-10   Supplying the SA password

The installation process must connect to the existing SQL Server installation. Enter the password to the system administrator, or SA account. See Figure 6-10. After an SQL Server installation this password will be blank.

I personally had many problems at this point in the installation. My problems began when I aborted an installation about two-thirds completed. The installation did not complete due to another problem I had. Every time I attempted to continue past this screen, I kept getting an error message that said, "Unable to log on to SQL Server. Make sure the SQL Server Service can be started and that the sa password supplied is correct." I would check the SQL Server service and it would be running. It was started by the installation. I could log on to the SQL Server through all the tools such as ISQL/W. The only way I was able to fix the problem was to do a complete reload of Windows NT and SQL Server.

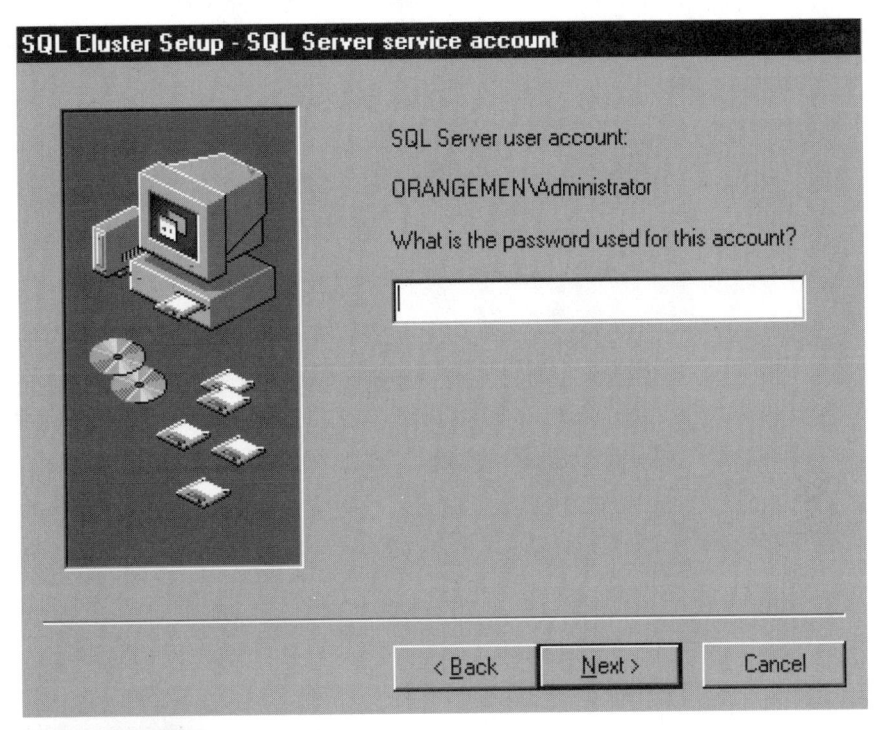

FIGURE 6-11 Supplying the SQL Server service password

Enter the password for the account under which the SQL Server is configured to run. See Figure 6-11. If the service is configured to run with the System account, this screen will not appear. In order for the Cluster support for SQL Server installation to proceed beyond this point, the username and password the SQL Server service is running under must be the same on both cluster nodes. If they are different, use the Services program from Control Panel to configure the username and password for the service by double-clicking on the MSSQL Server service. The password is not supplied from the account database when a username is selected. It must be entered for security purposes. To determine whether the username and password are correct, select the service and then the "Start" button. This will attempt to start the service. If no error messages appear, the service has started successfully. One common configuration problem is that the account configured to run the service does not have the privilege to run as a service. This privilege can be granted through the policies menu in User Manager.

Chapter Six • Windows NT Cluster Server Guidebook

FIGURE 6-12 Supplying the SQL Executive service password

Enter the password under which the SQL Executive account is configured to run. See Figure 6-12. When doing an SQL Server installation, it is not an option to specify an account for this service. It will be configured to run under the System account. The SQL Executive service must run with the same username and password on both nodes in the cluster. To guarantee this, use a domain account rather than a local account if the computers are not configured to be domain controllers. If the password is changed in the account database, it must also be changed through the Services program in Control Panel. This screen will not appear if the SQL Executive is running under the System account.

Six • Clustering SQL Server **167**

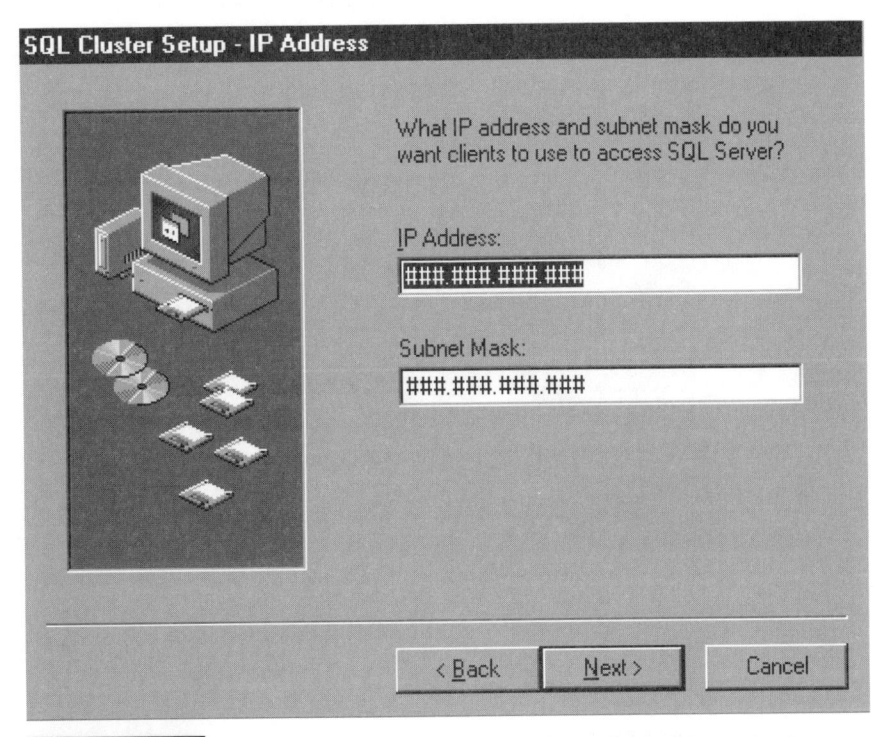

FIGURE 6-13 Supplying the virtual server TCP/IP address and subnet mask

Each symmetric virtual server has a unique name and address. Enter the TCP/IP address and subnet mask that will be allocated to the virtual server. See Figure 6-13. This should look familiar. The information in this screen is used to create an IP Address resource in the cluster. The TCP/IP address entered here is the address that will be exposed on the network for the virtual server. For example, although not commonly used, it is possible to connect to a SQL Server in ISQL by using an TCP/IP address. Programmers could use the address when developing applications. Although this is not good practice, it demonstrates that the SQL Server name and TCP/IP address are interchangeable. Names are there for our benefit. As far as the computer is concerned, it is just extra work to resolve the name to a TCP/IP address.

Since the virtual server is associated with a TCP/IP address, and this resource can move between cluster members, it is now possible to see the foundation for how cluster support for SQL Server works.

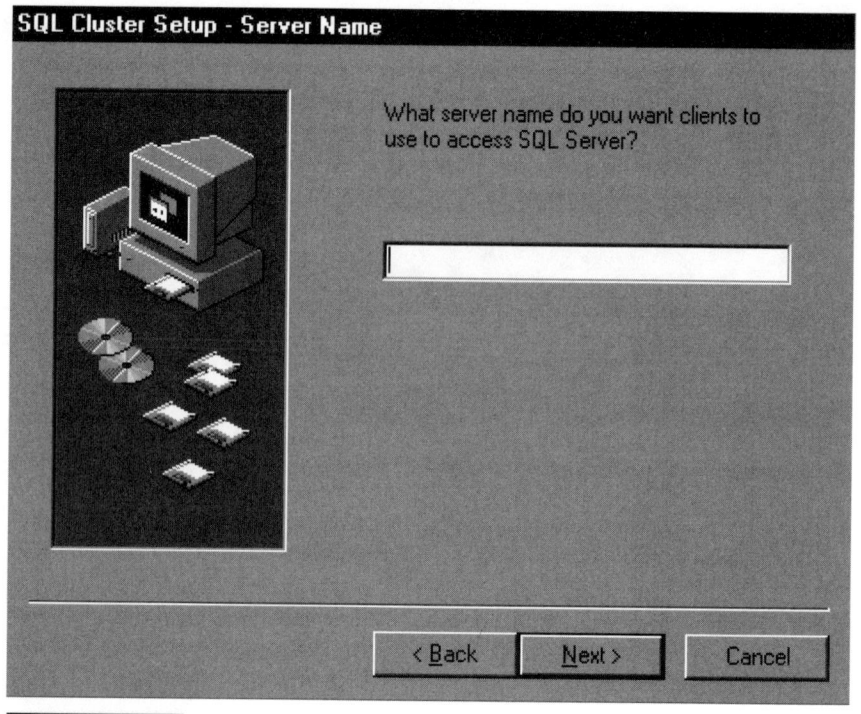

FIGURE 6-14 Supplying the virtual server name

Every virtual SQL server must be assigned a unique name. Enter the name by which this virtual server will be known. See Figure 6-14. This is the name that users will enter in ISQL or administrators will register in Enterprise Manager. This name is used to define a network name resource in the cluster. The network name is the SQL Server to which clients and applications connect. This network name resource has a dependency of the IP address entered in Figure 6-13.

FIGURE 6-15 Completing the installation

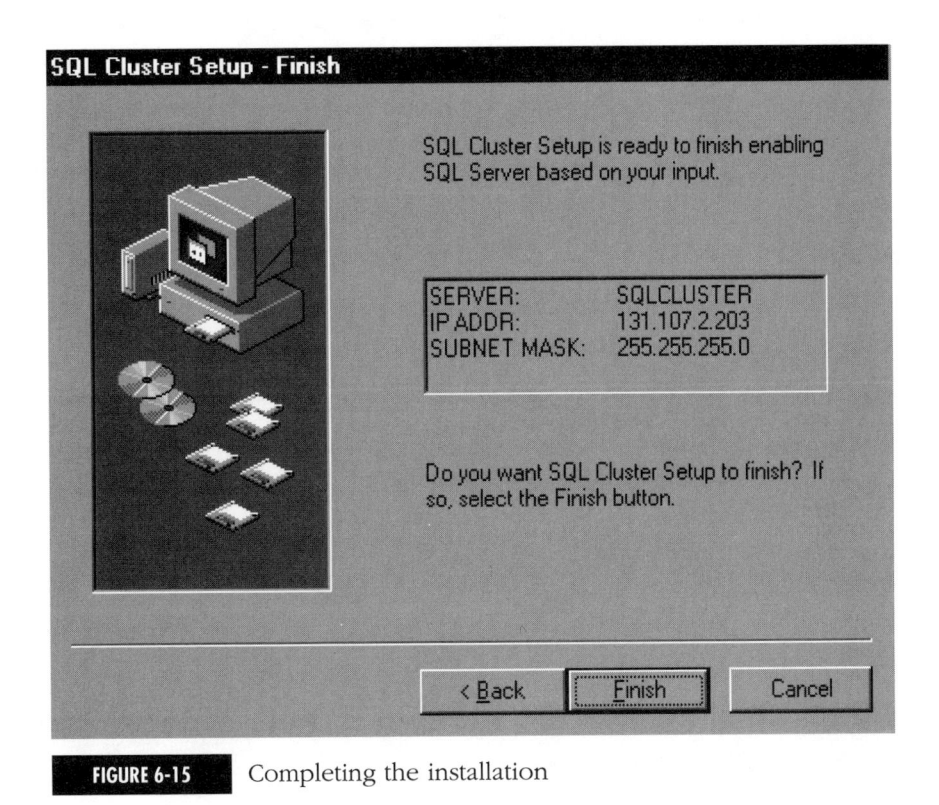

Verify the server name, IP address and subnet mask, and select "Finish." The installation completes unattended at this point. When the installation is complete, the virtual server will not be accessible because the resources created to support the cluster will be offline. To test the virtual server, run Cluster Administrator and bring online any resources in the group that have the same name as the server name supplied in Figure 6-15. Once the resources are brought online, it will not be necessary to bring them online again, even after a system reboot, unless there is a resource failure or if they are manually taken offline. This step is necessary only once.

Cluster Support for SQL Server Modifications

When cluster support for SQL Server is installed, various changes are made both to Windows NT and to the cluster configuration. The most significant change to the operating system is the addition of three services. These new services can be viewed with the Services program in Control Panel. Two of the services replace the normal SQLServer and SQLExecutive services. The

FIGURE 6-16 Examining the virtual server installation

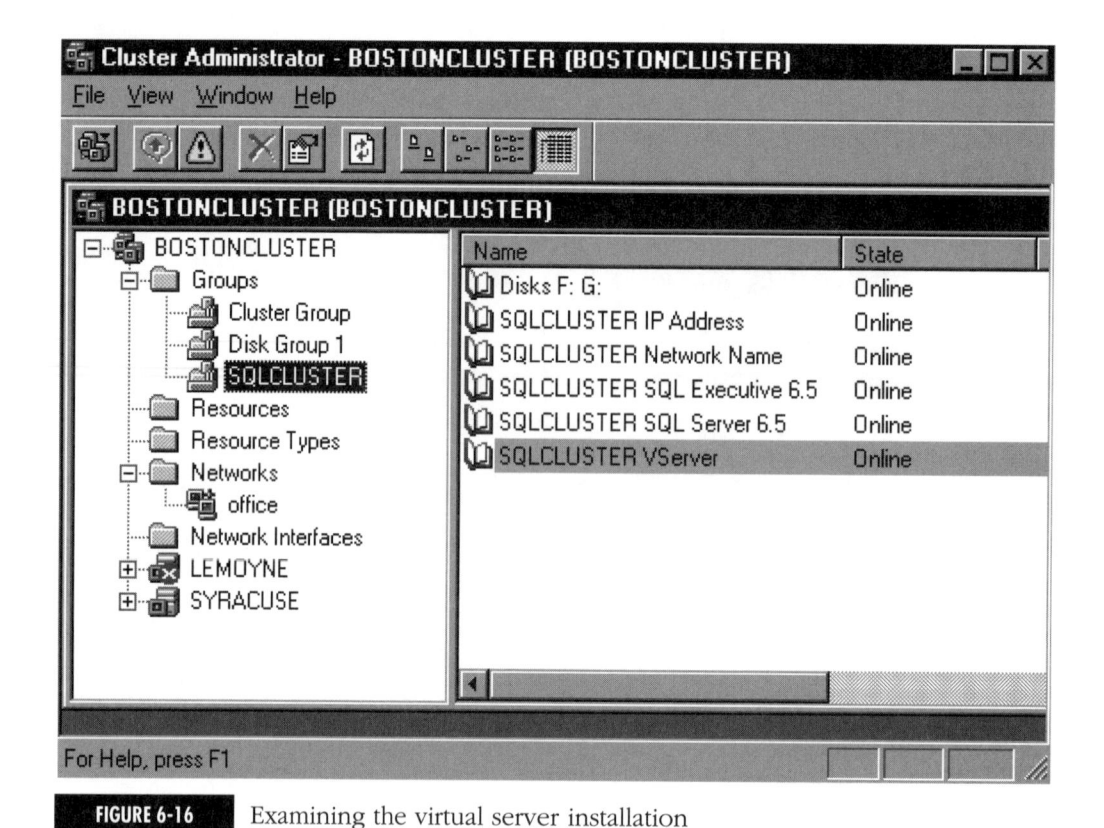

names are MSSQLServer$*name*, where *name* is replaced by the virtual server name created during the SQL cluster support software installation. The third service is named VSrvSvc$*name*, again replacing *name* with the name of the symmetric virtual server created. It is interesting that only this service is defined as a generic service in the cluster. The SQLServer and SQLExecutive services are not cluster resources, in the sense that they are not generic service resources. There are, however, two new resource types in the cluster configuration. See Figure 6-16.

The software installation creates a new cluster group based on the name supplied for the virtual server. There are six resources in this group. The first is the physical disk resource. The installation moves the necessary disk resource into the group, which could lead to many other resources being automatically moved to this group if the same disk is used to store other resources such as file shares. This forces all the resources to be running on the same node as the virtual server. In order to distribute the processing load, it is necessary to have a separate disk on the shared SCSI bus for SQL Server processing. This allows the SQL virtual server resource to be located on a cluster node independently from other cluster resources. In order to balance the load, make one node the preferred owner for the SQL virtual server group and the other node the preferred owner for the other resource groups. To review how to define preferred owners for cluster groups, refer to Chapter 4. The next two resources are standard IP address and network name resources. These create a unique endpoint on the network that can move between cluster nodes. The next two resources are types that have not been introduced earlier.

The resource titled SQLCLUSTER SQL Executive 6.5 is a resource of type SQL Executive 6.5. It is directly linked to the new service created during the installation process. When the SQL Executive resource is taken offline, the service is automatically stopped. When the resource is brought online, the service is started. The proper administrative interface to the SQL Server services is through the Cluster Administrator utility, not the Services program. One issue with managing the SQL Server and SQL Executive services is that many methods appear to manage the services, but the only method that actually brings the resource online is Cluster Administrator, For example, the services can still be controlled through the SQL Service Manager. The problem with this is that if the SQL Executive resource is offline, the SQL Service Manager does not bring the resource online when it starts the service. The resource must still be brought online via the Cluster Administrator utility. It becomes a two-step process to actually start the SQL virtual server. If the resources are first brought online via Cluster Administrator, the services are started at the same time without administrator intervention.

The next resource in the group is SQLCLUSTER SQL Server 6.5. This resource has a type of SQL Server 6.5. The resource takes the place of the standard SQL Server service and is associated with the service named MSSQLServer$*name*, where is replaced by the virtual server name created during the SQL cluster support software installation. The administration of this resource is performed identically to the SQL Executive resource. It is managed through the Cluster Administrator utility.

The last resource is the SQLCLUSTER Vserver resource. This resource has a type of generic service.

SEVEN

Clustering Exchange Server

Exchange Server is one of two major applications; the other is SQL Server, released by Microsoft in an Enterprise Edition which provides cluster aware support for installation into a Microsoft Cluster Server environment. It also shares with SQL Server an increasing role as a line of business application whose functionality is essential to corporate workflow. Designed to enhance user access to a wide variety of resources by removing the technical obstacles between the user and the resource, Exchange is itself enhanced by Cluster Server's promise of "high availability." Achieving the cluster "high availability" promise for Exchange Server is the topic of this chapter.

Exchange Server – Overview

Microsoft Exchange Server, as its name implies, facilitates the flow of information within and between organizations. More than simple messaging, it combines a secure and reliable information store with a robust directory database and the necessary services, connectors, and agents to provide authorized users with convenient enterprise-wide access to corporate information resources. It provides server-side services to a broad range of clients communicating over native MAPI, SMTP, POP3, IMAP4, NNTP and HTTP messaging protocols. The focus is on comprehensive and powerful convenience.

Hierarchically, Exchange establishes an inverted tree structure defining a solitary Exchange Organization at the top, comprised of one or more Exchange Sites, each consisting of one or more Exchange Servers. Logically, the site is the unit of administration. The practical reality is that resources exist on individual servers—sometimes more than one—to insure availability and fault tolerance. Scalability is insured by the distributed granularity of the Exchange topology: additional sites or servers can be deployed at any point to redress load or performance issues.

Each server maintains its own information stores and a dynamic copy of a shared directory services database, which weaves the server's NetBIOS name into the internal name for all local exchange database objects. This creates a coupling so strong that changing the server's NetBIOS name will incapacitate Exchange server. The core functionality of Exchange Server is established at installation by the creation and registry of five Windows NT services (System Attendant, Directory, Information Store, Message Transfer Agent, and Event Services). Additional functionality, such as connectors or Advanced Security, can be supported with the deployment of the appropriate Windows NT services. All Exchange components are stored in an extensive set of file system folders established during installation, some of which are shared to facilitate inter-component communication. Single seat organization-wide administrative capability is provided by an optional module, Admin.exe, which provides a powerful graphical interface for configuring the properties of individual Exchange objects.

As Microsoft Exchange has increasingly become an essential component of mainstream corporate workflow, the issue of service availability has grown. With the failure of an Exchange Server, the user mailboxes and non-replicated public folders on that server will be unavailable until that server is returned online. Any connectors uniquely homed on the failed server will also be down. Users homed on other Exchange Servers will not be affected by the remote server failure unless they must access a resource uniquely homed on the failed server. Users whose mailboxes are homed on the failed server cannot access the Exchange Server, but if they are configured for offline client operation, they can continue working with the resources that were offline enabled at the time they last synchronized the offline store with the server store. No updating of these offline resources is possible until the server is brought back on line.

Microsoft Exchange Server has been available in both a Standard Edition and an Enterprise Edition from its first release. Prior to version 5.5, the significant difference between the two editions was the ability and product license to install intersite connectors. With version 5.5, the Enterprise Edition adds cluster awareness to Exchange Server, taking a significant step to ensuring high availability. Note that not all Exchange components and services are cluster aware. The design goals for Exchange Cluster Server include hardware failure protection and high availability and are met with the current active/standby clustering model. For this version of Exchange and Cluster Server, the goals specifically did not include user load balancing (which would require active/active clustering) or dynamic backup capability (available on some third-party products).

Installing Exchange Server, Enterprise Edition

Installation of Microsoft Exchange Server, version 5.5, Enterprise Edition, into a Microsoft Cluster Server environment is a two-stage process. In the first stage, Exchange Server Enterprise Edition is installed onto the primary node of an existing cluster. This is a full installation, with Exchange's Executable, database, component and support files installed to the shared cluster drive(s), Exchange resources are created in the cluster resource group, system libraries and extensions are installed into the primary node's local Windows NT System32 folder, and Windows NT services are created and registered on the primary node. This results in a viable Exchange Server installation on the primary cluster node, but not one that will survive being failed over, for there is no Exchange awareness or capability on the secondary cluster node. The second stage of the installation process remedies this by installing system libraries and extensions into the secondary node's local Windows NT System32 folder, and creating and registering Windows NT services on the secondary node.

The installation process begins automatically when you place the Exchange Server Enterprise Edition CD-ROM in the drive. (If it does not start automatically, it can be initiated by running Launch.exe in the root of the CD-ROM.) A helpful menu system appears (Figure 7-1) with options to move to a sub-menu of installation choices, to open and review the Exchange Server Release Notes, to move to a sub-menu of documentation choices (including an html document specifically about clustering Exchange Server), to move to a sub-menu of online resource choices, or to exit the installation program. Both the Release Notes and the "Clustering with Exchange Server" web document call attention to the required pre-existing cluster environment which must be in place before a clustered installation of Exchange Server can be successful. These topics are discussed in the next section before moving on to setup, proper.

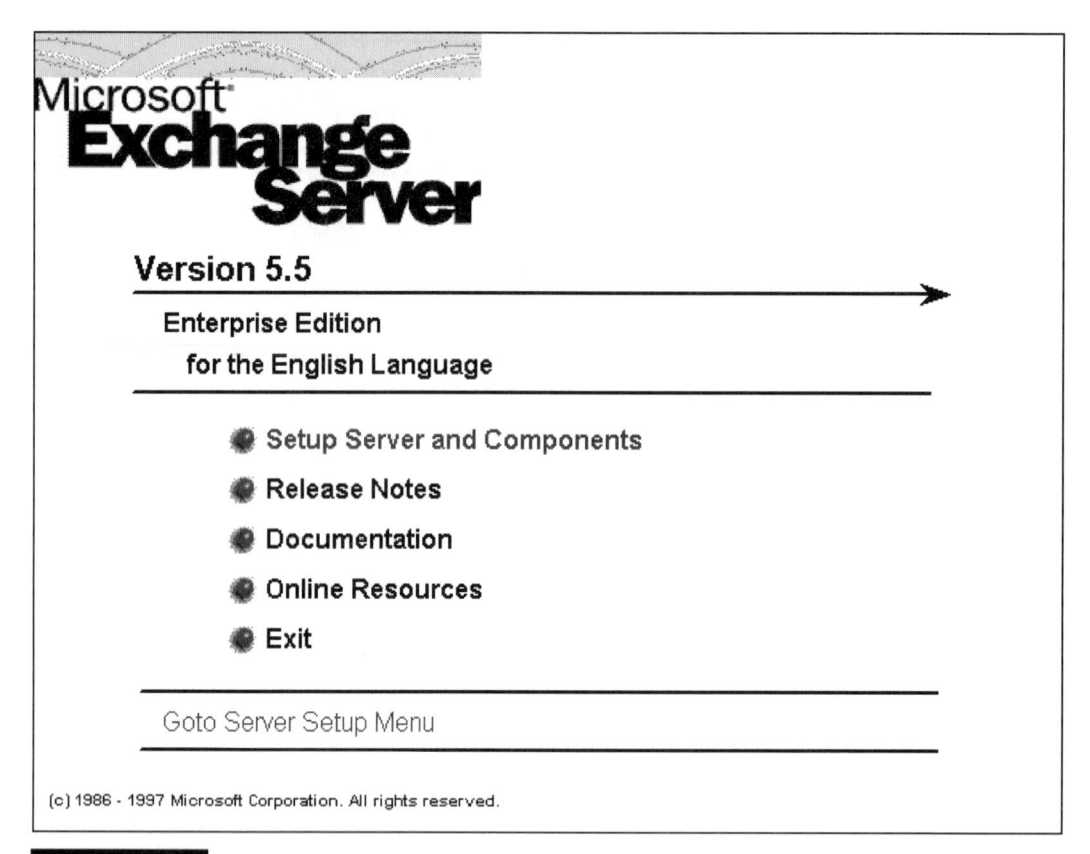

```
Microsoft
Exchange
       Server

Version 5.5
   Enterprise Edition
   for the English Language

      ● Setup Server and Components
      ● Release Notes
      ● Documentation
      ● Online Resources
      ● Exit

   Goto Server Setup Menu

(c) 1986 - 1997 Microsoft Corporation. All rights reserved.
```

FIGURE 7-1   Microsoft Exchange initial installation menu

Pre-setup Considerations

An Exchange Cluster Server is created by installing Exchange Server into an existing MSCS cluster; there is no way to add clustering services to an existing Exchange Server. The existence of a viable cluster is one pre-installation requirement and there are additional required conditions to ensure that the cluster will properly support Exchange:

- The cluster server hardware should be symmetrical. The processor type and capability, installed memory and local hard drive configuration should be the same on both nodes of the cluster. Further, it must be adequate to support the cluster OS and all applications, whether or not cluster aware, which might be running on either node at any given time. In addition to the basic requirement that a failed over application be able to find, configure, and launch the necessary local resources in

a compatible environment, Exchange optimizes its use of hardware resources based upon a static, point-in-time analysis of the server on which it is running. Performance and, possibly, function may be impaired following fail over, depending upon the degree of divergence from hardware symmetry.
- The cluster server hardware should be approved for cluster use in the hardware compatibility list (HCL) found at http://www.microsoft.com/hwtest/hcl. Microsoft will not provide support for non-complying hardware.
- The cluster hotfixes must be installed prior to installing Exchange Server. The setup documentation which accompanies Exchange Server states that the "Roll-up" hotfixes must be downloaded from ftp://ftp.microsoft.com/bussys/winnt/winnt-public/fixes/usa/NT40/hotfixes-postSP3/roll-up and installed. However, a document in the FTP site corrects that; the "Cluster" hotfixes, not the "Roll-up" hotfixes, are required, and may be downloaded from ftp://ftp.microsoft.com/bussys/winnt/winnt-public/fixes/usa/NT40/hotfixes-postSP3/roll-up/cluster. The user is cautioned not to install the "Roll-up" hotfixes if the "Cluster" hotfixes have already been installed. The hotfixes are available as a single, platform-dependent file (clusfixi.exe for Intel platforms, clusfixa.exe for Alpha platforms) which can be launched to install the upgrades. Alternatively, the separate hotfixes can be extracted from the file by using the /x parameter. Individual hotfixes can then be installed by typing the specific Executable name.
- Exchange Server 5.5, Enterprise Edition, is the only version of Exchange which is cluster aware. It must be installed on the shared cluster drive(s) of an active cluster node in order to take advantage of cluster services. It is possible to install Exchange Server, Enterprise Edition, onto a non-cluster server, or to install Exchange Server, Standard Edition, onto a non-shared (non-cluster) drive of a cluster node. Both will yield viable Exchange servers, but neither will provide any of the benefits derived from clustering. Should the server fail, the Exchange resources are unavailable until the problem is resolved. It is also possible to install Exchange Server, Standard Edition, onto the shared cluster drive of an active cluster node (the non-cluster-aware standard edition setup program does not prevent it), but failover of the non-cluster-aware Exchange Server installation results in its destruction and corruption of its files due to Standard Edition's inability to virtualize its network name. Exchange Server, Standard Edition, is not intended for a multisite, multiserver environment and is, by design, utterly unsuited for deployment in a clustered server environment. Unless specifically stated otherwise, further references to Exchange Server will mean version 5.5, Enterprise Edition exclusively.

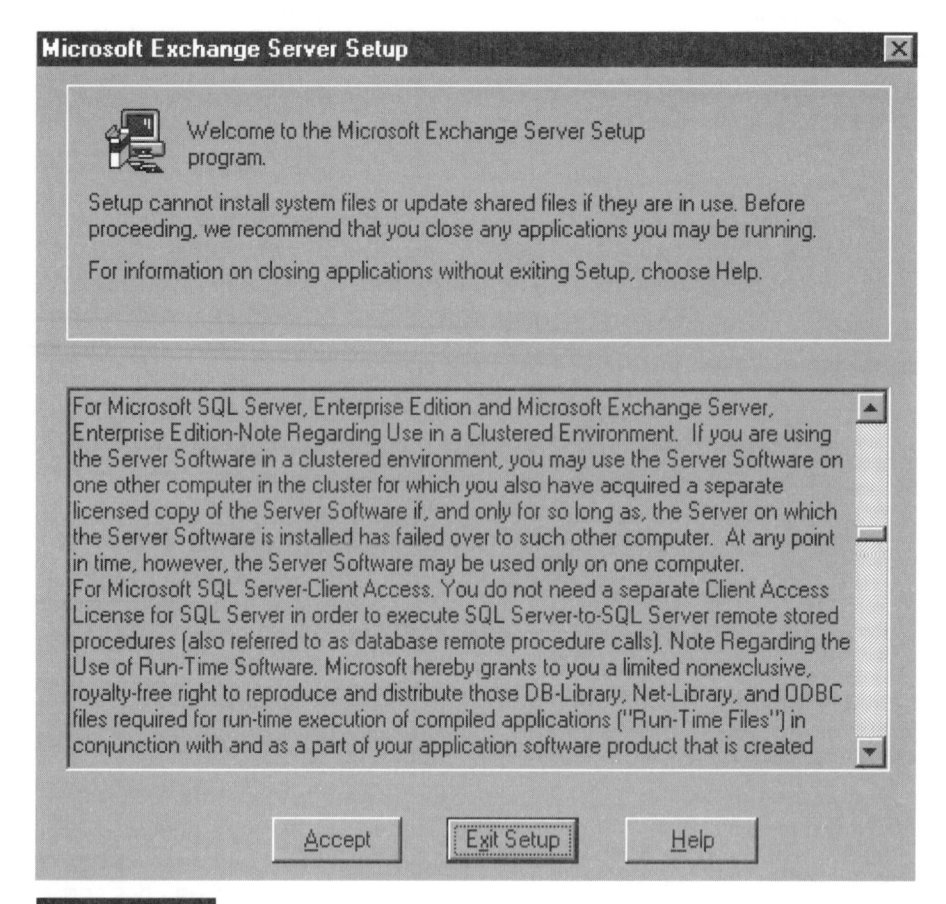

FIGURE 7-2 License agreement acknowledgement screen

- Installation of the Enterprise Edition of Exchange Server into a cluster requires two server licenses for Exchange, even though only a single instance of Exchange can be running at any point in time. This requirement is made part of, and detailed in, the online license agreement, shown in Figure 7-2, which must be agreed to in order to continue the installation process. It appears that this licensing requirement foreshadows migration to an active/active cluster support mode, where each node hosts an active Exchange Server installation capable of being failed over to the other node. Microsoft has indicated that the future of Exchange Cluster Server lies in that direction.

Seven • Clustering Exchange Server **179**

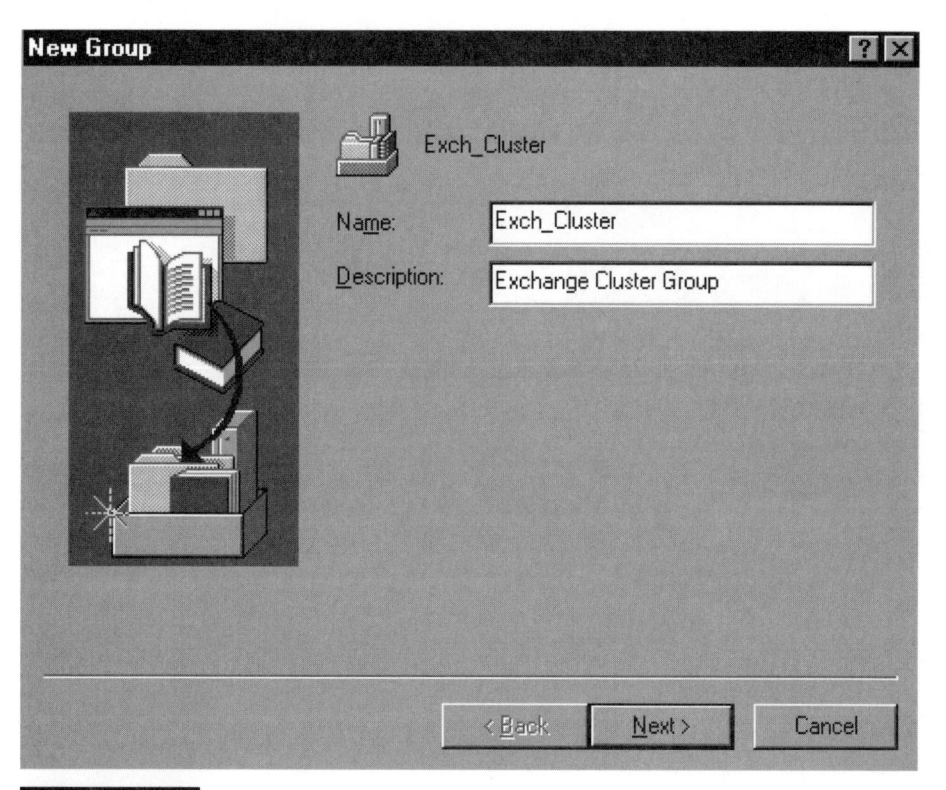

FIGURE 7-3 Creating the Exchange Server cluster group

A cluster resource group must be created and configured to support the cluster aware installation of Exchange Server. This resource group contains the Exchange components and defines the administrative and fail over unit for the Exchange Cluster Server. An IP Address resource, a Network Name resource, and a disk resource are all required to be created and configured online in the exchange resource group prior to launching the Exchange setup program. To create a resource group, in Cluster Administrator, choose the FILE menu button, then NEW, and GROUP to open the New Group dialog box (Figure 7-3). Enter the name for the cluster resource group in the Name: field; it is good policy to also provide a definitive description. This name is used almost exclusively within the cluster environment—it is exposed only in the Exchange environment early in the setup process, to identify the cluster resource group for installation, so it does not enter into the naming convention consideration for the Exchange topology. If more than one Exchange Cluster Server installation is administered, it is still a good idea to choose a uniquely definitive name to help avoid administrative confusion. It is easier to deal with

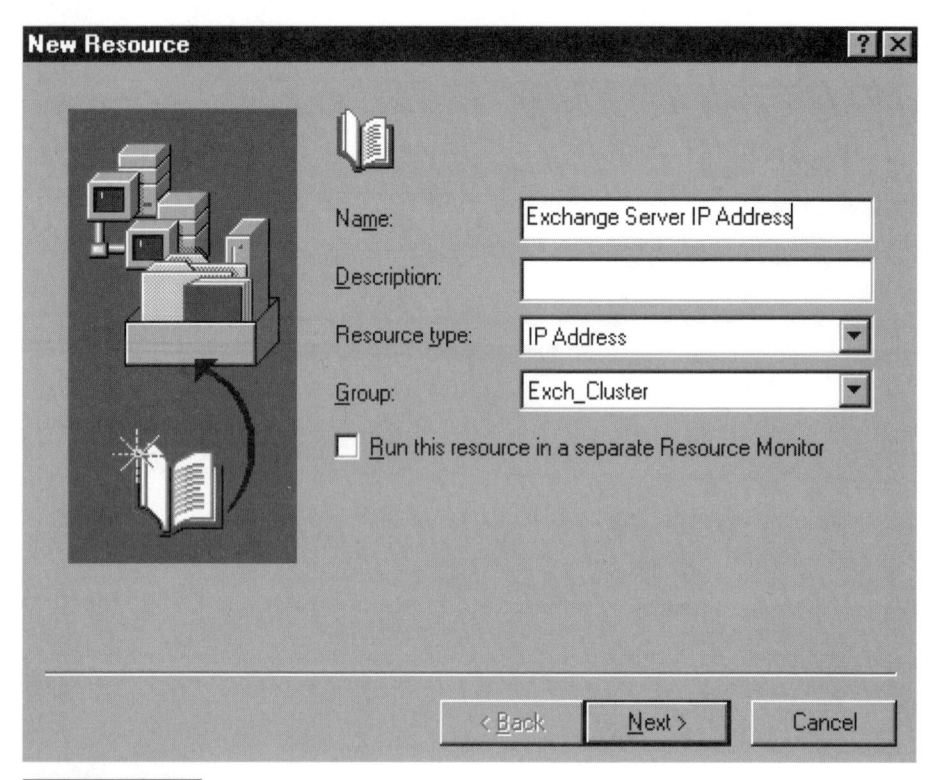

FIGURE 7-4 Creating the Exchange Server IP address resource

Exch_Cluster_Boston and Exch_Cluster_Dallas than two Exch_Cluster's, which will force a review of the (hopefully present) description to uniquely identify the latter two.

To create the IP Address resource, in Cluster Administrator, choose the FILE menu button, then NEW, and RESOURCE to open the New Resource dialog box (Figure 7-4). Enter the name for the IP Address resource in the Name: field and add an optional description. This name is used exclusively in the cluster environment and is not exposed in Exchange, so the same general comments made about the cluster resource group name also apply here. Choose IP ADDRESS for the Resource type. Be sure the Group field identifies the Exchange cluster resource group created earlier.

TCP/IP Address Parameters

Exchange Server IP Address

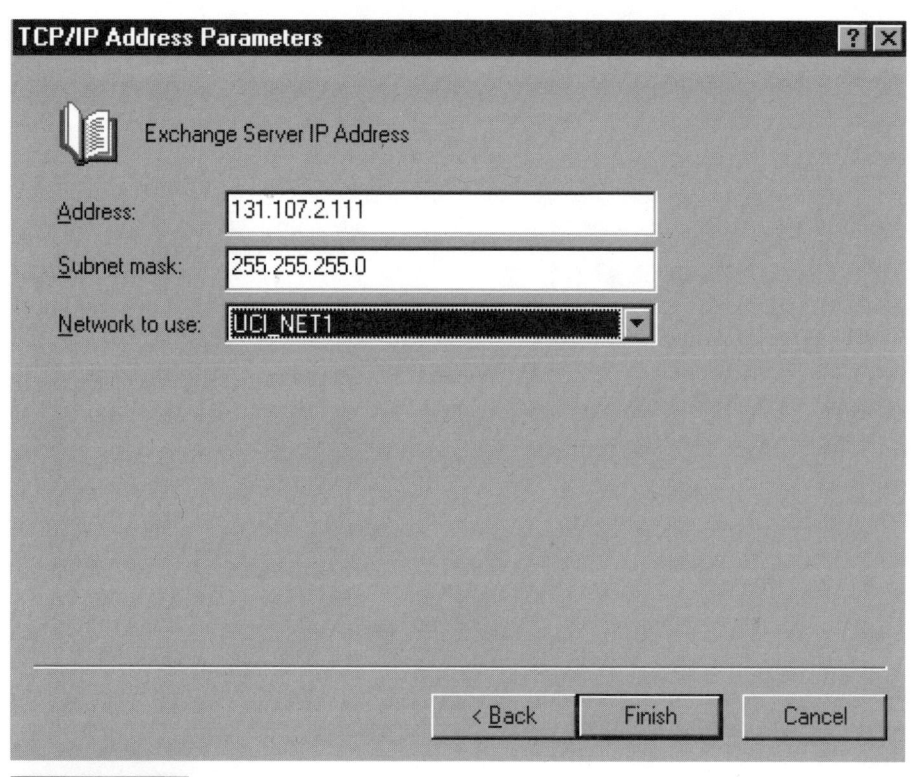

Address: 131.107.2.111
Subnet mask: 255.255.255.0
Network to use: UCI_NET1

FIGURE 7-5 Defining the IP address resource parameters

The default values are acceptable for the Possible Owners dialog box and Dependencies dialog box (the IP Address resource has no dependencies) which follow. In the TCP/IP Address Parameters dialog box (Figure 7-5), enter the unique IP address and subnet mask assigned to the Exchange virtual server. This IP address is fully exposed in the intranet/Internet environment and must be handled just as the IP address of a non-clustered Exchange server is handled. Also, identify the appropriate network for client access (if more than one network is available). Choose Finish to close.

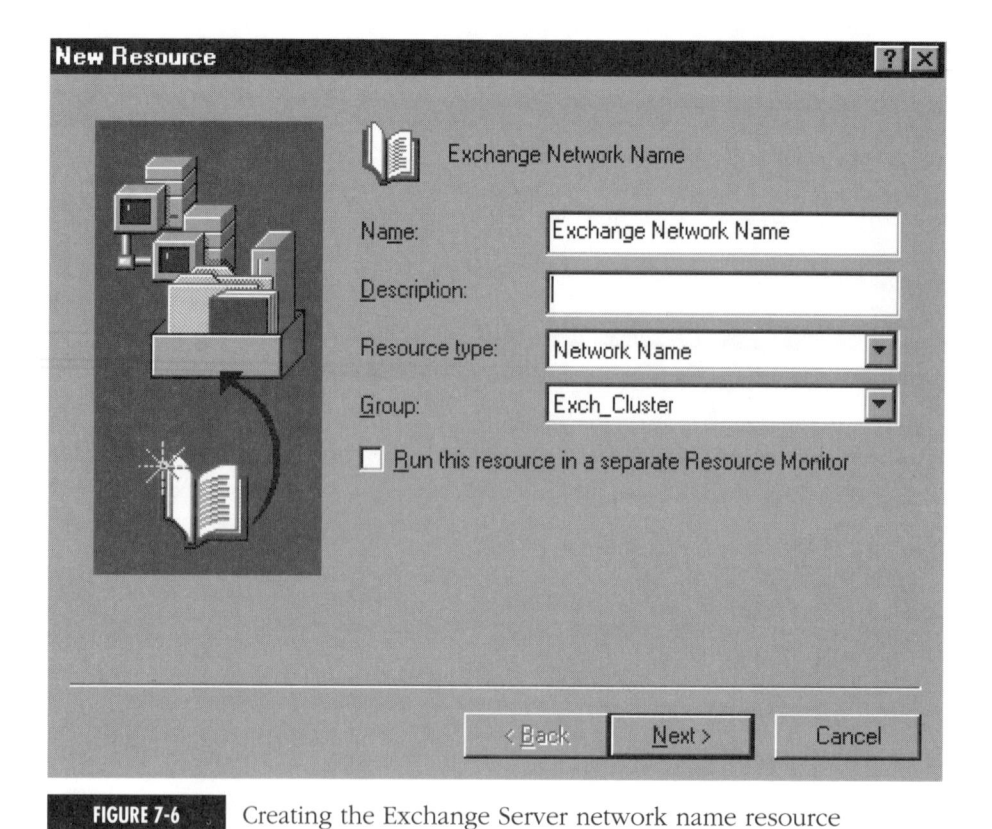

182 Chapter Seven • Windows NT Cluster Server Guidebook

FIGURE 7-6 Creating the Exchange Server network name resource

To create the Network Name resource, in Cluster Administrator, choose the FILE menu button, then NEW, and RESOURCE to open the New Resource dialog box (Figure 7-6). Enter the name for the Network Name resource in the Name: field and, again, add an optional description. This name is the name of the cluster administrator resource object itself, whose resource type is Network Name. It is not the NetBIOS name of the virtual Exchange server. This name is used exclusively in the cluster environment and is not exposed in Exchange, so once again, the same general comments made about the cluster resource group name also apply here. Choose Network Name for the Resource type. Be sure the Group field identifies the Exchange cluster resource group created earlier.

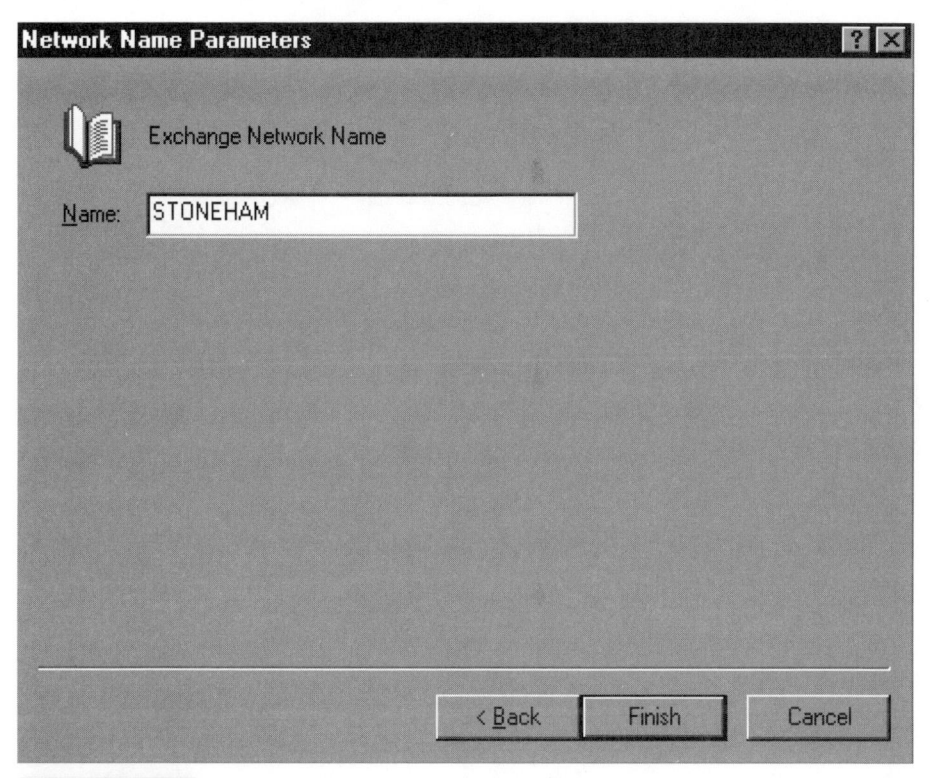

FIGURE 7-7 Defining the network name resource parameter

Once again, the default values are acceptable for the Possible Owners dialog boxes, but this time the Dependencies dialog box requires an entry, and enforces this with an error message and the disabling of the Next button until the Network Name resource is declared dependent upon the IP address resource. In the Network Name Parameters dialog box (Figure 7-7), enter the unique NetBIOS name assigned to the Exchange virtual server. This server name is fully exposed in the Exchange and network environments and must be handled just as the server name of a non-clustered Exchange server is handled. It is, in fact, a server name which will be listed in Network Neighborhood or another browser list. It is the Exchange Server name which is shown in the Exchange Admin.exe program and it is the name which forms a part of the internal object names in the Exchange Directory Services database. This name should be subject to the same naming convention/suitability consideration accorded any other server name. Choose Finish to close.

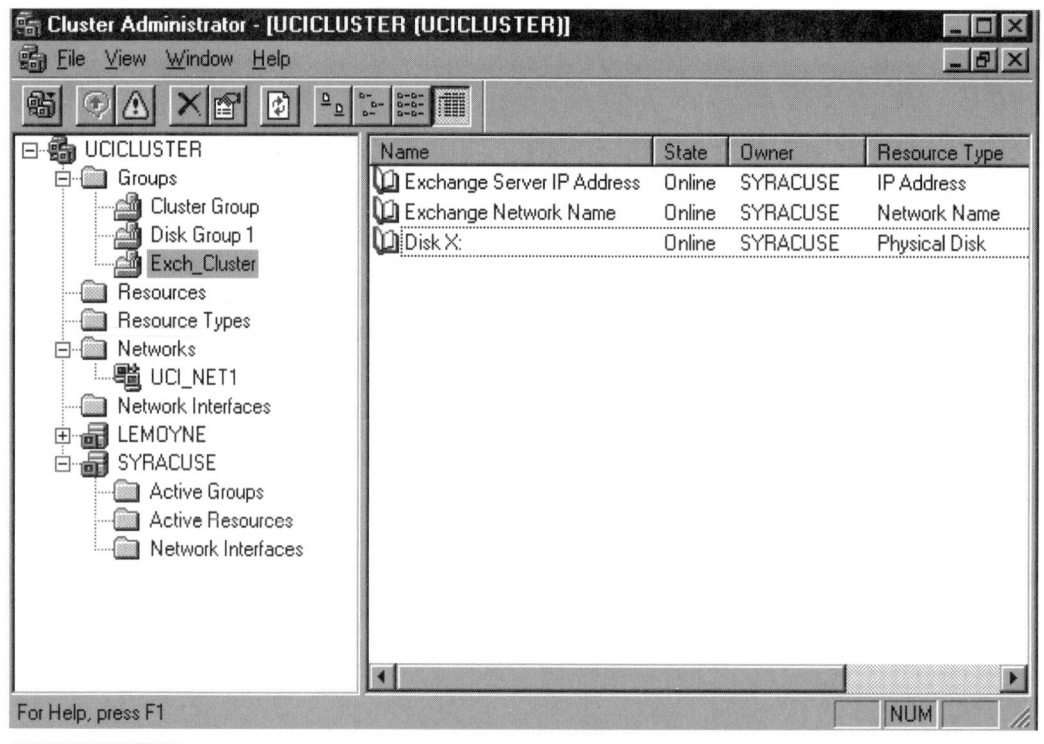

FIGURE 7-8 Cluster Administrator view of required Exchange Server cluster resources

The final step in this cluster resource group preparation is to move the shared disk resource into the Exchange resource group. The view in Cluster Administrator should look like Figure 7-8, with an active, fully configured Exchange cluster resource group containing an IP Address resource, a Network Name resource, and a shared cluster disk resource. The cluster is now ready to support Exchange Server.

The discussion to this point has largely focused on the cluster aspects of this Exchange Server installation. It may need to be restated that the underlying purpose of this entire process is to create an Exchange Server—one enhanced to cluster-supported high availability operation—but still, at the core, an Exchange Server. The standard planning and analysis procedure used to support the deployment of a non-clustered Exchange Server is fully applicable to the clustered Exchange Server. However, the E.C.S. deployment is probably a complete replacement for an existing Exchange Server, made to gain the benefits derived from clustering, rather than a topologically new site/server or a load-balancing scalability install, which are the reasons for most non-clustered Exchange Server installations. A complete replacement install has significant server namespace and existing resource preservation/

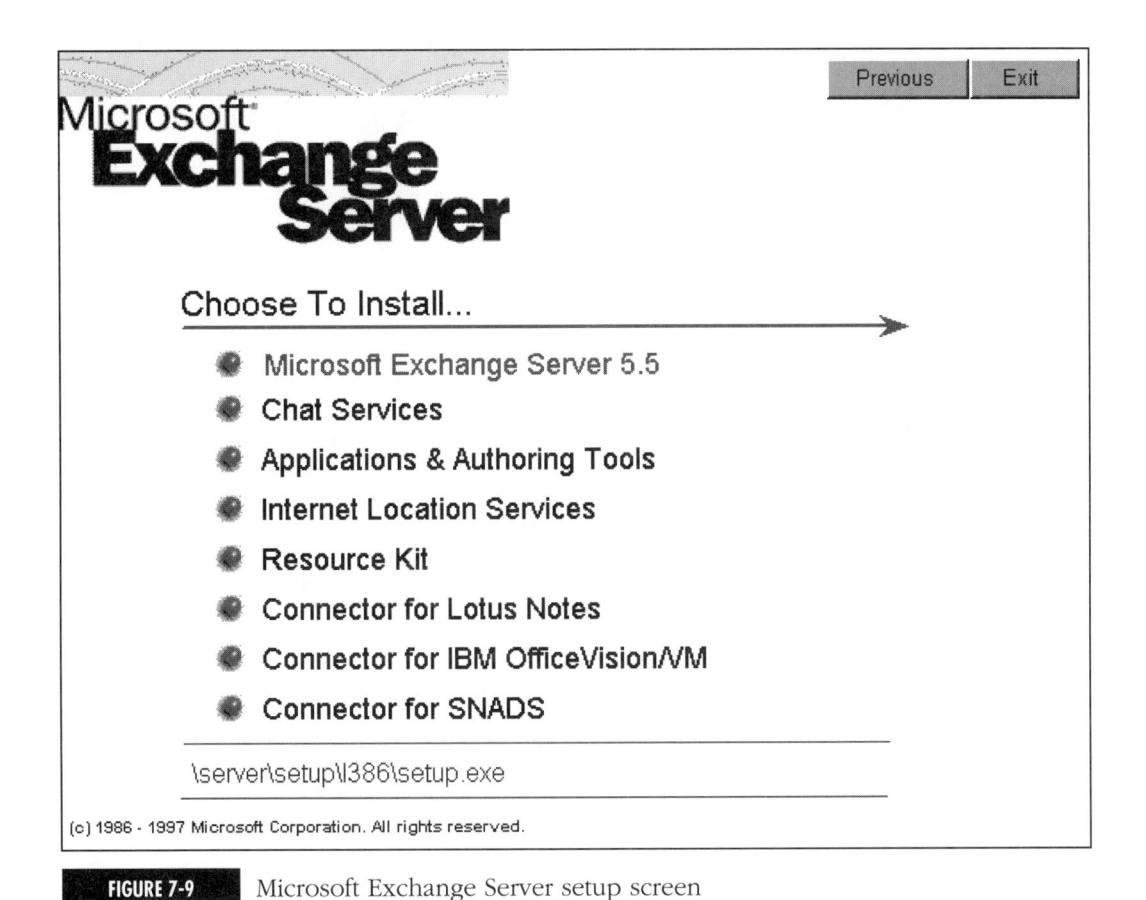

FIGURE 7-9 Microsoft Exchange Server setup screen

migration implications that simply do not apply to the new site or site extension deployment. This server's role in the Exchange topology must be well-defined prior to installation.

Setup—Primary Cluster Node

Following the activity and involvement of the pre-setup section, the actual setup of Exchange Server into a Cluster Server environment is an anti-climax. This is largely because the process is well-defined and executes reliably. From the top-level of the Exchange Server installation menu (Figure 7-1), the "Setup Server and Components" option opens a sub-menu of choices, as shown in Figure 7-9. Choosing "Microsoft Exchange Server 5.5" launches the server setup program appropriate to the installation platform (Intel or Alpha). As shown in the lower portion of the illustration, this can also be

FIGURE 7-10 Clustered Exchange Server installation—Primary node

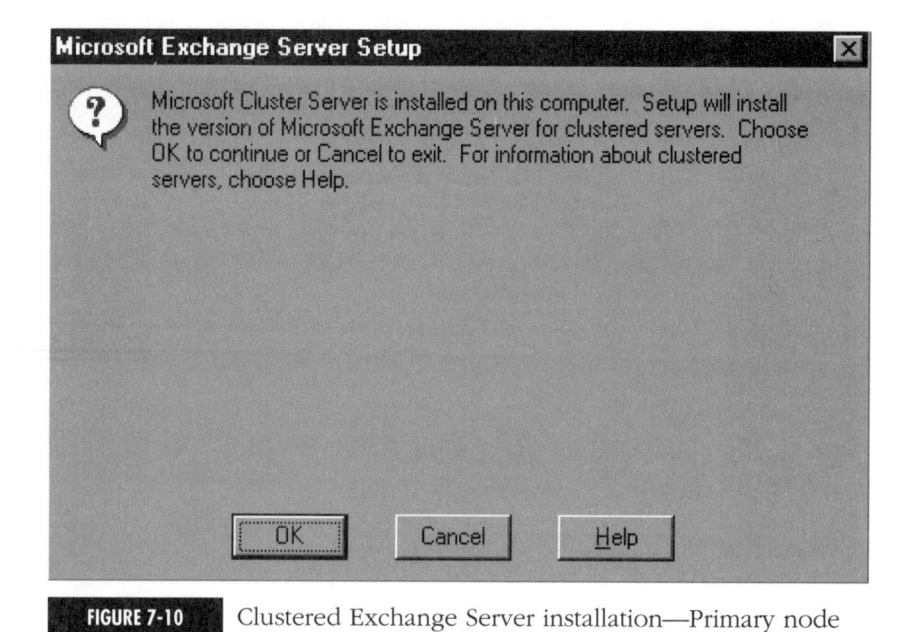

launched by running CD:\server\setup\I386\setup.exe or CD:\server\setup\alpha\setup.exe, as appropriate.

The cluster-aware setup program detects that it is running on an active cluster node and confirms this by displaying the informational dialog box shown in Figure 7-10. Choosing "Help" for more information about clustered servers opens the Help dialog box, providing a hot link to basic information on Cluster Servers and a reminder to make sure that Enterprise Edition is installed on symmetrically configured Cluster Servers.

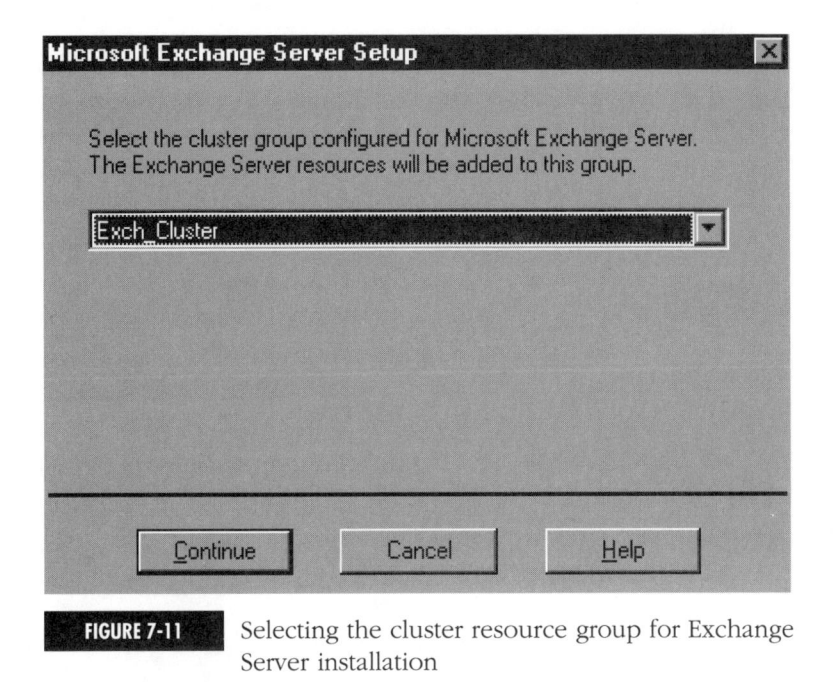

FIGURE 7-11 Selecting the cluster resource group for Exchange Server installation

The setup program next requires identification of the cluster resource group into which it will install exchange resources (see Figure 7-11). A choice from the drop down box of all cluster resource groups is offered. This is the single point, mentioned earlier, where the name of the cluster resource group is exposed in the Exchange Server Environment.

Selection of a resource group not currently active on the local node results in the error message shown in Figure 7-12. In a simple environment, the common cause triggering this message is the attempt to install Exchange on the secondary (non-active) cluster node before installing it on the primary (active) cluster node. In a more complex clustering environment, with multiple shared disk resources, it is clearly important to recognize that active and passive states are not attributes of cluster nodes, solely, but of binary combinations of cluster nodes and shared disk resources. The salient point is that Exchange Server must be installed first on the active cluster node (with respect to the target disk resource) before it can be installed on the inactive cluster node.

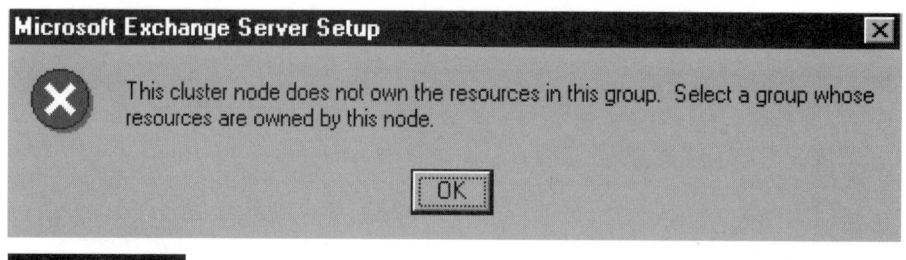

FIGURE 7-12 Message displayed if active node does not own the resource group selected for installation

The setup program continues, requiring (among other things) a site services account and password. It will default to the administrator account used for the install, but this should not be accepted; use a dedicated account for this purpose. This portion of the process is indistinguishable from a non-clustered install until the installation type (minimum, typical, complete/custom) dialog box is displayed (Figure 7-13).

FIGURE 7-13 Exchange Server installation type and target directory dialog box

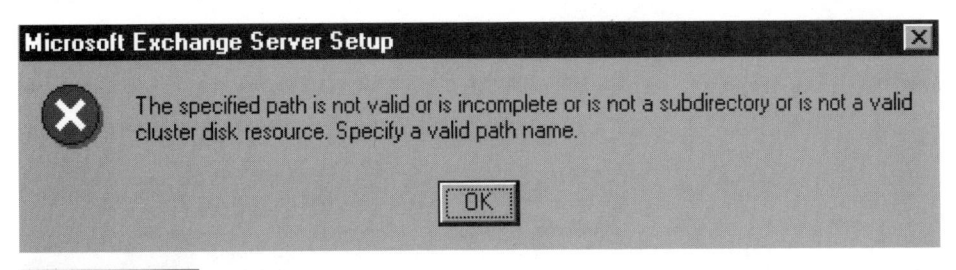

FIGURE 7-14 Message displayed if target directory is not located on a shared cluster disk

The difference at this point between a cluster-aware installation and a non-cluster installation is not readily apparent until an unacceptable action is attempted, which causes the cluster aware setup program to define the operational environmental rules in place. This dialog box, in addition to allowing the choice of installation scope, displays the installation directory for the Exchange Server files (in this case, X:\exchsrvr) on the shared SCSI cluster disk. An attempt to specify an alternative installation directory, via the Change Directory button, pointing to a non-cluster disk, generated the error message shown in Figure 7-14.

The fourth explanation for the error—that the proposed directory is not a cluster disk resource—is the operative one; it makes the point that whatever continuity exists between a failed cluster node and its surviving twin, exists solely on the shared cluster drive(s). Installation to a shared cluster drive, specifically one identified as a disk resource in the Exchange resource group, is mandatory and will be enforced by the system.

Setup proceeds, supporting a complete installation, all components installing to the shared cluster drive, as shown in Figure 7-15. The install then copies Exchange Executable, database, component and support files to the shared cluster drive, establishes cluster resources in the Exchange cluster resource group, copies system libraries and extensions to the local \System32 directory, and creates and registers Windows NT services on the primary node. Finally, the setup program uses two dialog boxes to declare itself finished and provide reminders to run Setup on the secondary node and to run Performance Optimizer on the active node (Figures 7-16 and 7-17).

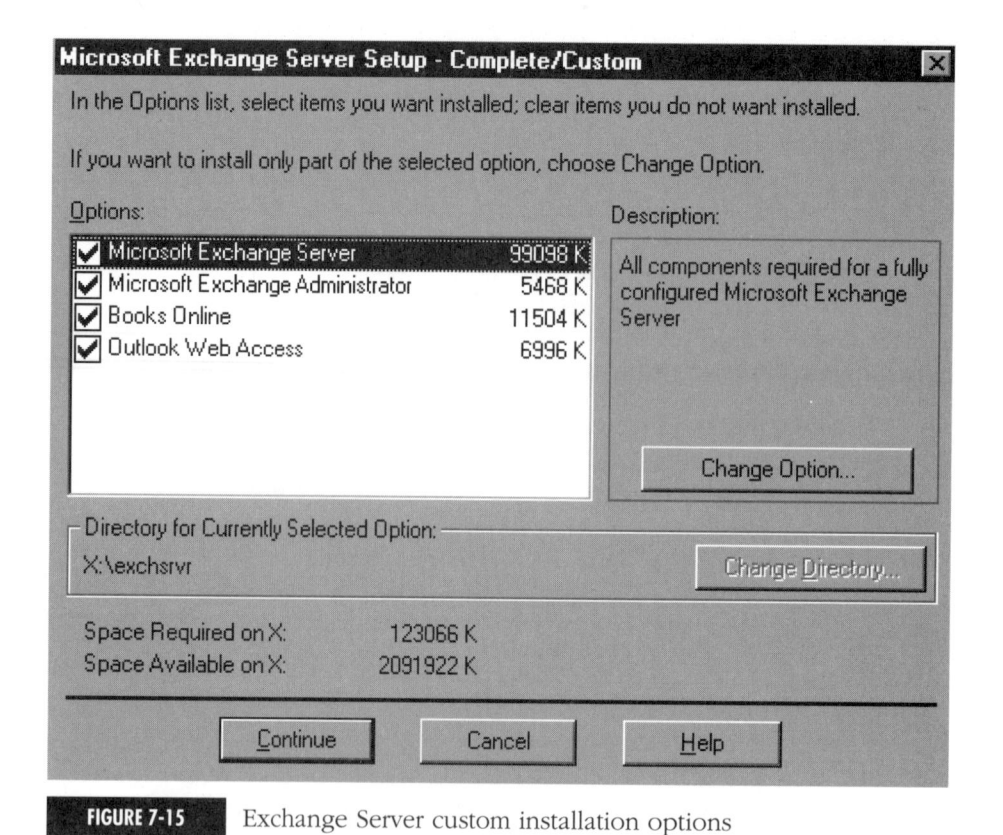

FIGURE 7-15 Exchange Server custom installation options

Except for running Performance Optimizer, installation on the primary node is complete and the Exchange server is available for use, but only on the primary node. Until Setup is completed on the secondary node, fail over of the Exchange installation will be fatal, so proceed directly to the setup of the secondary node.

Seven • Clustering Exchange Server

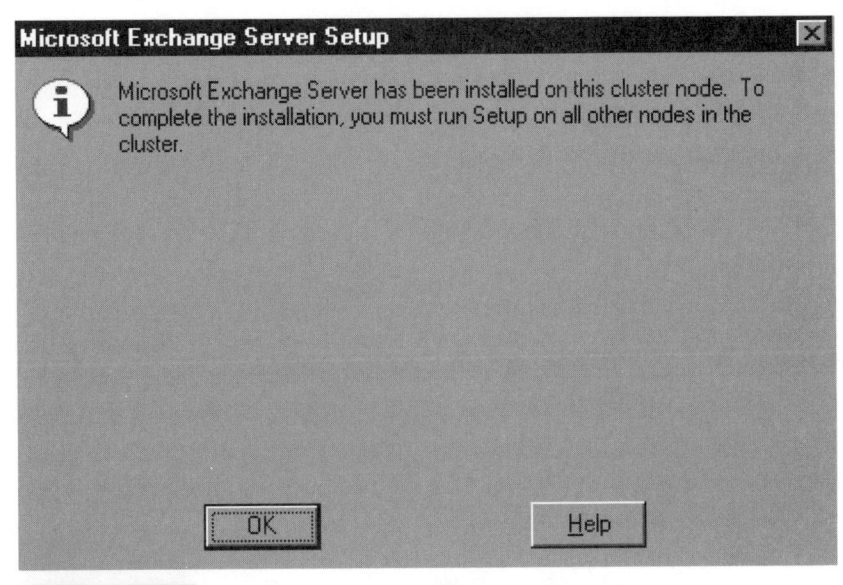

FIGURE 7-16 Reminder to run Exchange Server setup on secondary node

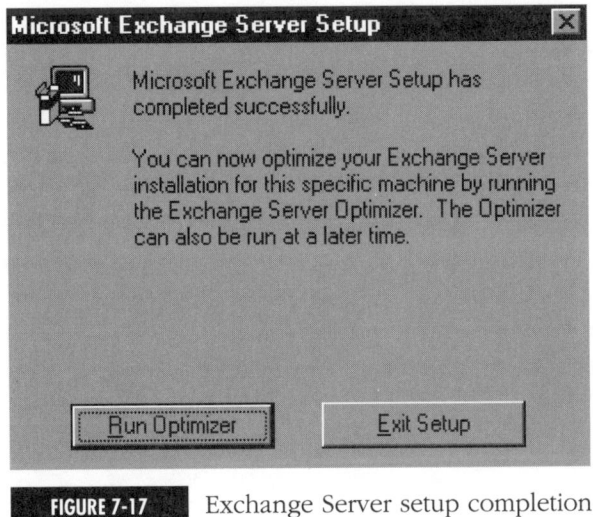

FIGURE 7-17 Exchange Server setup completion message—Primary node

FIGURE 7-18 Clustered Exchange Server installation—Secondary node

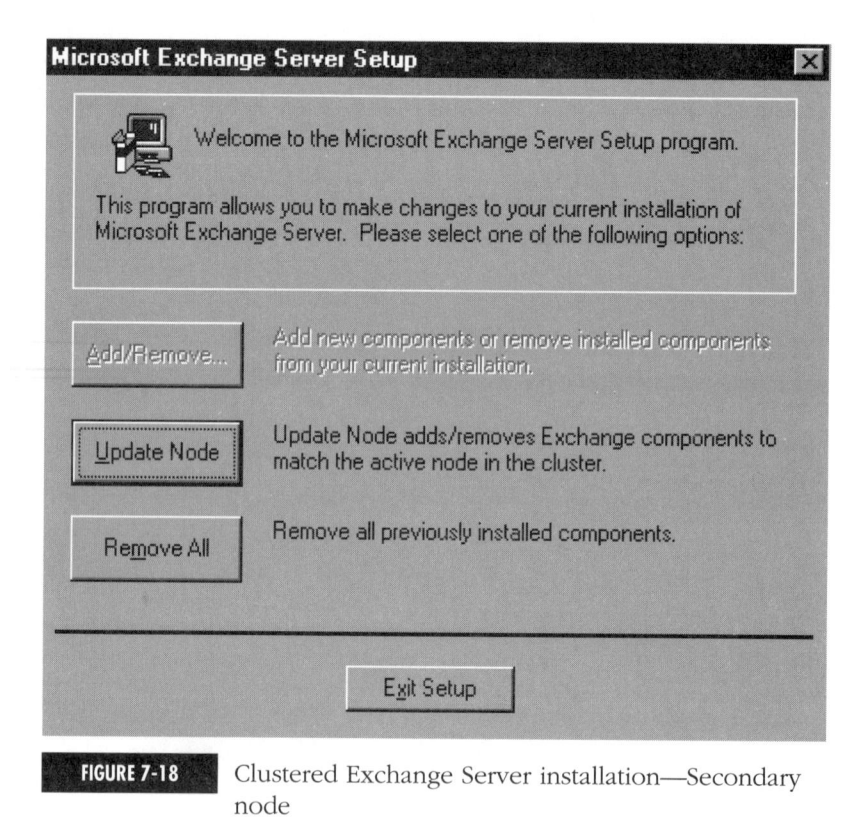

Setup—Secondary Cluster Node

Running setup on the secondary node is a straightforward process, requiring only knowledge of the Exchange site service account login ID and password, and access to the primary (active) Exchange Cluster Server and the Exchange setup program. The Welcome screen (Figure 7-18) provides two choices: Update Node, which duplicates the primary node's local Exchange environment (system libraries and extensions, services) on the secondary node, and Remove All, which permits removal of Exchange functionality from the server.

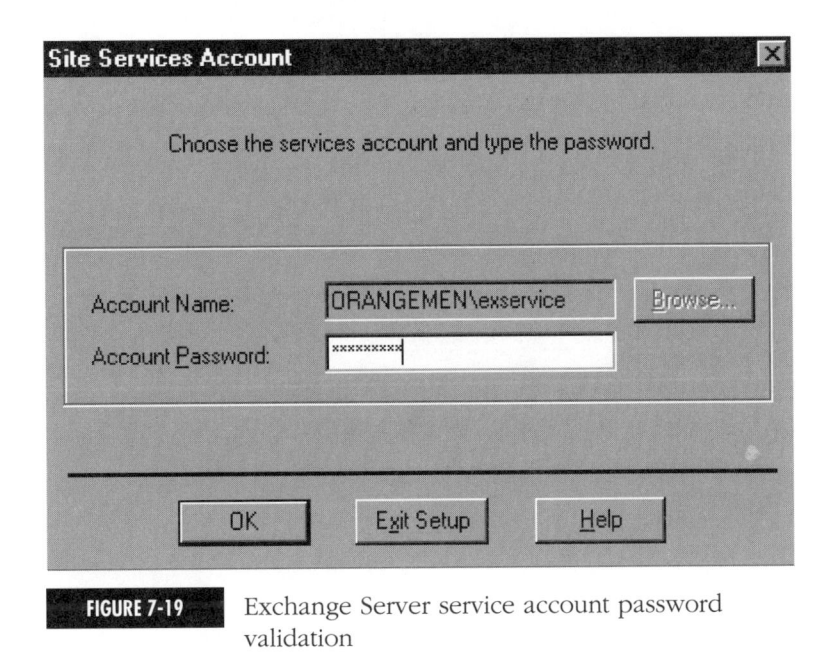

Seven • Clustering Exchange Server   **193**

FIGURE 7-19   Exchange Server service account password validation

Note that the option to Add/Remove Exchange components is not available on the secondary node. All such initiating configuration decisions are restricted to the active Exchange Cluster Server node, which is the only node that can access the Exchange files on the shared cluster disk; the secondary node is slaved to the primary configuration via Update Node. The administrator is required to supply the Exchange site service account password to demonstrate his or her right to administer this installation (Figure 7-19).

FIGURE 7-20 Exchange Server setup completion message—Secondary node

After copying system libraries and extensions to the local \System32 directory, and creating and registering Windows NT services on the secondary node, the Exchange setup program declares its successful completion in Figure 7-20. Note that, unlike the analogous dialog box at the end of primary node setup, there is no suggestion to run Performance Optimizer on the secondary node. If Performance Optimizer has been run on the active node, the logical extension of the symmetrical server hardware assumption is that there is no reason to run it again on the secondary node—it's identical. More practically, the secondary node cannot access the shared cluster disk, has no administrative access to the Exchange environment, and therefore has no resources to optimize, nor an Executable to run.

The Exchange Cluster Server is now installed, functional, and capable of failing over from one cluster node to the other as required by component failure or administrator intervention. To clients, the clustered Exchange environment is indistinguishable from a non-clustered environment in the Exchange Administrator window (Figure 7-21), but administration of the clustered Exchange environment has some singular differences which must be observed. They are discussed later in this chapter.

Replacing an Existing Exchange Server

Typically, an Exchange Cluster Server is either a new Exchange Server in a new or an existing site, or a complete replacement for an existing, non-clustered Exchange Server. The setup already outlined suffices for the new serv-

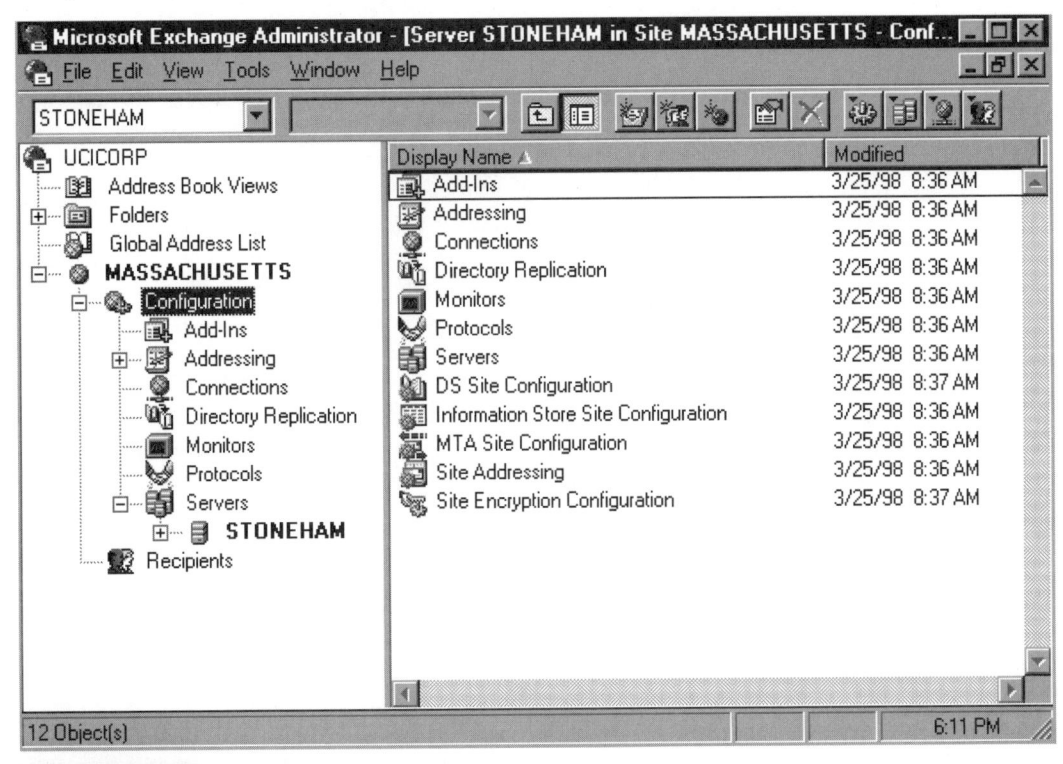

FIGURE 7-21 Exchange Administrator view of clustered Exchange Server

er scenario—just populate with recipients. The replacement scenario, however, requires some additional effort. It can be accomplished in one of two ways: by moving mailboxes from the existing, non-clustered Exchange Server to the new Exchange Cluster Server in the same site, or by using disaster recovery techniques to restore the existing Exchange Server objects and resources into the new Exchange Cluster Server framework. The former method is conceptually easier and completes without an interruption in service, but requires, at least temporarily, two servers: both the old and new servers must be online simultaneously. The latter method requires no additional hardware beyond the target server, but must be planned and implemented differently than outlined above, involves an interruption in service, and relies upon disaster recovery techniques with which many administrators feel less comfortable.

To move users, set up the new Exchange Cluster Server in the same site as the existing Exchange Server, and ensure that directory replication on both old and new servers is up to date. In the Exchange Administrator program, highlight all the mailboxes on the existing Exchange Server, then the Tools menu, select Move Mailbox, identify the Exchange Cluster Server as the target server, and the contents of the selected mailboxes will be moved from the old server to the new one. (This process can take some time to complete.) The existing public folders created and owned by the users, originally on the old Exchange Server, do not move with the mailboxes. It is necessary to rehome the public folders separately. One way to do this is to replicate all the public folders on the original Exchange Server to the new Exchange Cluster Server. Once replication has completed (be sure the new replicas show a recent Last Received Time in the Public Information Store\Folder Replication Status tab and match the original values in the Total K and Total number of Items columns of the Public Information Store\Public Folder Resources tab) the instances can be removed from the original Exchange Server Public Information Store and rehomed on the new Exchange Cluster Server. If the old Exchange Server was the first server installed into the site, it will also be necessary to rehome the Site Folders (Offline Address Book folders, Schedule+ Free/Busy folders, Organizational Forms folder) and reset the Offline Address Book server and Routing Calculation server to the new Exchange Cluster Server (see Knowledge Base article Q152959 for further details). The result is that the resources of the original server are now completely duplicated on the new server. Note that it is not possible to maintain the same Exchange Server name for the new server: it must have a distinct (although virtual) network name of its own, which becomes its Exchange Server name. This, of course, impacts each useris messaging profile, which identifies the useris home server. As long as the old server remains online and in the site, the next time the users log into email, their messaging profiles will automatically be updated to identify the new server. So it is important that the old server not be removed from the site until all users have logged into email once, subsequent to the migration. The old server can then be retired.

To replace an existing, non-clustered Exchange Server using disaster recovery techniques, no additional hardware beyond that needed to form a cluster is required: the original server can be reinstalled as one node in the cluster. It does, however, require additional planning and installation steps. The original Exchange Server must be upgraded to Exchange version 5.5, then backed up and taken offline. (If the server is going to be reused in the new environment, the upgrade to NT 4.0 Cluster Server can be done at the same time.) The cluster resources must be prepared, as described previously, except that the Network Name resource must match the NetBIOS name of the original Exchange Server. Using the Command Prompt, change directory to the platform-appropriate subdirectory of the Exchange Server 5.5 Enterprise Edition CD and run Setup.exe in Recovery Mode (using the /r parameter, eg: CD:\Server\Setup\I386\setup.exe /r). Recovery Mode tells the setup program to install a new exchange environment, but that the Directory and Information Store databases will be restored from a previous backup. Complete the setup of the primary node as before, and run

Performance Optimizer without restarting services. Using the Cluster Administrator program, bring the Exchange Server System Attendant resource online. Next, restore the Directory and Information Store databases to the shared cluster disk, again without starting services after completion of the process. Using the Cluster Administrator program, bring the Exchange Server Directory resource online. Now right click the Exchange Server Information Store resource, choose Properties/Registry Replication tab, and force a new registry checkpoint by removing the existing Root Registry Key entry and adding the following new entry: SYSTEM\CurrentControlSet\ \Services\MSExchangeIS. Choose OK twice to return to the Cluster Administrator program main window, and bring the Exchange Server Information Store resource online. (This process can take some time to complete, particularly with large information stores, since the system must first recover the databases prior to bringing the resources online. It is possible the default startup timeout interval—600 seconds—will expire and Cluster Administrator will post a resource failure message. Ignore this message and let the process complete recovery, and bring the IS resource online.) Finally, select the Exchange Server resource group name and bring the entire resource group online. Installation of the primary node is complete. Run Setup.exe on the secondary node and choose Update Node, as before. Installation and replacement is complete.

Supporting Exchange Server, Enterprise Edition

Supporting an Exchange Cluster Server, for the most part, is very similar to supporting a non-clustered Exchange Server. The bulk of the daily administrative workload is still accomplished as before, through the Exchange Administrator program, Admin.exe, and clients should note no difference, except increased availability. The two most significant differences are the need for a two-step setup process (primary node and then secondary node update) whenever Exchange services are installed or removed, and the general use of Cluster Administrator instead of Control Panel/Services to start and stop Exchange services. These issues, and a few other one-time changes, are discussed in the next several sections.

Administration—Operational Differences

WHERE TO RUN ADMIN.EXE

Generally, run Exchange's Administrator program, Admin.exe, on any convenient NT computer except an Exchange Cluster Server. By default, Admin.exe is installed for each node in the cluster, but, like most other Exchange components, Admin.exe's Executable is physically installed on the

FIGURE 7-22 Message displayed when attempting to run Exchange Administrator from the passive node

shared Exchange disk resource (in \Exchsrvr\bin). Thus, each node has a valid shortcut for the Exchange Administrator program, but only the active node, which controls the shared disk resource, can successfully access and run the program. The inactive node, without access to the shared disk resource, simply cannot find the Executable (Figure 7-22).

The problem with running the Administrator program on the active node of a clustered Exchange Server is that the node may not remain the active node. Fail over of the Exchange group resource, and consequent loss of access to the shared disk resource, will cause an Administrator program running locally on the clustered Exchange Server to crash, even if the node itself remains up. In contrast, an Administrator program connected to the Exchange Cluster Server, but physically running on some other Windows NT Server or Workstation, will experience only a server-specific interruption in activity (and may display component or server access or timeout errors), but is otherwise unaffected, and resumes activity once the Exchange environment is restarted on the other (now active) node.

STARTING, STOPPING AND PAUSING EXCHANGE SERVICES

In a typical non-clustered environment, Exchange components implemented as NT services are configured to start automatically with server startup. Individual Exchange services can be stopped, restarted, or paused manually using Control Panel/Services, Server Monitor/Services or Net Stop and Net Start commands. In the clustered environment, these Exchange services are configured for manual startup on both nodes, and the cluster software methodically starts the services (in dependency order) on the active node only. Generally, Exchange services in a clustered environment should only be stopped and restarted using the Cluster Administrator program (see Figure 7-23) to take them offline and bring them online, respectively. This is the only reliable means to change the state of clustered services. The cluster resource manager recognizes five resource states: online, online pending, offline, offline pending, and failed. Note that, using Control Panel/Services, a clustered service, when started, is specifically not online and a clustered ser-

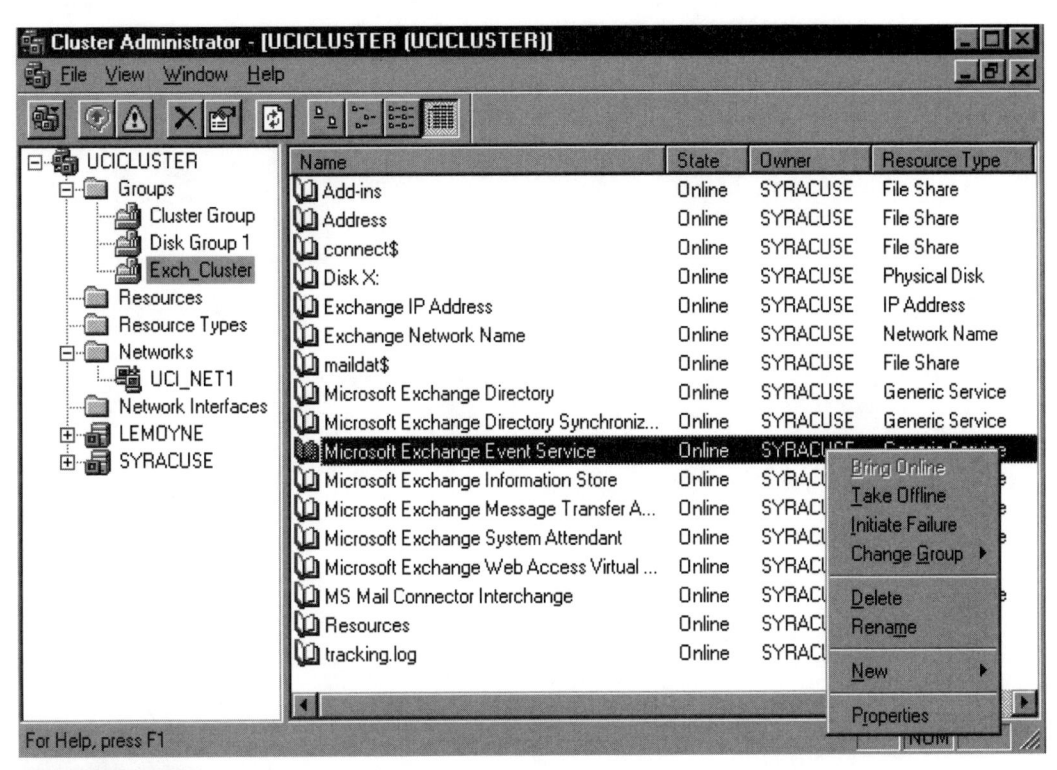

FIGURE 7-23 Managing Exchange Server services with Cluster Administrator

vice which is stopped is specifically not offline. From the perspective of Cluster Services, a stopped service which is not offline must have failed, and this triggers an appropriate corrective response from the cluster, which may involve a service restart or a full resource group fail over. The administrator of a mixed clustered and non-clustered Exchange environment must be particularly careful with regard to stopping and restarting Exchange services.

One exception to the above rule is the Key Management Server service. The KM Server creates and manages the public and private keys to enable Advanced Security digital signing and encryption of messages. For security, the KM service requires entry of a specific password at each and every service initialization, or it will not load. The password can be read from a floppy disk or entered manually, but in either case, it will not typically be so readily available that automatic restart of the KM service is possible or desirable. When installed in a clustered environment, the KM Server resource is configured not to restart in the event of service failure or fail over (see Figure 7-24). This also means that failure of the KM Server service cannot trigger a fail over of the cluster group, since Affect The Group is a sub-

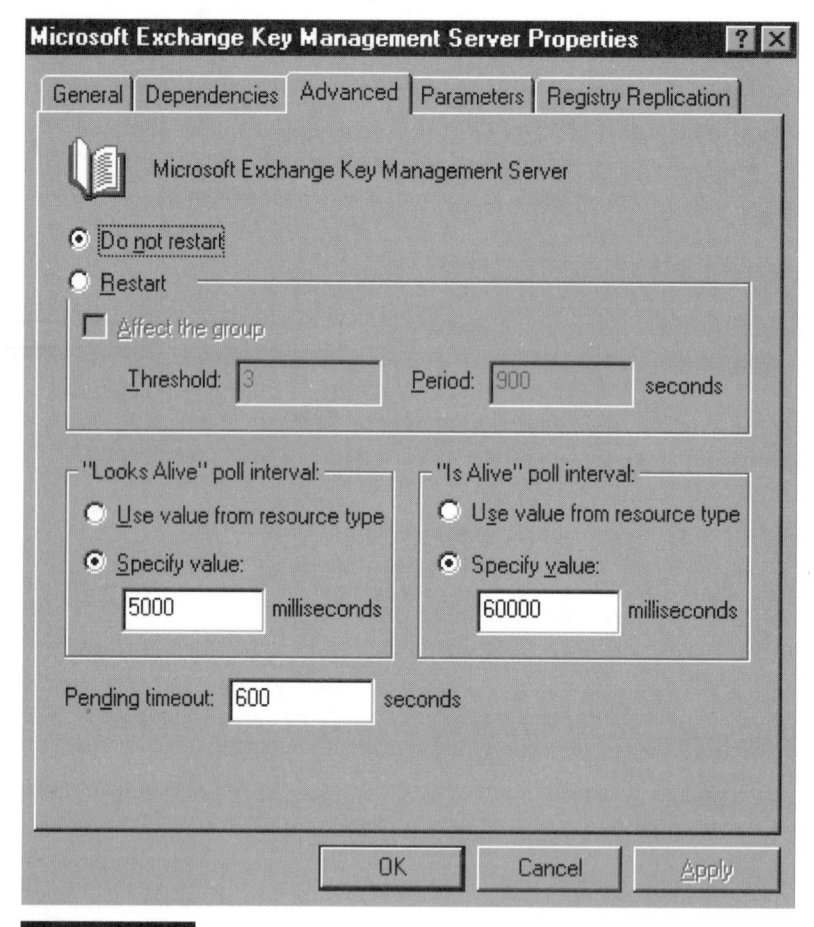

FIGURE 7-24 Default settings for the Key Management Server resource

option of the Restart option. So in this case, the KM service can be stopped and restarted using any method, without adversely affecting the clustered Exchange environment. Microsoft recommends starting the clustered KM Server service via Control Panel/Services, and then using Cluster Administrator to bring the resource online. Moreover, Microsoft does not recommend installing KM Server into a cluster environment in the first place, since the security requirements defeat the fail over capability of the resource.

A second exception to the above rule results from the lack of a Paused service state within the Cluster Administrator program. There are times when a service needs to be paused in order to support a specific process (for example, in order to cycle a manual Dirsync process, with Exchange server as the Dirsync Server, the Directory Synchronization service must be paused at specific points in the process). In order to achieve this, it is necessary to take the resource offline in Cluster Administrator (service is stopped and offline), restart the service outside of Cluster Administrator (service is started but still offline), then pause the running service (service is paused and still offline). When the process requiring the service pause is complete, just Continue the service and then bring it online.

SERVER MONITORS

Server monitors defined in the Exchange Administrator program are prevented from taking actions to restart services or servers when an Exchange Cluster installation is involved. The role of server monitors is to monitor specifically defined services on one or more Exchange servers in an organization. An Exchange administrator defines a series of responses, triggered by the server monitor when an abnormal condition is detected on one of the monitored Exchange servers. The responses range from, at the minimum, a pop-up message on one or more operators' consoles and escalate, with the passage of time, through sending email alerts, launching specified processes, and attempting to restart the affected service or restarting the Exchange server on which the service runs.

This activity of server monitors is duplicated in regard to the capabilities and responsibilities of the Cluster Service itself, and might, if permitted, block the Cluster Service's ability to insure resource availability. Imagine the Cluster Service trying to take resources offline in preparation of fail over, while server monitors attempt to restart those same resources! To avoid this possibility, the server monitor properties pages have been made cluster aware, so that if an Exchange Cluster Server is added to the list of monitored servers, the Actions tab options are disabled and appear grayed out, as shown in Figure 7-25. It is recommended that the Exchange administrator run dual sets of server monitors—one for non-clustered servers for which restart actions are supported, and one for clustered servers for which restart actions are disabled. It is also up to the Exchange administrator to insure that any process launched by a server monitor does not independently attempt to stop or restart services, in conflict with Cluster Server actions.

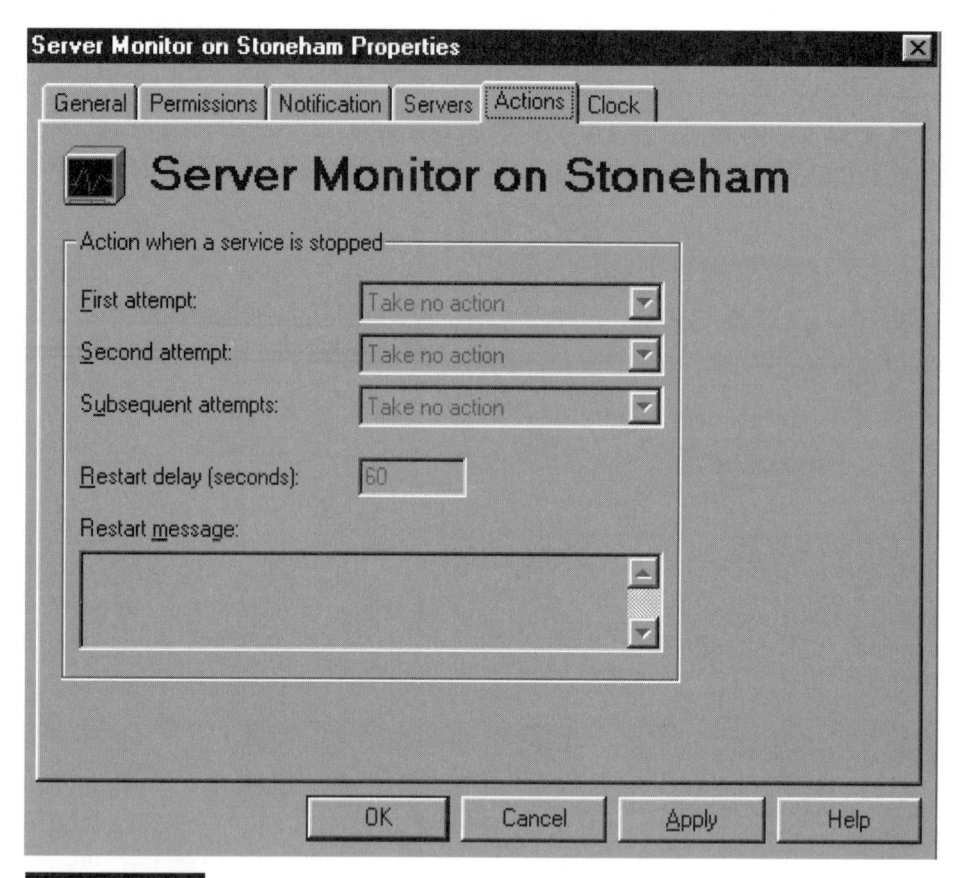

FIGURE 7-25 Server Monitor actions disabled for clustered Exchange Server

ADDING AND REMOVING EXCHANGE COMPONENTS

Once Exchange Server has been installed on both nodes and Performance Optimizer has been run, the Exchange installation is fully and optimally functional, but it may not be complete, or remain so. It is a common administrative task to add or remove messaging connectors or other components as workflow, needs, and capabilities change. Some components (Internet Mail Service [IMS], Internet News Service [INS], Microsoft Mail [PC] Connector, Lotus cc:Mail Connector, Exchange Scripting Service, Key Management [KM] Server) are implemented as distinct Windows NT services, while others (Site Connector, X.400 Connector) are not. Whenever one of the Exchange NT services is installed or removed on the primary node, Setup.exe/Update Node must be run on the secondary node, as during the initial Exchange cluster install.

Microsoft's Exchange Server 5.5 Resource Guide contains a list of Exchange components which are not supported in a cluster environment:

- Dial-up connection services including: Dynamic RAS Connector, dial-up Internet Mail Service, dial-up Internet News Service
- Microsoft Exchange Connector for IBM OfficeVision OV/VM (PROFS)
- Microsoft Exchange Connector for Lotus Notes
- Microsoft Exchange Connector for SNADS
- Microsoft Mail for AppleTalk Networks (now Quarterdeck Mail)
- Microsoft Outlook Web Access (OWA)
- X.400 Connector using X.25
- X.400 Connector using TCP/IP.

Fortunately, unsupported does not necessarily mean unstable, and some of the components can be fixed (OWA & X.400•TCP/IP), although others cannot (MS Mail for Appletalk, see Knowledge Base article Q175563). The inability of the component process to properly resolve the virtual Exchange Server resources distinctly from the physical cluster node resources appears to be the common, defining problem.

The issue with using the X.400 connector over TCP/IP in a cluster environment lies in how the remote Exchange Server is identified. If identified by IP address, an MTA communication failure results because the physical IP address of the cluster node gets substituted for the Exchange Server IP address. The solution is to identify the remote server by Exchange Server name, not IP address, on the X.400 Stack tabs of both Exchange servers. The MTAs will then connect properly.

A workable solution for Outlook Web Access is to install Internet Information Server (IIS) on both cluster nodes. Outlook Web Access will then by default establish a virtual IIS root (IIS 3.0) or instance (IIS 4.0) on the shared disk resource. After updating the secondary cluster node, each node will have an Exchange IIS virtual directory pointing identically to the shared disk. A client's browser access against the Exchange Server's virtual network name resolves properly to the IIS virtual directory via the active node.

For the remaining unsupported components, reliability testing in a non-production setting which emulates your production environment will illuminate the field support issues. Following the logic of the problems outlined above, the failure of the component process to properly resolve virtual from physical resources, may suggest fruitful avenues of investigation.

EIGHT

Cluster Performance

System performance probably generates more work and headaches for a system administrator than any other system support task. The four dreaded words to a system administrator are, "The system is slow." What is the definition of "slow?" A good definition of the word is, "Something is perceived to be moving at a rate that is less than expected." There are two key words here: "perceived" and "expected." When this definition is applied to computer system performance, the client base is usually the group that states that a system is running "slow." The first decision of an administrator is to determine whether the system is actually processing at a rate that is less than of what it is capable. If the answer is "yes", then steps must be taken to correct the problem. This is reactive performance tuning. In a perfect world, administrators are able to do pro-active performance tuning, which is fixing potential performance issues before they become an issue, but we all know the time is often unavailable to perform this task.

Before we delve into the world of Windows NT and cluster performance, let's spend a few more minutes on the definition of "slow." As you all know, it is difficult to set client expectations on system and network response time. You cannot explain to a user that his screen display is really a SQL query that travels over the routed network to a server that supports 30 other SQL users, all accessing the same disk. The client is concerned with how fast his data displays. In a previous career, I managed a data center that supported approximately 300 users. Getting the users to have a reasonable perception of response time was a difficult task. The problems generally arose when a new application was loaded, or more clients were added to use existing applications. The existing clients noticed a degradation in their response time; therefore the system was now "slow." How do you correct a slow system? Of course most systems will degrade, at least slightly, as more applications or clients are added. Along with the increased system load, now the network is supporting more traffic. I met a person once who had a very novel idea that he used, which I must state in print that I am NOT suggesting you implement. To address the above problem of clients' experiencing degraded response times as new users or applications were added, this individual actually configured a system so that it would not perform as well as it possibly could. He mistuned the system! As new users and applications were added, he repaired his tuning mistakes. This did correct users' perceptions of systems being slower, as they now generally experienced response times similar to what they had always experienced. The client base did not know that the system was performing slower than possible, because they had nothing else with which to compare the response time.

Analyzing the performance of a cluster is an extension of analyzing the performance of any Windows NT computer. Notice that I use the word, "analyze," as opposed to "tune." I make this distinction because, for the most part, Windows NT is considered to be self-tuning! For example, logic has been built into the operating system to allocate and de-allocate memory to processes as needed to minimize page faulting. Other operating systems I have worked with made the administrator define memory usage limits on a per user basis. We will discuss this in greater detail in the following pages, but for now let's assume that what we are going to do is bottleneck analysis. In other words, we will determine which system resource or resources are limiting performance.

In order to properly determine bottlenecks and successfully correct them, it is important that the administrator know something about the applications that are running on the system being analyzed. Are the CPU intensive applications, such as a CAD application? Are they I/O intensive applications, such as SQL Server? In addition, it may be necessary to have some knowledge about how those applications are being used. For example, SQL Server consumes a fair amount of memory and can generate numerous disk I/Os, but if users are issuing commands such as sorts on data, SQL Server will also consume more processor time. It is impractical to be familiar with every command your user base executes, but try to be familiar with the tasks that are performed regularly.

Analyzing System Performance

To analyze system performance, it is important to understand the basics of the operating system. I break down performance analysis into four categories that should be examined in a specific order. The reason for the specific order will be clear later. The categories that I use are:

- Memory utilization
- Disk I/O
- CPU utilization
- Network.

Network is a very ambiguous term here. Do we mean throughput on the cable? If so, that is not system performance, it is network performance analysis. We can look at network traffic, by protocol, to and from a system. This is useful in pinpointing some CPU and memory usages.

At first, it might seem important to ask about the types of the different components, such as "Are the disks SCSI or IDE?" or "How much memory is in the system?" Although this is useful information to have, we want to determine the limiting resource. It will not change our performance analysis process if we are examining an eight megabyte system or a sixty-four megabyte system. Also, the method I use to show you to analyze disks is not concerned with SCSI and IDE disk access times. It is important to know the existing hardware when the final outcome of the performance analysis is a hardware upgrade. This is not a cop-out. The last resort to alleviating bottlenecks is always to increase the hardware resource.

One more statement should be made about the philosophy of performance analysis: There is always a bottleneck on a system. The definition of a bottleneck is, "the resource that limits the ability of other resources to perform at a faster rate." The question that must be asked is, "Are users content with their current level of response?" If so, performance analysis does not need to be made at the current time.

Memory

What is Virtual Memory?

To properly analyze memory and determine whether it is a bottleneck on a system, it is necessary to understand the concept of virtual memory. The word, "virtual," means not real. Virtual memory, therefore, is memory that is not "real." It is a method employed by the operating system to give processes the capability to utilize approximately four gigabytes of what appears to be memory. Virtual memory is not unique to Windows NT. It is a widely used method of allowing more programs to run on a system than will fit into physical memory.

Windows NT is a 32-bit operating system. The largest number that can be represented using 32 bits worth of storage is approximately 4.3 billion. Since memory addresses are stored in 32 bits, 4.3 billion is also the total amount of memory, in bytes, that the operating system, or an application program, can reference. While this is an architectural limit, how many systems have 4.3 gigabytes of memory? In order to take advantage of the total range of addresses regardless of the amount of physical memory on the system, the concept of a virtual address space is used. The virtual address space is the range of possible addresses. In the case of Windows NT, the size of the virtual address space is 4.3 billion. I stated earlier that an application program can reference the entire 4.3g address range. Actually, one portion of the virtual address space is allocated to the application which the user is running, and the rest is allocated to the operating system. See Figure 8-1.

Virtual Address Space

Address 0

User Space

System Space

Address 4.3g

FIGURE 8-1 Virtual memory allocation

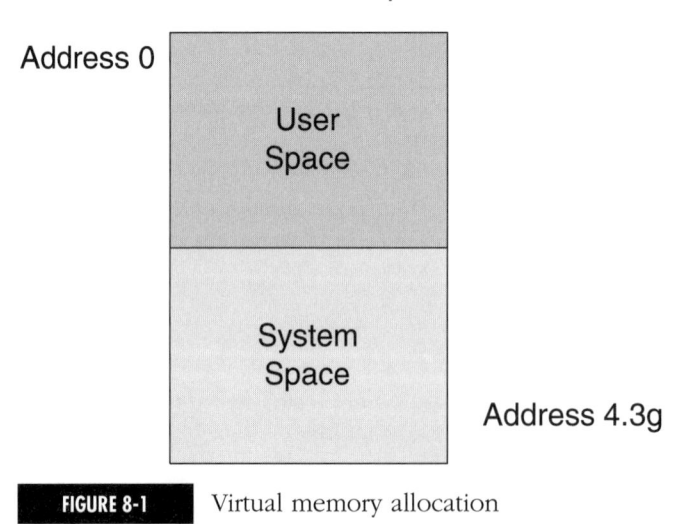

In previous versions of Windows NT, the virtual address space has always been allocated half, or 2g, for the user and the other 2g for the operating system. In Windows NT Server, Enterprise Edition, there is now an option to allocate 3g for the user space. This allows applications to become 50 percent larger, while taking away 50 percent from the operating system. This is not a performance penalty for the operating system, since it never used all of the virtual memory allocated.

Now we have a user space that can potentially address 2-3gb of memory, and this is on a per user basis. Should we all run out and buy stock in memory chip manufacturers? The concept of virtual memory solves this problem. The next concept to discuss is a page table. A page table is actually a translation table that takes a virtual address space address and returns the actually memory location the virtual address references. Every process running on the system will have its own virtual address space, and every virtual address space will have an address location 100. In order for the processes to be protected from each other, their address 100 must be a unique location in physical memory. It is the page table that stores this information. See Figure 8-2.

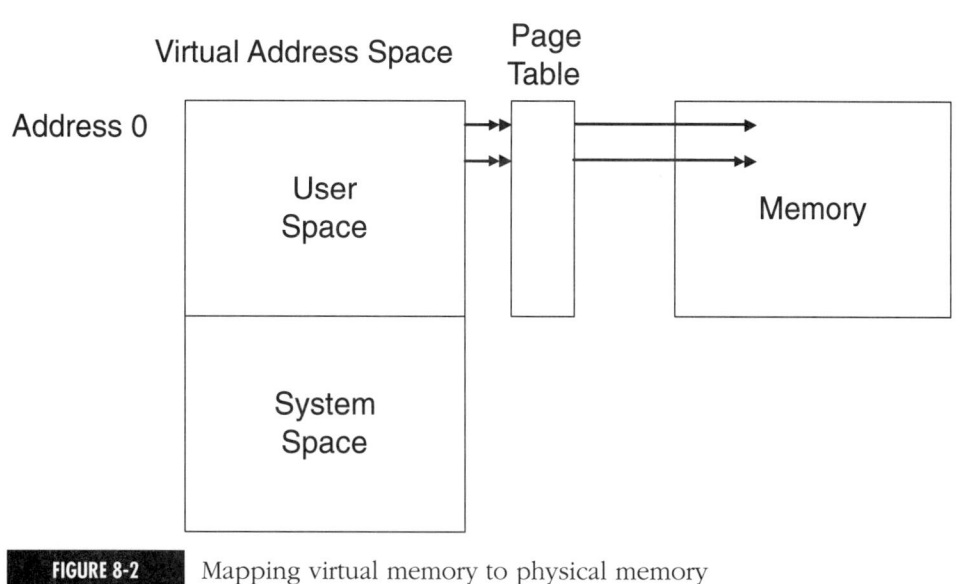

FIGURE 8-2 Mapping virtual memory to physical memory

The page table holds the actual memory address that corresponds to a virtual address. When a program is executed, it must be loaded into memory. As it is loaded, the page table is populated with the memory locations.

There are many advantages to a virtual memory model, such as memory for a given program, which does not need to be contiguous. Also, the virtual memory model makes it simple to share memory. For example, every process has a system space where the operating system code is referenced. While there is a separate page table for each user space, there is only one system space page table that all processes share. Every process now has the same pointers to physical memory in the system space. The memory is shared!

Paging

Physical memory is divided into logical units called pages. The size of a page varies with the hardware platform. Currently, the DEC Alpha uses 8192 bytes per page, while all other hardware platforms use 4096 bytes per page. Various events force data to be moved between disk and memory. This process is called paging. Paging is vital to the workings of a virtual memory operating system, though extensive paging can overload the processor and disk resources.

Although a process may have access to 2-3gb of virtual address space, Windows NT puts a limit on how much physical memory a process can own. The amount of memory currently "owned" by a process is known as its working set. Depending on the activity of the process and the amount of free memory on the system, Windows NT will increase a process working set as needed. Here is how it works. A user runs Excel. As the program is paged into memory, the page table for the process is updated with the proper memory locations. At this point, the user may have a working set size of 1 mgb. Next, the user creates a large spreadsheet. Windows NT allocates memory for the spreadsheet and updates the process page table. For this example, let's assume there is plenty of free memory, so the operating system simply increases the size of the working set for the process. When the user closes the spreadsheet, the memory allocated to store it is released. When the user exits the Excel program, the memory used to store it is released. If we examined the users' working set at this time, we would have no idea of the load they had put on memory earlier. One useful piece of information that can be retrieved from various monitoring tools is the peak working set for a process. This will tell us the largest demand that the process had placed on the system's memory resource.

Page Faulting

For the next example, let's assume the same user has just loaded the Excel program, but this time when he creates the new spreadsheet, the system does not have sufficient free memory to increase the working set size of the process to the total amount needed. For example, the operating system may allocate memory to store half the spreadsheet, but will not let the process have any more. Examine Figure 8-3.

FIGURE 8-3 Soft page faulting

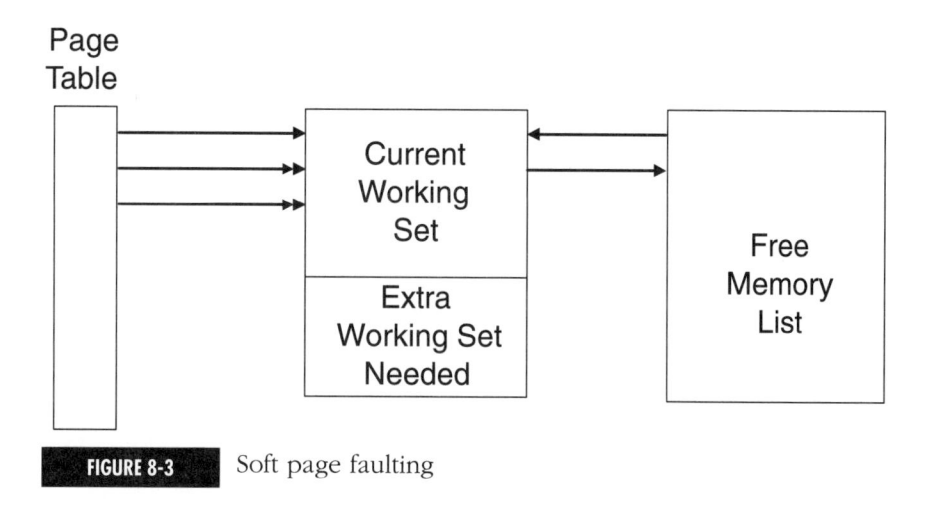

The operating system protects itself from running out of physical memory by restricting processes from allocating more memory when the amount of free memory is low. But what happens to the user running Excel that needs more memory? The operating system plays a juggling game. When the user process is not allowed to extend its working set any further, for every page of memory that it receives from the operating system, it must give one back. The page of memory given up by the process goes on the end of the free page list. This sounds worse than it is. The process retains its pointer in the page table for the page that it gives back to the operating system; it is just not part of the process working set any longer. If the process requests access to that page at a future time, the operating system must return it to the working set. This is the definition of a page fault.

There are a couple of different situations that could arise if a page given up by the process is needed again. For the first example, assume that the page released by the process is on the free page list. This is simple. The operating system gives the page back to the working set of the process, but in turn it may require another one to be released. Since the requested data is still in memory on the free page list, this is known as a soft page fault.

For our second example, assume the data in the page released by the process contains part of the Excel program. Before the process can request that the page be returned, there is a large demand on memory and the page is allocated to another process. The free page list is a common pool of memory to be used for all processes. At this point, the operating system must retrieve the Excel program from disk. This is known as a hard page fault. Hard page faults have a larger impact on performance since they involve disk I/O, one of the slower hardware components.

Page Table

Figure 8-4: Hard page faulting

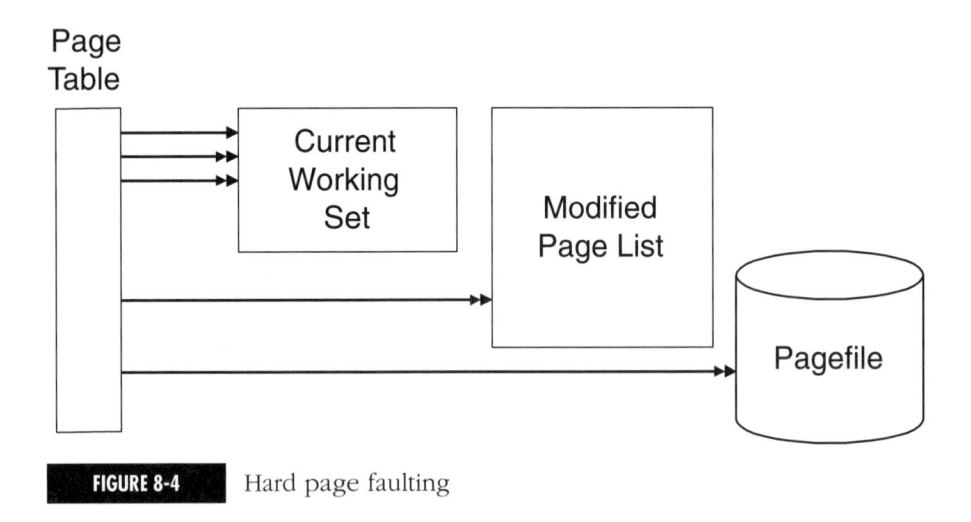

For the last example, assume that the page given up by the process does not contain a portion of the Excel Executable; instead, it contains part of the spreadsheet which the user is building. Unfortunately, if this page is placed on the free page list, works its way to the top, and is allocated to another process, the data is lost. If the page of memory released by the process has been modified by the user, the page is stored in a special location called the modified page list. The modified page list is a portion of physical memory dedicated to storing this type of data. See Figure 8-4. Since the modified page list is a fixed amount of memory, it could possibly be completely full. At this point, the data in the modified page list is copied to disk to a special file known as a page file, named pagefile.sys. During this whole process, the page table for the process still has a pointer to the data no matter where it is and can always retrieve it. If the data is retrieved from the modified page list, it is a soft page fault. If it is retrieved from the page file, it is a hard page fault. It is very important that the page file not fill up. If this happens, the modified page list will fill up next. Finally, processes will begin to hang when they need to place data in the modified page list.

Memory Pools

The Windows NT operating system has reserved areas of memory called pools. These pools of memory are used to store critical, operating system data structures. There are two types of pooled memory: paged and non-paged. The non-paged pool area is where the operating system stores its most critical information because the data is always guaranteed to be in memory, since it cannot be paged out. The sizes of the paged and non-paged pool areas are defined by the operating system, but they can be overridden in the registry. In certain situations, the system may need to create something in non-paged pool and not have sufficient memory to do so. This is called a non-paged pool failure. Non-paged pool failures usually mean that an application cannot perform its requested task.

In many situations, non-paged pool failures are associated with a misbehaving program with a "memory leak." Such a program is one that repetitively does something to allocate memory, but never frees the memory when completed. Memory leaks can be hard to find and worse, they will disappear, at least temporarily, if the system is rebooted. The Processes tab in Task Manager is a good place to start when examining memory problems.

Analyzing Memory

As mentioned earlier, page faulting occurs when a process requires more memory than its working set. If the working set for a process is large enough, the process will not page fault. Remember, however, that the working set is the amount of physical memory that a process can own, so arbitrarily allocating large working sets would severely impact how many processes the operating system can support. In a virtual memory operating system some page faulting is expected. The goal is to keep the number of page faults low.

Other operating systems I have worked with allow the system administrator to define working set values on a per user basis. This is beneficial to the administrator who dedicates the time to monitoring each user and application to determine optimal working set values. The Windows NT operating system takes a different approach; it decides on working set values and will then increase or decrease the working sets of processes as they are running in an effort to minimize page faulting. For example, a process that is generating a high number of page faults will get an increase in its working set, whereas a process that is generating no page faults may get its working set size reduced. Since working set sizes determine the extent of page faulting that occurs by adjusting the working sets for processes, Windows NT is sometimes classified as self-tuning. This is the reason for the earlier statement that in Windows NT performance analysis is performed more than performance tuning.

When analyzing memory, ask the following questions:

- Is the system generating too many page faults?
- If so, which process is generating the largest number of page faults?
- Can the amount of free memory be increased?

Performance Monitor

Standard Windows NT comes with a monitoring tool called Performance Monitor. It is useful for collecting all kinds of data, but it does not do any analysis. The interpretation of the data collected by Performance Monitor is left to the administrator. There are some standard documented values that can be compared against the data supplied by Performance Monitor to determine whether the various components of the system, CPU, memory and disk, are performing within acceptable limits.

Performance Monitor does not know anything about activity that occurred before it is started. For example, a user may call and say the system is sluggish. You start Performance Monitor and everything looks fine. The system could have had a page fault rate of fifty per second when the user noticed the system degradation, but if Performance Monitor was not running at that time, it did not collect that spike in page faults. So, should Performance Monitor be left running all the time? Some say that this in itself generates a system load. Performance Monitor has a sample interval that defines how often it should take a snapshot of the performance data. If there is a concern about Performance Monitor itself degrading the system, increase the sample interval. If you have ever taken a statistics course, you know that the more samples of data that you have, the more accurate the result. Increase the sample interval and accept the less accurate result.

Performance Monitor returns current, minimum, maximum and average data for data being collected. As a rule, be concerned about average numbers that are over acceptable limits. There will often be spikes, but if they are short, they will have only a slight impact on performance. Average numbers must be generated properly. For example, collecting data over a twenty-four hour period and looking at the average is useless information if the systems are used only eight or nine hours per day. The start and stop times for performance monitor data collection should parallel system usage.

Views

Performance Monitor supports four different "views" of the data it collects. The first and most common view is the chart view. The chart view is a graphical display of collected data.

Second is a log view. The log view is not actually a view of data at all, but is a mechanism to record data to a file to be examined at a later time, possibly in a chart.

The third view is a report. This provides very simplistic reporting of either real-time data or data retrieved from a log. To generate professional-looking reports, experiment with saving collected data as a comma-separated value (CSV) file, or a tab-separated value (TSV) file, and then importing the data into Excel or Access.

The last view is an alert. This view is very useful if implemented properly. An alert is a counter and a threshold value for that counter. As Performance Monitor runs, it compares the data collected to the threshold for defined alerts. If the data exceeds the threshold, Performance Monitor can be configured to send a message to another computer in reference to the problem counter. The messages appear as a pop-up window, similar to the "Send Message" utility. This is handy for an administrator who manages many systems, as all systems could be configured to send alerts to the computer the administrator normally uses.

Counters

Counters are the raw data that is collected by Performance Monitor. Most counters provide detail on the minimum, maximum, and average values collected for the counter since Performance Monitor was started. Average values are the most important when looking for trends in system performance. Remember to get a large enough sample so that the average numbers show realistic data. For example, monitoring between the hours of eight and nine a.m. will give different results from monitoring between the hours of twelve a.m. and one p.m. if your office follows a normal lunch schedule.

There are a couple of counters that are not collecting by default. For example, disk I/O counters are not automatically collected. The argument is that collecting performance data for disks can itself contribute to system degradation. Therefore, it is necessary to manually activate the collection of disk counters by issuing the command, "Diskperf –Y." If the disk configuration includes disk RAID sets, the command is "Diskperf –YE." This enables the collection of disk counters until manually disabled with the command "Diskperf –N."

Another component that is not configured for performance data collection by default is the TCP/IP protocol stack. In order to collect and view TCP/IP traffic, it is necessary to load the SNMP, Simple Network Management Protocol, software that ships with Windows NT.

Objects and Instances

When a system is monitored, it is actually monitoring the behavior of its objects, such as processes, threads, memory, etc. In Windows NT, an object is the standard mechanism for identifying and using system resources. There are object types and instances of objects. An example of an object type is a process. When a process is created by the operating system, it has actually created an instance of the process object.

In the Performance Monitor utility, an object can loosely be defined as a category of counters. For example, when the "Process" object is selected, all counters pertinent to analyzing the performance of a process will be made available.

Depending on the object selected, one or more instances may be available for monitoring purposes. For example, the process object will have an instance for every process currently running on the system. This is useful when it has already been determined the system as a whole is overloaded, and the next step is to narrow it down to a specific process. The administrator can simply select a process, such as SQL Server, and monitor various activities, such as its page faulting rate and user time consumption.

Some objects contain an instance named "Total." This provides an easy method to get resource usage for all instances of the object. For example, an administrator might want to know the total of all process working sets. This is easily obtained by selecting the process object, the total instance, and the working set counter.

Certain objects and their associated counters are present on all systems. Other counters, however, are application specific. For example, SQL Server and Exchange Server will install new objects and counters when the software is loaded.

Analyzing Disk Activity

The disk hardware is one of the slowest hardware components of the overall system. Because it is slow by nature, a bottleneck in the disk subsystem is magnified. Thankfully, faster disk configurations are appearing on a regular basis, but this does not help if money has already been invested in a disk configuration that cannot be replaced every six to twelve months. Disk hardware generally consists of two components: the disk and the controller. It is usually the disk that is the source of a bottleneck if there is one, but do not discount the possibility of the controller as a potential bottleneck. With the number of devices that can be connected to a SCSI bus, it deserves to be analyzed.

Lazy Writes

Since the disk subsystem is one of the slower parts of the computer, the less time the operating system spends transferring data to or from the disk, the better the system will perform. The amount of data a program usually reads or writes is relatively small. Approximately seventy to eighty percent of the total time a disk access takes is hardware-related. The hardware time involved does not change significantly based on the size of the disk I/O being performed. Therefore, if larger amounts of data can be transferred between memory and disk at one time, the average time per disk I/O is reduced. This is the concept of a lazy write. An application program issues writes to the disk. The operating system lets the application think the disk write is completed, but actually the data is saved in memory. At a later time, when there is enough data, or when the system is less busy, the data is written to the disk. This mechanism limits the number of times the disk hardware is accessed. Depending on the application, slight risks can arise from lazy writing. For example, assume an application uses two files to store data. The application could issue two writes, one to each file; one may get written, and the other could be cached by the lazy write mechanism. Now assume there is a power failure. The second file was never actually updated, and now the files are out of sync.

The action on lazy writing is the default for the Windows NT operating system. It is the responsibility of the application developer to disable lazy write support within the application.

The act of lazy writing can lead to confusing displays in Performance Monitor. For example, a program that is performing lazy writes will show little or no disk activity for a period of time, then show a large spike on disk data transfers. At first glance, this may seem to be a problem, but in reality it is not. One lengthy disk access will take less time overall than the same amount of data broken up into smaller disk I./Os.

Another misleading feature of lazy writing is that it makes the processor resource appear busier. This is because the operating system is not issuing a large number of disk I/Os that can cause the processor to wait for the I/O to complete before it resumes processing. For example, a processor running an application updating a file may appear fifty percent busy without lazy writing enabled and ninety-five percent busy with lazy-writing enabled. The information that is not available is that the application would complete much faster with lazy writing enabled because the processor is more efficient by saving the disk writes and performing a large number of writes at one time. For example, the application may run for five minutes without lazy writing enabled with processor time accounting for fifty percent, or two and one-half minutes. With lazy writing, the application may complete in two minutes, with the application accounting for ninety-five percent of the time. Has a processor bottleneck been introduced to alleviate a disk bottleneck.? No. Lazy writing will make better use of the processor because the waiting by the processor on disk I/Os to complete has been minimized. The application still consumes the same amount of processor time, but over a smaller elapsed time period. Since applications will use the processor at a greater rate with lazy writing enabled, application response times can be impacted in unforeseen ways. The main idea is that more of the potential processor time is available to applications, which should increase throughput.

It is useful to know if an application supports lazy writing or not, especially when evaluating the disk subsystem in Performance Monitor.

Disk Queues

All the different types of disk hardware can make evaluations confusing. For example, which is closer to being a bottleneck, a disk with a 12 millisecond access time performing 25 I/Os per second, or a disk with a 15 millisecond access time performing 20 I/Os per second? There are algorithms to calculate the average response time for a disk and compare that value to acceptable ranges. It is not necessary to perform those calculations. It is possible to determine how busy any disk is by examining its queue length. A disk queue is the number of outstanding I/Os that have been issued to a disk but are in a waiting state because the disk is busy serving another I/O request. The nice feature about the disk queue length is that it is not necessary to know the relative speed of the disks being analyzed. A disk with a 10 millisecond access time and a queue length of 1 is just as overloaded as a disk with a 15 millisecond access time and a queue length of 1.

Disk queues can be examined at the physical disk and logical disk levels. To determine whether or not a disk is a bottleneck, examine the physical disk queue length. Once it is determined that a specific disk is overloaded, examine the queue length of each logical drive on the disk. This may help determine which application is the cause of the excessive I/O requests.

> Object: Physical Disk or Logical Disk
> Counter: Current Disk Queue Length
> What to look for: The average queue length should be less than 2 for the physical disk.

File System Caches

The file system cache is a portion of physical memory reserved for frequently used file system data, which is any information that is necessary to retrieve a file from disk. The directory entry for a file is an example of data that can be stored in the file system cache. The NT file system is a b-tree directory structure. Think of it as like an inverted tree with many branches, with files at the very end of the smallest branches, like leaves. To locate a file on a disk, it is necessary to traverse the entire tree from top to bottom, eventually reaching the file entry. Every branch is a possible disk I/O. It is possible for one file access to generate 3 or more disk I/Os. The file system cache stores recently and frequently used portions of the tree. Any time the file system, or "tree" data, can be located in memory, as opposed to reading the data from the disk, performance will be improved. Again, this is because the disk is one of the slowest, if not the slowest, hardware components.

The memory resource is critical to file system caching. If the amount of free memory on a Windows NT system drops below 4MB, the memory allocated for file system caching is reclaimed by the operating system, to solve the shortage of available memory.

Object: Memory
Counter: Cache bytes
What to look for: This is the size of the file system cache. It should not be zero.

Object: Cache
Counter: MDL Read Hits %
What to look for: This is the percentage of time that data is found in the cache. Anything over 70% is good.

Analyzing Processor Activity

The processor is probably the easiest of the major components of the hardware to analyze. Every process running on the system is competing for processor time. There is an operating system component called the scheduler that decides which process uses the processor. A process uses the CPU for a period of time known as a time slice. When a process has used its time slice, the scheduler will move another process into the CPU. The scheduler makes its decision based on the priority of all processes waiting to use the CPU.

The main question when examining the CPU resource as a potential bottleneck is, "How busy is the processor?" This is represented as a percentage value, such as sixty percent. If your processor shows one hundred percent busy, you may feel that you are getting your money's worth from the system, but this is not the case. As a general rule, a processor should not average more than seventy to eighty percent busy.

When analyzing processor performance, ask the following questions:

- Is the processor averaging more than seventy percent busy?
- Is there a processor queue? If not, the CPU is probably not a bottleneck at this time.
- If yes, is the majority user time or privileged time?
- If privileged time, is there a memory or disk resource bottleneck?
- If user time, what process is consuming the majority of the CPU resource?
- Can the amount of CPU activity be reduced?

User Time

Processor usage is divided into two categories: user time and privileged time. User time is generally considered to be running application code, not operating system code. For example, the amount of processor time spent executing instructions from a program such as Excel is classified as user time. This should be the majority of processor usage.

> Object: Processor
> Counter: User time
> What to look for: This value should be 60% or more of total processor time in use. If it is less, this is a sign of excessive operating system overhead such as paging, disk activity or interrupts.

Privileged Time

Privileged time is processor time consumed running operating system code as opposed to user application code. Examples of privileged time include performing disk I/O and handling page faults generated by a user process. It is easy to get led down the wrong path here. Overloaded memory and disk resources can generate what appear to be processor bottlenecks by generating a lot of privileged mode activity. This is the reason that the memory and disk resources should be analyzed before the processor resource. Problems that are discovered with the disk and memory components should be resolved before doing a thorough analysis of the processor.

> Object: Processor
> Counter: Privileged time
> What to look for: The value should be 40% or less of total processor time in use.

Processor Queue

A processor queue is the list of threads that are waiting to use the processor while it is occupied. The processor queue length is the best measure of whether the CPU is a bottleneck or not, even better than processor utilization. Here is why. A program that performs no I/O and does only calculations can make the processor appear to be between ninety and one hundred percent busy, especially if it is the only process that currently needs the CPU. To the untrained observer, a processor bottleneck may be declared; however, one doesn't necessarily exist. What if the processor queue length is zero? This means there are no jobs waiting to use the CPU. Can there really be a bottleneck if no processes are getting blocked from using the processor? In the situation where a processor does show ninety to one hundred percent busy, but the processor queue length is low, the CPU is not currently a bottleneck; however, adding new applications or users could lead to creating a processor bottleneck.

The one situation where the processor can be considered a bottleneck with no processor queue is when one extremely intensive CPU application is running, such as a CAD application. The response time of the application in this case will correlate directly with the speed of the processor.

Object: System
Counter: Processor Queue Length
What to look for: The average queue length should be less than .2.

Analyzing Network Activity

It does not matter how well the cluster nodes are running if the network between the client and the server is experiencing performance problems. Network performance can be impacted by numerous factors. The network might be busy because of large print jobs being transmitted or numerous file transfers. The network can also be impacted by malfunctioning devices introducing "noise" to the cable. Since Ethernet is single-channel, meaning that only one device transmits successfully at any point in time, a faulty network device can slow an entire network segment.

Network Monitor

The Network Monitor utility has functionality similar to a network sniffer. It collects network traffic and does basic analysis, such as which node is sending the most data, or which node is destination for the majority of the network traffic. The Network Monitor utility does not take the place of components such as sniffers. There is information necessary to network administrators that Network Monitor does not provide, such as the rate of collisions on the cable. A collision occurs when two systems attempt to use an Ethernet cable at the same time. When this happens, there is no guarantee that either packet will reach its destination. The sending systems can detect a collision and resend the packet in question. The number, or rate, of collisions is useful to determine what kind of true throughput is achieved on an Ethernet segment. On a 10MB Ethernet segment, 3-4MB of throughput is what can be expected normally.

Network has two distinct components. First is the Network Monitor agent, which collects the data from the network. The second piece of the software is the Network Monitor tool, which accepts information from the Network Monitor agent and displays it graphically.

There are two versions of the Network Monitor utility. The first one ships with Windows NT. This version of Network Monitor has only the capability to examine and analyze the network traffic to or from the node on which it is installed. This is useful for examining whether the network for a given server is busy, but it does not give any information regarding the overall load on the network cable.

The second version of Network Monitor is bundled in with Microsoft's Systems Management Server product, which is part of the BackOffice suite of products. This version of Network Monitor is a more complete solution in that it monitors all traffic on a network segment. It also has the capability to monitor remote network segments by attaching to remote Network Monitor agents. This can be useful in a support desk situation where clients are on various network segments.

Cluster Performance

The first step in analyzing a cluster's performance is to view each cluster member independently. The Windows NT environment on each node is totally separate. The only normal communications that occur between nodes are the heartbeat packets used to determine whether cluster members are online or offline. The amount of network traffic is minimal. Recall that the Cluster Server software can use a separate cable for cluster communications. This includes the heartbeat messages and any cluster group movement between members due to a failure or a request initiated by the Cluster Administrator utility.

To achieve best performance, balance the load between cluster members. Let's briefly review each primary system component and discuss possible balancing techniques.

Memory

The primary clue that a memory bottleneck exists is page faulting. If both cluster members are similar in hardware configurations, first split the load of four applications by placing two on each processor. However, this does not take into account the memory consumption and processing characteristics of the individual applications. One poorly written application can generate as many page faults as three or more efficiently designed programs. By using Task Manager and Performance Monitor, the amount of page faulting for each application can be determined.

Should applications be allocated between cluster members to minimize page faulting or to balance the amount of free memory? There is a performance penalty when the amount of free memory drops below 4MB. Memory normally used for file system caching is reclaimed, disabling caching for the most part. It should be a high priority to guarantee that both cluster members have at least 4-6MB of free memory.

If a resource is moved between cluster nodes to relocate a portion of the page faulting activity, the potential exists for an increase in disk I/O. This will occur if the page faults incurred by the cluster member are hard page faults. If the cluster member is already incurring waits on disk I/Os, reconsider moving the cluster resource. Processor activity will increase with the number of page faults because a page fault is an operating system routine. If the processor is already recording a high percentage of privileged time, again reconsider moving the application.

Disk I/O

Keep in mind when analyzing disk I/O performance that "Less is more." The fewer disk I/Os that are performed, the better system performance will be. Since a disk can be accessed by only one cluster member, balancing the I/Os between cluster members is not an option. Even if it were, splitting I/Os to a single disk between two or more computers does not make the disk hardware work any less. Actually, it would possibly make it work more because the various computers would probably be reading data at different locations on the disk!

The goal is to spread the I/Os across the different physical disk resources to achieve the lowest possible I/O wait times, not to balance the number of I/Os. Balancing the number of I/Os across the different disk resources does not take into account variables such as the relative speed of each disk or the size of the disk I/O being performed. To accomplish this, first monitor the disk queue length of each of the disk resources. If disk queues are out of balance, even them out by moving applications between disks. One of the problems with a tool such as Performance Monitor is that it does not supply information on what are sometimes called "hot" files. These are the target of the majority of the disk I/Os. There is no clean way to determine which application is generating the disk I/Os, since I/O rates cannot be monitored by process. If the physical disk resource is divided into multiple logical drives, the counter "Logical Disk" in Performance Monitor will display the amount of disk I/O to each logical drive. This should help to determine which applications are generating the most disk I/Os.

If possible, take advantage of file system caching to alleviate any disk I/O problems. Experiment with locating the more I/O intensive applications on the cluster member that has more memory available. The cluster member should have a larger file system cache, which may in turn reduce disk I/Os.

Processor

You may recall that processor time consists of user time and privileged time. Privileged time occurs when the operating system is performing work outside the applications that are currently running. Page faulting and disk I/O are good examples of events that consume privileged time. If the memory and disk I/O resources have already been analyzed and the load allocated between the cluster members, the processor privileged time is inherently balanced between processors.

Privileged time is not generally the largest consumer of processor time. If it is, this is a problem that needs to be analyzed. Generally, the majority of processor time should be in user mode. This is the time spent actually executing the code of the applications that are currently running.

The goal is to allocate cluster resources between the cluster members and balance the amount of processor time used. This will give the best possible response times to clients of all applications.

If a situation arises where one application is considered to have a higher degree of importance, an arbitrary decision must be made regarding how much more of the processing load must be shifted to one of the cluster members. As a rule, a processor should never be loaded to the point where it runs continually busy seventy percent of the time or more.

NINE

Cluster Troubleshooting

Troubleshooting is one of the most aggravating tasks an administrator must perform, but at the same time, one of the most gratifying. All the time invested and mistakes made are forgotten as the adrenaline rush from solving a new problem occurs. As we gloat over our success, we ponder whether we should document our victory or let the same problem challenge the troubleshooting skills of someone else.

In my opinion, troubleshooting should be a methodical process. I have seen many individuals troubleshoot by randomly trying various combinations until the problem goes away. This usually works, but being methodical can narrow down the possible cause of the problem faster. I use what I once heard called "the divide and conquer" method, which involves making one change that eliminates one possible cause of the problem. For example, if a client cannot access a server, you may want to use the "ping" utility to verify potential connectivity between the client and the server. If the ping utility is successful, the network is functional, and you move on to another test. If the test fails, the network may be having a problem. Next, attempt to ping devices between the client and the server such as routers to isolate the segment or router that may be malfunctioning.

Successful troubleshooting requires knowledge in many areas, such as NetBIOS, network protocols, network hardware, computer hardware, Windows NT security, and Window NT performance. To test and eliminate various components as potential problems, it is necessary to know what tool to use. For example, the ping utility tests the ability of two computers to communicate via TCP/IP. The "NET VIEW \\computername" command, however, tests NetBIOS connectivity. If TCP/IP is the only protocol loaded, the "net view" command, if successful, proves that both TCP/IP and NetBIOS are functional.

Portions of this chapter will repeat material from previous chapters. Some new information will also be provided. The goal of this chapter is to give a cluster administrator consolidated information on how to troubleshoot various cluster problems that could arise.

Troubleshooting Tools

Successful troubleshooting begins by using the correct tool for the problem. Windows NT provides many such tools. Each one is useful for testing one or more components of the operating system.

Disk Administrator

A successful installation of Cluster Server requires that both cluster members assign the same drive letters for the partitions on the shared SCSI bus. This is accomplished with the Disk Administrator utility. The same feature of Disk Administrator that allows the administrator to properly configure drive letters also allows drive letter problems to be introduced. If an administrator changes drive letter assignments to a device on the shared SCSI bus, but fails to perform the same configuration on the other cluster member, problems will result. The Disk Administrator utility can be used to view drive letter assignments. If a mismatch in drive letters occurs, use the "Assign drive letter" option under "Tools" to again make the drive letters consistent between cluster members. Disk Administrator can also be used to determine which cluster member has control of a disk. See Figure 9-1. This is useful when there are problems bringing resources, such as the quorum resource, online. The cluster member that has control of the disk will properly display the partition information of the disk. The cluster member that does not have control of the device will display an entry for the device with the text, "Configuration information not available."

FIGURE 9-1 Examining disk configuration with Disk Administrator

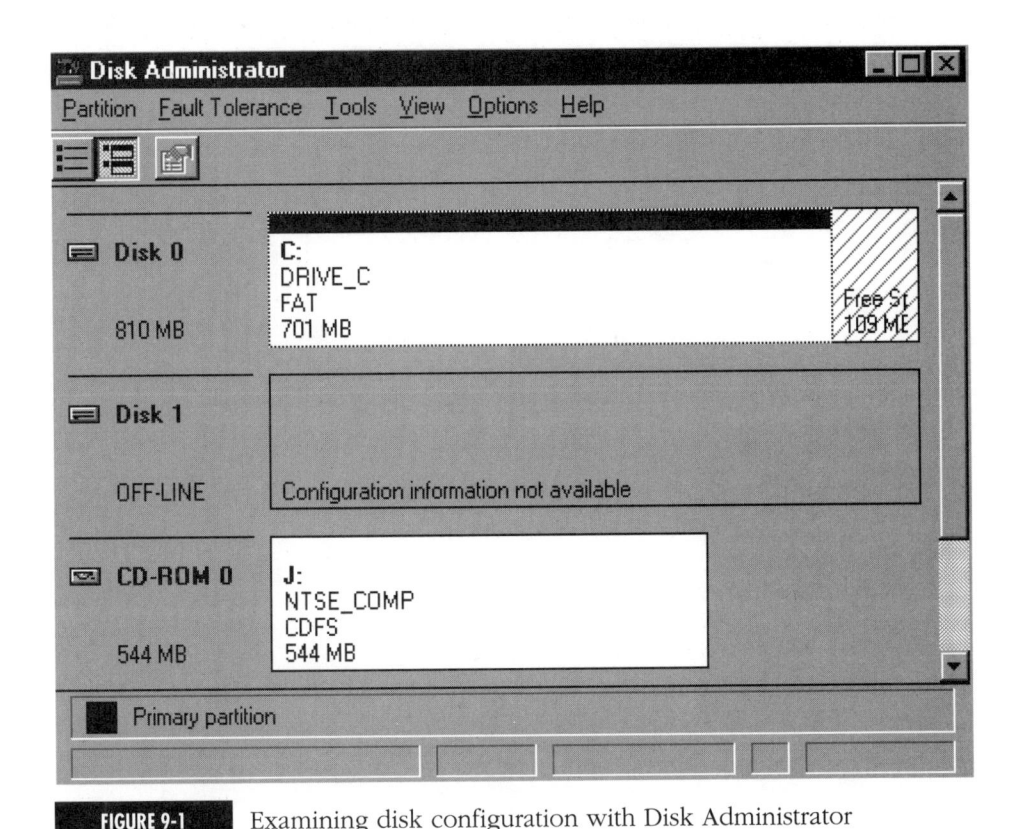

Task Manager

The Task Manager program allows the administrator to perform a quick view of the operating system and its current load. Task Manager is invoked by right-mouse clicking on the taskbar and selecting the "Task Manager" option. Task Manager allows three different views of the operating system. The first one is the "Applications" view, which shows what Windows applications are running. This view can be used to terminate a malfunctioning application by highlighting the application and selecting the "End Task" button. This view is the equivalent of the Windows task list.

The second view offered by Task Manager is the "Processes" view. See Figure 9-2. The "Processes" view displays all processes currently running on the system. The amount of activity that is displayed for a process is the amount of activity by the process since it was created. If the Task Manager utility is closed, it has no effect on the counters. For example, the CPU time displayed for a process will be the total amount of CPU time the process has consumed since the process was created. Processes created by the Cluster

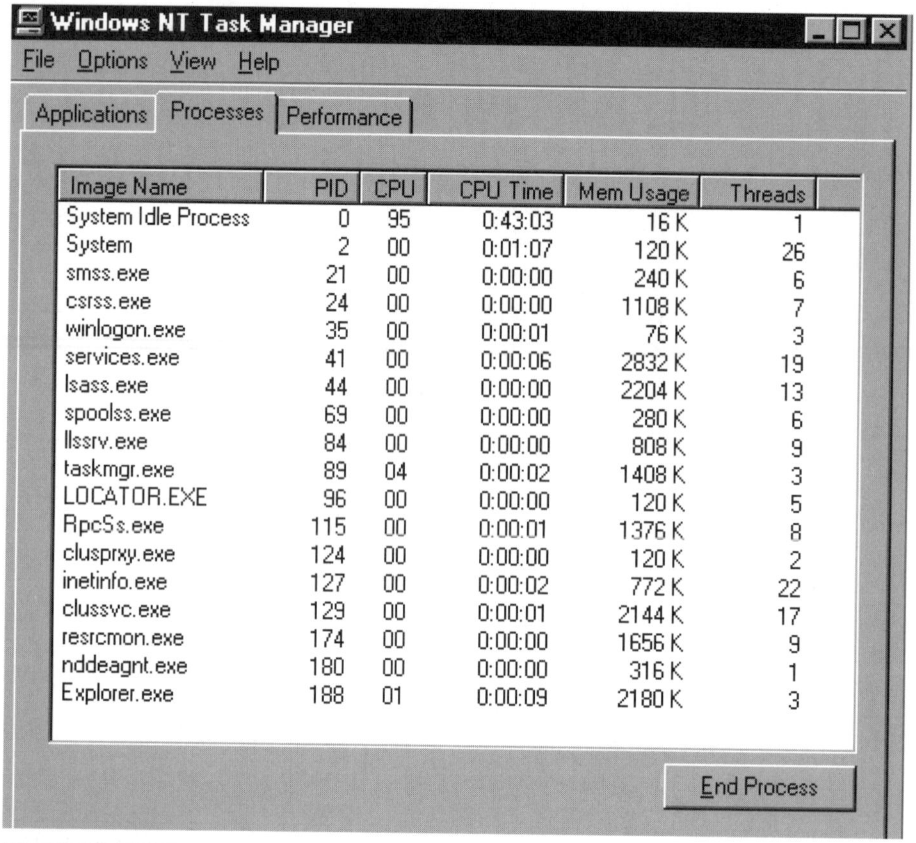

Windows NT Task Manager

File Options View Help

Applications | Processes | Performance

Image Name	PID	CPU	CPU Time	Mem Usage	Threads
System Idle Process	0	95	0:43:03	16 K	1
System	2	00	0:01:07	120 K	26
smss.exe	21	00	0:00:00	240 K	6
csrss.exe	24	00	0:00:00	1108 K	7
winlogon.exe	35	00	0:00:01	76 K	3
services.exe	41	00	0:00:06	2832 K	19
lsass.exe	44	00	0:00:00	2204 K	13
spoolss.exe	69	00	0:00:00	280 K	6
llssrv.exe	84	00	0:00:00	808 K	9
taskmgr.exe	89	04	0:00:02	1408 K	3
LOCATOR.EXE	96	00	0:00:00	120 K	5
RpcSs.exe	115	00	0:00:01	1376 K	8
clusprxy.exe	124	00	0:00:00	120 K	2
inetinfo.exe	127	00	0:00:02	772 K	22
clussvc.exe	129	00	0:00:01	2144 K	17
resrcmon.exe	174	00	0:00:00	1656 K	9
nddeagnt.exe	180	00	0:00:00	316 K	1
Explorer.exe	188	01	0:00:09	2180 K	3

End Process

FIGURE 9-2 Displaying process list with Task Manager

Server software can be monitored for activity. The processes pertinent to the Cluster are:

- Clussvc.exe (This is the main cluster service.)
- Clusprxy.exe
- Resrcmon.exe

Use the "Processes" display to determine if any of the cluster related processes are logging any CPU activity. The cluster processes will not log any activity unless a request is sent to the process. For example, the clussvc process logs CPU activity when the Cluster Administrator utility is executed and makes a connection to the Cluster Service. A resource monitor logs CPU time when one of the resources it manages has activity. There is other process-related data that can be displayed, such as the number of page faults. To add or remove columns from the window, use the "View" menu

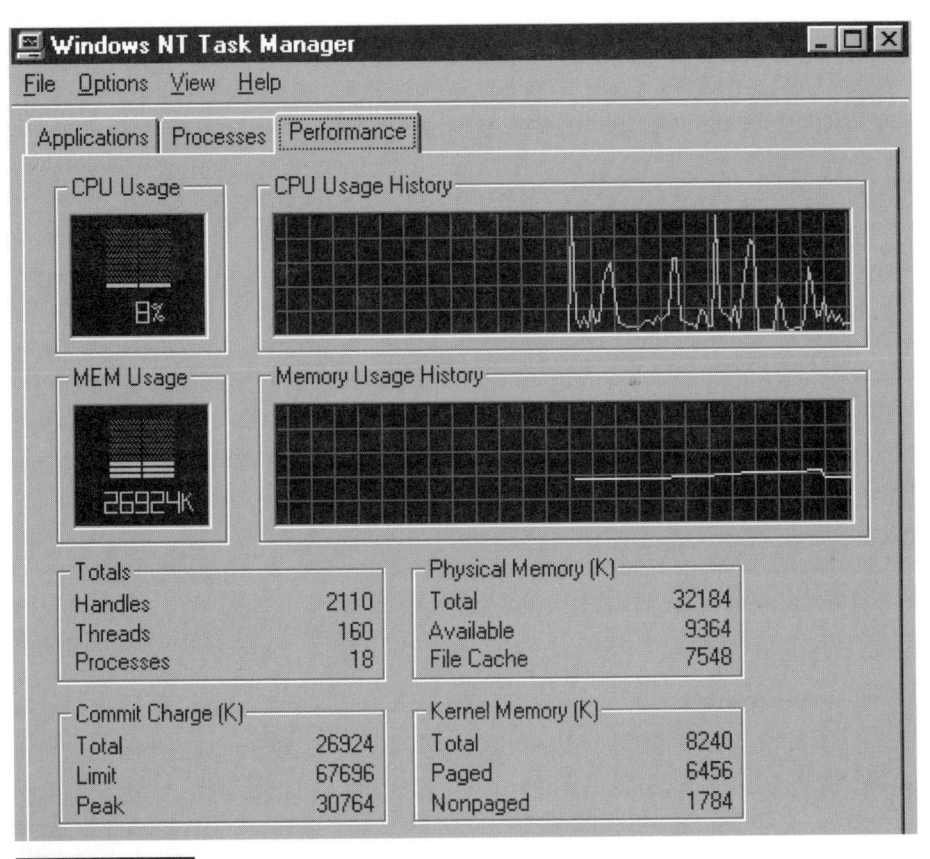

FIGURE 9-3   Examining system performance with Task Manager

option and then the "Select Columns" option. Make changes to the fields displayed by selecting and de-selecting the appropriate fields.

The "Performance" display gives a quick overview of the load on various system resources such as processor and memory consumption. See Figure 9-3. Use this display to determine if the system is being overloaded. If it is, further analysis with Performance Monitor may be necessary.

Useful items in the performance display include the size of the file cache and the number of handles. The file cache keeps certain data read from the disk in memory. If this data is needed again, a disk I/O is saved. When free memory is limited, the size of the file cache is reduced. The impact is more physical disk activity, which is slow compared to retrieving the same data from memory.

The amount of available memory is important. There should always be at least 4 to 6MB of free memory on a system.

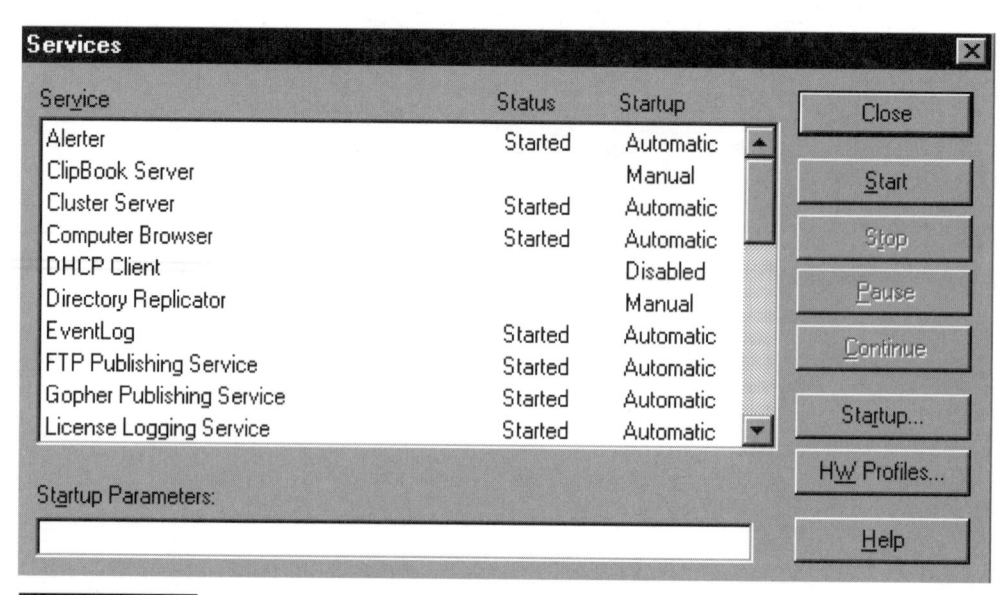

Services option in Control Panel

FIGURE 9-4 Displaying service list with the Services program

The Services option in Control Panel can be used to verify that the Cluster related services are running. See Figure 9-4. These services include the Cluster Server, the Remote Procedure Call Service, and the Time Service. The Cluster Server and RPC Service should have a status of "Started." The exception is the Time Service, which is started by the Cluster Server software when necessary. Services have configuration information that is accessed by mouse-clicking twice on the specific service. See Figure 9-5. For example, if it becomes necessary to change the password for the account under which the Cluster Server service is running, it must be changed in User Manager and also in the Service properties.

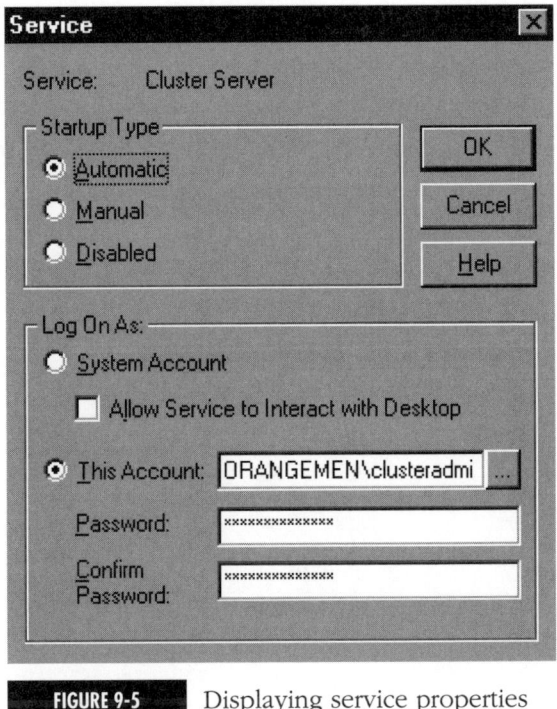

FIGURE 9-5 Displaying service properties

Services also have the option of accepting one or more startup parameters. The Cluster Service has parameters to fix certain problems that may arise. The parameters are discussed in more detail later. To pass a startup parameter to a service, do the following:

1. Stop the service by highlighting the service and selecting the "Stop" option.
2. Enter the data to be supplied to the service in the Startup Parameters box on the Services screen. See Figure 9-4.
3. Restart the service by selecting the "Start" option.

Startup parameters are not saved. If the service is stopped and started, it will run without the startup parameter. To restart the service with the startup value, the data must be re-entered into the Startup Parameters box.

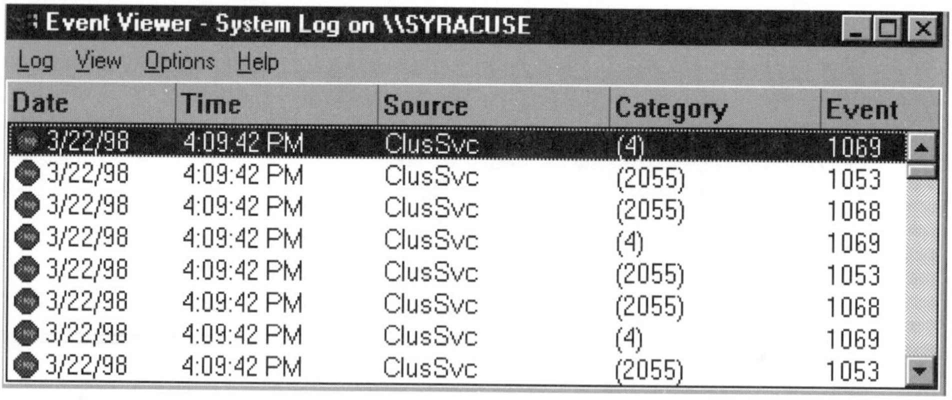
Event Viewer - System Log on \\SYRACUSE
Log View Options Help
Date Time Source Category Event
3/22/98 4:09:42 PM ClusSvc (4) 1069
3/22/98 4:09:42 PM ClusSvc (2055) 1053
3/22/98 4:09:42 PM ClusSvc (2055) 1068
3/22/98 4:09:42 PM ClusSvc (4) 1069
3/22/98 4:09:42 PM ClusSvc (2055) 1053
3/22/98 4:09:42 PM ClusSvc (2055) 1068
3/22/98 4:09:42 PM ClusSvc (4) 1069
3/22/98 4:09:42 PM ClusSvc (2055) 1053

FIGURE 9-6 Displaying recent system events with Event Viewer

Event Viewer

The Event Viewer utility displays the Windows NT logging files. It is located in the Administrative Tools group. There are actually three logs that can be viewed through Event Viewer. The Cluster Server software writes messages into the system log. See Figure 9-6.

The cluster administrator should review the logs in Event Viewer regularly, even when there are no noticeable problems. If there is an entry in the event log, the detail can be displayed by double-clicking on the entry. See Figure 9-7.

Net Helpmsg

The command "net helpmsg error-number," when issued from a command prompt, displays the text message of the error number supplied. This is very useful because often, program error handling displays only an error number. See Figure 9-8.

Nine • Cluster Troubleshooting 233

Event Detail

Date: 3/22/98   Event ID: 1053
Time: 4:09:42 PM   Source: ClusSvc
User: N/A   Type: Error
Computer: SYRACUSE   Category: (2055)

Description:
Cluster File Share 'share1' cannot be brought online because the share could not be created.

FIGURE 9-7 Displaying event details

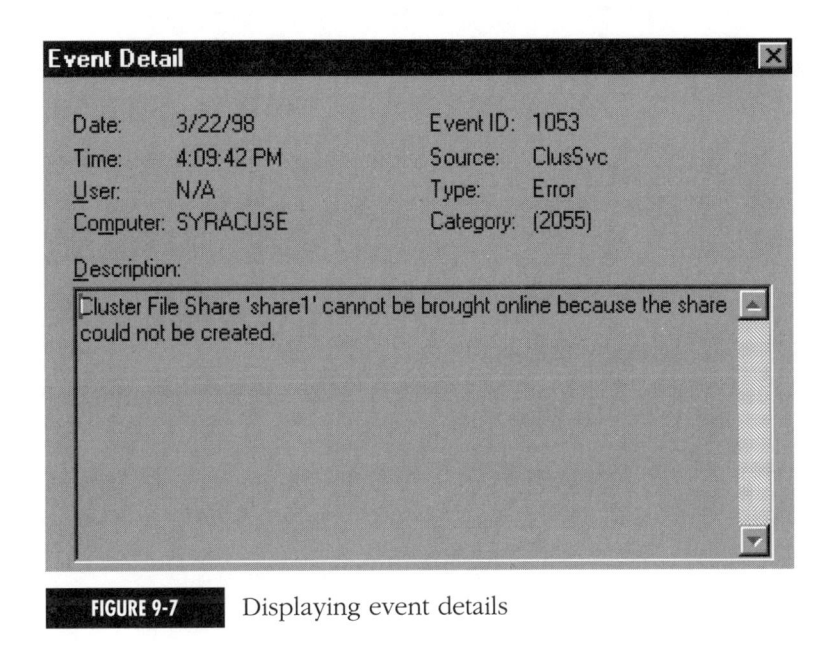

In this example, the error number to be translated is 5. The error text for error number 5 is "Access is Denied." This utility works for most errors encountered.

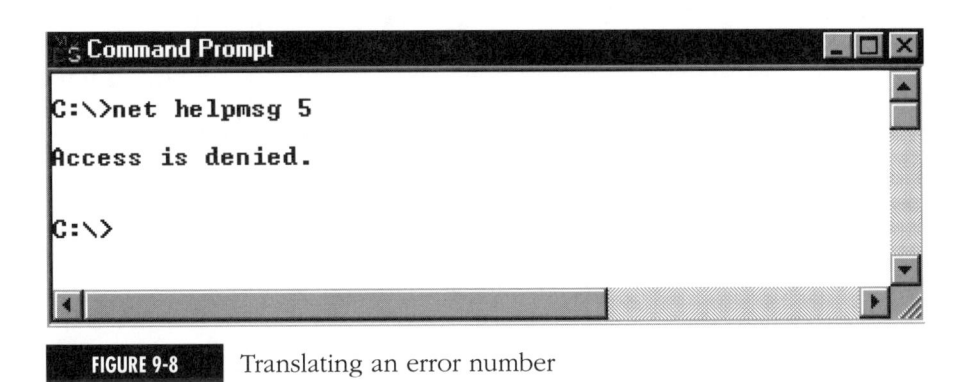

Command Prompt

```
C:\>net helpmsg 5

Access is denied.

C:\>
```

FIGURE 9-8 Translating an error number

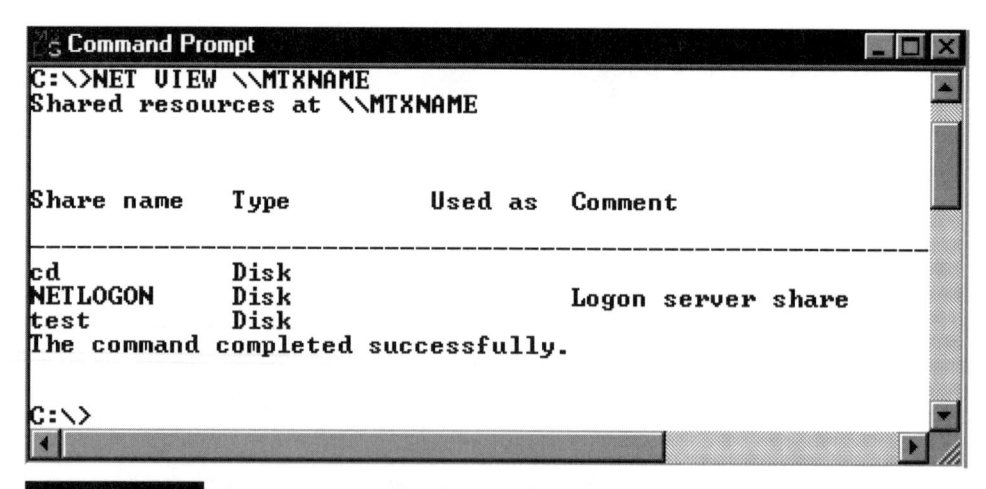

```
Command Prompt
C:\>NET VIEW \\MTXNAME
Shared resources at \\MTXNAME


Share name    Type          Used as   Comment
-------------------------------------------------------
cd            Disk
NETLOGON      Disk                    Logon server share
test          Disk
The command completed successfully.

C:\>
```

FIGURE 9-9   Displaying the file shares offered by a network name resource

Net View

The command, "net view \\computername," or, "net view \\network_name," tests the ability to connect to a server with NetBIOS. See Figure 9-9. This is useful in testing whether file share resources are available or testing the validity of any cluster network name resource. If the command fails, it does not prove that NetBIOS is not functioning. The problem could be with NetBIOS name resolution. To test whether NetBIOS name resolution is the problem, issue the command, "net view \\ip_address." This command is new with Window NT V4.0. If this command works and the first one does not, NetBIOS is functional, but NetBIOS name resolution is not working properly.

Ping Utility

The ping utility is a TCP/IP connection test. Since the cluster server software works only with TCP/IP protocol, it is the only protocol that must be tested to troubleshoot cluster problems. To test whether TCP/IP is functional between a client and the cluster, or between cluster members, issue the command, "ping host_name," where host_name is the name of the system that is encountering connection problems. If the command is successful, TCP/IP is functional. If the command is not successful, some of the possible problems are:

- An invalid TCP/IP address, subnet mask, or router entry on the server or client
- A network failure between the client and the server
- Host name resolution is not working properly.

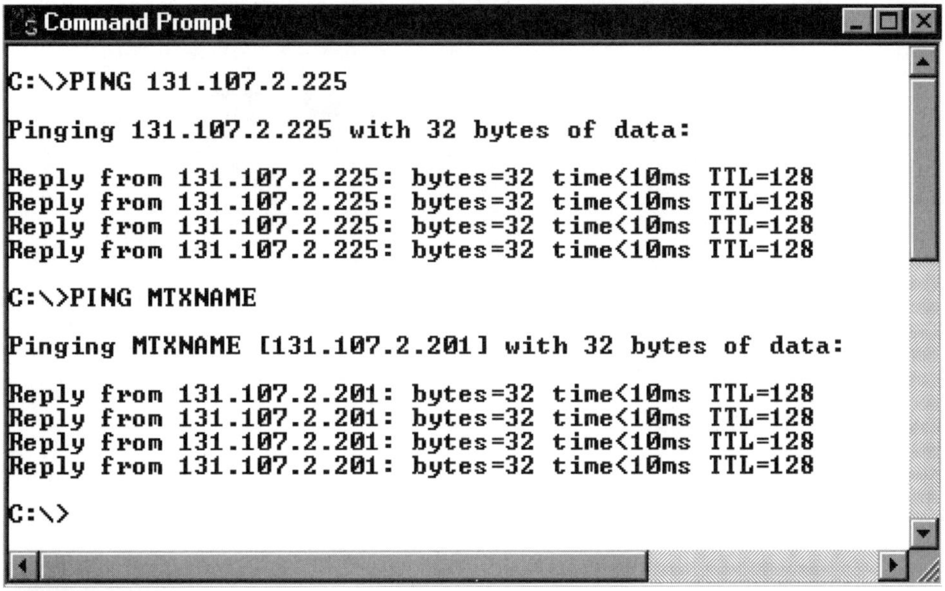

```
Command Prompt

C:\>PING 131.107.2.225

Pinging 131.107.2.225 with 32 bytes of data:

Reply from 131.107.2.225: bytes=32 time<10ms TTL=128
Reply from 131.107.2.225: bytes=32 time<10ms TTL=128
Reply from 131.107.2.225: bytes=32 time<10ms TTL=128
Reply from 131.107.2.225: bytes=32 time<10ms TTL=128

C:\>PING MTXNAME

Pinging MTXNAME [131.107.2.201] with 32 bytes of data:

Reply from 131.107.2.201: bytes=32 time<10ms TTL=128
Reply from 131.107.2.201: bytes=32 time<10ms TTL=128
Reply from 131.107.2.201: bytes=32 time<10ms TTL=128
Reply from 131.107.2.201: bytes=32 time<10ms TTL=128

C:\>
```

FIGURE 9-10 Testing an IP address resource with the "ping" command

To determine if host name resolution is the problem, issue the command, "ping address," where address is the TCP/IP address of the system being tested. If pinging by TCP/IP address is successful, but pinging by name fails, the problem is with host name resolution.

A slight anomaly occurs when testing network name and IP address resources with the ping utility. In Figure 9-10, the IP address resource of 131.107.2..225 is tested. Also, the network name of MTXNAME, which has a dependency on the same IP address resource is tested. The test is successful, but notice the TCP/IP address that replies to the test. It is not the TCP/IP address of the resource, but the actual TCP/IP address of the cluster member that currently owns the tested resources.

Performance Monitor

Performance Monitor is covered extensively in a previous chapter, but there are a couple of counters to mention in regards to troubleshooting.

Network Monitor

Network Monitor is a graphical utility that functions like a network sniffer. It can provide information such as the overall load on a network segment and the source and destination addresses of each packet. This is useful in determining whether data is moving between the client and the server. The network monitor utility is covered more thoroughly in the chapter on performance.

Windows NT Diagnostics

FIGURE 9-11 Displaying device IRQs with the Diagnostics program

Windows NT Diagnostics has numerous screens to view various operating system-related data. See Figure 9-11. One display I find useful is the Resources display. This tab displays the settings of the devices for which Windows NT has assigned an IRQ and loaded a device driver. If there are problems getting Windows NT to recognize a device, check Windows NT Diagnostics to determine whether another device is using the same hardware settings and is stopping the device in question from being loaded.

Nine • Cluster Troubleshooting   **237**

Cluster Logging

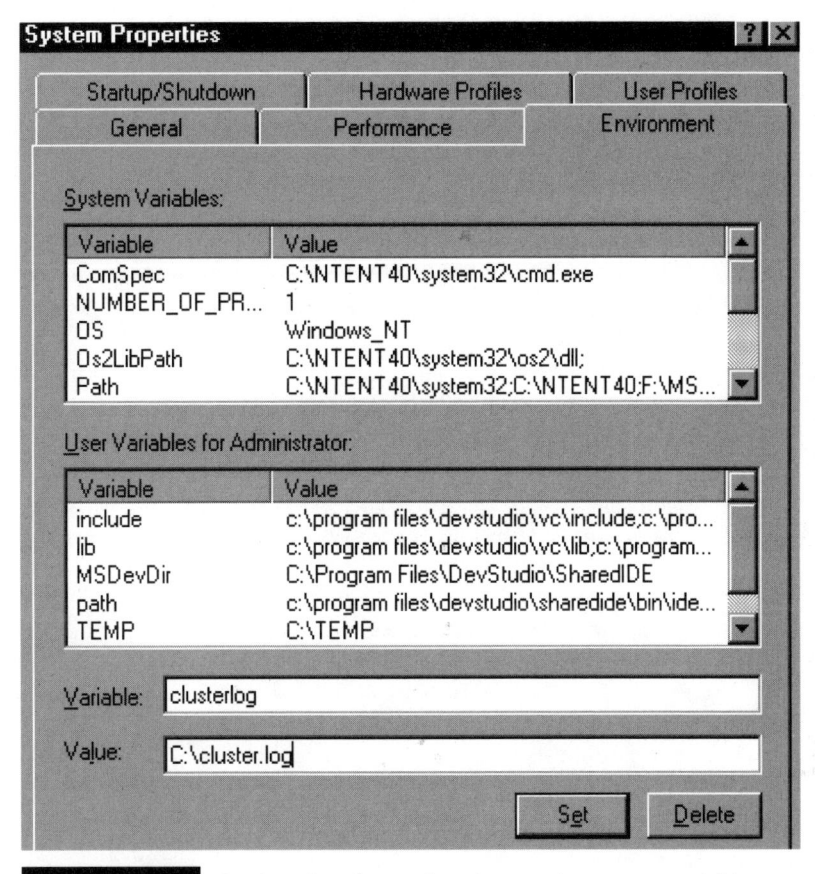

FIGURE 9-12   Setting the cluster logging environment variable

The Cluster Server can write detailed information to a file regarding significant events or problems. This is known as cluster logging. Cluster logging is not enabled by default, probably due to the extra load it can introduce to the disk. To enable cluster logging, an environment variable must be defined. To define this variable, access the System option from Control Panel and select the Environment tab. There are two sets of environment variables displayed. See Figure 9-12. The system variables are environment variables that are available system-wide. The user environment variables are available only to the current logged-on user. To enable cluster logging, do the following:

- Select the System Environment area by mouse-clicking anywhere in the System Variables display.

- Erase the data in the Variable and Data boxes and add the system environment variable CLUSTERLOG with a value that represents the path and filename the Cluster Server software should use to record events and error messages, and select the "Set" button. Verify that the entry appears in the System Variables window.
- Restart the system for cluster logging to take affect.

The environment variable must be a system environment variable. A user variable will not work because the Cluster Service is usually running under a different user name. Make sure to enable cluster logging on all nodes in the cluster. The cluster log is overwritten each time the cluster member is restarted. The cluster log file has a maximum size of 8MB. If the log file reaches this limit, cluster server will start overwriting the data in the file. The 8MB limit on the log file can be overridden by adding the value ClusterLogSize in the HKEY_LOCAL_MACHINE\System\CurrentControlSet\ClusSvc\Parameters. The ClusterLogSize parameter has a type of DWORD, and it should specify the maximum size for the log file.

Cluster Troubleshooting

Troubleshooting on a cluster requires familiarity with both the Windows NT and cluster configurations. Also, knowledge of any applications, such as SQL Server, that are integrated into the cluster is an absolute necessity. There is no way to list every possible problem you will encounter and the resolution to that problem, because every implementation will be slightly different. Also, there will be problems that have never occurred before that you may encounter, as clusters become more widely implemented. What follow are some checklists for possibly resolving various problems. Also, some of the standard issues and problems that have been prevalent with Cluster Server to date are included.

Windows NT Configuration Checklist

The following is a basic checklist of configuration rules to determine whether the target Windows NT computers can install and form a Windows NT cluster:

- Windows NT Server, Enterprise Edition and Service Pack 3 must be installed on both nodes.
- Both computers must be members of the same domain. Valid configurations include:
  - Both computers are member servers of a domain.
  - Both computers are backup domain controllers in a domain.
  - One computer is the primary domain controller, the other is a backup domain controller.
- Both computers must be in the same domain.

- A computer can be a member of only one cluster.
- Each member must have a common SCSI bus, and a disk not on the shared bus to store the operating system.
- The shared SCSI device must be formatted NTF.

Windows NT Procedure Checklist

Various tasks that can be performed on a standalone server without severely impacting the operating system can have very negative affects on the cluster. Some of these tasks include:

- Repartitioning – If the partition scheme of a disk on the shared SCSI bus is changed, make sure both cluster members are rebooted to update their disk information.
- Repartitioning – Make sure all disk resources are removed before repartitioning the target disk.
- Computer Names – The name of a cluster member cannot be changed after installing the cluster server software. To change the computer name, the cluster server software must be removed before the name can be changed. Then, reinstall cluster server, joining the already existing cluster.
- TCP/IP addresses – The TCP/IP address of an IP address resource should not be changed if a Network Name resource has the IP address as a dependency. The network name and IP address are automatically registered with WINS, and unexpected results might occur if the address is changed.
- Do not modify logical drive letters after cluster server has been installed.
- Make sure to re-apply Service Pack 3 whenever files are loaded from the Windows NT Server, Enterprise Edition distribution after the original operating system installation. If service packs are not reapplied, problems previously repaired by the service pack can reappear. A more serious potential problem is that an operating system component might cease to function totally. When in doubt, reapply the service pack.

Installation Problems

Installation problems are usually due to the shared SCSI bus configuration.

Cluster Server Installation Fails on First Node

If the cluster installation fails on the first node of the cluster, check the following:

- Does the cluster name used already exist? A removed or aborted installation may have already registered the cluster name and IP address with a WIN Server. Check the WINS database, and if there is an entry for the cluster name, remove it.
- If the installation fails when the username and password for the Cluster Service are supplied, verify that:
  - The username and password are accurate
  - The account does not have the "User must change password at next logon" box checked
  - The account has the privilege to log on as a service
  - The account has administrative privilege.
- If the installation fails to display any shared SCSI devices, either the SCSI bus and devices are not configured properly or the Windows NT system drive is on the shared SCSI bus. Cluster Server does not allow the bus that contains the disk on which the operating system is installed to be used as a shared bus.

Cluster Server Installation Fails on Second Node

If the Cluster Server installation fails on the second node, check the following:

- Is the first node of the cluster running? Verify a successful installation of the first node by running Cluster Administrator.
- Is the cluster name resource reachable? Open a command prompt on the second node and ping the cluster name and cluster IP address. If this fails, there is a network problem, possibly either with the TCP/IP address or subnet on one of the cluster members, or the cluster address and subnet mask.
- Is there an outdated entry for the cluster name in the WINS database from a previous installation? If so, delete it.

SCSI Device Problems

Because the cluster server uses SCSI configurations in a very atypical manner, many problems arise in this area. Most problems appear at hardware configuration time.

SCSI Bus or SCSI Device Not Recognized

If problems occur while attempting to get the SCSI bus or a SCSI device recognized by the hardware, check the following:

- If the entire bus is not functional, verify the following conditions:
  - Is the SCSI bus properly terminated?
  - Have SCSI cabling specifications, such as distance limitations, been violated?
  - Are both SCSI controllers on the shared bus exactly the same type? It is not guaranteed that two different SCSI controllers will support the shared bus. In fact, I have never been successful with that type of configuration.
  - No two devices, including controllers, can share the same SCSI ID.
  - The SCSI controllers in the cluster members that support the shared SCSI bus must be configured at SCSI IDs 6 and 7.
  - Is the SCSI controller recognized by Windows NT? Use Windows NT Diagnostics to verify that the SCSI controller is known by the operating system. If not, two possible problems are an IRQ conflict or a plug-and-play problem.
  - If there are multiple SCSI controllers in a cluster member, make sure that only the SCSI controller that contains the cluster member's boot disk has its BIOS enabled. If the BIOS is enabled on multiple controllers, very obscure errors can occur. For example, someone received the message, "Not enough disk space," when attempting to load Internet Information Server even though there was over 1gb free on the installation drive.

- If a specific SCSI device is not functional, check the following conditions:
  - Does the SCSI device have power? External SCSI devices must be powered on before the operating system boots in order to detect their existence.
  - Verify that the SCSI ID does not conflict with another device on the bus. The SCSI IDs assigned to the various devices can usually be viewed with the software used to configure the SCSI controller.
  - If the messages, "Device not Ready," or, "Device timeout," appear after a long delay when the second cluster member is booting, disable the option on the SCSI controller to scan for SCSI devices. The

first cluster member has taken control of the SCSI bus, and the second computer is attempting to detect the devices on the bus but is getting blocked by the first system. Disabling the SCSI device scan has no negative impacts on Windows NT or Cluster Server.

Cluster Member Connectivity Problems

Disks Do Not Fail Over Successfully

- Verify that the SCSI bus is connected to both cluster members.
- Run Disk Administrator on the cluster member the disk will not fail over to and check the configuration. The physical disk should appear in Disk Administrator with the message that configuration information is not available. This at least proves that Window NT is aware of the disk's existence.

When the Cluster Server software is installed, it displays SCSI disks on all buses other than the system SCSI bus. There can be only one shared SCSI bus, so all other devices are considered to be local. The problem is that Cluster Server does not know which bus will be the shared bus, so it displays all options. The installation by default configures all SCSI devices found on any non-system SCSI bus as a shared disk. It is the responsibility of the administrator to remove devices from the Cluster Server configuration for all except one bus. If this is not done, resources could be defined on disks, and the disks will not fail over between cluster members because they are not on the shared SCSI bus.

Resources are sometimes intentionally configured on local disks, but the application the resource offers must be installed on local disks on both cluster members. For example, if both cluster members have a local drive D:, a resource can be created with its file location as the D: drive. In this case, the application must be installed on the local disk of each cluster member. The cluster concept is used to fail over the availability of the application and not data, since data is on a local disk and is unavailable to be moved between cluster members.

Quorum Resource Fails

If the device that holds the quorum resource fails and cannot be brought online, the Cluster Service will not start. It can be started with a special parameter that starts the Cluster Service without a quorum resource. Then the administrator can use the Cluster Administrator utility to select a new quorum resource. To correct a quorum resource failure, implement the following:

1. Shut down one cluster member. Only one node should be running.
2. Use the Services option from Control Panel to stop the Cluster Service if it is running.
3. In the Startup Parameters box, enter "-fixquorum," then start the Cluster Service.
4. Use the Cluster Administrator utility to modify the properties of the cluster and select a new quorum resource.
5. Use the Services option in Control Panel to stop and restart the Cluster Service. This clears the fixquorum parameter that was passed. It is not necessary to clear anything from the Startup Parameters box, because anything entered is not saved.
6. Reboot the second cluster member.

This works as long as there is more than one physical disk on the shared SCSI bus. The fixquorum parameter does not bring the quorum disk online. Therefore, it is not possible to move the quorum resource from one partition to another on the same disk, since the disk is offline.

Quorum Disk or Quorum Log is Corrupted

If the quorum disk or quorum log becomes corrupted, the cluster server software will attempt to correct the problem by resetting the log file. This can be determined by examining the Window NT event log and looking for the message, "The log file quolog.log was found to be corrupt." The source of the message is the Cluster Service. If the quorum log cannot be reset, the Cluster Service will fail to start. If the Cluster Server software fails to determine that the quorum log is corrupt and starts, the message, "ERROR_CLUSTERLOG_CORRUPT," will be entered in the cluster log. To correct this problem, do the following:

1. Use the Service option from Control Panel to stop the Cluster Service if it is started. Do this on both cluster members.
2. On one node, enter "-noquorumlogging" in the Startup Parameters box for the Cluster Service and start the service. This starts the Cluster Server software without quorun logging, which means that the cluster files on the quorum disk will not be open.
3. Run a disk repair utility, such as CHKDSK, against the quorum disk. If the disk shows errors, allow CHKDSK to fix them. If CHKDSK reports no errors, the quorum log itself is probably corrupted. Delete the file quolog.log and any temporary files from the MSCS directory on the quorum disk.
4. Use the Services program to stop and restart the Cluster Service.

The only potential problem with the above procedure is that the quorum log stores cluster configuration changes until they can be communicated to all nodes. When the Cluster Service is configured to start without a quorum log, it is possible that recent configuration changes to the cluster could be lost. But, since the quorum log is corrupted anyway, starting the cluster with a quorum log is the best solution.

Second Node Cannot Connect to Shared Devices

When the second cluster member is started, it establishes a connection to the shared devices. This can be verified by running the Disk Administrator utility on the second node. The shared SCSI devices should be included with the caption, "Configuration information is not available." If the shared disks fail to appear:

- Verify that the drive letters assigned to the drives are the same on both cluster members.
- Perform all the SCSI device and bus checks discussed previously.

Client – Cluster Connectivity Problems

All communications between clients and the cluster members will occur via TCP/IP. Most connection issues can usually be attributed to TCP addressing or name resolution problems.

Client Cannot Connect to Virtual Servers

A virtual server consists of a TCP/IP address and a network name. If a client is having problems connecting to a virtual server:

1. Attempt to ping the TCP/IP addresses of both cluster members and the cluster IP address. If the test fails, there is a network problem, possibly TCP/IP addressing.
2. Attempt to ping the TCP/IP address associated with the IP address resource the virtual server uses. If this test fails, but step 1 is successful, there is a problem with the IP address resource. Check to see if it is online, and make sure that the address has not been changed.
3. Attempt to ping the network name of the virtual server. If the client is on a different subnet from the cluster members, this will test name resolution mechanisms such as WINS and DNS. If the client on a remote subnet fails this test, verify that a name resolution mechanism is available and that an entry for the virtual server network name exists.
4. If the client has problems accessing file shares, verify that the user has been granted access to the share and is not getting "Access denied" messages.

Clients Cannot Access a Group That Has Failed Over

If a client is using a resource, and the resource fails over to the other cluster member, communications will be temporarily interrupted by the cluster transition. Also, depending on the application, the client may need to manually reconnect. This is application dependent. If the client cannot reconnect to the resource, verify that it is online. The cluster software has the capability to use two network adapters, one for client access and the other for cluster communications. It is possible that the network adapter used for client access on the second cluster member is misconfigured or not functional. The cluster will be able to fail over the resources on its private network segment, but the resources will be unavailable to clients.

Clients Cannot Access a File Share Resource

If a client cannot access a file share resource, consider the following:

- File share resources use a virtual server. Perform the troubleshooting for virtual servers discussed earlier.
- Verify that the user has access permissions to the share.
- If the message, "Conflicting credentials," appears, the user is attempting to establish connections to the same server using different usernames and passwords. Windows NT does not support that feature.

Group and Resource Failure Problems

Group and resource failure problems occur when the resource and group failure mechanism does not function as expected.

A Resource Fails But is Not Brought Back Online

When a resource fails, the cluster server will attempt restart it unless:

- The "Don't Restart" option is selected in the Advanced page of the resource properties.
- A resource dependency is offline.
- The resource has reached its failure threshold. A resource has a threshold defining how many failures to accept for the resource and when to restart it. If the threshold is reached, and the resource cannot be moved to another cluster member, the resource will go into a "Failed" state and must be brought online manually.

A Group Cannot Be Brought Online

When a group is brought online, the Cluster Service attempts to bring all the resources in the group online. If one or more resources cannot be brought online, the group will have a warning symbol next to it denoting this fact. The resource failures must be examined individually. If none of the resources in a group can be brought online, verify access to the disk on the shared SCSI bus that the group uses. Perform all the SCSI device troubleshooting is necessary.

A Group Will Not Move or Fail Over to Another Node

If a group will not automatically or manually move to another cluster member, check the following questions:

- Can the other node accept all the resources in the group? The cluster member must be configured as a possible owner of every resource in the group.
- Do the properties of the resources have the "Affect the group" option selected? This option notifies the group to fail to the other cluster member. Also check the threshold for the resources. The resource threshold defines how many times the resource should be restarted on the same node before it is failed over to another cluster member. There is also a group threshold value that defines how many total resource failures can occur before the group is failed over to another member. For example, let's assume a group with 6 resources. If each resource fails twice, no resource has reached the default threshold of three. However, the total of twelve failures does exceed the default group threshold of ten and the group will be failed over to another cluster member.
- Is the group failing over to another cluster member, then immediately failing back? The Cluster Server software allows group to be returned to their preferred owner in the cluster, if one is defined.

A Group Fails Over But Will Not Fail Back

If a group successfully fails over to another cluster member but does not automatically failback to the original cluster member, consider the following:

- Make sure that the Prevent Failback option is not selected in the group properties.
- If failback is enabled, is it configured to occur only during specific hours of the day. If so, has that time occurred?
- Are preferred owners defined for the group? The Cluster Server software will failback groups to their preferred owners only.

A Group Fails Immediately When Brought Online

If a group fails immediately when it is brought online, one or more resources are not starting properly, reaching their threshold, and are affecting the group. Instead of bringing the group online, bring the resources online one at a time to determine which resource or resources are the cause of the problem.

General Cluster Issues

The Cluster Service Will Not Start

If the Cluster Service fails to start, it could be due to a problem with the account used by the Cluster Service. An easy method to verify that the account and password are valid is to log in with them. If the system rejects the login attempt, possibly the password has been changed and not updated in the service properties. Reset the password in both User Manager and in the service properties. If this is the case, make sure that the account has not been locked out by the operating system. Use the User Manager program to verify that the "Account locked out" option is cleared. If it is selected, clear it.

The next most common problem is that the password has expired. This is easily recognized during a login attempt. If Windows NT requests a password change during the login process, this will stop the service from starting, since the service has no capability to respond to the operating systems request. The problem can be resolved by again using the User Manager program. Make sure that the "User must change password at Next Logon" box is cleared and that the "Password never expires" box is checked for the service account.

The Message, "RPC Server is Unavailable," is Displayed

This message can occur when Cluster Administrator is used to connect to a cluster. Two possible causes are listed below.

- Has the system just completed rebooting? If so, the Cluster Server software probably has not started yet. Wait a minute or two and try the Cluster Administrator utility again.
- Attempt to connect to the cluster by TCP/IP address instead of the cluster name when entering Cluster Administrator. If the connection by TCP/IP address is successful, the problem may be in the WINS or DNS databases. Verify that there are no invalid entries for the cluster in the WINS and DNS servers.

Cluster Administrator Fails to Connect to a Node

If the Cluster Administrator utility cannot establish a connection to a node:

- Make sure that the Cluster Service and RPC Service are both started.
- Attempt to connect by TCP/IP address. If this succeeds, name resolution is not working.

A Running Application Cannot Be Closed

If a Windows application is configured as a generic application resource in the cluster, when the resource is brought online, the application will open on the desktop. If the application is closed on the desktop, the Cluster Server software will automatically restart it and the application will reappear on the desktop. To properly close the application, use the Cluster Administrator utility and take the resource offline.

Troubleshooting by Resource Type

This section provides various tests to perform when troubleshooting a specific resource type, such as a file share resource.

Troubleshooting a Physical Disk Resource

If one or more of the cluster members will not recognize a physical disk resource or bring the disk resource online, check the following items:

- The disk on the shared SCSI bus should not be repartitioned if the cluster has disk resources referencing the physical disk. To repartition a disk, first remove any disk resources for the disk in Cluster Administrator. This could require that the quorum device be relocated if the disk to be repartitioned currently is the quorum resource.
- If the disks have been repartitioned, both cluster members must be rebooted to recognize the changes.
- Make sure drive letters for the disks on the shared SCSI bus are consistent on all cluster members.
- The Cluster Server software stores disk signatures for the disks on the shared SCSI bus in the registry. For this reason, it is not possible to restore a backup of a Windows NT system running Cluster Server to another computer. The disk signatures will not match and the Cluster Server software cannot access the devices on the shared bus. The new cluster member will need Windows NT and Cluster Server installed. Then any applications which the Cluster Server will offer as resources can be restored.
- When the second server in a cluster boots, registry information from the

existing cluster member is written to the registry of the joining cluster member. This may include updated disk signature information. The registry information should update successfully within 60-90 seconds. If one or two disk signature error messages have been logged, but the cluster is functioning properly, this is probably the cause of the message.

Troubleshooting an IP Address Resource

Although TCP/IP networking can be very complex, an IP address resource is fairly simple because it has no dependencies and the data, which consists of a TCP/IP address and subnet mask, is easy to troubleshoot using standard TCP/IP testing procedures.

The most common problem with IP address resources is misconfigured data for the IP address resource. This can be either the TCP/IP address or subnet mask. Verify that the subnet mask is proper and that the TCP/IP address is in the proper subnet. If necessary, reconfirm the data with the network administrator, or whoever is responsible for handing out TCP/IP addresses. The one test that can be used for an IP address resource is the ping utility. Use it to test access to the IP address resource from a computer on the same subnet and also from a computer on a remote subnet. If the local test is successful, but the remote test fails, this is probably an invalid subnet, assuming the physical network is functional. The Cluster Server software does not complain if addresses and subnet masks are configured for the IP address resource. In fact, an IP address resource with an address for an entirely different subnet can be configured and brought online successfully. It would be nice if the software compared the IP address settings against the TCP/IP configuration at the operating system level and warned of any discrepancies.

Troubleshooting a Network Name Resource

To troubleshoot a network name resource, check the following items:

- Network name resources are used as NetBIOS names and host names. They have a dependency on an IP address resource, so the first check should be that the IP address resource is online.
- If there is no noticeable problem with the IP address resource, try to ping the network name. If this is successful, TCP/IP is functioning properly. A delay of approximately 60-90 seconds before the ping test is successful shows that the system initiating the test is configured to use a DNS Server, and there is no entry in the DNS database for the network name resource. Although there may be entries in a WIN server for the network name, DNS is checked before WINS when a ping test is issued. This can be confusing, because if the "net view \\network_name" command is used to test the network name, it may respond more rapidly because the "net view" command uses NetBIOS name resolu-

tion, which does not use a DNS until last in its name resolution sequence.
- If network name resources are constantly created and deleted (perhaps this is a test cluster), another potential problem exists. The Cluster Server software automatically registers network name resources with the WIN Server configured for the cluster member. If the WIN Server then replicates its database to other WIN Servers, and subsequently the network name is deleted or modified by the cluster administrator, some WIN Servers will have wrong information in their databases regarding the network name. Always check the WIN Server that is used by the system that is experiencing problems with the network name. If necessary, delete the WINS database entry or force a WINS database replication to occur.

Troubleshooting a File Share Resource

To research a file share resource problem, check the following items:

- File share resources have dependencies on a network name and physical disk resource, so the first step in troubleshooting is to check the functionality of these two resources. Make sure both dependent resources are online.
- If the problem occurs when bringing the file share resource online, verify that the directory exists. Also check the local file security if the directory is on an NTFS formatted partition. If there is no access to the directory with NTFS security, the Cluster Service cannot bring the resource online.
- If users are encountering problems, such as saving or writing to files, the problem may also be at the NTFS permission level. Even if the file share resource is created with the proper user access, the permissions at the NTFS level can possibly restrict access further. The actual access which users will have to file share resources will be the most restrictive permissions granted to the file share resource and to the files and directories via NTFS.

Troubleshooting a Generic Service Resource

Generic services are a pretty simple resource. The complicated work has been performed by making a program run as a service. If a generic service resource is not functioning properly, check the following items:

- Is the generic service attempting to run a service that does not support running in a cluster such as DNS, DHCP or WINS? These services cannot be configured as a generic service resource.
- If the service logs in with a specific account, manually attempt to login with the account to make sure that the password has not been changed or that the password has not expired.

- If the generic service resource functions properly on one cluster member, but fails on the other, does the service require information from the registry that may not be getting replicated properly?

Troubleshooting a Generic Application Resource

To troubleshoot a generic application resource, check the following items:

- A generic application resource does not require any dependent resources, but there is a good chance that it has a dependency on a physical disk resource. Make sure the disk resource is functioning properly.
- If the application works on one cluster member, but not on another, check to see if the application stores information in the registry. If it does, check the properties of the resource to verify that registry replication has been configured.
- Since virtually any program can be installed as a generic application resource, this introduces the possibility of configuring a malfunctioning program to run as a cluster resource. Run the program interactively and observe its behavior. Does it open a window? Does it end in error? Does it run to completion and end? If the answer is "yes" to any of these questions, check the following when troubleshooting the resource:
    - If the program is a Windows application, the checkbox, "Allow application to interact with desktop" must be checked. If the box is not selected, and the application is a Windows application, it does not fail when brought online. It will be running in the background, not having been able to open a window.
    - If the application resource continues to restart and eventually goes into a failed state, it could be one of two problems. The Cluster Server software will restart any resource that fails. If the application ends with an error, this is considered a failure and the application is restarted. If the application ends normally, this is also considered a resource failure and the application is restarted. In either case, the application will eventually reach its failure threshold and either be failed over to another cluster member or placed into a failed state.

Troubleshooting a Print Spooler Resource

To troubleshoot a print spooler resource, check the following items:

- A print spooler resource is dependent on a physical disk and network name resource. Verify that these dependent resources are functioning properly, in the same group as the print spooler resource, and are online.
- Make sure that access to the disk and directory used by the print spooler has not been restricted through NTFS permissions. Also check

that the disk that contains the spool directory is not full. This will cause print jobs to hang.
- Check the LPR port mapping for the print device in question. The LPR port must be created for each cluster member. If the print spooler works from on cluster member, but not the other, this could be the problem.
- The printer driver must be manually loaded on each cluster member. If the print spooler functions properly on only one of the cluster members, this could also be the problem.

Troubleshooting an IIS Virtual Root Resource

To troubleshoot an IIS virtual root resource, check the following items:

- An IIS virtual root resource has a dependency on an IP address resource. Verify that it is functioning properly.
- If the IIS resource does not work with a domain name, such as www.ucicorp.com, does it work by using the TCP/IP address? If so, the problem is with name resolution and DNS.
- If the resource is a WWW or FTP virtual root, the allowed access can be Read or Execute. The granted access must be "execute" in order for a client to run a program in the directory.
- If the resource functions properly on only one of the cluster members, verify that the directory used is on a shared disk. If it is a local disk, the directory must exist on both cluster members.

Troubleshooting an SQL Server Resource

To troubleshoot an SQL Server resource, check the following items:

- Clustering support for SQL Server uses a network name and disk resource as dependencies. Verify that they are functioning and online.
- When clustering support for SQL Server is installed, it replaces the standard SQL services of MSSQL Server and SQL Executive. Use the Service option from Control Panel to determine whether the original SQL services have been started, and stop them if necessary. The proper method to start and stop a clustered SQL Server is to take the SQL associated resources offline or bring them online.

- If the SQL virtual server resource functions properly on one of the cluster members, but not another, make sure that the username and password used for the SQL Server service account are identical on both nodes.

Troubleshooting a Distributed Transaction Coordinator Resource

To troubleshoot a distributed transaction coordinator resource, check the following items:

- Verify that the problem is not with the Transaction Server software or with the database server, such as SQL Server, that the transaction coordinator is accessing.
- A distributed transaction coordinator resource has dependencies on a disk and a network name resource. Verify that both dependent resources are functioning properly.

Troubleshooting a Message Queue Server Resource

To troubleshoot a message queue server resource, check the following items:

- Verify that the problem is not with the Message Queue Server software.
- A message queue server resource has a dependency on a disk and a network name resource. Verify that both of these resources are functioning properly.
- The message queue server software has various settings that can stall the message queue. This is specific to the software and is not a cluster issue.

TEN

The Future for Cluster Server

Microsoft Cluster Server, like most software products, is guaranteed to change as the product evolves. The first release provides a solution for the problem that IS managers consider their area of greatest concern: high availability of applications.

As Cluster Server matures as a product, software products will be tailored to take advantage of its features by incorporating the cluster API into the application. Although there is no guarantee of a product's features until it is officially released, Microsoft has definitive plans for Cluster Server and various products such as SQL Server and Exchange Server.

The Future for Microsoft Cluster Server

With Windows NT 5.0 on the horizon, Cluster Server will undergo some changes. Known as Microsoft Cluster Server "Phase 2", the next release already has some features defined. First, a major requirement for developing cluster-aware applications is a globally accessible, programmable naming service with which clients can interface to locate cluster-based resources. The current plan is to use the Active Directory Services of Windows NT 5.0 as the cluster naming service.

Load Balancing

Another component of the current version of Cluster Server that will be addressed is the load-balancing functionality. Currently, any load-balancing must be manually configured by the administrator by placing the applications in groups and using the preferred owner property to force groups to run on certain nodes. The problem with this method of load balancing is that the administrator must constantly re-evaluate the cluster member performance information and make adjustments in order to maintain a cluster where all cluster members are working at approximately the same rate.

A future release of Cluster Server is planned that will allow administrators to specify performance-related failover policies for cluster groups through the Cluster Administrator utility. The administrator will specify Performance Monitor counters that will trigger group failovers to other cluster members. For example, the administrator will be able to configure such that if the processor queue length rises above 1, the Cluster Server software should move the IIS virtual root resource to another cluster member. As the number of cluster members increases from the current limit of two, it may be necessary to have a method to rank cluster members, either statically or dynamically, according to the amount of processing a cluster member should accept in relation to other cluster members.

As more "cluster aware" applications are developed, it will be possible to spread the workload for a single application over multiple servers in a cluster. This satisfies one of the four major features which clustering software should offer: scalability. Microsoft Transaction Server, along with distributed transaction coordinator resources, is a step in this direction.

APPENDIX A

Resource Dependency Table

The Cluster Server software will not allow resources to be created unless the proper dependent resources have already been defined. In the shared nothing cluster model that Microsoft Cluster Server implements, group and resource planning is very critical because it is the method available to perform any load balancing of processing load between the cluster members. What follows is a table of resource types and their associated dependencies. When reviewing the table and performing any preliminary planning, remember two basic rules:

1. A resource can be a member of one group only.
2. A resource and all its dependent resources must reside in the same group.

CLUSTER RESOURCE	REQUIRED DEPENDENCIES
Distributed Transaction Coordinator	Physical Disk and Network Name
Exchange Server	
File Share	None *
Generic Application	None
Generic Service	None
IIS Virtual Root	TCP/IP Address
IP Address	None
Network Name	TCP/IP Address
Message Queue Server	Physical Disk, Network Name, SQL Server, and Distributed Transaction Coordinator
Physical Disk	None
Print Spooler	Physical Disk and Network Name
SQL Server	
Time Service	None

* The file share resource usually uses a physical disk resource, but it is not a required dependency.

APPENDIX B

The Cluster API

Tools of the Microsoft Cluster Administrator use the cluster API to administer the cluster and monitor its state. Application developers can also use this API to create "cluster-aware" applications. The API provides functions to perform management and monitoring of the cluster, nodes, groups, resources, and the cluster configuration.

Cluster Management Functions

The *cluster management* functions allow a cluster-aware application or a resource DLL to perform a wide variety of maintenance and management tasks on a cluster. Functions in this group are used to receive notification of cluster-related events, enumerate through objects of the cluster, and both obtain and set information about the cluster configuration.

Most of the cluster management functions require the developer to invoke the function *OpenCluster,* which returns a handle to the cluster (type **HCLUSTER**). This handle is used in subsequent calls to the API, including many of the API functions described in the following paragraphs. The API function *CloseCluster* closes the cluster handle, not the actual cluster itself.

Cluster-aware applications can use the functions *CreateCluster-NotifyPort, RegisterClusterNotify,* and *GetClusterNotify* to receive notification of cluster related events. Events for which an application can receive notification include changes in cluster and individual node state (for example, nodes added and deleted) and changes in the state of resources. In general, to implement this capability in an application, a developer first invokes *OpenCluster* to receive a handle to the cluster, then passes that handle to the

CreateClusterNofityPort function. This function is also passed a bitmask indicating the events for which the application will receive notification. Alternatively, an application can use *RegisterClusterNotify* to add or remove from the list of notification events. The function *CloseClusterNotifyPort* should be used when an application is no longer interested in receiving notification of cluster events.

Another group of cluster management functions allows an application to enumerate through a list of cluster-related objects, such as node, resource types, resources, and groups. These functions are *ClusterOpenEnum*, *ClusterEnum*, and *ClusterCloseEnum*. To include this functionality in an application, a developer must first invoke *OpenCluster* to receive a cluster handle, then pass that handle to *ClusterOpenEnum*, along with a bitmask indicating which objects are to be enumerated. The *ClusterOpenEnum* function returns another handle, which is subsequently passed repeatedly to *ClusterEnum* to retrieve information about each object. Once this list has been enumerated, the developer should call *ClusterCloseEnum* to release resources consumed by the functions.

The final group of functions in this category includes *GetClusterInformation* and *GetClusterQuorumResource*, which are used to get information about the cluster. Also included are functions that allow an application to change the cluster configuration, such as *SetClusterName*, *SetClusterQuorumResource*, and *SetClusterTime*.

Node Management Functions

The node management functions allow an application to monitor and manage the individual nodes in a cluster and to change their state. Using functions in this group, it is possible to develop an application that monitors the state of an individual node or nodes in the cluster and that controls nodes by pausing, resuming, or evicting them from the cluster.

All of the functions in this category require a handle to a node (type **HNODE**), which is returned by the function *OpenClusterNode*. Note that this function, in turn, requires a handle to the cluster, which is returned by the function *OpenCluster*. Once an application is no longer interested in a particular node in the cluster, it should invoke the function *CloseClusterNode*. Note that this function releases only the handle used by the application; it does not actually "close" the node.

Once a handle to a node has been obtained, an application can use the function *GetClusterNodeState* to obtain the state of a node in the cluster. The function returns a code indicating whether the cluster is *up*, *down*, *paused*, or is currently *joining* the cluster.

An application can also control a node in the cluster using the functions *PauseClusterNode*, *ResumeClusterNode*, and *EvictClusterNode*. The *PauseClusterNode* function requests that a node temporarily suspend its cluster activity. A node's activity can be later resumed by invoking *ResumeClusterNode*. To delete a node from the configuration database, an application can use the function *EvictClusterNode*.

Group Management Functions

The group management functions allow an application to manage a cluster's groups and group members and to change group state. The operations implemented by these functions fall under the domain of the resource manager and failover manager component of the cluster service. Some of the operations are executed on the system that owns the affected group or resource; other operations are executed on the system that is hosting the affected group or resource.

Functions in this category allow applications to be developed that create and delete cluster groups, establish a name for a group, establish a preferred node list for a group, bring groups online and offline, move a group's resources from one node to another, and obtain the state of a cluster group.

As is the case with other API function groups, these functions require the application to open and obtain a handle that is used in subsequent API functions. The function *OpenClusterGroup* opens a group and returns a handle to it. It requires the developer to pass the cluster handle returned from the *OpenCluster* function. The *CloseClusterGroup* should be invoked when the application is no longer interested in a group.

To obtain the current state of a group, an application uses the function *GetClusterGroupState*. This function returns a code indicating fully or partially online, offline, or has failed.

To enumerate through the resources of a cluster group, an application must first invoke the function *ClusterGroupOpenEnum*, which opens a group enumeration and returns a handle to it. An application subsequently invokes *ClusterGroupEnumResource*, which enumerates the resources in a group, returning the name of one resource with each call.

Cluster groups can be brought offline using the function *OfflineClusterGroup*. Groups can be brought back online from an application using the function *OnlineClusterGroup*.

Cluster groups can also be created and managed from an application. To create a cluster group, an application can use the function *CreateClusterGroup*, which adds a group to a cluster and returns a handle to the newly added group. The function *SetClusterGroupName* establishes a name for a group, and the *SetClusterGroupNodeList* establishes the preferred node list for a group. *DeleteClusterGroup* removes a group from a cluster. Finally, *MoveClusterGroup* moves a group and all of its resources from one node to another.

Resource Management Functions

The largest category of cluster API functions includes functions related to the management of cluster resources. These functions allow an application to manage the resources in a cluster and to change their state.

To begin monitoring and/or managing resources in a cluster, an application must first invoke *OpenCluster* to obtain a handle to the cluster. This handle is subsequently passed to the *OpenClusterResource* function, which opens a cluster resource and returns a handle to it. When an application is no longer interested in a resource, it should invoke the *CloseClusterResource* function, which closes a cluster resource by invalidating its handle.

The list of resources can be enumerated using the functions *ClusterResourceOpenEnum*, *ClusterResourceEnum*, and *ClusterResourceCloseEnum*. The *ClusterResourceOpenEnum* function opens an enumeration object and returns a handle which should subsequently be repeatedly passed to the *ClusterResourceEnum* function, which enumerates objects relating to a resource in a cluster, returning the name of one object with each call. *ClusterResourceCloseEnum* closes a cluster enumeration object by invalidating its handle.

Functions are also available within this category to obtain the state of a resource and bring a resource online or online. The *GetClusterResourceState* function returns the current state of a resource as a code indicating whether the resource is inherited, initializing, online, offline, or failed. An application can bring a resource online or offline using the functions *OnlineClusterResource* and *OfflineClusterResource*.

There are several functions in this category that enable an application to create, delete, and modify resources in the cluster. Resource types can be created and deleted using *CreateClusterResourceType* and *DeleteClusterResourceType*. Resources can be created and deleted using the *CreateClusterResource* and *DeleteClusterResource* functions. A name can be established for a resource using the function *SetClusterResourceName*.

To indicate which node or nodes a resource can run on, an application can use the *AddClusterResourceNode* function. To move a resource from one group to another, applications should invoke the function *ChangeClusterResourceGroup*.

Dependencies between two resources can be queried, established, and removed using functions that fall within this category. To determine if a resource is dependent upon a second resource, an application can use the *CanResourceBeDependent* function. To manage the dependency between two resources, the API provides the functions *AddClusterResourceDependency* and *RemoveClusterResourceDependency*.

To initiate resource failure, an application should invoke the *FailClusterResource* function.

Configuration Database Management Functions

Recall that Windows NT Clusters provide a cluster-wide configuration database that is similar to the Win32 system registry, but it is replicated across all of the nodes of a cluster. To access and update this database, the clusters API provides functions that are similar to the functions used to access and update the system registry. Additional functions are provided to permit multiple updates to be committed automatically.

The list of cluster keys can be enumerated using *ClusterRegEnumKey*. Values for a particular key can be enumerated using *ClusterRegEnumValue*.

The *ClusterRegOpenKey* opens a cluster registry key, returning a handle to the key (type **HKEY**). Subsequent calls use this handle. For example, *ClusterRegQueryValue* retrieves the name, type, and data components associated with a value for an open cluster registry key. *ClusterRegSetValue* sets a value for a cluster registry key. *ClusterRegCloseKey* releases the handle of a cluster registry key.

Keys can also be created and deleting using *ClusterRegCreateKey* and *ClusterRegDeleteKey*. To remove the value of the key without removing the key itself, an application can use the *ClusterRegDeleteValue* function.

GLOSSARY

ARP	Address resolution protocol. The method by which TCP/IP converts TCP/IP addresses to MAC addresses in order to properly address a network packet.
Backup Domain Controller (BDC)	A computer running Windows NT Server that holds a copy of the domain account database. The backup domain controller can validate logon requests against their read-only copy of the user account information.
Bottleneck	In system performance terms, the hardware component, usually disk, memory or processor, that hinders performance of a system. It is sometimes referred to as "the limiting resource."
Client/server	An application design method that divides its processing into a front end (client) and a back end (server).
Cluster	A group of two or more independent computers that are addressed and used as a single system.
Cluster API	A set of program routines that allows application developers to interface with the Cluster Service and perform tasks such as creating new resources and initiating a failure on a resource.
Cluster-aware application	An application that includes Cluster API routines capable of interfacing with the Cluster Service.
Cluster.Exe	A command line program to allow an administrator to perform cluster administration. The Cluster.Exe program is useful in situations where a series of similar commands are going to be issued.
Cluster log	A log file of important cluster events and errors. To implement cluster logging, it is necessary to define the environment variable CLUSTERLOG to the path where the log file should be stored.
Cluster member	A computer runnning Windows NT Server, Enterprise Edition and Microsoft Cluster Server.
Cluster service	A component of the Cluster Server software that is implemented as a Windows NT service. The Cluster Service manages all aspects

of the cluster's operation and manages the configuration database. Each node in a cluster runs an instance of the Cluster Service.

Cluster transition The time necessary to relocate resources and groups to the proper cluster members when a cluster member exits or rejoins the cluster. Depending on the number of resources that must be moved, cluster transition ranges from 5 to 30 seconds. During this time, all user processing is suspended.

Dependency The requirement of one resource needing another resource in order to function properly. A resource does not contain all its configuration information. For example, a network name resource logically represents a computer name on the network, but a computer name is really a representation of a TCP/IP address. The network name resource does not have a TCP/IP address as part of its properties. What it does have is a dependency on an IP address resource to fulfill the address require-ment.

Disk mirroring A disk fault-tolerant method that writes data simultaneously to two disks using the same disk controller. The disks operate in parallel, storing and updating the same files. Disk mirroring protects against a disk failure and file corruption generated by a hardware malfunction. It does not protect against a software-generated corruption such as a file being opened and modified with the incorrect tool, such as Notepad.

Disk striping A disk configuration where multiple disks are treated as one logical disk. Data is written across the disks as opposed to filling one disk and moving to the next as with a volume set. Disk striping provides no fault tolerance.

Disk striping with parity Similar to disk striping except that one disk in the set will store parity information. If a member disk of a stripe set with parity fails, the parity information in conjunction with the data available from the remaining disks can be used to regenerate the data that was stored on the failed disk.

Distributed lock manager Software used in a shared resource cluster model to coordinate user activity on multiple cluster members to concurrent access to a file.

Distributed transaction coordinator resource A cluster resource capable of functioning as a coordinator in a Microsoft Transaction Server environment. The Transaction Server product allows for guaranteed transaction processing, in chronological order.

DNS Domain Name Server	An industry-standard method of providing name resolution. A static database of computer names and TCP/IP addresses is maintained on one or more DNS servers. In order for a client to use DNS for resolution, it must contain a software component referred to as a DNS resolver. This is included in most TCP/IP implementations.
Domain	There are two definitions. In Windows NT, a domain is a logical group of computers that share a security account database. In TCP/IP, a domain is a logical group of computers for naming purposes, such as ucicorp.com.
Dynamic Link Library (DLL)	A file that is a library of functions that one or more programs can share. The addition of new resource types to the cluster is generally implemented by providing a DLL with the program routines necessary to support a resource type.
Dynamic load balancing	A method of allocating the application load between cluster members based on the current processing load of the members. As the processing activity on cluster members changes, application resources can be dynamically relocated to the lesser used processor to provide the best possible client response times.
Failback	The action of moving a resource back to the cluster member designated to be the resource's preferred owner. By default, resources are owned by their preferred owners, so a failback will occur only if the resource has been moved from its preferred owner. This would probably be the result of a failover.
Failover	The process of taking one or more resources offline on one cluster member and bringing them online on another cluster member.
Failover threshold	The number of times a resource failure is allowed before the resource is moved to another cluster member.
Failure	When a resource stops functioning properly. Cluster resource failure are detected by either the IsAlive or LooksAlive timers.
Fault tolerant	The capability to offer uninterrupted availability in the event of a hardware or software failure.
File share resource	A standard shared directory that is accessible via the normal NetBIOS naming convention, or UNC name, such as \\server\share. Implemented by the Cluster Server as a resource.
File system cache	A portion of physical memory that the operating system uses to store file system data such as directory and file header informa-

tion. The goal of the cache is to reduce the amount of actual disk I/O the operating system performs.

Generic application resource A standard batch file or Executable file that is supported by the Cluster Server software as a resource.

Generic service resource A Windows NT service that is supported by the Cluster Server software as a resource. Not all Windows NT services are capable of running as a generic service resource.

Group A logical organization of resources. A resource is not failed from one cluster member to another, whereas groups are. Allows the administrator to place dependent resources into one unit to guarantee that a resource and all its dependent resources will always be owned by the same cluster member.

Heartbeat A message sent between cluster members to notify each of the others' existence. If heartbeat messages are not received from a cluster member, it is considered to have gone offline and all resources that it owned are failed over to the remaining cluster members.

Host name An alpha-numeric representation of a TCP/IP address. Host names are used by TCP/IP utilities such as FTP, telnet and ping.

IIS virtual root resource A cluster resource to be used with Internet Information Server that supports a unique WWW, FTP and GOPHER service. Cluster Server does not support virtual roots containing access information.

IP address resource A valid TCP/IP address that is supported as a cluster resource.

IsAlive timer Compared to the LooksAlive timer, this is a more thorough check of a resource.

Lazy write An operating system method of minimizing physical disk access. When an application issues a disk write, the data is held in memory, but the application is notified that the write has completed. The operating system then performs the physical disk I/O at a time when the system is less busy.

LPR A method by which printing is supported over a TCP/IP network. Consists of a server, or daemon, and a TCP/IP addressable printer.

LooksAlive timer A timer that triggers a quick check by the Cluster Server software to determine if resources that are considered to be online are actually available.

Glossary

Message queue server resource
A cluster resource capable of performing the role of server in a Microsoft Message Queue Server environment. Message Queue Server is a message delivery mechanism used by programmers to transport application independent messages across a network with guaranteed delivery, even if the target computer is not currently available.

NetBIOS name
An alphanumeric name that is used by clients to reference a computer on the network. NetBIOS names are used as the server in a UNC name.

Network name resource
A cluster resource that offers a valid host or NetBIOS name on the network.

NTFS
NT file system. A file system supported by Windows NT that supports user level security with access control lists.

Offline
The state of a resource or group that classifies it as unavailable. When used in context with a cluster member, offline implies that the cluster member may not be booted, or that the Cluster Service on the node in question may not be functioning properly.

Online
The state of a resource or group that classifies it as available. When used in context with a cluster member, online implies that the other cluster members are receiving heartbeats from the cluster member in question.

Page fault
The function performed by the operating system when data needs to be mapped into memory. Excessive page faulting is a sign that the system does not have enough memory to support its current workload.

Paging
An operating system event where data is moved between disk and memory.

Paused
The state of a cluster member in which it does not accept any new connections. Administrators can place a cluster member in this state before shutting it down to minimize the effect of cluster transition on the client base.

Physical disk resource
A disk attached to the shared SCSI bus to store shared directories and applications to be implemented as cluster resources.

Possible owners
A list of cluster members that are capable of supporting a specific resource. A resource can be failed over only to a cluster member that appears in this list.

Preferred owner

The cluster member that should own a group when both the group and cluster member are online. A preferred owner is the cluster member a resource will be failed back to if and when the cluster member returns to an online state. Static load balancing of resources is accomplished by having one group per cluster member and by defining a different preferred owner for each group.

Primary domain controller (PDC)

A computer running Windows NT Server that maintains the account database used by the Windows NT domain.

Print spooler resource

A print spooler that is supported as a cluster resource. The print spooler resource can support one or more print queues. Printers typically shared in this manner will be network printers (lpr), as opposed to local attached printers, since the print server function can move between cluster members.

Private network

A network segment used by cluster members strictly for cluster communications traffic, such as heartbeat packets and resource failover.

Process

The object used by the operating system to execute a program. A process is allocated system resources such as memory, and is therefore a common focus of performance analysis. A process has one or more threads.

Public network

The network segment used by clients to gain access to the cluster and its related resources.

Quorum

Means "majority." Guarantees that all cluster members participate in a single cluster. This is accomplished by allowing only the cluster member that owns the quorum resource to create the cluster. A cluster member that does not own the quorum resource can join only an existing cluster. Avoids what is known as a "partitioned cluster," where both cluster members that boot at the same time create a cluster, since they do not detect one already in existence.

Quorum resource

The disk that signals to a booting cluster member whether the cluster already exists and therefore it should join the cluster, or whether the cluster must be created.

RAID

Redundant array of independent disks. A storage mechanism that uses two or more disks to provide one logical disk that provides varying levels of performance improvement and fault tolerance. RAID can be implemented at the hardware or software levels. Microsoft Cluster Server supports only hardware RAID on the shared SCSI bus.

Glossary

Registry — The set of files that Windows NT uses to store all configuration information. Can be viewed and modified only with a registry editor, such as the REGEDT32 utility.

Resource — A physical or logical entity managed by a cluster member. A resource offers a service to clients in a client/server application.

Resource DLL — A set of routines that facilitates communication between a resource and the Cluster Service.

Resource monitor — A cluster software component that provides communication between one or more resources and the Cluster Service. The resource monitor is also used to determine whether a resourc has failed by using the IsAlive and LooksAlive timers to poll the resource.

Restart — The action performed by the cluster software when it is determined that a resource has failed due to a lack of response from the IsAlive and LooksAlive timers. The cluster will re-execute the command used originally to bring the resource online.

Scalability — The capability to incrementally add one or more systems to an existing cluster when the cluster reaches its processing capacity.

SCSI bus — The connection media used to daisy-chain SCSI devices that are serviced by the same controller. There are various SCSI specifications, such as SCSI2 and wide SCSI. Each specification uses a different hardware bus.

SCSI device — A device connected to a SCSI bus. Each device requires a unique SCSI id. Examples of SCSI devices include disks, CDROMs, tape drives, and scanners.

SCSI id — The logical address assigned to every device on SCSI bus. The basic rule is that every device on a SCSI bus requires a unique SCSI bus, thus limiting the number of devices that can be supported on one bus.

SCSI termination — The mechanism of dissipating an electronic signal in order to prevent bounce back on a cable. Termination is used on various busses, including SCSI and Ethernet.

Service — An application that runs on a Windows NT system that is not associated with the desktop or the currently logged in user. A service is the equivalent of a daemon from the UNIX environment.

Service pack	An update to the operating system that corrects documented problems. Whenever files are loaded from the operating system distribution media, the service pack must be reapplied because the files which the service pack had repaired could be overwritten.
Shared nothing cluster model	An implementation of a cluster that does not allow resources to be accessed simultaneously by multiple cluster members. This is the cluster model implemented by Microsoft Cluster Server.
Shared resource cluster model	An implementation of a cluster that supports multiple cluster members simultaneously accessing the same resource, such as a file. While this implementation allows for more dynamic load balancing, the overhead involved in supporting the resource access is high.
Static load balancing	A method of load balancing processing activity between computers where the administrator is required to manually assign which applications should execute on which processors. This method does not automatically move applications between processors based on current processing loads.
Thread	An execution context of a process. A process that is multi-threaded has multiple independent execution contexts at one time.
Time service	A resource supported by the Cluster Server software that maintains consistent time settings between cluster members.
UNC	Universal Naming Convention.
Virtual memory	The mechanism by which operating systems allow processes to address more memory than is possibly available on the system.
Virtual server	A collection of resources that supply the appearance of a Windows NT Server to clients. A virtual server generally refers to all the resources, such as an IP address and network name resource, necessary to run a specific application.
WINS Windows Internet Naming Service	A WIN Server is a name resolution server that supports dynamic use a WIN Server for name resolution, the host must be capable of being a WINS client. Currently, only Microsoft operating systems support WINS client functionality.
Working set	The amount of physical memory that a process is allowed to reserve for ownership. Process working sets may be adjusted by the operating system depending on current available memory on the system.

INDEX

A
account information 39
active/active configuration
 defined 9
 SQL Enterprise 154, 156-57, 160
active/passive configuration
 defined 9
 SQL Enterprise 154, 156
Add Printer 92, 94-96
Admin.exe 197-98
API call 17-18
APP IDADDRESS 69
APPSERVER 69
ARP
 defined 257
 IRP address resource 72
 network name resource 80
auditing 132-35

B
Back Office 222
backup 149
Backup Domain Controller 257
boot delay time 15-16
Bring Online 68
building a cluster 25-55

C
cache 13
capacity planning 27
Change Group 71
client-cluster connectivity problems 244-45
cluster
 API 21, 267-71
 building 25-55
 defined 7-23, 257
 implementing resources 57-117
 management 119-49
 performance 205-24

 troubleshooting 225-53
Cluster Administrator
 Close 121
 cluster object 121
 Domain Name Server 121, 259
 heartbeats 125-26
 installation 51-55, 120-26
 multiple network adapters 124-25
 naming rules 121
 Open Connection 121
 options 121
 Permissions 123
 properties 122
 quorum resource 124
 Rename 121
 resource permissions 122
 traffic 124-26
 WINS 121
cluster API 21, 267-71
cluster-aware application 21
cluster logging 237-38
cluster management functions 267-68
cluster name resource 81
Cluster Network Driver 19
cluster node management
 evict node 128
 pause node 127-28
 start/stop cluster service 128-29
 Y cable 128
cluster resources
 distributed transaction coordinator 115-17
 file-share 81-88
 generic application 103-107
 generic service 96-102
 group objects 58-66
 IIS virtual root 110-14
 IP address 72-77
 network name 77-81
 physical disk 107-109
 print spooler 88-96
 resource objects 67-71

Index

Cluster Service 16-21
  Communications Manager 19
  Database Manager 17
  Event Processor 17-18
  Global Update Manager 19
  Node Manager 18-19
  offline state 16
  online state 17
  paused state 17
  Resource Manager 19
cluster transition
  distributed lock manager 13, 258
  group objects 63
Cluster.Exe
  advantages of 135
  Cluster 136
  Cluster Group 138-39
  Cluster Network 145-47
  Cluster Node 137
  Cluster Resource 140-43
  Cluster Resourcetype 144-45
  defined 257
Communications Manager 19
configuration 57-117
configuration database management
    functions 271

D

daemon 8, 96
Database Manager 17
date setting 22
de-installation of cluster member 53-55
dependency 67, 258
design of cluster 26
Dirsync server 200-201
disk activity
  disk queues 218
  file system cache 218-19
  lazy write 216-17
Disk Administrator 226
disk controllers 28
disk fault tolerance 26-27, 259
Disk Group 1, 58
disk I/O performance 223
disk queues 218
disk redundancy 2-3, 8
  backup schedule 2
  disk mirroring 2, 258
  disk striping 2-3, 258
distributed lock manager
  advantages of 13

caching 13
cluster transition 13
defined 11, 258
disadvantages of 12
relocation of lock block 12-13
resource table 11
distributed transaction coordinator
    resource
  creating resource 116-17
  defined 115, 258
  Microsoft Distributed Transaction
      Coordinator 115
  name dependency 117
  Resource Manager 115
  SQL Enterprise Manager 117, 151
  Transaction Manager 115
  troubleshooting 253
Domain Name Server
  Cluster Administrator 121
  defined 259
  IIS virtual root resource 110-12
  IP address resource 72
Dormant State 18
drive letters
  group objects 58
  installation 32-33
dynamic link library
  defined 259
  file-share resource 84
  resource monitor 21
dynamic load balancing 259

E

Event Processor 17-18
Event Viewer
  security 132, 135
  troubleshooting 232
Evict Node 128

F

failback
  defined 21, 259
  group properties 65-66
failover
  defined 259
  file-share resource 82, 85, 87-88
  group properties 65
  print spooler resource 91
  protection 4, 8-9
  Resource Manager 20
  SQL Enterprise 154

Index

SQL Exchange 177, 198
fault tolerance 57, 60
file-share resource
  access 82, 245
  creating resource 83-87
  defined 81-82, 259
  dependency 85-86
  device path 82
  directory path 82
  dynamic link library 84
  failover 82, 85, 87-88
  IP address resource 85
  load balancing 81
  names 84, 87
  NetBIOS sessions 87
  network name resource 85
  Network Neighborhood 87
  network share point 86
  ownership 84-85
  Parameters page 86
  Resource Monitor 84
  SCSI device 82
  static load balancing 82
  troubleshooting 250
  UNC name 86
  User Limit 87
  using resource 87
file system cache 218-19, 259
Forming State 18

G

generic application resource
  configuration 106-107
  creating resource 104-107
  defined 103, 260
  load balancing 105
  New Resource 104
  registry 106-107
  replication 107
  Task Manager 106-107
  troubleshooting 251
generic service resource
  access token 97
  configuration 99-102
  defined 96, 260
  dependencies 101
  Microsoft SQL Server 98
  names 99-100
  NetBios requests 96
  ownership 100-101
  REGEDIT 98
  REGEDT32 98

  registry 102
  SCSI device 100-101
  service resource object 98
  startup parameters 101
  troubleshooting 250-51
  wrapper 96-97
Global Update Manager 19
group management functions 269-70
group objects
  cluster transition 63-64
  creating groups 60-63
  defined 58
  dependencies 60
  Disk Group 1, 58
  drive letters 58
  fault tolerance 60
  load balancing 60
  maintenance 63-64
  pause node 64
  planning groups 58-60
  possible ownership 62
  preferred ownership 60-62
  removing member 64
  requirements for failover 59
  setting properties 65-66
  standard cluster groups 58
  working with 63-64
group properties
  failover 65
  failback 65-66
group and resource failure problems 245-47

H

hard page fault 211-12
hardware configurations 26
hardware requirements installation
  bus reset 29
  capacity planning 27
  compatibility lists 35
  compatability with software 28
  differential transmission 29-30
  disk controllers 28
  disk fault tolerance 26-27
  hardware compatibility list 28
  Microsoft Cluster Server requirements 27-31
  operating system 26
  peripheral device configuration 26
  RAID 26-27
  SCSI bus and device configuration 28-31
  SCSI ID 29

Index

signal convertor 30
single-ended transmission 29-30
trilink connector 29
Windows NT Server Enterprise Edition 27
Y cable 29
heartbeat
  Cluster Administrator 125
  defined 260
  Node Manager 18
hierarchical storage controller 8
HOSTS
  IIS virtual root resource 110, 112
  network name resource 80-81

I

IIS virtual root resource
  alias 114
  defined 110, 260
  dependency 113
  Domain Name Server 110, 112
  HOSTS 110, 112
  New Resource 113
  Parameters 114
  troubleshooting 252
  URL 112
  WINS 112
implementing resources 57-117
Initiate Failure 69
installation of Cluster Server
  account information 39, 50
  Cluster Administrator 51-52
  design 26
  drive letters 32-33, 48
  file location 38
  first cluster member 33-47
  hardware compatibility lists 35
  hardware requirements 26-31
  hardware and software configurations 25
  multiple clusters 52
  names 37, 52
  network adapter 42-44
  new cluster 36
  NHLOADER 33
  password 39, 50
  physical arrangement 51
  preliminary steps 25, 32-33
  problems 240
  quorum resource 41
  removal 53-55
  second node 47-51
  secondary cluster members 36
  secondary node installation 47-50
  Setup program 33
  shared SCSI disk 40
  software requirements 31-32
  subnet mask 45
  TCP/IP address 45
  timeout 47
  trusts 39
InstallShield 54
Internet 110-14, 161
Internet Information Server 67
IP address resource
  ARP 72
  creating resource 74-76
  defined 72, 260
  Domain Name Server 72
  file-share resource 85
  network name resource 79-81
  Network to Use 75
  Ping utility 76
  RFC 826 73
  TCP/IP protocol 72
  translation 72
  troubleshooting 249
  verification 76
  Windows Internet Name Server 72
IsAlive timer
  defined 260
  interval 22
  resource object 70

J

job completion timeout 90
Joining State 18

K

Key Management Server 199-202

L

lazy write 216-17, 260
LMHOSTS 80-81
load balancing
  file-share resource 81
  generic application resource 105
  group object 60
  shared nothing model 14
lock block
  distributed lock manager 11-13
  future releases 256

Index 277

multiple computers 11-13
relocation of 12-13
single computer 10-11
LooksAlive timer
  defined 260
  interval 22
  resource object 70
LPR port 91-93, 260
LPT1 port 91-92

M

member connectivity problems 242-44
Member Search 18
memory
  analysis of 213
  cluster 222-23
  hard page fault 211-12
  memory pool 212-13
  page faulting 210-12
  paging 210
  virtual memory 207-209
memory pool 212-13
message queue server
  defined 261
  troubleshooting 253
Microsoft Cluster Server overview 16-23
Microsoft Distributed Transaction
    Coordinator 115
Microsoft Internet Information Server
    110-14
Microsoft Windows NT Diagnostics 236
mirroring 2, 258
multiprocessor 3-4

N

names
  Cluster Administrator 52, 121
  cluster backup 149
  file-share resource 84
  generic service resource 99-100
  group objects 61
  IIS virtual root resource 112
  installation 37
  print spooler resource 89, 95
  SQL Enterprise 160, 166-68
  virtual server 23
Net Helpmsg 232-33
Net View 234
network activity 221-22
network adapter 42-44
Network Monitor 221-22

troubleshooting 235
network name resource
  ARP 80
  cluster name resource 81
  creating resource 78-81
  defined 77, 261
  dependency 79
  DHCP 81
  file-share resource 85
  HOSTS 80-81
  IP address resource 79-81
  LMHOSTS 80-81
  NetBios 81
  troubleshooting 249-50
  WINS server address 81
Network to Use 75
NHLOADER 33
node management functions 268-69
Node Manager 18-19
NTFS format 40, 261

O

offloading from file or application server
    26

P

page faulting 210-12, 261
paging 210, 261
partitioned cluster 15
pause node
  cluster nodes 127-28
  group objects 64
performance
  analysis 207
  cluster performance 222-24
  disk activity 216-19
  memory 207-213
  network activity 221-22
  Performance Monitor 214-16, 223
  processor activity 219-21
  speed 205-206
Performance Monitor
  counters 215
  disadvantages of 223
  objects and instances 215-16
  page faulting 222
  troubleshooting 235
  views 214
physical arrangement 51
physical disk resource
  creating resource 108-109

defined 107, 261
New Resource 108
troubleshooting 248-49
poller thread 22
possible ownership 62, 261
preferred ownership 60-62, 261
primary domain controller 262
print queue 88-96
print spooler resource
  Add Printer 92, 94-96
  client access 93
  configuring device 91-96
  creating resource 88-91
  defined 88, 262
  dependency 88-89
  failover 91
  job completion timeout 90
  names 89, 95
  New Resource 88
  ports 91-94
  printing driver 94-96
  splitter cable 92
  spool folder 90
  troubleshooting 251-52
  UNIX server 93
printing driver 94-96
privileged time 220, 224
processor activity
  analysis of 219
  cluster performance 224
  privileged time 220, 224
  processor queue 220-21
  user time 220, 224
processor queue 220-21

Q
Quantum disk 40
Quorum Disk Search 18
quorum resource
  Cluster Administrator 124
  defined 15-16, 262
  installation 41
  Node Manager 18-19
  physical disk resource 107
  troubleshooting 242-44

R
RAID 26-27, 262
REGEDIT 98
REGEDT32 98, 149

removing nodes 53-55
replication server 3
requirements of data processing system 4
resource dependency 265-66
resource failure 20
resource management functions 270-71
Resource Manager 19-21
  distributed transaction coordinator
    resource 115
  failback 21
  failover 20
Resource Monitor 21-22
  defined 263
  file share resource 84
  IsAlive timer 22
  LooksAlive timer 22
  resource objects 67
resource object
  APP IDADDRESS 69
  APPSERVER 69
  Bring Online 68
  Change Group 71
  configuration 68
  defined 67
  Delete 71
  dependency 67
  drag-and-drop 71
  fault tolerance 67
  implementation 67
  Initiate Failure 69
  IsAlive timer 70
  LooksAlive timer 70
  Properties 71
  Resource Monitor 67
  restarting 69
  SCSI disk 67
  standard resources 67
  Take Offline 69
  working with 68-71
resource sharing 4, 9
resource table 11
restoring backup 149
RFC 826 73

S
scalability 4, 8, 263
SCSI device problems
  bus and device 241-42
SCSI installation
  bus and device configuration 28-31
  bus reset 29
  differential transmission 29-30

Index

disk controllers 28
drive letters 32-33
ID 29
NTFS format 40
shared disk 40
signal convertor 30
single-ended transmission 29-30
Y cable 29
secondary node installation 47-50
security
  accounts and groups 129
  auditing access to data 132-35
  changing account 130-31
  changing password 131-32
  domain controller 129
  Event Viewer 132, 135
  file share resources 132
  NTFS 132-33
  privileges 131
  SID 129
  User Manager 131, 134
service resource object 98
Setup program 33
shared nothing cluster
  advantages of 14
  defined 9, 14, 264
  disadvantages of 14-15
  load balancing 14
  resource failover 14-15
shared resource cluster
  defined 9, 264
  distributed lock manager 11-13
SID 129
software requirements installation
  Windows NT Server Enterprise Edition 31-32
  WINNT32 31
  WINNTUP 31-32
spool folder 90
SQL Enterprise
  active/active configuration 154, 156-57, 160
  active/passive configuration 154, 156
  client applications 153-54
  cluster support 161-71
  cluster support for SQL Server modifications 169-71
  database 152
  defined 151
  device 152
  distributed transaction coordinator resource 117
  failover 154

hot fix 160
installation of Edition 6.5, 155-60
installation of virtual server 163
IP address resource 171
master device 158
Microsoft Cluster Server support 152-54
MSDTC 152
named pipes 159
names 160, 166-68
network name resource 171
network protocols 159
physical disk resource 170
replication 155
SCSI disk 152, 157
SQL Executive 152
SQLCLUSTER SQL Executive 6.5 resource 171
SQLCLUSTER SQL Server 6.5 resource 171
SQLCLUSTER SQL VServer resource 171
symmetric virtual server 152, 157
testing 169
troubleshooting 252-53
upgrade to Edition 6.5 155
SQL Exchange
  adding components 202-203
  Admin.exe 197-98
  Advanced Security 174
  cluster awareness 175, 177, 179, 186
  connectors 174
  defined 174-75
  Directory 174
  Dirsync server 200-201
  disaster recovery 196-97
  Event Services 174
  failover 177, 198
  hot fix 177
  Information Store 174
  installation of Edition 5.5 175
  IP address resource 180-81
  Key Management Server 199-202
  Message Transfer Agent 174
  multiple shared disk resource 186
  network name resource 182-83
  Performance Optimizer 189-90, 193, 196-97
  pre-setup considerations 176-85
  primary cluster node 185-91
  Remove All 192
  removing components 202-203
  replacing existing exchange server 194-97
  secondary cluster node 192-94

server license 178
server monitors 201
shared disk resource 184
starting, stopping, pausing Exchange
   Services 198-201
supportable components 203
supporting Exchange Server 197-203
System Attendant 174
troubleshooting 252-53
Update Node 192-93
star coupler 7
startup parameters 101
startup problems 247
static load balancing
   defined 264
   file-share resource 82
   shared nothing model 14
striping 2-3, 258
subnet mask 45
symmetric virtual server 152
synchronization 22
   to resource access 15

T
Take Offline 69
Task Manager 227
Time Service 22, 264
time setting 22
tracking cluster members 18
Transaction Manager 115
transaction processing 3
troubleshooting
   client-cluster connectivity 244-45
   cluster logging 237-38
   cluster member connectivity 242-44
   Disk Administrator 226
   distributed transaction coordinator
      resource 253
   Event Viewer 232
   file share resource 250
   general problems 247-48
   generic application resource 251
   generic service resource 250-51
   group and resource failure 245-47
   IIS virtual root resource 252
   installation problems 240
   IP address resource 249
   message queue server resource 253
   Microsoft Windows NT Diagnostics 236
   Net Helpmsg 232-33
   Net View 234
   Network Monitor 235

network name resource 249-50
Performance Monitor 235
physical disk resource 248-49
Ping utility 234-35
print spooler resource 251-52
SCSI device 241-42
SQL service resource 252-53
Task Manager 227
Windows Nt configuration 238-39

U
Uninterruptable Power Supply 2
UNIX server 93
upgrades
   hardware and software 147-48
   multiple SCSI adapter 148
   rolling upgrade 148
URL 112
User Limit 87
user time 220, 224

V
VAXCluster 7-8
virtual memory
   advantages of 209
   defined 207-209, 264
virtual server
   client-cluster connectivity problems 244
   defined 23, 264
   resource objects 67
volume shadowing 8

W
web site 110-114
WINNT32 31
WINNTUP 31-32
WINS
   Cluster Administrator 121
   defined 264
   IIS virtual root resource 112
   IP address resource 72
   network name resource 81
   troubleshooting 240
wrapper 96-97

Y
Y cable
   cluster node management 128
   SCSI installation 29